ERIC W. GRITSCH

MARTIN—
GOD'S COURT JESTER

Luther in Retrospect

FORTRESS PRESS   PHILADELPHIA

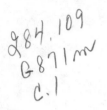

Dedicated to
My Students, the Reformers of My Teaching

and to
My Mate Ruth, the Midwife of This Book

√ Library of Congress Cataloging in Publication Data

Gritsch, Eric W.
  Martin—God's court jester.

  Bibliography: p.
  Includes indexes.
  1. Luther, Martin, 1483–1546. 2. Reformation—
Biography. I. Title.
BR332.5.G74 1983   284.1'0924 [B]   83–48004
ISBN 0–8006–1753–3

K129D83   Printed in the United States of America 1–1753

CONTENTS

PART II: Neuralgic Heritage

PART III: Ecumenical Legacy

"I shall for the time being become a court jester."

Martin Luther, "To the Christian Nobility," 1520. *WA* 6:404.24–25; *LW* 44:123.

"What else was Luther than a teacher of the Christian church whom one can hardly celebrate in any other way but to listen to him?"

Karl Barth, "Luther Jubilee" (*Lutherfeier*), *Theologische Existenz heute* 4 (1933):11.

"If there is any sense remaining of Christian civilization in the West, this man Luther in no small measure deserves the credit."

Roland H. Bainton, *Here I Stand* (1950), 22.

"The ultimate mystery of Luther's effectiveness was his own vitality."

Joseph Lortz, *The Reformation in Germany* (1968) 1: 483.

PREFACE

Who was Martin Luther? Popular images abound: a frustrated apostate monk who taught a lesson in Christian freedom to a totalitarian Christian culture; a German divine who argued with the devil and taught Germans how to persecute the Jews; a verbose priest-professor who was a workaholic with a sense and taste for the infinite in nature, music, and language; a family man who adored children, animals, food, and sex, with a fascinating psyche expressed in such phenomena as anal fixation and constipation; the proto-Protestant whose slogan "Here I Stand" became the battle cry of a movement forever pledged to fight hierarchical clericalism and to defend the common priesthood of all believers. These are but a few of the many images.

In 1916, a frustrated Lutheran depicted Luther as an unwelcome stranger among Lutherans in America, most of whom made little effort to get to know him. The most conservative Lutherans even charged him with heretical opinions. Luther's visit in America, described in *Little Journeys With Martin Luther* by a Lutheran pastor calling himself "Brother John," was totally unsuccessful. The anonymous author, who seems to have had his fill of Lutheran strife, dedicated the book "to the pieces of the Church of to-day for the sake of the peace of the Church of to-morrow."[1]

Would Luther be welcome today, five hundred years after his birth? In America, Germany, or wherever? One has to know him in order to answer the question; he certainly has left much material for those who want to try. His massive literary corpus consists of more than four hundred and fifty treatises, some of them quite voluminous, in addition to more than three thousand sermons and twenty-six hundred letters. The Weimar edition of Luther's works, consisting of more than a hundred oversized volumes published since 1883, is still incomplete.

All kinds of Luther scholars have produced innumerable studies, ranging from analyses of minute details of Luther's life and thought to bold judgments regarding his place in the annals of history. Since the First International Congress for Luther Research in Aarhus, Denmark, in 1956, more than a hundred Luther scholars have met periodically to assess and share new research findings. The result is an almost unfathomable "Lutherania."

Luther employed sagacious scholarship and creative wit to talk and think his way through the complex historical events which, to a considerable degree, he helped to create. Luther scholars know only too well how difficult, if not impossible, it is to weave Luther's diverse works and ideas into an easily discernible and systematic whole. I have learned during my long association with Luther that attempts to pin him down are seldom successful, because of the speed, intensity, and creativity with which he lived and worked.

Luther's self-image of "court jester" (*Hofnarr*) is quite an appropriate one. More than any other man of his day, Luther appears to have worn his heart on his sleeve, tipping his cap to the troubled consciences of common folk, ringing his bells to warn the mighty in both church and world of God's unyielding power, and tapping his feet to the tune of the gospel's cheering and chilling news of Christ's lordship in a world nearing its end. And yet, whether as God's court jester or as Rome's boar in the vineyard, Luther—at his best and worst—was a biblical theologian (Luther scholars like to call him a professor of Old Testament)[2] who tried to restore the authority of the gospel in sixteenth-century Christendom, thus becoming entangled in a complex web of historical events which would rapidly change the shape of Christianity.

This book tries to distill, as it were, the historical Luther as well as the most significant research findings into a condensed retrospective which aims to be both an introduction to and an appraisal of Martin Luther. I resolved to write this book after engaging in a public disputation with the Roman Catholic Luther scholar Albert Brandenburg on "The Success and Failure of Martin Luther as a Reformer of the Church."[3] The disputation took place in 1977 at the Fifth International Congress for Luther Research in Lund, Sweden. Twenty years of teaching Luther to budding theologians, busy pastors, and curious congregations; twelve years of work as director of the Institute for Luther Studies at Gettysburg; and the five-hundredth anniversary of Luther's birth have impelled me to attempt what the institute has pledged to undertake: "a critical assessment of Martin Luther in terms of his significance for ecumenical Christianity and the contemporary world."

I have tried in part 1 to offer a historical profile showing why Luther became the leader of a reform movement within the church catholic. Part 2 describes what I think has become Luther's neuralgic heritage: the considerable pain he has caused along the curves of many Christian nerves. Part 3 suggests what might be considered Luther's ecumenical legacy. The final chapter sketches the history of Luther interpretations. A time chart, "Luther and the World, 1483–1555," is appended.

Luther's works are listed in English in the endnotes with the year of their publication, and with the original title in parenthesis when cited for the first time. All quotations appear in translation either from English editions or from the author. The endnotes list the original source first, usually the

Weimar edition; the same procedure also applies to quotations from other sixteenth-century sources. Biblical citations are from the Revised Standard Version. Other works are cited by author and title. Full data are available in the bibliography. Frequently cited works appear in abbreviation. Both the endnotes and the bibliography list only sources used by the author.

The word *Anfechtung* has been used in the original throughout the book. Luther sometimes rendered it in Latin as *tentatio*, "temptation," but its contextual meaning varies. It was one of Luther's favorite words to describe the attacks of Satan and/or struggle with God.

On the eve of St. Martin,
10 November 1982,
EWG

ACKNOWLEDGMENTS

I am grateful for the assistance given to me in the production of this book to the following persons and institutions: The Board of Directors of the Lutheran Theological Seminary at Gettysburg, for a sabbatical leave in 1980/81; the president and dean of the seminary, for making it possible to receive a Faculty Support Grant from Lutheran Brotherhood; the Lutheran Brotherhood, for their efficient handling of the grant; the staff of the seminary library, for their courteous cooperation in securing books; my "doctor father," Professor Emeritus Roland H. Bainton, and Carl J. Peter, Dean of the School of Religious Studies and Professor of Systematic Theology at the Catholic University of America—a partner in the Lutheran/Roman Catholic Dialogue and a colleague in the Washington Theological Consortium—for reading the final draft and making helpful suggestions; Norman A. Hjelm, Senior Editor and Director of Fortress Press, for supporting the project from beginning to end; Harold W. Rast, Executive Editor, for his efficient editing of the final draft; my students, for their sustained interest in Martin Luther; the Institute for Luther Studies, whose annual Martin Luther Colloquia with visiting Luther scholars has provided significant stimuli; the Fifth International Congress for Luther Research, for inviting me to engage in a public debate which this book continues; and last, but certainly not least, my spirited personal critic, editor, and typist Ruth C. L. Gritsch, who piloted my authorship through dangerous waters.

ABBREVIATIONS

ARG   *Archiv für Reformationsgeschichte*. Gütersloh: Bertelsmann, 1903– .

BC   *The Book of Concord*. Translated and edited by Theodore G. Tappert. Philadelphia: Fortress Press, 1959.

BS   *Die Bekenntnisschriften der evangelisch-lutherischen Kirche*, 3d ed., rev. Göttingen: Vandenhoeck & Ruprecht, 1930.

CR   *Corpus Reformatorum. Philippi Melanthon's Opera*. Edited by Carl B. Bretschneider and H. E. Bindseil. Halle: Schwetschke, 1834–60.

DRTA.JR   *Deutsche Reichstagsakten unter Kaiser Karl V. Jüngere Reihe*. Edited by Historische Kommission bei der Bayrischen Akademie der Wissenschaften. Gotha, 1893– . Photomechanical reprint. Göttingen: Vandenhoeck & Ruprecht, 1967.

EA var   *D. Martini Lutheri opera latina varii argumenti ad reformationis historiam imprimis pertinenta*. Frankfurt and Erlangen: Heyder & Zimmer, 1865–73.

LW   *Luther's Works*. American Edition. Edited by Jaroslav Pelikan and Helmut Lehmann. Philadelphia and St. Louis: Fortress Press and Concordia Pub. House, 1955–

LWC   Jaroslav Pelikan. "Luther the Expositor." *Luther's Works*, Companion Volume. St. Louis: Concordia Pub. House, 1959.

MA.I   Carl Mirbt and Kurt Aland, eds. *Quellen zur Geschichte des Papsttums und des römischen Katholizismus*, 6th ed., vol. 1. Tübingen: J. C. B. Mohr, 1967.

SD   Otto Scheel, ed. *Dokumente zu Luthers Entwicklung bis 1519*, 2d ed. rev. Tübingen: J. C. B. Mohr, 1929.

SJ   Preserved Smith and Charles M. Jacobs, eds. *Luther's Correspondence*, 2 vols. Philadelphia: Muhlenberg, 1913–18.

SML   Otto Scheel. *Martin Luther. Vom Katholizismus zur Reformation*, 3d ed., rev., 2 vols. Tübingen: J. C. B. Mohr, 1917–21.

TRE   *Theologische Realenzyklopädie*. Edited by Gerhard Krause and
         Gerhard Müller. Berlin and New York: Walter De Gruyter,
         1976–   .

WA   *Luthers Werke*. Kritische Gesamtausgabe. [Schriften.]
         Weimar: Böhlau, 1833–   .

WA.BR   *Luthers Werke*. Kritische Gesamtausgabe. Briefwechsel.
         Weimar: Böhlau, 1930–   .

WA.DB   *Luthers Werke*. Deutsche Bibel. Weimar: Böhlaus Nachfolger,
         1906–61.

WA.TR   *Luthers Werke*. Tischreden. Weimar: Böhlaus Nachfolger,
         1912–21.

PART 1

HISTORICAL PROFILE

1

THE POWER OF VOCATION

But perhaps you will say to me, "Why do you, by your books, teach throughout the world, when you are only a preacher in Wittenberg?" I answer: I have never wanted to do it and do not want to do it now. I was forced and driven into this position in the first place, when I had to become Doctor of Holy Scripture against my will. Then, as a Doctor in a general, free university, I began, at the command of pope and emperor, to do what such a doctor is sworn to do, expounding the Scriptures for all the world and teaching everybody. ("Commentary on Psalm 82"[:5], 1530. WA 31/1:212.6–13; LW 13:66)

EDUCATIONAL AND SPIRITUAL FORMATION

Sometime in the fall of 1511 or in the spring of 1512, the young Augustinian friar Martin met with his vicar-general, John Staupitz. The meeting took place under a pear tree in a garden just north of the Wittenberg Black Cloister, where monks were permitted to spend their prescribed recreation time. "Herr Magister, you must become a doctor and a preacher. Then you will have something to do," Staupitz told Luther. Luther objected, citing no less than fifteen reasons why he should not be called to preach and teach. Staupitz reproached him, "Do not be wiser, my friend, than the whole convent and the fathers." A frightened Luther burst out, "Herr Staupitz, you will bring me to my death! I will never endure it for three months." But Staupitz persisted: "Don't you know that our Lord God has many great matters to attend to? For these he needs wise and clever people to advise him. If you should die, you will be received into his council in heaven, because he too has need of some doctors."[1]

This encounter under the pear tree at the end of Luther's formal academic education reflects his self-image as a reformer of the church catholic. "I would not exchange my doctor's degree for all the world's gold," he declared twenty years later.

For I would surely in the long run lose courage and fall into despair if . . . I had undertaken these great and serious matters without call or commission. But God and the whole world bears me testimony that I entered into this work

2

publicly and by virtue of my office as teacher and preacher, and have carried it on hitherto by the grace and help of God.[2]

Luther's sense of vocation was deeply grounded in his academic training—the bridge from slavery to freedom in the medieval world for those not born into nobility. He was born into a family which treasured economic and social status.

The Luther family (with various spellings: Ludher, Luder, Lueder, Lutter, Lauther, probably derived from the German first name, Lothar) belonged to a particular Thuringian community of peasants known as "the inheritance tax people" (*Erbzinsleute*). They were a group of families who lived in a village or a farm, owning land in common; they shared fields, meadows, water, and woods. Unlike other citizens they paid a small inheritance tax, based on real-estate value, to ecclesiastical and secular authorities rather than paying a tax based on a feudal landlord's individual assessment. The Luthers lived in the village of Möhra, near Eisleben. Heine Luther, Martin's paternal grandfather, was known to have a farm in Möhra.[3] Martin's father, Hans, married Margarethe Lindemann, the daughter of a highly educated burgher family in nearby Eisenach.[4] Shortly before 1483, Hans and Margarethe Luther moved to Eisleben, the capital of the county of Mansfeld and a thriving copper-mining town which offered healthy young men opportunities to earn a reasonable income. Hans had moved because he was not the youngest son and therefore could not inherit the family farm. Soon after his arrival in Eisleben he managed to start a small smelting enterprise of his own.[5]

Martin was born on the eve of St. Martin, 10 November 1483, shortly before midnight. He was the second of four sons and the brother to four sisters born later.[6] The next day he was baptized in the Church of Saints Peter and Paul by Pastor Bartholomy Rennebecher.

The parents were determined to see one of their older sons take up a vocation which would yield wealth and status in the medieval feudal society. To achieve this goal, Martin was enrolled very early in the Latin Grammar School at Mansfeld, where his parents had moved in 1484. The boy had to be carried to school, since he was not old enough to walk.[7] Luther went to school in Mansfeld until he was fourteen, completing the first part of the medieval curriculum, the *trivium*, which consisted of Latin grammar, logic, and rhetoric. Strict spiritual formation accompanied academic learning: the children learned to pray before and after every meal; they learned to recite a confession of sins, the Apostles' Creed, the Lord's Prayer, and the Hail Mary; and they were frequently asked to commit to memory a whole psalm from the Vulgate Bible. Before Martin was twelve, he could read and speak Latin, appreciate the rhetoric of Roman prose and poetry, and he knew elementary musical theory, especially hymnody and liturgy.

Although few details are known about Martin's years at the Mansfeld school, he emerged from it ready for further academic training. Since his father had friends and business connections in the large city of Magdeburg (about twenty-five to thirty thousand inhabitants) north of Eisleben, he sent Martin and Hans Reinecke, the son of a family friend, to live in Magdeburg with the "Brethren of the Common Life" (*Fratres communis vitae*), a non-monastic order which cherished the simple, apostolic Christian life and placed great emphasis on education, Bible study, and pastoral care.[8] While in Magdeburg, Luther was a welcome visitor at the home of Dr. Paul Mosshauer, one of his father's business associates who had been in the foundry business and had now become an official at the archbishop's residence. Since Luther spent only one year in Magdeburg (from the fall of 1496 or the spring of 1497 until the end of that year),[9] nothing is known about his education there.

One of the customary ways for young students in Germany to earn part of their room, board, and tuition was to sing, going from door to door. Although Luther's father certainly had the means to pay for Martin's education, Luther later fondly recalled his years as a "crumb collector," someone who sang for a morsel of bread. "I too was such a crumb collector once, begging from door to door, especially in my beloved city of Eisenach—though afterwards my dear father lovingly and faithfully kept me at the University of Erfurt, by his sweat and labor helping me to get where I am."[10]

"Beloved Eisenach" provided Luther with further academic and spiritual formation at the parochial school of St. George. Some of his mother's relatives as well as the husband of the sister of Luther's paternal grandmother, Conrad Kutter, a sacristan at St. Nicholas Church, lived in Eisenach. Eventually, Luther lived with the family of Heinrich Schwalbe and took their son Caspar to school with him, having been asked to be a sort of big brother to Caspar. Luther may also have lived for a while in the home of Mrs. Ursula Cotta, who had liked his singing and had asked him to stay in her home.[11] Heinrich Schwalbe had been mayor of Eisenach and was serving on the city council. Thus Luther met a number of interesting people in the Schwalbe home, among them some Franciscan monks who impressed the adolescent student with their talk of penance and the art of dying.[12] Luther also had a cordial relationship with the Eisenach priest John Braun, a grandfatherly figure, and with some teachers at the school of St. George. There was much joking and singing at the Braun parsonage, where students and teachers frequently met for a convivial evening.[13]

Little is known about Luther's actual schooling in Eisenach, but Philip Melanchthon's somewhat uncritical summary does provide some evidence. Young Martin is described as an expert in Latin studies who had outstripped his companions in eloquence, languages, and poetic verse.[14]

In any event, the eighteen-year-old Luther was quite ready to begin his higher education at Erfurt University, and his record for the next four years at Erfurt (1501–1505) seems to substantiate Melanchthon's judgment. In less than two years Luther received the baccalaureate degree in liberal arts, ranking thirtieth in a class of fifty-seven; two years later he completed graduate work for the master's degree, ranking second in a class of seventeen.[15] Both degrees entitled the twenty-one-year-old Luther to teach in a school of liberal arts.

The years in Erfurt also taught Luther severe academic discipline combined with strict rules of moral behavior. Students had to live in a dormitory (the *Burse*), and they spent all day in classes or in preparation for them; they were allowed to mingle with women only on special occasions, probably only at weddings; and they could consume only a prescribed amount of beer. However, the young scholar enjoyed reading the classic authors of the Greco-Roman world taught by the beloved professor Jodocus Trutvetter, known as "Doctor Eisenach," who spiced his philosophical lectures with illustrations from the ancient classics and who often disclosed his dislike for scholastic subtleties. Luther also studied Aristotelian physics, metaphysics, and ethics with Professor Trutvetter, learning his progressive interpretation of the proper distinction between the realm of faith and the realm of reason.

The Erfurt faculty's method of teaching was the "modern way" (*via moderna*), which was based on the systematic thought of the British theologian William of Occam (ca. 1285–1349). In contrast to the adherents of the "old way" (*via antiqua*), whose system was based on that of Thomas Aquinas (1225–74), which assigned human reason a decisive place in theology, Occamists stressed the contrast between faith and reason. Whereas faith relates to divine revelation, reason is tied to the realm of this world. The struggle between the *via antiqua* and the *via moderna* eventually resulted in a separation of theology from philosophy, of divine truth from human experience, especially with the investigation of nature through scientific experiments.[16]

Luther did not feel that he had been called to become a theologian or philosopher after completing his training for the degree of Master of Liberal Arts. Instead, he followed his father's advice and, in spring 1505, enrolled in the School of Law at Erfurt. Continuing to live in the dormitory with his friends, he did some obligatory teaching and began to immerse himself in the study of canon law. Nor did he have any intention of becoming a celibate monk. Much later, in 1521, he told his father, "You had learned from numerous examples that this way of life [to be a monk] turned out sadly for many. You were determined, therefore, to tie me down with an honorable and wealthy marriage."[17] Why, then, did Luther enter the Black Cloister of the Reformed Congregation of Augustinian Hermits in Erfurt on 17 July 1505?

Although the question cannot be answered with complete historiographi-

cal satisfaction, there is sufficient evidence to suggest that Luther had had a
traumatic experience and that fear of death drove him into the monastic
life.[18] He told his father, in a letter dated 21 November 1521:

> I remember very well that after we were reconciled and you were [again] talking
> with me, I told you that I had been called by terrors from heaven and that I did
> not become a monk of my own free will and desire, still less to gain any
> gratification of the flesh, but that I was walled in by the terror and the agony of
> sudden death and forced by necessity to take the vow. Then you said, "Let us
> hope that it was not an illusion and a deception."[19]

The "terrors from heaven" and the "agony of sudden death" refer to what
Luther experienced during a severe thunderstorm on 2 July 1505. Thirty-
four years later, a guest at Luther's table recorded Luther's account of it.

> "Today is the anniversary of my entrance into the convent at Erfurt," Luther
> said, and he began to tell the story of how he had taken his vow: how almost
> fourteen days before, on the road near Stotternheim not far from Erfurt he was
> so frightened by a thunderbolt that in terror he shouted: "Help, Saint Anna, I
> will become a monk" . . . "The day before St. Alexius [July 16] I invited some of
> my best friends to a farewell party, as on the next day they were to lead me to
> the monastery." To those he left behind, however, he said: "Today you see me for
> the last time." "In tears they led me away. My father was very angry about my
> vow, but I persisted in my determination. I never considered leaving the
> monastery. I had died completely to the world until God's proper time and the
> young fellow Tetzel forced me to leave it, and Dr. Staupitz incited me against the
> pope."[20]

Even though Luther failed to find peace in the monastery of the
Augustinian Hermits, he was nevertheless a fine example of academic and
spiritual formation. He was awed by the drama of initiation into monastic
otherworldliness. When he took the monastic vows in the fall of 1506, he was
elated, for he had been promised the peace of mind and the state of grace
due to a friar who dedicates his entire life to serving God and the church. In
preparation for the priesthood, Luther had to concentrate on the liturgy of
the Roman Mass as interpreted by the well-known Tübingen theologian
Gabriel Biel in his *Exposition of the Canon of the Mass (Espositio canonis
missae)* of 1499. Luther later remarked, "When I read it my heart bled."[21]
He quickly received the holy orders of subdeacon and deacon, and on 3 April
1507 he was ordained priest. It was the high point of his young life. Luther's
father came to Erfurt with twenty horsemen to attend the ceremony and
donated twenty guilders to the monastery. Luther recalled his fright when
he celebrated his first Mass on 2 May 1507: "When I stood there during the
mass and began the canon [the consecration of bread and wine] I was so
frightened that I would have fled if I hadn't been admonished by the prior."[22]
The power of the priesthood was awesome to him, for no one else had the

power, through the Sacrament of the Altar, to bring Christ to the people. But when, during the festive dinner, the new young priest explained to his father that his vocation was the result of the thunderstorm experience two years earlier, Hans Luther countered, "Let us hope that it was not an illusion and a deception," and added a little later, "Have you not also heard that parents are to be obeyed?" Luther much later admitted that he had never heard anything so striking from anyone. But, "I heard only a man, and boldly ignored you; though in my heart I could not ignore your word."[23]

The young priest followed a grueling schedule during those early years in the monastery. Besides the terrible living conditions, there were spiritual exercises and a tough academic program to follow. A monk lived in a small cell with one window and no heat and was cut off from communication with the world. He had to obey the strict dress code of the Augustinian Friars, which was to wear a long white dress with a black cowl and hood girded by a leather sash. Even during their short sleeping hours, the friars were not permitted to undress. Hourly prayers and daily masses in addition to academic work were intended to keep the friars constantly alert and prepared for a life of chastity, poverty, and obedience. The two simple meals a day were supposed to be endured, not enjoyed.

Luther was determined to do his best. He studied hard, tried to mortify his flesh by fasting and praying, and fulfilled his priestly duties of celebrating Mass and hearing confession. He was praised by friend and foe alike as an exemplary monk.[24] His own words best depict the spiritual and academic pressures he was under:

> When I was a monk I was unwilling to omit any of the [prescribed] prayers, but when I was busy with public lecturing and writing I often accumulated my appointed prayers for a whole week, or even two or three weeks. Then I would take a Saturday off, or shut myself in for as long as three days without food and drink, until I had said the prescribed prayers. This made my head split, and as a consequence I couldn't close my eyes for five nights, lay sick unto death, and went out of my senses. Even after I had quickly recovered and tried again to read, my head went 'round and 'round. Thus our Lord God drew me, as if by force, from that torment of prayers. To such an extent had I been captive![25]

Given those living conditions and the lack of modern medicines, especially aspirin, it is no wonder that the young Luther underwent what researchers have dubbed "the monastic struggle." Yet despite all of the pressures, Luther continued the daily grind imposed on him by the Augustinian order. He took the course of advanced theological studies (the *studium generale*) which was taught by Father John Nathin, who was a student of Gabriel Biel and who presented the modernist thought of Occam, and he did the spiritual exercises for the mortification of the flesh which centered on the daily "offices" of prayer and on the sacrament of penance, usually exercised in private confession. Luther may have absorbed much theology and learned to deal with the new theological questions posed by Occamism, but he was more exposed to the teaching of traditional systematic theology as outlined in Peter Lombard's four books, especially *The Sentences (Libri IV Sententiarum)*, the textbook of medieval theology since the twelfth century.

When looking back on these years of study, Luther was thankful that he had been forced to become well-acquainted with the Bible. The rules of the Augustinian Hermits required frequent reading of the Bible. Luther had been given a personal copy, bound in red, when he entered the monastery, and he later boasted that he was one of the few monks who read the Bible frequently and with care.[26] Yet the Hermits' great emphasis on ascetic discipline and their attempts to appease God, the judge of life, in the world of flesh, evil, and death obscured for Luther the biblical message of mercy and redemption in Christ. "I shuddered all over that word and at the name of Jesus Christ," he told his students during his lectures on Genesis.

> For I thought that He had been represented as my Judge, not as my Savior. I admired and respected a priest arrayed in his long vestment or bringing a sacrifice for the living and the dead more than I admired and respected the doctrine concerning Christ together with the promises and the sacraments. I thought that this doctrine was of no concern whatever to me.[27]

Luther went beyond the requirement. He memorized whole portions of the Bible and diligently used existing exegetical methods. "I read the Bible diligently," he recalled. "Sometimes one important statement occupied all my thoughts for a whole day."[28] Whereas Luther's teachers stressed a study of the Bible seen in light of ecclesiastically approved commentaries, Luther wrestled with biblical texts in order to get answers to his own spiritual questions and was frequently plunged into despair. On 18 January 1518, he wrote to his friend George Spalatin:

> It is absolutely certain that one cannot enter into the [meaning of] Scripture by study or innate intelligence. Therefore your first task is to begin with prayer. You must ask that the Lord in his great mercy grant you a true understanding of his words, should it please him to accomplish anything through you for his glory and not for your glory or that of any other man. . . . You must therefore completely despair of your own diligence and intelligence and rely solely on the infusion of the Spirit. Believe me, for I have had experience in this matter.[29]

Luther found this kind of approach to Bible study confirmed in the writings of the great church father Augustine rather than in the scholars of the Middle Ages. What Augustine had to say in his work *On the Spirit and the Letter (De spiritu et litera)* decisively shaped Luther's early struggles with the Bible.[30]

Luther was such a good academician that his superiors, at the behest of Vicar-General Staupitz, sent him to the University of Wittenberg in the fall of 1508. He was to replace Father Wolfgang Ostermayer, the Augustinian professor of moral philosophy, and lecture on Aristotelian ethics. He simultaneously continued his studies for the last two degrees before the doctorate: the Biblical Baccalaureate (*Baccalaureus Biblicus*), which would make him a specialist in biblical studies, and the Master of Sentences (*Sententiarius*), which would entitle him to lecture on *The Sentences* by Peter Lombard (a systematic discussion of Christian doctrines). Wittenberg awarded him the *Baccalaureus Biblicus* in the spring of 1509, and Erfurt made him a *Sententiarius* that same fall after his return from Wittenberg.

The twenty-six-year-old rising star of the Augustinian Hermits encountered his first political challenge as a loyal member of the Erfurt convent when the Roman and German ecclesiastical authorities proposed to merge the Conventional and Reformed Augustinians. Whereas the Reformed— among them Erfurt—pressed for strict spiritual discipline and high academic standards, the Conventional wing favored a less rigorous, rather lax adherence to the Augustinian rule. Luther made it well-known that he favored the Reformed position. With the approval of Vicar-General Staupitz, the three most obstinate convents—Erfurt, Nuremberg and Kulmbach— decided to send Luther and another friar to Rome, since Luther and his Erfurt teacher John Nathin had been unsuccessful in persuading the Archbishop of Magdeburg to oppose the merger.

It took almost forty days to make the 850-mile journey from Saxony to Rome, and it was Luther's only trip abroad. The appeal failed; the head of the Augustinian order, General Epidis, rejected the petition. But that journey, during the winter of 1510/11, made a lasting impression on Luther. He was especially struck by the confusing bureaucracy and by the general moral decay.

> My chief concern when I departed for Rome was that I might make a full confession [of my sins] from my youth up and might become pious, although I had twice made such a confession in Erfurt. In Rome I encountered the most unlearned men. Dear God, what could the cardinals be expected to know when they were so overloaded with business and political affairs? We who study every day and are occupied every hour have trouble enough.[31]

Much of what Luther later had to say about Rome would be influenced by the sights and sounds he had experienced in that decaying capital of Christianity.

After their return, Luther and Lang changed their minds and agreed with Staupitz, who had managed a compromise between the feuding wings of the Augustinian Hermits in Germany. The Erfurters, however, stubbornly clung to their independence. Luther and Lang openly defied their immediate superiors in a vote on the matter and were consequently sent to Wittenberg into a kind of exile. Vicar-General Staupitz, however, had approved the move, for he had come to know Luther well by 1511. He appointed Luther subprior of the Wittenberg monastery with the responsibility of supervising academic studies there.

Although Luther had finished all the required academic work for the doctor's degree, he was unable to pay the necessary fee to obtain it. But Staupitz told Elector Frederick of Saxony that Luther would be a lifelong professor of Holy Scripture, and Frederick agreed to put up the required fifty guilders. Staupitz received the money in Leipzig when he and Luther traveled there on 9 October 1512; the receipt for the fifty guilders from the electoral treasury is the oldest sample of Luther's handwriting we have.[32]

The day Luther was awarded the doctorate, 19 October 1512, was indeed a festive one. Luther's Erfurt superiors were there; there was a solemn speech by the president of the university; Luther swore allegiance to the Roman church, promising not to teach vain and strange doctrines, especially those the church had condemned; he received the doctoral ring depicting the trinity, a Bible, and the biretta; and he gave a brief lecture and supervised a disputation. A banquet concluded the festivities, which had taken place in the Castle Church. Many of Wittenberg's two thousand to twenty-five hundred inhabitants lined the streets to observe the traditional doctoral procession while the church bells rang out. Luther had found his place in life—to be a professor of theology with the special assignment of interpreting Holy Scripture (*lectura biblica*).

In another ceremony on 21 October, Luther became a member of the theological faculty of Wittenberg University, having promised to be faithful to the rules and regulations and to tend the interests of the department of theology. He became the official successor to Staupitz, who had had to relinquish teaching because of his increasing administrative duties as vicar-general of the Augustinian Order. Beginning with the winter semester of 1513/14, Luther lectured two to three hours every week throughout his life, with scheduled interruptions for vacations and holy days and very few unscheduled interruptions due to illness, the plague, exile, and travels. In addition, he was required to preach at the monastery as well as in the Town Church (*Stadtkirche*), though not regularly.[33]

In Luther's classroom students used biblical texts printed with extra space between lines and with wide margins so that they could add their notes, or "glosses." Interlinear glosses were brief explanations, mostly of a grammatical or philological nature, of individual words and phrases in the text; marginal glosses depicted the text's meaning according to church fathers and ecclesiastic tradition. The students used a separate notebook to record Luther's own extensive interpretations ("scholia") of biblical texts. The scholia were brief studies of either words or whole passages which Luther interpreted in the light of other interpretations and in which he disclosed the theological meaning of the text.[34]

Luther shared these biblical labors with successive generations of students for thirty-three years. He was first and foremost a biblical scholar and teacher, intent on guarding the proper distinction between the Word of God and human tradition. This was the focus of his whole career.

ANFECHTUNGEN AND BREAKTHROUGHS

Throughout his life, Luther was subject to bouts of anxiety ranging from simple doubts to deep depressions, which he labeled *Anfechtungen*.[35] These *Anfechtungen*, especially those he suffered while in the monastery, have tempted some Luther interpreters to engage in long-distance psycho-analysis. But research has made it clear that Luther's inner, personal experiences cannot be separated from his theological perceptions, his scholarly work, and especially his study of the Bible. "I didn't learn my theology all at once," Luther said, "I had to ponder over it ever more deeply, and my spiritual trials *(Anfechtungen, tentationes)* were of help to me in this, for one does not learn anything without practice."[36]

Luther was a child of his age, sensitive to the inexplicable trials and tribulations besetting medieval society. "Dear Doctor, our Lord God treats people too horribly," he once complained to Staupitz in the Erfurt monastery. "Who can serve Him as long as He strikes people down right and left, as we see He does in many cases involving our adversaries?"[37] There were plagues for which there was no medical help; there was magic and sorcery, concrete evidence of the devil's work; and there was the fear of a life after death subject to God's wrath. Such fears made Luther feel like a soldier in a panic-stricken army, frightened by the sound of a driven leaf (Lev. 26:36). God appeared to be an unjust judge, mysterious in his predestination of people and in his toleration of the devil's work.

Staupitz and other father confessors attempted to help Luther find some consolation. When Luther asked him, "Why does God seem so unjust?" Staupitz answered, "Dear fellow, learn to think of God differently. If he did not treat them [people] this way, how could God restrain those blockheads? God strikes us for our own good, in order that He might free us who otherwise would be crushed."[38]

One of the ways Luther did search for a gracious God was through the sacrament of penance. Theologians like Staupitz saw penance not so much as an effort to please an angry God, but rather as a spiritual exercise concentrating on God's love for his sinful creatures expressed through the cross of Christ. Luther gave Staupitz credit for his own understanding of penance *(poenitentia)*. "I accepted you as a messenger from heaven," he told Staupitz in a letter dated 30 May 1518,

> When you said that *poenitentia* is genuine only if it begins with love for justice and for God, and that what they [the Occamist theologians] consider to be the

final stage and completion [namely, the love of God] is in reality rather the very beginning of *poenitentia*. Your word pierced me like a sharp arrow of the Mighty [Ps. 120:4]. As a result, I began to compare your statements with the passages of Scripture which speak of *poenitentia*. And behold—what a most pleasant scene! Biblical words came leaping toward me from all sides, clearly smiling and nodding assent to your statement. They so supported your opinion that while formerly almost no word in the whole Scripture was more bitter to me than *poenitentia* (although I zealously made a pretense before God and tried to express a feigned and constrained love for him), now no word sounds sweeter or more pleasant to me than *poenitentia*. The commandments of God become sweet when they are read not only in books but also in the wounds of the sweetest Savior.[39]

Whereas even the revisionist theologians of the Occamist school like Gabriel Biel viewed salvation as the process from contrition through fear of God to absolution as evidence of the love of God, Luther learned from Staupitz and from his study of Scripture that God's love is truly revealed in the wounds of Christ rather than in a reward for a contrite heart. What school theologians asserted to be the completion of the penitential process—the experiencing of divine love and mercy—Luther discovered to be the beginning of penance. Accordingly, the commandments of God already disclose his love for his sinful creatures, who are saved not through their own attempts to fulfill the commandments, but through faith in the Christ who fulfilled the commandments on their behalf.

Sometime during his early years as priest-professor in Wittenberg, Luther learned that penance means a change of mind (in Greek, *metanoia*) from doing something to please God to yielding to his mercy in Jesus Christ. Whether Luther's experience of spiritual change, a "conversion," was gradual or traumatically sudden may never be fully known. Numerous studies have been written about the date and circumstances of this transition from Roman Catholicism to the "evangelical" stance which formed the impetus of the Reformation. A variety of factors could have influenced the young Luther: his increasing doubt about the spiritual value of Aristotelian methodology, even when modified or criticized by the modernist theology of William of Occam and his disciples; his study of the church fathers, especially Augustine; his relaxation with Latin poetry and prose, especially Ovid, Vergil, and Plautus; his identification with German mystics, particularly John Tauler and the "German Theology" (*Theologia Germanica*), which Luther edited with praise in 1516;[40] his contact with other Augustinian friars, whom he visited after 1515 when he was elected district vicar of the eleven monasteries in the Congregation of the Reformed Augustinians in central Germany; and above all, his intensive Bible study, particularly Psalms and the letters of Paul.

Anyone in Luther's position, with the kind of responsibilities he had, could have *Anfechtungen*. In a letter dated 26 October 1516 to John Lang, his close friend and now prior to the Erfurt monastery, Luther described his hectic life.

> I nearly need two copyists or secretaries. All day long I do almost nothing else than write letters; therefore I am sometimes not aware of whether or not I constantly repeat myself, but you will see. I am a preacher at the monastery, I am a reader during mealtimes, I am asked daily to preach in the city [town] church, I have to supervise the study [of novices and friars], I am a vicar (and that means I am eleven times prior), I am caretaker of the fish[pond] at Leitzkau [source of income for the monastery], I represent the people of Herzberg at the court in Torgau [in a dispute between parish and prince], I lecture on Paul [Galatians], and I am assembling [material for] a commentary on the Psalms. . . . I hardly have any uninterrupted time to say the Hourly Prayers and celebrate [mass]. Besides all this there are my own struggles with the flesh, the world, and the devil. See what a lazy man I am![41]

Luther himself later linked his breakthrough to radically new insights to the intensive work on biblical texts he performed in the "tower room" (*Turmstube*) of the Wittenberg monastery, where his study was located; thus the event has become known as the "tower experience." In a table talk dating from the summer of 1532, Luther said, "The Holy Spirit unveiled the Scriptures for me in this tower," adding in other table talks that this experience took place in the monastery's "heated room," "the secret place of the monks," and "lavatory" (*cloaca*).[42] But Luther never gave either a definite date or a specific place. Luther research has produced extensive documentation for early as well as for late dates—sometime between 1513 and 1518—but chances for a scholarly consensus on the matter are very slim since the sources simply do not yield conclusive evidence.

Scholars have also found it exceedingly difficult to reach a consensus concerning the relationship between Luther's early theological formulations reflecting this change of mind and the assertions made by late medieval scholastic theologians like William of Occam.[43] Luther described his experiences of the period from 1517 to 1519 in the Preface to his complete edition of Latin works in 1545. After reminiscing about the publication of the Ninety-five Theses in 1517, about his encounters with Cardinal Cajetan in Augsburg in 1518, and with the theologian John Eck at the Leipzig Debate in 1519, Luther described a particular exegetical struggle with Paul's Epistle to the Romans:

> I had indeed been captivated with an extraordinary ardor for understanding Paul in the Epistle to the Romans. But up till then it was not the cold blood about the heart, but a single word in Chapter 1 [:17], "In it the righteousness of God is revealed," that had stood in my way. For I hated that word "righteousness of God," which, according to the use and custom of all the teachers, I had been taught to understand philosophically regarding the formal

or active righteousness, as they called it, with which God is righteous and punishes the unrighteous sinner.

Though I lived as a monk without reproach, I felt that I was a sinner before God with an extremely disturbed conscience. I could not believe that he was placated by my satisfaction. I did not love, yes, I hated the righteous God who punishes sinners, and secretly, if not blasphemously, certainly murmuring greatly, I was angry with God, and said, "As if, indeed, it is not enough that miserable sinners, eternally lost through original sin, are crushed by every kind of calamity by the law of the decalogue, without having God add pain by the gospel and also by the gospel threatening us with his righteousness and wrath!" Thus I raged with a fierce and troubled conscience. Nevertheless, I beat importunately upon Paul at that place, most ardently desiring to know what St. Paul wanted.

At last, by the mercy of God, meditating day and night, I gave heed to the context of the words, namely, "In it the righteousness of God is revealed, as it is written, 'He who through faith is righteous shall live.'" There I began to understand that the righteousness of God is that by which the righteous lives by a gift of God, namely by faith. *And this is the meaning: the righteousness of God is revealed by the gospel, namely, the passive righteousness with which merciful God justifies us by faith, as it is written, "He who through faith is righteous shall live." Here I felt that I was altogether born again and had entered paradise itself through open gates.* There a totally other face of the entire Scripture showed itself to me. Thereupon I ran through the Scriptures from memory. I also found in other terms an analogy, as, the work of God, that is, what God does in us, the power of God, with which he makes us strong, the wisdom of God, with which He makes us wise, the strength of God, the salvation of God, the glory of God.

And I extolled my sweetest word with a love as great as the hatred with which I had before hated the word "righteousness of God." Thus that place in Paul was for me truly the gate to paradise.[44]

This recollection, written by the sixty-two-year-old Luther, may not be as precise as scholars would like to have it. Its most significant aspect, however, is Luther's new understanding by 1519 of the phrase "the righteousness of God." As a professor of biblical theology, as preacher at the monastery and at the Town Church, Luther had used all his vocational skills to discover what it means to be righteous before God. His first lectures on Psalms (1513–15) already disclose how he wrestled with the question of righteousness in the context of his quest for the difference between biblical and scholastic theology. By employing traditional exegetical methods as well as insights gained from Augustine, Luther could depict the Psalms as the christological hymnbook of the Bible.[45] God appears both as judge and as savior in Christ—a disclosure of his contrariness as the Creator who demands judgment through the law and as Redeemer who promises mercy through the gospel. God cannot be appeased by such human virtues as monastic humility. Rather, God offers peace through Christ's atonement to those who

suffer the existential *Anfechtung* of sin, which is the desire to live without
God. Luther, therefore, saw true humility as his own nothingness before the
God who wants to be trusted rather than appeased. Thus, *Anfechtung* and
faith belong together, because that is the way in which God disclosed himself
in Christ. As Luther put it in his exposition of Ps. 69:3 ("I am weary with my
crying . . ."):

> Nothing is safe where everything is safe, nothing so sick as when everything is
> healthy; there is no temptation when all is temptation, no persecution when all
> is persecution. Thus the devil now fights the church with the greatest
> persecution, because he fights with no persecution but rather with security and
> idleness. Therefore woe to us, who are so snatched away by present things and
> foolishly do not see the devil's trap![46]

Luther's lectures on Romans (1515–16), on Galatians (1516–17), and on
Hebrews (1517–18) reveal his intensified search for the proper meaning of
righteousness.[47] Does righteousness belong to God rather than to the
creature, thus being an alien righteousness? Or is righteousness something
which the creature has to attain through good works, thus living out an active
righteousness meriting salvation? What is the proper interpretation of the
Latin genitive "of God" (*Dei*)?

In these lectures Luther rediscovered the ancient prophetic insight into
the covenant between God and Israel: one becomes righteous by trusting
only in God's love for his creatures. "The righteous shall live by faith" (Hab.
2:4). One is righteous "by faith alone," that is, by yielding to God, the only
source of a never-ending relationship. Luther, therefore, rediscovered the
God who, like a loving father, loves his children without first asking whether
or not they deserve it. Why the shift from the just, wrathful God to the
merciful, accepting Father? Because the righteousness which God demands
for salvation is the righteousness of Christ who atoned for sinful creatures.
There are, then, "two kinds of righteousness," according to a Palm Sunday
sermon so entitled, preached by Luther—probably in 1519—as an
exposition of Phil. 2:5–6.

> The first is alien righteousness, that is the righteousness of another, instilled
> from without. This is the righteousness of Christ by which he justifies through
> faith, as it is written in 1 Cor. 1 [:30]: "Whom God made our wisdom, our
> righteousness and sanctification and redemption. . . ." The second kind of
> righteousness is our proper righteousness, not because we alone work it, but
> because we work with that first and alien righteousness. This is that manner of
> life spent profitably in good works, in the first place, in slaying the flesh and
> crucifying the desires with respect to the self, of which we read in Gal. 5 [:24]:
> "And those who belong to Christ Jesus have crucified the flesh with its passions
> and desires." In the second place, this righteousness consists in love to one's
> neighbor, and in the third place, in meekness and fear toward God.[48]

Luther felt "born again" because he had focused his attention on what God did in Christ rather than on what he, Luther, could do for God. Faith is the bond which unites the church, the bride, with Christ, the bridegroom, just as "a man shall leave his father and mother and be joined to his wife, and the two shall become one. This is a great mystery" (Eph. 5:32). Luther called this union the result of a "cheerful change and argument" (*fröhlicher Wechsel und Streit*) in his treatise, "The Freedom of the Christian" (1520), dedicated to Pope Leo X.

> Christ is God and man in one person. He has neither sinned nor died, and is not condemned, and he cannot sin, die, or be condemned; his righteousness, life, and salvation are unconquerable, eternal, omnipotent. By the wedding ring of faith he shares in the sins, death, and pains of hell which are his bride's. As a matter of fact, he makes them his own and acts as if they were his own and as if he himself had sinned; he suffered, died, and descended into hell that he might overcome hell. . . . Who then can fully appreciate what this royal marriage means? Who can understand the riches of the glory of this grace? Here this rich and divine bridegroom Christ marries this poor, wicked harlot, redeems her from all her evil, and adorns her with all his goodness.[49]

Luther's *Anfechtungen* and breakthroughs were intimately linked to his vocation as priest, professor, administrator, and counselor. He experienced his greatest *Anfechtung* when he discovered the wide divergence between scholastic theology and Holy Scripture; and he made his greatest breakthrough when he began to appropriate the existential character of biblical theology into the foundation of both private and public life with God.

COMMITMENTS

Luther used the traditional medieval method of public disputation to make his insights known. On 25 September 1516, on the occasion of the examination of Bartholomew Bernhardi—one of Luther's students and dean of the liberal arts faculty—for the degree of Master of Sentences, the Wittenberg theological faculty was drawn into a debate about a classic issue: the relationship of the human will to the grace of God in the process of salvation.[50] As one of Luther's adherents, Bernhardi argued that the human will can only turn to evil and that salvation comes only through the grace of God. Augustine had held this view and had rejected the position of the British monk Pelagius, who taught a doctrine of free will (that one can say yes or no to the offer of God's grace) and who denied the doctrine of original sin (that Adam's sin is trasmitted to everyone through conception and birth). Luther, who cherished the view of Augustine, used Bernhardi to revive that ancient controversy by attacking any and all versions of Pelagianism or "semi-Pelagianism" contained in traditional medieval scholastic theology.

Although the majority of the theological faculty opposed Bernhardi's stance at the time of the disputation, Luther's power of conviction and his skills as a teacher soon prevailed. "Our theology and St. Augustine are progressing well," he wrote to his friend Lang on 18 May 1517,

> and with God's help rule at our University. Aristotle is gradually falling from his throne, and his final doom is only a matter of time. It is amazing how the lectures on *The Sentences* are disdained. Indeed no one can expect to have any students if he does not want to teach this theology, that is, lecture on the Bible or on St. Augustine or another teacher of ecclesiastical eminence.[51]

Dean Andreas Bodenstein von Carlstadt was persuaded to study Augustine, and when he did he was so enthralled with the new theology that he defended it in fifty-one theses in April 1517.[52] On 4 September 1517, Luther presided at another public disputation at the awarding of the degree of Biblical Baccalaureate to his student Franz Günther. Günther defended some theses against scholastic theology which had been written by Luther. A defense of the position of salvation by grace alone, the theses attacked Aristotelian methodology, the scholastic notion of free will, and the reliance of theologians on philosophical speculation. They affirmed instead the biblical view of penance as trust in Christ's atonement, salvation by predestination rather than by good works, and the proper distinctions between law, will, and grace. All ninety-seven theses, Luther contended, contained "nothing that is not in agreement with the Catholic church and the teachers of the church."[53]

Luther soon discovered the dangerous interrelation between theological assertions and ecclesiastical practice. If an effort of human will can appease God, as official theology taught, then money can become the embodiment of human will. Moreover, Johann Gutenberg's invention of the printing press in 1450 had made possible the beginnings of a credit system which led to the establishment of banks as centers of trade and finance. Soon there developed a symbiotic relationship between the new money market and the well-established, ecclesiastic practice of granting an "indulgence" (an excuse from punishment for a sin) for any human effort of penance and/or satisfaction—from joining a crusade to giving money to the church. Both the doctrine and the use of "indulgences" had become complex and controversial.[54] Normative doctrine understood an indulgence to be a partial or total remission of punishment due to a sin already forgiven by a priest. To obtain an indulgence, the penitent had to do a good work, including making cash payments; the punishment thus avoided included time spent in purgatory. Priestly admonitions to do good works, as well as popular belief in the efficacy of prayers for the dead, did much to encourage the sale of indulgences, which funded various ecclesiastical causes. The crude efforts of Bishop Albrecht of Mainz to use the sale of indulgences to finance his advancement to archbishop prompted Luther to warn the Wittenbergers of the ecclesiastic abuse of indulgences and to ask the theological faculty to debate the issue. In a sermon preached on 24 February 1517, Luther attacked the sale of indulgences by the Dominican monk John Tetzel, whom Bishop Albrecht had authorized to start an indulgence-sales campaign in the neighboring lands of Mainz, Magdeburg, Halberstadt, and Brandenburg. Luther concluded the sermon:

> Would that I were a liar when I say that indulgences are rightly so called, for to indulge means to permit, and indulgence is equivalent to impunity, permission to sin, and license to nullify the cross of Christ. Or, if indulgences are to be permitted, they should be given only to those who are weak in faith, that those who seek to attain gentleness and lowliness through suffering, as the Lord here says [Matt. 11:28], may not be offended. For not through indulgences, but through gentleness and lowliness, so says he, is rest for your souls found. . . . They teach us to dread the cross and suffering, and the result is that we never become gentle and lowly, and that means that we never receive indulgence nor come to Christ. Oh, the dangers of our time! Oh, you snoring priests! Oh, darkness deeper than Egyptian! How secure we are in the midst of the worst of all our evils![55]

When Luther discovered that Bishop Albrecht's official instructions to his indulgence preachers included the permission to forgive sins previously committed on earth by people whose souls now suffered pain in purgatory, he drafted his famous Ninety-five Theses, dated 31 October 1517, as the basis for a "disputation on the power and efficacy of indulgences." The theses were an invitation to correct an abuse on the basis of a proper biblical understanding of the sacrament of penance.

> 1. When our Lord and Master Jesus Christ said, "Repent" [Matt. 4:17], he willed the entire life of believers to be one of repentance.
> 42. Christians are to be taught that the pope does not intend that the buying of indulgences should in any way be compared with works of mercy.
> 62. The true treasure of the church is the most holy gospel of the glory and grace of God.
> 91. If, therefore, indulgences were preached according to the spirit and intention of the pope, all these doubts [about the real power of indulgences] would be readily resolved. Indeed, they would not exist.
> 94. Christians should be exhorted to be diligent in following Christ, their head, through penalties, death, and hell;
> 95. And thus be confident of entering into heaven through many tribulations rather than through the false security of peace [Acts 14:22].[56]

Unaware of the intricate arrangements between Bishop Albrecht, the Roman Curia, and the Fugger banking house in Augsburg,[57] Luther sent a copy of the Theses, along with a covering letter, to the bishop on 31 October 1517.

What can I do, excellent Bishop and Most Illustrious Sovereign? I can only beg you, Most Reverend Father, through the Lord Jesus Christ, to deign to give this matter your fatherly attention and totally withdraw that little book (the episcopal *Instructions* used by Tetzel and the other salesmen) and command the preachers of indulgences to preach in another way. If this is not done, someone may rise and, by means of publications, silence those preachers and refute the little book. This would be the greatest disgrace for Your Most Illustrious Highness. I certainly shudder at this possibility, yet I am afraid it will happen if things are not quickly remedied.[58]

This was not the voice of a revolutionary who was intent on opposing the church. Rather, it was the voice of a priest-professor who spoke "out of love and zeal for truth and the desire to bring it to light."[59] Luther even tried to prevent the dissemination of the Theses, for he was afraid they might be used to cause political strife between Elector Frederick and Bishop Albrecht.[60] However, the Theses quickly became a manifesto for a growing movement which called for reform of the church from top to bottom, and Luther was drawn into a controversy intimately linking theological opinion and hierarchical authority. First John Tetzel, the chief promulgator and defender of indulgences, tried to malign Luther by writing 106 theses defending the indulgence traffic and charging Luther with heresy. Then John Eck, professor of theology at the University of Ingolstadt in Bavaria, attempted to expose weaknesses in Luther's argumentation by publishing *Obelisks* (from the Greek *obeliskos*, "little dagger"), which Luther countered quickly with *Asterisks* (from the Greek *asteriskos*, "little star"). Finally, Bishop Albrecht officially requested that Rome stop Luther's movement by summoning him to a hearing and charging him with heresy.[61]

These events placed considerable strain on Luther's regular schedule of teaching and preaching in the spring of 1518. But he missed neither his classes nor his assigned preaching of the catechetical Lenten sermons at the Town Church. He did not hesitate to share with his congregation his apprehensions regarding the indulgence traffic. "So far has this childish veneration and holiness gone," he declared on 17 March 1518, "that they have started this game of excommunication, and the letters are flying about like bats, all because of a trifling thing."[62]

The debate over indulgences was not "a trifling thing." Rather, it disclosed deeply rooted problems in medieval Christendom, ranging from questions of theological method to authority in the church and the world. To clarify his position, Luther drafted "Explanations of the Ninety-five Theses" early in 1518, still hoping for cooperation from other theologians and from Rome.

Because this is a theological disputation, I shall repeat here the declaration usually made in the schools in order that I may pacify individuals who, perhaps, are offended by the simple text of the disputation.

First, I testify that I desire to say or maintain absolutely nothing except, first of all, what is in the Holy Scriptures and can be maintained from them; and then what is in and from the writings of the church fathers and is accepted by the Roman church and preserved both in the canons and the papal decrees. But if any proposition cannot be proved or disproved from them I shall simply maintain it, for the sake of debate, on the basis of the judgment of reason and experience, always, however, without violating the judgment of any of my superiors in these matters.

I add one consideration and insist upon it according to the right of Christian liberty, that is, that I wish to refuse or accept, according to my own judgment, the mere opinions of St. Thomas, Bonaventura, or other scholastics or canonists, which are maintained without text and proof. I shall do this according to the advice of Paul to "test everything, hold fast to that which is good" (1 Thess. 5:21).[63]

Although Luther's bishop, Jerome Schulze of Brandenburg, forbade the publication of the "Explanations," Luther published them in August 1518 and sent copies to the bishop, to Vicar-General Staupitz, and, through Staupitz, to Pope Leo X. Meticulously explaining one thesis after another, Luther used the image of pilgrimage to make the point that the church needed "theologians of the cross" rather than "theologians of glory."

A theologian of the cross (that is, one who speaks of the crucified and hidden God), teaches that punishments, crosses, and death are the most precious treasury of all and the most sacred relics which the Lord of this theology himself has consecrated and blessed, not alone by the touch of his most holy flesh but also by the embrace of his exceedingly holy and divine will, and he has left these relics here to be kissed, sought after, and embraced. . . . Many make pilgrimages to Rome and to other holy places to see the robe of Christ, the bones of the martyrs, and the places and remains of the saints, which we certainly do not condemn. But we lament the fact that we do not at the same time recognize the true relics, namely, the sufferings and crosses which have sanctified the bones and relics of the martyrs and made them worthy of such great veneration.[64]

The "Explanations" did not prevent Bishop Albrecht, John Tetzel, and the Dominican Order from lobbying in Rome for a hearing that charged Luther with heresy. Luther, however, felt liberated, and for a while he signed his letters "friar Martin Eleutherius" (from the Greek word for "free").[65]

Many students and younger theologians supported Luther's call for a return to biblical theology and to the early church fathers, especially to Augustine, but older theologians did not. Professor Jodocus Trutvetter in Erfurt disassociated himself from his former student even though Luther had tried to persuade him to join the new theology. Vicar-General Staupitz, however, made certain that the new Wittenberg theology would get a hearing in the Augustinian Order. On 25 April 1518, he invited Luther to attend the plenary meeting of the order in Heidelberg, and to prepare a set of theses on sin, free will, and grace. These theses were Luther's theological and philosophical farewell to Aristotle as the foundation of Christian doctrine. They also foreshadowed the thoroughly biblical foundation for what Luther called "a theology of the cross," as formulated in theses 19 and 20:

> 19. That person does not deserve to be called a theologian who perceives and understands the invisible nature of God through God's own works (Rom. 1:20).
> 20. But he deserves to be called a theologian who comprehends what is visible and world-oriented in God through suffering and the cross.[66]

True theology does not concentrate on such human efforts or virtues as godliness, wisdom, and justice to please God. The recognition of these things does not make one worthy or wise.

> Because men misused the knowledge of God through works, God wished again to be recognized in suffering, and to condemn wisdom concerning invisible things by means of wisdom concerning visible things, so that those who did not honor God as manifested in his works should honor him as he is hidden in his suffering. As the Apostle says in 1 Cor. 1(:21), "For since, in the wisdom of God, the world did not know God through wisdom, it pleased God through the folly of what we preach to save those who believe." Now it is not sufficient for anyone, and it does him no good to recognize God in His glory and majesty, unless he recognizes Him in humility and shame of the cross. . . . For this reason, true theology and recognition of God are in the crucified Christ.[67]

The Heidelberg meeting won converts to Luther's cause of theological and academic reform. George Spalatin, court chaplain and confidant of Elector Frederick, had already joined Luther's movement in 1516, persuading the prince to approve a complete overhaul of the university curriculum in accordance with Luther's ideas. The new curriculum stressed classical languages, especially Greek and Hebrew, and the study of original sources from classical antiquity as rediscovered by the Humanist movement. Luther's own view on the matter of reform is clearly expressed in a 9 May 1518 letter to his old Erfurt teacher Trutvetter:

> I simply believe that it is impossible to reform the church unless canon law, decretals, scholastic theology, philosophy and logic are completely eradicated the way they are done now, and are replaced by other studies. That is the conviction which has so far propelled me; and I pray daily to the Lord that the purest study of the Bible and the holy fathers be revived as fast as possible.[68]

On Exaudi Sunday morning, 16 May 1518, Luther preached a sermon in the Wittenberg Town Church "On the Virtue of Excommunication." Its content was clear and to the point: every Christian has an external and internal relationship to the church. The external relationship involves participation in sacramental life and in other outward ecclesiastical activities; the internal relationship is one of faith, hope, and love. Whereas the external relationship can be put under the church's ban, the internal relationship cannot. Only God can judge one's faith, hope, and love. Consequently there is just and unjust excommunication. Excommunication is just when church members refuse to participate in sacramental life and become notorious public sinners; God can nevertheless save such members through grace and penance. But excommunication is unjust when church members are punished for pursuing righteousness and truth in the face of ecclesiastic arrogance and power. Luther was quite candid about unjust excommunication:

> Concerning the unjust excommunication, you must be very much on guard not to give up or omit, and to do or say that for which you are excommunicated, provided you can do so without sin. Since righteousness and truth belong to the internal relationship to the church, they are not to be yielded because of external excommunication, even though death might follow. He who is afraid of [external] excommunication may suffer the worst excommunication: he must patiently endure such excommunication and die for it; he should not be afraid of missing the eucharist, Christian burial and entombment. These are incomparably inferior matters when compared to giving up righteousness. He who dies excommunicated, without remorse and despising excommunication, will not be condemned. Contrition and humility absolve him from everything, even though his body be exhumed and drowned. Blessed is he who died unjustly excommunicated, for he will be crowned in eternity for the righteousness which he preserved even though he had to endure such a heavy whipping.[69]

Luther's academic reforms in Wittenberg were intimately linked to demands for ecclesiastic reforms, particularly the reform of the sacrament of penance which had been widely abused even before the offensive indulgence traffic in Germany.[70] But his attack on the indulgence traffic made Luther a popular figure among people from all walks of life, and both academic Wittenberg and civic Wittenberg were proud of the spirited, thirty-four-year-old priest-professor. The doctor of theology had become a reformer.

2

MANDATE TO WITNESS

At Worms I had to appear before the Emperor and the whole realm, though I already knew well that my safe-conduct was worthless, and all kinds of strange wiles and deceit were directed at me. Weak and poor though I was there, yet this was the disposition of my heart: If I had known that as many devils as there were tiles on the roofs at Worms took aim at me, I would still have entered the city on horseback. ("Letter to the Princes of Saxony," 1524. WA 15:214:21–26. LW 40:53).

DEFIANT DEFENDANT

Luther quickly learned what it meant to oppose ecclesiastic authority. Not only were John Tetzel, the Dominican Order, and Archbishop Albrecht asking the Roman Curia to investigate Luther and charging him with heresy,[1] the chief justice of the Roman Curia, Auditor-General Bishop Jerome Ghinucci, also requested the Master of the Sacred Palace, Silvester Mazzolini (known as Prierias, the name of his home town), for an expert evaluation of Luther. Entitled "A Dialogue Against the Presumptuous Conclusions of Martin Luther About the Power of the Pope," Mazzolini's evaluation declared Luther's teaching erroneous and heretical mainly because Luther had questioned the church's unquestionable right to control faith and morals.

Luther received a copy of "Dialogue" early in August 1518 together with a summons to appear in Rome for a hearing within sixty days, and simply had the "Dialogue" reprinted with the addition of a statement presenting his own position, in which he cited Paul, Augustine, and canon law. He contended that canon law cannot go beyond Scripture and the church fathers, and warned Prierias to be better prepared for theological battle.

Behold, reverend father, I have responded to you very quickly and in two days, because your refutation seems trifling; therefore, I have answered it extempore with whatever came uppermost in my mind. If, after that, you wish to hit back, be careful to bring your Thomas Aquinas better armed into the arena, lest perchance you not be treated as gently again as you are in this encounter. I have foreborne to render evil for evil.[2]

But Prierias was not interested in good theological debate. Replying in November 1518, he merely told Luther to have more respect for Roman dignitaries and to recant his obviously erroneous views.[3] Luther again had the reply reprinted, this time without comments. He later recalled how nervous he had been when he realized that Prierias represented the mighty power of the pope. "Then I thought, 'Good God, has it come to this that the matter will go before the pope?' "[4] Luther had looked forward to a good theological battle, but instead confronted blunt power.

What saved Luther from the full blast of the Roman Curia's fury was politics: the empire needed both money and men from Germany to fight the threatening Turkish invasion from the south. The Holy Roman Emperor Maximilian I, from the House of Hapsburg, had convened the Diet of Augsburg in the summer of 1518 to make certain that German princes would support a crusade against the Muslims, who had so far been victorious in their march north. Saxony's Elector Frederick was one of the most powerful German princes; moreover, Emperor Maximilian I was old, and Frederick's vote for a successor in the near future was vitally important. Thus Luther's clash with Rome occurred at an inconvenient time for Rome, a time of decisive political constellations in Europe. Spain, France, and England had become the most powerful nations in the empire; the House of Hapsburg had acquired dominance by increasing its influence through political marriages;[5] Germany consisted of many independent political territories, with Frederick (called "the Wise") the most powerful of its princes. Therefore the question for Rome was: Would Frederick sacrifice Luther for the cause of political unity against the Muslim threat? Or would he protect Luther and his reforms, which had a chance to succeed after centuries of apathy and abuse?[6]

Luther did not hesitate to ask for Elector Frederick's protection and assistance. "My Spalatin," he wrote to Frederick's trusted counselor,

> I now need your help more than ever, or rather, it is the honor of almost our whole University that needs it along with me. This means that you should use your influence with the Most Illustrious Sovereign and Doctor Pfeffinger [treasurer] that our Sovereign and His Imperial Majesty [Maximilian I] obtain for me from the Pope the return of my case, so that it is tried before German judges.[7]

The Wittenberg faculty tried to help Luther by appealing to the patriotism of Charles von Miltitz, a Saxon politician who was a member of the Curia and who was being sent to Saxony to persuade Elector Frederick to release Luther to Roman authorities. "A German must not be deserted by a German, especially when laboring under such a calamity; for we should feel much better about the future if the pope knew about this man's integrity, piety, and erudition." They also wrote another letter to Pope Leo X directly, asking that Luther be excused from the long journey to Rome because of illness and the perils along the way.[8]

As a gesture of conciliation toward Elector Frederick, Rome agreed to hold a hearing in Germany, to take place in Augsburg on 12 October 1518, after the adjournment of the diet. Since Emperor Maximilian I had urged Pope Leo X to stop Luther before he gained a large following, the pope instructed the papal legate to the diet, Thomas de Vio (known as "Cajetan"), to conduct the hearing but not to get involved in a disputation. The pope also politely asked Elector Frederick to cooperate in the matter, while at the same time instructing the Roman general of the Augustinian Hermits to make sure that Luther's provincial superior, Gerhard Hecker, have Luther arrested and brought to Rome.[9]

Luther was protected on the journey to Augsburg by Elector Frederick's letters of safe conduct, and lawyers from the Saxon court were sent along to advise him, but he was plagued by *Anfechtungen*. He feared death and political intrigue. He bore up well, however, showing reverence for Cajetan and displaying his usual sagacity at crucial points, such as during a conversation on the use and abuse of indulgences. The hearing, which began on 12 October and ended on 14 October 1518, focused on Cajetan's demand for Luther to recant and Luther's determination to demonstrate the orthodoxy of his views.[10]

Luther managed to get Cajetan to discuss what the Roman Church meant when it taught that Christ through his death acquired a treasure of merits for believers. Citing Pope Clement VI's 1343 bull, *Unigenitus*, Cajetan accused Luther of teaching "a new and erroneous doctrine" in the "Explanations of the Ninety-five Theses" by asserting that the sacrament of penance is not efficacious unless there is faith. Luther had written, "For it is not because the pope grants it that you have anything, but you have it because you believe that you receive it. You have only as much as you believe according to the promise of Christ."[11] This statement, Cajetan told Luther, was a new and erroneous doctrine because every communicant could not be guaranteed to receive God's grace. When Luther pressed the issue of whether in *Unigenitus* the power to disseminate Christ's merits was ascribed to the power of the pope or to the gospel, Cajetan refused to continue the discussion. He insisted Luther appear only to recant his views. Luther, however, could not bring himself to recant and tried to prolong the discussion. He felt that the meaning of "treasure" and its relationship to Christ and "merit" in *Unigenitus* needed to be further clarified in light of his own thesis 62 (of the Ninety-five Theses): "The true treasure of the church is the most holy gospel of the glory and grace of God."[12] Are believers justified by faith in the gospel or by obedience to the pope? When Cajetan got so excited that he screamed at Luther, Luther asked for a recess to think things over.

On the next day, 13 October, he appeared in the company of Staupitz, four imperial counselors, a notary, and another person functioning as witness. He delivered a formal oral declaration affirming his loyalty to the Roman Church but adding a request for further discussion because, he said, Cajetan seemed unwilling to go beyond the demand for simple obedience. He declared himself willing to be examined by any theological faculty chosen by Rome, such as the faculty of Paris or Louvain. Upon Staupitz's request, Cajetan agreed to accept Luther's arguments in writing. Luther had written these in systematic order, again focusing on the differences between Scripture and the bull *Unigenitus*.[13] The meeting ended when Cajetan rejected Luther's views but promised to take the matter to Rome for further investigation. All attempts to move Luther to recant had failed. Staupitz released Luther from his vow of obedience, hinting that Christ rather than the church was in charge of the matter.[14]

Rumors spread that Luther would be arrested. Convinced that Rome was out to get him, Luther agreed to leave Augsburg on 22 October, but first sent another appeal and a polite farewell note to Cajetan.[15] "I sought nothing in this hearing," he said, summarizing the events in a published report,

> except the true meaning of Scripture, which those so-called holy decretals, if they are not actually corrupt, certainly obscure for us in many places with their distorted and malevolent words and hide, as it were, the brightest sun with a cloud. This I will some day treat in greater detail, especially if some Roman flatterers should oppose me. God willing, I will then distinguish myself as a jurist and theologian, even though I shall hardly please anyone, especially not the flatterers of the Roman Curia, for I have recently longed to play war with them as Joshua waged war against the people of Ai (Josh. 8:3–29).[16]

After his return to Wittenberg he discovered that Cajetan had been instructed as early as 23 August 1518 to bring him to Rome, by force if necessary. "It is incredible that such a monster (the papal *Breve* with the instructions) should come from a pope, especially from Leo X," Luther wrote to Spalatin on the day of his return.[17] Though frustrated and disappointed, he was still eager to continue the debate on the abuse of indulgences. Since the pope apparently failed to provide the pastoral leadership and justice demanded by his office, Luther decided to follow tradition and appeal to a general ecumenical council. "The Appeal for an Ecumenical Council" was drafted by a lawyer, John Auer, and was solemnly read aloud by Luther on Sunday afternoon, 28 November 1518, in the Holy Spirit Chapel of the Wittenberg Town Church. This juridical act was modeled after other such appeals previously made by the University of Paris and other academic institutions on various issues. Presenting a list of grievances, especially that of having been accused of heresy without proper hearings, the "Appeal" closed with a call for a council "at a safe place, where I can go, or send my attorney,

> to prove that the citations and procedures on the part of tyrannical judges and authorities are unjustified and unjust, and to be relieved of future threats such as ban, suspension, and other ecclesiastical punishments, accusations of heresy and of apostasy; also from all future burdens to be imposed upon me and my followers. I heartily ask that my appeal be granted by anyone who is empowered to give it to me, and I promise to follow to the best of my ability all legal procedures to which I and my followers are entitled.[18]

Luther's "Appeal," which reached a wide audience after printers published it without his consent, made the situation even more dangerous for the Wittenberg professor since canon law prohibited such a procedure in the case of heresy. "You have only the cross to expect," Staupitz wrote to Luther in December of 1518 from his retirement home in Salzburg, Austria. "Leave Wittenberg while there is still time, and come to me so that we might live and die together."[19] Luther was quite willing to leave Saxony to spare the elector and the university embarrassment and trouble. But he refused to recant, even though Rome sent Charles von Miltitz to persuade the elector to hand Luther over to Roman authorities.

In January 1519, Elector Frederick arranged a meeting between Luther and Miltitz in the house of court chaplain Spalatin in Altenburg, attended by a lawyer and several other officials of the Saxon court. Miltitz failed to convince Luther that his views on indulgences were wrong, and a compromise was reached. Luther promised to keep silent if his adversaries remained silent, and Luther's case was to be settled through arbitration, probably by the Archbishop of Salzburg. Luther also agreed to make a written statement of his position once more for the pope to show that he was not really a heretic. His non-polemic position paper, which never reached the pope, asserted that he had taught nothing which would detract from the honor of the Roman Church.[20]

Miltitz left Saxony convinced that he had avoided an impending religious schism. "We separated amicably," Luther wrote to his friend John Egranus in Zwickau, "with a kiss (a Judas kiss!) and tears—I pretended that I did not know they were crocodile tears."[21] After Miltitz's return to Rome, he sent a report to Elector Frederick declaring the compromise of Altenburg would pave the way for a good resolution of Luther's case.

The death of Emperor Maximilian I on 12 January 1519 only increased Elector Frederick's influence in the case of Luther. Both the young Spanish regent Charles I and Francis I of France were vying for the imperial crown, and Pope Leo X supported Francis I. The pope was eager to secure Elector Frederick's vote for Francis I in the forthcoming election; he even went so far as to write a conciliatory personal letter to Luther on 29 March 1519, in which he interpreted the controversy about indulgences to be a quarrel between a learned Augustinian professor and a crude Dominican monk, and tried to seduce Luther to come to Rome.

> We, therefore, considering that the spirit indeed is willing, but the flesh is weak, and that many things are said in the heat of anger which must later be corrected by saner counsel, thank Almighty God who has deigned to enlighten your heart and vouchsafe that Christians who rely on your authority and learning may not be led into grave and pernicious errors in those things which concern the salvation of their souls. . . . Because of the benevolence with which we regard all learned men, especially those learned in divinity, we desire to hear and see you personally, so that you may be able safely and freely to make before us, the vicar of Christ, that recantation which you feared to make before our legate [Cajetan].[22]

When the letter arrived at the Saxon court, Elector Frederick withheld it from Luther, suspecting that Luther might become even more defiant than he already was. Luther was only aware of another attempt by Miltitz to stage a hearing in Germany—this time in Koblenz, where Cajetan and Miltitz were visiting the Archbishop of Trier. Luther declined Miltitz's written invitation. "If what you write is true about having to come after me with papal letter," Luther wrote Miltitz on 17 May 1519, "may God grant you that you come safely. I am very busy, serving many men, and I am not able to lose time and wander abroad without causing loss to many."[23] Rome's second attempt to silence Luther through diplomacy had failed.

Luther's request for an academic debate was granted in the summer of 1519. Duke George of Saxony, a staunch defender of the old religion, asked the reluctant theological faculty of Leipzig University to support John Eck in his attempts to silence the new Wittenberg theology and Luther in particular. An ever increasing number of students had matriculated at Wittenberg University; the nascent reform movement had set its hope on Luther and on the new Wittenberg faculty member, Philip Melanchthon, who was the best Greek scholar in Germany and who had joined the faculty at age twenty-one in the fall of 1518;[24] and Dean Carlstadt had continued the literary debate with Eck while Luther was busy defending himself against the attacks from Rome. When the Leipzig Debate finally took place (27 June to 14 July) after lengthy negotiations between Wittenberg and Leipzig theologians and politicians, it was one of the great events of the century,[25] full of pomp and circumstance.

Carlstadt and Luther were accompanied by the president of Wittenberg University, Duke Barnim of Pomerania, by Melanchthon, by several other colleagues, and by about two hundred students, most of them armed in one way or another. Eck's entourage was smaller, but Leipzig University

provided him with an honor guard of officials and students. The famous choir
of St. Thomas performed a Mass which had been composed for the occasion.

The debate itself, which was held at Pleissenburg, Duke George's castle,
gave Luther an opportunity to tackle the issue which eventually made him a
heretic in the eyes of Rome: whether or not the papacy is the divinely
instituted teaching authority for all Christians. In preparing for the debate,
Luther had completed extensive historical research regarding the origins and
growth of teaching authority in the first five centuries of church history. He
had read of the development of doctrine through the actions of ecumenical
councils, especially the Council of Nicaea, which initiated the formulation of
the trinitarian dogma in A.D. 325. He discovered that there were
discrepancies between the claims of canon law and the conciliar evidence. In
a letter to Spalatin on 13 March 1519, he had already expressed his first
doubts about the claims of papal authority:

> I am studying the papal decretals for my disputation. And, confidentially, I do
> not know whether the pope is the Antichrist himself or whether he is his
> apostle, so miserably is Christ (that is, the truth) corrupted and crucified by the
> pope in the decretals. I am extremely distressed that under the semblance of
> laws and the Christian name, the people of Christ should be so deluded. . . .
> Daily greater and greater help and support by virtue of the authority of Holy
> Scripture wells up in me.[26]

Although the Leipzig Debate was scheduled to deal only with the subject
of indulgences in the context of the relationship between sin and grace, Eck
made it clear that papal authority was the real issue. In a series of theses
published in December 1518 as blueprints for the forthcoming debate, Eck
had openly challenged Luther's thesis 22 of the "Explanations" of 1518: that
the pope cannot remit penalties in purgatory which, according to canon law,
should have been paid in this life. Luther had supported this thesis with the
statement that before Pope Sylvester (A.D. 314–35) Rome had no jurisdiction
over other churches, especially not over the Greek churches, and that
consequently indulgences could only be offered to people living under the
authority of Rome. Since he had been attacked first, Luther felt no obligation
to abide by his agreement with Miltitz to remain silent. So in February 1519
he answered Eck by publishing his findings concerning papal primacy in the
first five centuries and concluded his lengthy treatise with his own thesis 13
in response to Eck's challenge.

> The very callous decrees of the Roman pontiffs which have appeared in the last
> four hundred years prove that the Roman church is superior to all others.
> Against them stand the history of eleven hundred years, the text of divine
> Scripture, and the decree of the Council of Nicaea, the most sacred of all
> councils.[27]

The issue of papal primacy, which Cajetan had tried to avoid debating at

Augsburg, had now become the central issue at Leipzig. After Eck and Carlstadt debated the question of sin and grace without any significant results (27 June to 3 July), Eck and Luther engaged in the battle everyone had been expecting (4–13 July). Eck argued that Christ made Peter and his successors "vicars" in the earthly "church militant" until the end of time, when the earthly church would join the "church triumphant" (according to Matt. 16:18). Luther countered with the argument that such an interpretation restricted the lordship of Christ who had promised, according to Matt. 28:20, "Lo, I am with you always, to the close of the age." Luther made it quite clear that the real issue was the difference between the authority of Scripture and the authority of the Roman tradition which interpreted Scripture in a particular way. The five-day debate on papal primacy culminated in a clash between Eck and Luther on the authority of ecumenical councils. Since Luther had acknowledged the authority of the Council of Nicaea (A.D. 325) because it was not under the power of the Roman pontiff, Eck now pressed for his opinion on the authority of the Council of Constance (1415), which had condemned John Hus of Prague for denying papal authority. When Luther stated his view that councils were only the creatures of the infallible Word of God, Scripture, and could err, he needed to say no more. The church had never officially admitted that pope and councils could err in matters of faith and morals.

The appointed umpires of the debate, the universities of Paris and Erfurt, were unable to reach an official verdict immediately, even though many theologians on both faculties sided with Eck. Some of the hesitation may have been due to the excitement over the election of a new Holy Roman Emperor. The seven electoral princes, including Frederick of Saxony, had been persuaded to vote for the Hapsburg King Charles of Spain, who was finally elected on 28 June 1519. The solemn coronation of the young Spaniard, now Charles V, took place on 23 October 1519, in Aachen, where Charlemagne had been crowned the first emperor of the Holy Roman Empire in A.D. 800.[28] Everyone knew that Charles V would try to work in close cooperation with the pope to prevent a religious schism.

Eventually the University of Paris did issue its verdict on 16 April 1521— the day on which Luther entered Worms for his hearing before the diet—and condemned as heretical 104 of Luther's statements. The verdict was based in part on Luther's writings published after the Leipzig Debate, but the issue of papal authority was not directly addressed by the Paris theologians.[29] Erfurt then refused to issue a verdict on the grounds that Paris had not really done so and that Dominicans and Augustinians had been excluded from the list of eligible judges. However, several Erfurt theologians let it be known that they did not side with Luther. The universities of Cologne and Louvain also condemned a series of Luther's statements which, in their judgment, confused official teachings on sin and grace, on good works, on indulgences, and on other normative assertions including the primacy of the papacy as the highest teaching authority in the church. Their verdict was based on Luther's collected writings which had been published in the fall of 1518 by the famous printer John Froben in Basel, Switzerland.[30]

By this time Luther no longer cared for the judgment of the universities. In a report to Spalatin on 20 July 1519, he called the Leipzig Debate a "tragedy" and "complete fiasco."

> Since Eck and the people of Leipzig sought their own glory and not the truth at the debate, it is no wonder that it began badly and ended worse. . . . This is the fruit of human glory. I, who really restrain my impetuosity, am still not able to dispel all dislike of them, for I am flesh and their hatred was very shameless and their injustice was very malicious in a matter so sacred and divine.[31]

Although Eck seemingly emerged the winner of the Leipzig Debate, Luther won more support than did Eck. The Froben collection of his works had three more editions by the spring of 1520 and was smuggled to England, the Netherlands, France, and Italy. Luther was called the new Daniel who would liberate the people of God from their bondage to scholastic theology.[32] Moreover, his pleas for a fair debate based on evidence from historical sources was heeded by many scholars and theologians, and the Leipzig Debate was followed by lively literary feuds conducted by Luther and his followers against adherents of the status quo.

REFORMATION BLUEPRINTS

Luther's own literary production moved into high gear between the fall of 1519 and the spring of 1521. A secretary transcribed 116 sermons for publication, and Luther himself delivered sixteen treatises to the printers within six months of the Leipzig Debate. He was also working on his interpretation of Psalms, and finished his first lectures on Galatians.[33] Devotional discipline occupied Luther's mind for a while. His exposition of the Lord's Prayer in a personal prayer book and brief homilies on preparing to die, on repentance, on baptism, and on the ban became models of devotional life in the new Lutheran movement.[34] He was also concerned with economic justice. A treatise entitled "On Usury" summarized Luther's concerns and was communicated from the pulpit in the fall of 1519 and in the spring of 1520. He basically agreed with the view of canon law that interest rates of thirty to forty percent lead to economic injustice and thus defended the papally approved rate of four to six percent for substantial transactions involving money or property.[35]

The debate over papal primacy continued. Augustine Alveld, a Franciscan monk from Leipzig, defended the papacy as a divine institution in a treatise which appeared in the spring of 1520 under the title "Concerning the

Apostolic See." Using crude arguments, Alveld tried to prove his position from scriptural passages like Matt. 5:17–18 and 1 Cor. 10:6 to document the thesis that the papacy is prefigured in the Old Testament and fulfilled in the New Testament by Christ's promise of authority to Peter in Matt. 16:18.[36] Luther, whom Alveld had labeled a "wolf among sheep," a "madman," and a "heretic," let his research assistant reply to Alveld. But Alveld continued his attacks in another treatise, trying to incite common folk against Luther. Luther therefore countered with a treatise of his own entitled "On the Papacy in Rome," in which he presented a well-reasoned defense of his position that the papacy is a human rather than a divine institution. At the same time, he deplored the papal abuse of power, especially its claim to stand above emperors, kings, and princes. Luther's old enemy, the Dominican Sylvester Prierias, joined Alveld in attacking Luther in another widely circulated pamphlet. Luther had it reprinted with a preface containing the lament "Farewell, unhappy, hopeless, blasphemous Rome!"

> We have cared for Babylon and she is not healed. Let us then leave her that she may be the habitation of dragons, spectres, ghosts, and witches, and true to her name of Babel, an everlasting confusion, an idol of avarice, perfidy, apostasy, of cynics, lechers, robbers, sorcerers, and endless other impudent monsters, a new pantheon of wickedness.[37]

Having bid farewell to Rome in the spring of 1520, Luther turned his attention to the budding reform movement which had become quite visible. German nationalists like the knight Ulrich von Hutten, anti-clerical Humanists associated with Erasmus of Rotterdam, and artists like Albrecht Dürer supported Luther's cause for a variety of reasons. Luther nurtured the movement with four seminal publications in 1520, supplying a "Lutheran" stance, a defiant witness against the status quo: (1) The "Treatise on Good Works" (June); (2) the address "To the Christian Nobility of the German Nation Concerning the Reform of the Christian Estate" (August); (3) "The Babylonian Captivity of the Church" (October); and (4) "The Freedom of the Christian" (November).

"Treatise on Good Works"

This treatise was a response to basic concerns on the part of political friends, particularly at the court of Elector Frederick, such as: If one is justified by faith alone, why perform good works at all? Or why adhere to law and order when one is really not rewarded for doing good? Did not Luther's basic stance lead to the demise of the existing moral fabric of life in the world?

The substantial treatise, dedicated to Duke John, the brother of Elector Frederick, was originally intended to be a sermon to the Wittenberg congregation. Its basic thesis is that good works are the natural consequence of a truly trusting relationship between the faithful and God, grounded in the atonement of Christ. The divine mandate to do good, summarized in the Decalogue, can only be fulfilled when Christ has become the driving force within the faithful. Consequently "faith" is not a decision to try to do good or an assent to divine teachings mediated by the church, but rather the source of all relationships of life on earth. All of these relationships find meaning only in the relationship between God and the Christ whose death redeemed a sinful world. "Faith, therefore, does not originate in works; neither do works create faith, but faith must spring up and flow from the blood and wounds and death of Christ."[38] In this sense doing good is always the consequence of trust in God who wants believers to love others the way Jesus, a suffering servant, loved the world. This is the true meaning of the "first table" of the Decalogue, which commands that one should not have any other gods but should honor the Father of Jesus Christ and should worship God through him. That is the way the new Adam fights the old Adam in the name of Christ.

> Look! these are the three parts of man: reason, desire, and dislike. All man's works are done under the impulse of these. These, therefore, must be slain by these three exercises: God's governance, our self-mortification, and the suffering inflicted on us by other people. This is how we must honor God and make way for his works.[39]

Luther admonished his readers to return to this basic understanding of the Decalogue: the principal guide for life with God in the face of earthly conflicts which will end only when Christ returns at the end of time. Since the Roman Church has abused the Decalogue, Luther contended, common sense is to be used to resist Roman authorities. "We have to act as good children whose parents have lost their minds," Luther suggested in the context of his exposition of the Fourth Commandment (to honor father and mother).[40] One should know the difference between what is commanded for the maintenance of basic values in life and what is not commanded, namely, "the building of churches, beautifying them, making pilgrimages, and all those things of which so much is written in the ecclesiastical regulations."[41] Finally, one should know that original sin will never be eliminated by any commandment. "It may be checked, but it cannot be entirely uprooted except through death. It is for this reason death is both profitable and desirable."[42]

"To the Christian Nobility of the German Nation"

This address offered Luther's detailed analysis of the deformation of medieval Christendom. Officials of the Saxon court, Wittenberg intellectuals, and other influential Germans had requested the analysis. Luther cast himself into the role of court jester (*Hofnarr*) in the treatise, confident that he could win German princes to the cause of reform. Praising the newly elected Emperor Charles V as a divine sign for "a time of grace," Luther began by calling for the demolition of the three walls behind which the papacy had established its authority: the notion that there is a divinely instituted difference between clergy and laity; the claim that only the pope can interpret Scripture; and the assertion that only the pope can summon an ecumenical council and approve its actions. He then listed a great variety of ecclesiastical abuses which had contributed to the maceration of moral and political life. In this section Luther was following the tradition of listing German "grievances" (*gravamina*) against the Roman Curia.[43] He ended by offering proposals for reform, including suggestions for the educational and economic renewal of Germany.

The most revolutionary portion of the treatise dealt with the relationship between baptism and Christian responsibility in the world. Here Luther called on the Christian nobles to assume the leadership of the organized church as "emergency bishops" (*Notbischöfe*) because the pope and his bishops had betrayed the gospel. The princes are qualified to do this on the basis of their baptism, which commissioned them to a ministry of reform: "For whoever comes out of the water of baptism can boast that he is already a consecrated priest, bishop, and pope, although of course it is not seemly that just anybody should exercise such office . . . without the authority and consent of the community."[44] This view of the common ministry of all the baptized, especially of those in positions of leadership, was Luther's weapon against the "three walls of the Romanists." With princes constituting an emergency episcopate, the church should then hold an ecumenical council to deal with abuses and to institute reforms stressing the proper distinction between spiritual and temporal powers. Since Luther regarded the power of the Roman Church as the greatest threat to such a distinction, he concentrated his attack on the ecclesiastical hierarchy, and offered few criticisms of the German nobility. "The pope should restrain himself, take his fingers out of the pie, and claim no title to the kingdom of Naples and Sicily."[45] If the pope continued to exercise temporal authority, the Christian nobility should oppose him—though Luther shied away from saying "by force." He concluded:

> I know full well that I have been outspoken. I have made many suggestions that will be considered impractical. I have attacked many things too severely. But how else ought I do it? I am duty-bound to speak. If I had the power, these are the things I would do. I would rather have the wrath of the world upon me than the wrath of God. The world can do no more to me than take my life. . . . Therefore, just let them go hard at it, pope, bishop, priest, monk, or scholar. They are just the ones to persecute the truth, as they have always done. God give us all a Christian mind, and grant to the Christian nobility of the German nation in particular true spiritual courage to do the best they can for the poor church.[46]

"The Babylonian Captivity of the Church"

This was Luther's "prelude" to his most significant battle with the Roman Church, namely, regarding its sacramental system which, according to Luther, had been carefully constructed to have tyrannical control over every member of the church. Luther asserted that, just as the people of Israel had been liberated from the tyranny of the Babylonian empire, so must European Christians be freed from the tyranny of the Roman Church and return to the Scriptures as the highest authority for Christian life on earth. Combining biblical scholarship with polemics, Luther dealt extensively with the true and false understanding of sacraments, particularly the Lord's Supper and Holy Baptism. The Lord's Supper, Luther contended, had been perverted by a particular concept of the ordained ministry which ascribes metaphysical powers to priests in the ritual of the Mass and deprives the laity of full participation by withholding the cup and reserving it for priests. As a consequence the priestly celebration of the Mass and its elaborate ritual had become burdened with self-righteousness and nearly lost its pastoral significance for people in need of consolation. Common folk had been taught for centuries to view priests as superior people endowed at ordination with a "special gift" called *charism* and a "special character" described as "indelible."

Luther lashed out specifically against the doctrines of transubstantiation and concomitance (promulgated in 1215 and 1415). The doctrine of transubstantiation was intended to safeguard the mystery of Christ's presence in the eucharistic bread and wine. Using the categories of Aristotle's philosophy, the church taught that when an episcopally ordained priest recites the canon of the Mass (Christ's words at the Last Supper, "This is my body . . .") the "substances" of bread and wine (their generic identity or essential being) become the true body and blood of Christ while their "accidents" (their properties, such as quantity and chemical composition) remain the same. The transubstantiation occurs when the rite is properly performed, that is, when the priest correctly enacts the prescribed liturgy regardless of his faith or that of the recipient. Thus the rite communicates the true body and blood of Christ "through the function itself" (*ex opere operato*) without regard to the feelings or convictions of priests and parishioners. The doctrine of concomitance stated that the whole Christ is truly present in a single element or "species," be it the bread or the wine, and thus allowed for "communion in one kind," that is, offering only the bread to lay people. This doctrine was intended to safeguard the consecrated wine from being spilled or otherwise endangered by careless handling.

Luther declared that these doctrines denigrated the mystery of the Eucharist rather than enhancing its meaning as a consoling sacrament, and moreover that they undermined the true meaning of baptism since baptism enables every Christian to join a common priesthood to witness in the world. Baptism is the truly royal sacrament through which the Holy Spirit is given, thus transforming sinful unbelievers into faithful servants of God. Every baptized member of the church is a priest in this sense, although there are and will always be some who are called to the special, ordained ministry of Word and sacrament. But no one has a special status before God; to make special vows in order to please God or to create a special class of people smacks of self-righteousness and is unscriptural. If one uses Scripture as the norm, Luther argued, only two sacraments, namely, Holy Baptism and the Lord's Supper, have been given to the church, for only these two have been duly mandated by Jesus as "promises" of salvation with "signs" attached to them. Jesus mandated baptism in the words "Go therefore and make disciples of all nations, baptizing them . . ." (Matt. 28:19) and promised that through the sign of water people will be saved (Mark 16:16). He also told his disciples, "Do this . . ." when he invited them to the supper before his death (1 Cor. 11:23–26), and he promised forgiveness of sins through the signs of bread and wine.

> Baptism, however, which we have applied to the whole of life, will truly be a sufficient substitute for all the sacraments which we might need as long as we live. And the bread is truly the sacrament of the dying and departing; for in it we commemorate the passing of Christ out of this world, that we may imitate him. Thus we may apportion these two sacraments as follows: baptism may be allotted to the beginning and the entire course of life, while the bread belongs to the end and to death. And the Christian should use them both as long as he is in this mortal frame, until, fully baptized and strengthened, he passes out of this world, and is born into the new eternal life, to eat with Christ in the kingdom of his Father.[47]

"The Freedom of the Christian"

This devotional booklet was dedicated to Pope Leo X and written as a goodwill offering. Luther had promised to make the gesture during his discussions with the papal emissary Miltitz regarding ways of reconciling with Rome. But the booklet contains no compromises; while not polemic in tone, it clearly presents Luther's celebration of the freedom of the gospel, God's liberating power in the face of tyranny and adversity. True Christian freedom, Luther argued, consists in complete trust in God who in Christ has made Christians subject to no one, on the one hand, and yet subject to all, on the other. By faith and trust in God, Christians are freed from all earthly bondage; yet by love and sacrifice, they are bound to their neighbors in need.

> Although the Christian is thus free from all works, he ought in this liberty to empty himself, take upon himself the form of a servant, be made in the likeness of men, be found in human form (as Christ was, Phil. 2:5–11), and to serve, help,

and in every way deal with his neighbor as he sees that God through Christ has dealt and still deals with him. This he should do freely, having regard for nothing but divine approval.[48]

CONDEMNED AND CONCEALED

While Luther was busy constructing the theological platform of the reform movement, Rome was trying Luther in absentia. On 9 January 1520, the case against him was reopened in order to find evidence to support the charge of "suspicion of heresy." Unlike Miltitz, Eck had provided a rather clear picture of Luther's views to the Curia after the Leipzig Debate. Thus Luther was no longer seen as a bright young theologian who had difficulties with certain teachings of the church; at issue was the ecumenical question of the proper relationship between the Word of God disclosed in Scripture and the authority of the church manifested in pope and general council.

Pope Leo X ordered a careful investigation of Luther's teachings, appointing Cardinals Pietri Accolti (an expert in canon law) and Cajetan to lead the investigation, with Eck serving as theological advisor. Three papal commissions and four consistories of cardinals considered the evidence against Luther; they relied heavily on the judgments of the Cologne and Louvain faculties, which had condemned some of Luther's teachings after the Leipzig Debate. Finally, on 15 June 1520, the pope signed a bull threatening Luther with the ban unless he recanted certain views within sixty days. Entitled *Exsurge Domine* (from Ps. 74:22, "Arise O Lord . . ."), the bull listed forty-one assertions the church declared erroneous. These were Luther's assertions regarding the very doctrines he had wanted to debate: indulgences; penance; the relation of sin and grace; the right of the laity to receive not only the bread but also the wine in the Eucharist; good works; purgatory; and matters relating to papal teaching authority.[49]

A "wild boar in the vineyard of the Lord" was the bull's appellation for Luther, whose name was not mentioned; Pope Leo X wrote to Elector Frederick on 8 July 1520 identifying Luther as the "wild boar" and urging the prince to silence him. "If he persists in his insanity, and at the end of the term prescribed in the bull should be declared a heretic, then you should take care and zealously try to capture him and send him bound into our custody."[50] Since the letter would take until October 1520 to reach the Saxon court, Rome sent several messages by various means to gain Elector Frederick's cooperation with regard to Luther.

Frederick, on the other hand, tried to prevent Rome from acting too severely. In an official communication to Cardinal Rafael Riario, a friend of the family, Frederick assured Rome that he would adhere to the original agreement to have Luther tried in Germany by the respected Archbishop of Trier, one of his friends and an electoral prince. "I never had the purpose or wish of being other than an obedient son of the Holy Catholic Church," he declared diplomatically.[51] At the same time, he was also hoping to win Emperor Charles V's support for a fair trial of his famous professor. To this end, the Saxon court asked Luther to state his case to the emperor, which he did in a short letter dated 30 August 1520. Luther stressed that he had become a reformer against his will, that he had nothing but the truth of the gospel on his mind in the face of "superstitious human traditions," and that he should be given a fair chance to debate his views. "I ask for only one thing," Luther concluded, "that neither truth nor falsehood be condemned without being heard and defeated. Your Most Serene Majesty owes this to Christ, who has power over so many kingdoms."[52] The emperor did not respond.

John Eck, who had helped draft the bull, was charged with its public dissemination in Germany in September 1520. But people in various cities and towns tore down the posted bull as soon as it was put up. When Luther read a copy of it he immediately told Spalatin, in a letter dated 11 October 1520:

> I rejoice with my whole heart that for this best of causes I suffer evil, who am not worthy of being so tried. Now I am much freer; for I am certain at length that the Pope is the Antichrist and that the seat of Satan has been openly found. God will keep his own lest they be seduced with his specious impiety.[53]

Luther knew that the die was cast. Having just completed the non-polemical treatise "The Freedom of the Christian" for Pope Leo X, Luther now penned an angry attack on the "execrable bull of the Antichrist." With regard to his excommunication, Luther denied being worthy of it, and he then excommunicated "blasphemous Rome," leaving it to Christ which excommunication would be valid in the end. On 17 November 1520, Luther once more published a formal appeal for a general council, calling on secular authorities to force Rome to call one.[54]

There was news that all over Germany Roman authorities were encouraging the burning of Luther's writings. His friends, led by Melanchthon and young John Agricola, one of Luther's students, instigated a counteraction. On 10 December 1520, three months after Luther's deadline to recant, they posted a notice at the Wittenberg Town Church announcing a public burning of books on canon law and scholastic theology. The book-burning took place at the Elster Gate, the *Schindanger*, the traditional place for public punishment. Luther himself threw a copy of the bull *Exsurge Domine* into the bonfire after others had thrown in editions of canon law, handbooks on confession, writings by Luther's enemies, and some theological books. Students celebrated a mock funeral of canon law.

Luther felt that justice had been done in the face of the injustices leveled against him. In a public account entitled "Why the Books of the Pope and

His Disciples Were Burned," he listed thirty erroneous claims of papal power as evidence that the papacy represented the Antichrist rather than being the guardian of Holy Scripture. "I am willing to let everyone have his own opinion," Luther said in closing his case against the pope:

> I am moved most by the fact that the pope has never once refuted with Scripture or reason anyone who has spoken, written, or acted against him, but has at all times suppressed, exiled, burned, or otherwise strangled him with force and bans, through kings, and other partisans, or with deceit and false words, of which I shall convince him from history. Nor has he ever been willing to submit to a court of justice or judgment, but at all times bawled that he was above Scripture, judgment, and authority.[55]

Given Luther's theological and political position as well as his defiant refusal to recant, Rome had no choice but to follow through with the threat to ban the Wittenberg priest-professor. Luther, his friends, and many of his foes had already interpreted Rome's first bull as a kind of ban. On 3 January 1521, Pope Leo X ordered Luther banned in the bull *Decet Romanum Pontificem* ("It is fitting for the Roman Pontiff . . ."). The bull presented these reasons for banning Luther: he had refused to recant, and he encouraged others to follow his example; therefore he and they must suffer punishment. All ecclesiastical authorities were put under obligation to enforce the ban. Archbishop Albrecht of Mainz was appointed the official inquisitor and, if necessary, could ask Emperor Charles V for help against the new heresy.[56]

Despite Rome's fury, Elector Frederick had his way. Since the Diet of Worms was scheduled for the winter of 1520/21, Frederick conducted a series of careful negotiations with imperial counselors and with the emperor himself, and arranged a hearing for Luther before Emperor Charles V at that time.[57] The papal legate to the diet, Jerome Aleander, and other papal emissaries and delegates tried hard to avoid a hearing for Luther and pressed for a simple condemnation. That was the least Rome expected the diet to do after the church had banned Luther. But Aleander was quickly made aware of the anti-Roman sentiments that existed in Germany. "The whole of Germany is in full revolt," he wrote to Cardinal de Medici in Rome on 8 February 1521.

> Nine-tenths raise the war-cry "Luther", while the watchword of the other tenth who are indifferent to Luther is: "Death to the Roman Curia." All of them have written on their banners a demand for a council to be held in Germany. . . . If we delay any longer, it is to be feared that the Lutherans will gain such strength that the imperialists will fear to pass any edict against them, for they even now hesitate, in order, as they say, not to irritate the people. . . . A shower of Lutheran writings in German and Latin comes out daily. . . . Nothing else is bought here [in Worms] except Luther's books, even in the imperial court, for the people stick together remarkably and have lots of money. . . . I neither can

nor will relate all the many and great dangers to which I am hourly exposed. You won't believe me until (may God prevent it!) I am stoned or torn to pieces by these people, who, if they meet me on the street, always put their hands to their swords or grind their teeth, and, with a German curse, threaten me with death.[58]

On 6 March 1521, Luther was finally invited to Worms to appear before the diet. The emperor addressed him as "honorable, dear and pious Sir" and promised him safe conduct; he was requested to appear within twenty-one days. Luther was again plagued by *Anfechtungen* during the journey to Worms and his stay there—despite the good company of another Augustinian friar, John Petzensteiner, his good friend Nicholas Amsdorf, and three other companions, among them the lawyer Justus Jonas from Erfurt. Though triumphantly received wherever he stopped along the road, during the two weeks (2–16 April) of the journey, Luther's fortitude was severely tested. On 14 April he wrote to Spalatin from Frankfurt am Main:

> All the way from Eisenach to here I have been sick; I am still sick in a way which previously has been unknown to me. Of course I realize that the mandate of Charles [V, to confiscate Luther's books, dated 10 March] has also been published to frighten me. But Christ lives, and we shall enter Worms in spite of all the gates of hell and the powers in the air [Matt. 16:18; Eph. 2:2].[59]

When Luther appeared before Emperor Charles V and the diet at 4:00 P.M. on 17 April, at the episcopal residence next to the cathedral, he wore his habit and looked nervous. The emperor had appointed John von der Eck, an official at the court of the Archbishop of Trier, to be imperial "orator." Von der Eck asked Luther in Latin and in German to answer two questions: Did he confirm the authorship of books published under his name? Did he hold to their content, or was he ready to recant? Before Luther could answer, Jerome Schurf, Elector Frederick's lawyer, requested the reading aloud of the titles which Legate Aleander had brought to the hearing. Then Luther answered softly that the books had been authored by him, in addition to others not there. With regard to the second question, Luther requested one day to deliberate before responding because, he said, it would not be wise in matters of faith and salvation to confess something which had not been thoroughly thought through. The emperor granted Luther's request but admonished him, through his orator, to be penitent and aware of his errors and to return the next day at the same time to give an oral, not a written response.

On the next day Luther's voice was once more clear, and he spoke with fervor. He asked for forgiveness in case his behavior did not fully correspond with the noble etiquette required at such occasions, but he was only a lowly monk who did not know better. Then Luther separated his writings into three kinds: those which tried to teach good Christian piety, something acknowledged even by his opponents; those written against defenders of the papacy who had devastated the body and soul of Christendom; and those written against specific persons who had attacked him under the cover of Roman tyranny. But, Luther declared, all his writings enhanced rather than threatened Christian unity since conflict is part and parcel of the ministry of the Word of God. Finally, Luther insisted that his cause not be identified with political ambitions in Germany.

The imperial orator reminded Luther that his teachings appeared to be in line with previously condemned heretics and that he had been commanded to give a clear answer, not to debate issues. Thus pressed to give a simple answer, Luther, heavily perspiring because of the heat in the room, responded:

> Unless I am convinced by the testimony of the Scriptures or by clear reason (for I do not trust either in the pope or in councils alone, since it is well known that they have often erred and contradicted themselves), I am bound by the Scriptures I have quoted and my conscience is captive to the Word of God. I cannot and will not retract anything, since it is neither safe nor right to go against conscience. I cannot do otherwise, here I stand, may God help me, Amen.[60]

Luther's words adjourned the diet for a day. He was led from the room by members of the imperial entourage; his friends and a large crowd accompanied him to his quarters in the *Johanniterhof*, where Luther raised his arms like a victorious knight at a joust and shouted, "I made it through, I made it through!" (*Ich bin hindurch*). During the recess, on 19 April, the emperor pledged all his efforts to preserve the unity of Christendom.

A number of delegates who were charged to make a final attempt to persuade Luther to give in succeeded in creating an imperial commission. The commission was composed of two electoral princes, the Archbishop of Trier and Duke Joachim of Brandenburg; two princes, George of Saxony and the Margrave of Baden represented by his chancellor, Jerome Vehus; two bishops, Jerome Schulze of Brandenburg (Luther's superior) and Bishop Christoph von Stadion of Augsburg; and four representatives of other estates, including Grandmaster Dietrich von Cleen of the Knights of the Teutonic Order (an order dating back to the crusades with territorial holdings in Prussia)[61] and the Humanist lawyer Conrad Peutinger from Augsburg who had served as advisor to Emperor Maximilian I. When Luther met the commission on 24 April 1521, he was asked to consider a compromise which would not violate his conscience but could prevent further difficulties with pope and emperor. Luther in turn expressed his deep appreciation for the meeting, but insisted that any compromise must be judged by Scripture. If refuted by Scripture, he would cease resisting the church.[62]

In order to let Luther spell out the details of his position, the Archbishop of Trier arranged a meeting between Luther, Nicholas Amsdorf, and the Saxon court official Jerome Schurff on the one hand, and the imperial orator John von der Eck and the theologian John Cochlaeus on the other. But Luther and Cochlaeus failed to reach agreement' on the question of the difference between papal and biblical authority. In another meeting, the cautious Humanist Peutinger and Jerome Schurff tried again to move Luther towards a compromise, and Luther agreed to be judged by a general council. But even such a council, he declared, would have to abide by the authority of Scripture. Finally, the Archbishop of Trier met with Luther alone, but failed again to reach a compromise. On 25 April 1521, Luther was told by the imperial orator, John von der Eck, that the emperor would make a decision in his case, and that Luther had twenty-one days to return to Wittenberg under safe conduct. He was not to preach or write along the way so as to prevent unrest among the people. Luther promised to abide by the imperial mandate and on 26 April left Worms, surrounded by curious crowds.

Before Luther left Worms, someone in Elector Frederick's entourage alerted him to the elector's arrangements for hiding him safely until it had become clear what kind of verdict the Diet of Worms had in store for him. "I would have preferred to suffer death at the hands of the tyrants, . . . but I must not disregard the counsel of good men," Luther wrote to his artist friend in Wittenberg, Lucas Cranach.[63] When Luther and his imperial protectors reached Hesse on 29 April, he dismissed the safe-conduct team saying that he would be quite safe from then on. He also asked the imperial herald who headed the team to deliver a letter to the emperor. In the letter Luther once again summarized his position, emphasizing his conviction that the Word of God should be free in the church. He closed the letter with the humble petition to be heard by the church on the basis of Scripture. "With my whole heart I desire, of course, that Your Sacred Majesty, the whole Empire, and the most noble German nation may be served in the best possible way, and all be preserved in God's grace as happy people."[64] The emperor never received the letter.

When Luther reached Eisenach on 3 May 1521, he agreed to preach there because he said that the Word of God cannot be prohibited. The next day he and his two companions, Friar Petzensteiner and Nicholas Amsdorf, were ambushed on the road. It was Elector Frederick's staged kidnapping. Luther was taken to the Wartburg Castle in the Thuringian forest; the "kidnappers" let Friar Petzensteiner escape, and Amsdorf, who had been informed in advance, went on to Wittenberg.

On 26 May 1521, the Edict of Worms declared Luther guilty of high treason and called on everyone in the empire to assist in his capture. The priest-professor was labeled a demon in monk's garb, and anyone caught aiding and abetting him was to be arrested and tried for the same crime of high treason.[65]

So Luther, isolated at the Wartburg, had now gone "underground," so to speak. He grew a beard and posed as "Knight George" (*Junker Jörg*). Besides the elector, only a few trusted friends knew that he was alive and at the Wartburg, so rumors of his death circulated all over the country. He called the Wartburg, his home for almost a year, his "island of Patmos" (Rev. 1:9) in the "land of the birds." Plagued by various *Anfechtungen*, among them insomnia and constipation, Luther soon returned to the monastic habit of praying and working. The involuntary exile provided him with plenty of time to write. Melanchthon and other friends in Wittenberg and at the Saxon court kept in touch with him through letters and messengers, so various literary pieces found their way to printers in Wittenberg. Some of these pieces were published before Luther's return from exile in the spring of 1522, thus keeping people guessing whether or not they were published posthumously. "I am both very idle and very busy here," Luther mused in a 10 June 1521 letter addressed to Spalatin.

> I am studying Hebrew and Greek, and am writing without interruption. The man in charge of this place [Castellan Hans von Berlepsch] treats me far beyond what I deserve. The trouble from which I was suffering at Worms has not left me but rather has increased. I am more constipated than ever in my life, and despair of remedy. The Lord thus afflicts me, that I may not be without a relic of the cross.[66]

The lonely exile at the Wartburg frequently felt besieged by the devil, but the story that he once threw an inkwell at him was created by Luther hagiographers and tourist guides.[67]

But the time of solitude provided an opportunity for a variety of reflections which Luther immediately wrote down. Always at work on the Bible, he wrote the "Magnificat," an exposition of Luke 1:46–55, and dedicated the work to Elector Frederick's nephew, John Frederick.[68] He sent a beautiful pastoral letter, penned in the context of an exposition of Psalm 37, "to the poor little flock of Christ in Wittenberg," asking for understanding and intercession.[69] He produced a humorous admission of "errors" addressed to his Leipzig opponent, Jerome Emser, who had taken himself very seriously.[70] From the Wartburg also came a lengthy treatise warning against turbulence in Wittenberg and elsewhere during the winter of 1521/22.[71] Luther provided parishes with a collection of sermons for the Christian year.[72] But his greatest achievement in exile was the translation into German of the New Testament, known as the "September Bible" of 1522.[73]

Luther was particularly concerned at this time with matters of ecclesiastical practice which had become thorny issues: the sacrament of penance, with its practice of oral confession; the power of religious orders, safeguarded through the vows of chastity, poverty, and obedience; and the question of the Roman Mass, especially the practice of the secret or "private

Mass" with the priest the only one in attendance. He deplored the fact that Rome required an enumeration of individual sins during private confession. "I regard the secret confession of sins as a very precious and wholesome thing," he wrote in his treatise on the matter.

> It is just like celibacy. Christians ought to be quite grateful that private confession exists, and thank God from the bottom of their hearts that He has provided this gift. But it is regrettable that the pope demands it as necessary, just as he does with celibacy.[74]

Luther also settled the indulgences controversy with Albrecht of Mainz, who had become a cardinal in 1518. In the fall of 1521, when the cardinal announced a campaign to sell indulgences to visitors to his collection of relics in Mainz, Luther wrote an angry treatise "Against the Idol of Halle" and advised the cardinal, in a letter dated 1 December 1521, to stop the abuse. "If the idol [the sale of indulgences] is not taken down, my duty toward divine doctrine and Christian salvation is a necessary, urgent, and unavoidable reason to attack publicly Your Electoral Grace (as I did the pope) . . . and to show to all the world the difference between a bishop and a wolf."[75] The cardinal apologized within a few weeks, telling Luther:

> My dear doctor . . . I will see to it that the thing that so moves you be done away, and I will act, God willing, as becomes a pious, spiritual and Christian prince, as far as God gives me grace and strength . . . for I can do nothing of myself and know well that without God's grace there is no good in me, but that I am as much foul mud as any other, if not more.[76]

Although condemned and concealed, the reformer now seemed to have more power than the cardinal!

In a treatise on monastic vows, Luther offered his final conclusions on celibacy and religious orders, being aware of the fact that some monks in Wittenberg had left the monastery and had gotten married. Dedicated to his father, the treatise dealt not with the question of whether a vow ought to be kept, but with what vows are true vows.[77] "A vow is Christian and godly only when it is not destructive of faith. Faith remains unhurt only when a vow is regarded as a matter of free choice and not as necessary to attain righteousness and salvation."[78] To be a monk is to be like a farmer, that is, to have a Christian calling which is not really superior to other callings. Since the medieval church, however, linked monasticism with righteousness, monastic vows have to be judged a violation of biblical command, reason, and common sense. Concluding with an exposition of 1 Timothy 5, Luther recommended that only people over sixty should become monks so as to avoid the pitfall of a troubled conscience in the light of the freedom of the gospel. "It is the gospel in which you have to put your trust, and these vows, whatever the circumstances, whatever the intent, whatever the time they were uttered, are to be abandoned in complete confidence and a return made to the freedom of the Christian faith."[79]

When Luther heard that there was confusion and unrest in Wittenberg, he broke down and paid a secret visit there between 4 and 10 December 1521. Some unrest was brewing among students and monks, but life in the city seemed normal. Dean Carlstadt and Professor Melanchthon had begun to institute some reforms such as a reduction in the number of masses celebrated and Sunday worship with sermons. Luther had a good time with his friends, had himself painted as "Knight George" by Lucas Cranach, but avoided any public appearances.

When he returned to the Wartburg, he wrote a treatise on the Mass and dedicated it to his brothers of the Augustinian Order in Wittenberg. In quick, successive strokes he told them that the Mass must be disengaged from the power of the clergy since every person is a priest through baptism; that the Mass is not a "sacrifice" offered by reciting the words of institution, but rather a celebration of Christ's promise to redeem poor sinners; and that the Mass has nothing to do with the papacy. Properly understood, the Mass is the testament of the dying Christ who promises forgiveness through his death and resurrection.[80]

> We should make a real effort to revive the manner and form in which Christ instituted the mass, so that only a single mass is held each Sunday, as is presently done on Easter day. . . . And the death of Christ should be proclaimed publicly through the Word; he should be remembered. And there should be prayer and thanksgiving in the congregation. On the basis of the Acts and Epistles of the apostles, that is obviously how it is to be arranged.[81]

Luther's most significant reflections at the Wartburg were on biblical authority and "justification by faith," and appeared in his lengthy reply to the Louvain theologian Latomus. The reply offered a blueprint of Luther's biblical theology, which was grounded in the teachings of Paul and especially in the Epistle to the Romans. He told Latomus that theologians must take seriously the power of sin after baptism. Life in this world is never without sin. That is why God instituted "law"—the Decalogue, secular government with its rules and regulations, and the uneasy conscience which senses that things go wrong. It is the function of law to reveal sin (Rom. 3:20). But God in Jesus Christ defeats sin for those who believe in his mercy—good news, "gospel"—for the world. In Scripture and in theology, law and gospel must be properly distinguished as the "two testaments" of God through which he deals with sin. The first testament, the law, reveals the corruption of human nature, the evil which humans inflict on themselves when they do what they want; and it discloses divine punishment, the evil which God inflicts on his creatures because they disobey him. The second testament, the gospel, also does two things. It gives righteousness, namely, faith in Christ who dies for human sin (Rom. 3:28); such faith enables believers to do good works for their neighbors, thus avoiding self-righteousness. Righteousness is accompanied by grace, namely, the goodwill and mercy of God for those who believe in Christ; such grace enables believers to fight remaining sin and to look at God as the merciful Father of Jesus Christ. Thus life is a struggle between good and evil, between sin and grace. "Everything is forgiven through grace," Luther told Latomus,

> but as yet not everything is healed through the gift [of faith]. The gift has been infused, the leaven has been added to the mixture. It works so as to purge away the sin for which a person has already been forgiven, and to drive out the evil guest for whose expulsion permission has been given. In the meantime, while this is happening, it is called sin . . . But now it is sin without wrath, without the law, dead sin, harmless sin, as long as one perseveres in grace and his gift. . . . To be sure, for grace there is no sin, because the whole person pleases; yet for the gift there is sin which it purges away and overcomes. . . . God saves real, not imaginary, sinners, and he teaches us to mortify real rather than imaginary sin.[82]

Luther did not present a very systematic view of his biblical theology to Latomus, a theology which climaxed in "justification by faith alone," but he did suggest that the distinction of law and gospel was the best possible methodological (hermeneutical) principle of theological reflection. This distinction led to the assertion that a Christian is "simultaneously righteous and sinful" (*simul justus et peccator*). Thus Luther tried to express what Paul had argued in Rom. 4:7, when quoting King David (Ps. 32:1: "Blessed is he whose transgression is forgiven . . ."), namely, there is a difference between being accounted righteous by God and still being aware of one's sin.[83] Luther regarded the discernment of this difference as the most essential aspect of Christian life. The proper distinction between law and gospel guards against a theology of glory which relies on the certainty of rational conviction that God loves the sinner, and the distinction also leads to humble worship of the God who promises the sinner's salvation through Christ.

Luther labored hard to link the revival of biblical theology to parish reform. He consequently made the Bible available to common people in their own language. Having taught himself Hebrew and Greek, with the help of Philip Melanchthon, Luther translated the Old and New Testaments into a German which consisted of a variety of dialects. Eventually the "Luther German" (*Lutherdeutsch*) became the language of the land, the "High German" which ended the linguistic segregation between Upper, Middle, and Low German.[84] The Luther Bible was, above all, the instrument of religious renewal in Germany, changing simple baptized Germans into biblically trained "common priests" united by a common language.

3

SHEPHERDING A RENEWAL

So, since the pope, with his following, simply refuses to convoke a council and reform the church, or offer any advice or assistance toward that end, but boastfully defends his tyranny with crimes, preferring to let the church go to ruin, we, so shamefully forsaken by the pope, cannot go on and must seek counsel and help elsewhere and first of all seek and ask our Lord Jesus Christ for a reformation. These desperate tyrants, whose evil forces us to despair of a council and of a reformation, must not drive us also to despair of Christ or to leave the church without counsel and help; we must instead do what we can, and let them go to the devil as they wish. ("On the Councils and the Church," 1539. WA 50:512.13–22. LW 41:11)

NOTHING IS REAL UNLESS IT IS LOCAL

Luther's absence from Wittenberg and the resulting rumors of his arrest or even death spawned unrest in the Saxon countryside and elsewhere in Germany. The common people, particularly the peasants, applied much of what Luther had said about Christian liberty to their own liberation from feudal landlords. Luther had heard rumors of violence among his followers, and his isolation at the Wartburg increased his fear of the violence and lawlessness caused by a confusion of church reform with political causes. That is why Luther sent a treatise to Spalatin in December 1521 which left no doubt about where he stood on the matter of "insurrection and rebellion":[1]

(1) No Christian is sufficiently righteous to equate faith and rebellion; if rebellion occurs, everyone is to blame because everyone remains sinful.

(2) Prayer is the best way to ask God to change the tyranny of pope and prince.

(3) Christ himself has already begun an insurrection, which is carried out through the preaching of the gospel; evil must be slain through the Word of God. Moreover, the "last day," the end of the world, may not be far off since the pope has been revealed as the Antichrist and Satan is tempting Christians to take God's business into their own hands.[2]

(4) There is no need to wage a "Lutheran" revolution against pope and emperor.

Luther therefore told potential revolutionaries:

I ask that men make no reference to my name; let them call themselves Christians, not Lutherans. What is Luther? After all, the teaching is not mine. Neither was I crucified for anyone. St. Paul, in I Corinthians 3[:22] would not allow the Christians to call themselves Pauline or Petrine, but Christian. How then should I—poor stinking maggot-fodder that I am—come to have men call the children of Christ by my wretched name? Not so, my dear friends! Let us abolish all party names and call ourselves Christians, after him whose teaching we hold.[3]

But Luther's warning was not heeded. Wittenberg experienced several disturbances during the winter of 1521/22. Dean Carlstadt urged not only reform of theological studies at the university but also implementation of Luther's ideas in congregations. Melanchthon hesitated to undertake anything without Luther's consent, and Elector Frederick favored a period of careful reflection, discussion, and education rather than immediate concrete action. But Carlstadt and Gabriel Zwilling, a former Augustinian monk, continued their efforts to implement Luther's liturgical proposals.

Their main goal was to establish the distribution of both bread and wine to each communicant at Sunday Mass. Their demand for the "lay chalice" echoed the old battle cry of the Hussites in neighboring Bohemia and Moravia, where John Hus had created a reform movement on this issue before his martyrdom in 1415. Many of these "Moravian Brethren" (as the pacifist Hussites were known at the time of Luther) regarded Luther as the "John Hus of Saxony." Elector Frederick's political enemies, such as his cousin George of Saxony, saw in the demand for the lay chalice a resurgence of the old Hussite heresy which the Council of Constance had condemned in 1415. A large group of Wittenbergers, consisting of former monks, priests, faculty members, prominent citizens, and plain people, rallied around Carlstadt and Zwilling, and on Christmas Day 1521 Carlstadt celebrated the first "evangelical" Mass in the Castle Church.[4] He wore no vestments, spoke German, and offered the chalice to every communicant.

On 27 December 1521, three "prophets" from the Saxon town of Zwickau appeared in Wittenberg and claimed to have received revelations from God in visions. They prophesied the imminent end of the world and called for the abolition of all sacraments and other "externals," especially infant baptism. They proclaimed that the individual's reception of the Holy Spirit in heart and soul was much more important than all the externals of the church, which in any case had prostituted itself ever since Constantine embraced it in A.D. 313 and adopted Christianity as the state religion. These "Zwickau prophets" were strongly influenced by their pastor, Thomas Müntzer.

Initially sympathetic to Luther's cause, Müntzer had soon turned away and, advocating rebellion against the ecclesiastical and political status quo, had created his own movement with the help of radical Hussites and disenchanted peasants.[5] The three Zwickau prophets—Nicholas Storch, Thomas Drechsel (unemployed weavers), and Mark, a former Wittenberg student known as "Stübner" because his father ran a bath house, a *Stube*, soon moved on. But they had created enough unrest to threaten law and order in both Wittenberg and the surrounding area. Zwilling preached such incendiary sermons in nearby Eilenburg that riots ensued; he returned to Wittenberg, and on 12 January 1522, failed to prevent a mob he had excited from devastating a parsonage.

The small Roman Catholic contingent in Wittenberg—mostly monks loyal to their vows—became the target of jeering gangs who often stoned them and their lodgings. Since the Augustinians had been told by their superiors to follow Luther's advice and regard vows a matter of conscientious choice, many of them left the monastery and got married. Many also joined Zwilling in removing altars and destroying images. On 19 January 1522, Carlstadt celebrated his own marriage to a peasant girl in an elaborate wedding attended by all influential Wittenberg citizens.

It is therefore not surprising that Duke George of Saxony asked the imperial court in Nuremberg to issue a mandate against the Wittenberg reforms for the sake of preserving Christian unity and the laws of the land. On 20 January 1522, a mandate was indeed sent to Elector Frederick which prohibited any change in public worship and also forbade monks to renounce their vows. Elector Frederick, however, politely refused to allow any interference in the internal affairs of Electoral Saxony.[6]

Carlstadt and his followers succeeded in persuading the city council to institute radical reforms, which they did by "ordinances" on 24 January 1522.[7] They provided care for the poor as a remedy against begging, prohibited prostitution, and abolished "Roman abuses" in public worship by instituting the models of the Mass that Carlstadt and Zwilling had celebrated. But the unrest continued. Carlstadt and Zwilling justified it by claiming that the local parish had a right to cleanse itself of the pagan abuses manifested in medieval ecclesiastical regulations and practices such as fasting, going to confession, and praying to images.

When Elector Frederick failed to calm the unrest despite a meeting on 13 February 1522, between one of his emissaries and the leaders of the Wittenberg radical reform movement, Luther decided to return to Wittenberg. Correspondence with Melanchthon and others had kept him well informed about events there.[8] He left the Wartburg in opposition to Elector Frederick's advice. "Your Electoral Grace has already done far too much and should do nothing at all," he told Frederick in a letter written on 5 March 1522, on the way to Wittenberg.

God will not and cannot tolerate your worrying and bustling, or mine. He wishes the matter to be left [in his hands] and no one else's. May Your Electoral Grace act accordingly. If Your Electoral Grace believes, then Your Electoral Grace will be safe and have peace. If Your Electoral Grace does not believe, I at least do believe and must leave Your Electoral Grace's unbelief to its own torturing anxiety, such as all unbelievers have to suffer.

Inasmuch as I do not intend to obey Your Electoral Grace, Your Electoral Grace is excused before God if I am captured or put to death. . . . For Christ has not taught me to be Christian at another's expense.[9]

Immediately after his arrival on 6 March 1522, Luther again wrote to Elector Frederick to reiterate his earlier conviction that he, Luther, had had no choice in the matter. The Wittenbergers had asked him to return, Satan must be tackled on the spot, and a general rebellion in Germany must be avoided. "Even if I could not accomplish anything in this affair, and even if I seem ridiculous to my enemies when they hear of it, I have to do what I see and know I must do."[10]

Three days later, on Invocavit Sunday, 9 March 1522, Luther mounted the pulpit of the Town Church and preached the first of eight sermons which restored law and order in Wittenberg. "The summons of death comes to us all," he told a crowd stunned by his appearance,

and no one can die for another. Every one must fight his own battle with death by himself, alone. We can shout into another's ears, but every one must himself be prepared for the time of death, for I will not be with you then, nor you with me. Therefore everyone must himself know and be armed with the chief things which concern a Christian. And these are what you, my beloved, have heard from me many days ago.[11]

Luther then listed the armor which the Wittenbergers needed in the struggle to reform the church catholic: a sense of sinful separation from God who is known as merciful in Christ; a deep feeling of love which springs from faith in Christ; patience, which discerns the difference between that which is a "must" and that which is "free."[12] Such discernment, Luther insisted, is the foundation for reforms. Consequently, "images" are appropriate if they are not worshiped. Fasting is fine if it does not lead to self-righteousness. Private confession is good when it is perceived as assurance of God's love in Christ. Changes in worship must be accompanied by good teaching so that people know what they are doing. Worship and catechetics are inseparable. Even the issue of the lay chalice must be treated in the context of a wise discernment of what is a "must" and what is "free."

Although I hold that it is necessary that the sacrament should be received in both kinds, according to the institution of the Lord, nevertheless it must not be made compulsory nor a general law. We must rather promote and practise and preach the Word, and then afterwards leave the result and execution of it entirely to the Word, giving everyone his freedom in the matter. Where this is not done, the sacrament becomes for me an outward work and a hypocrisy, which is just what the devil wants.[13]

Luther chided the Wittenbergers for neglecting the weak among themselves. "If you will not love one another, God will send a great plague upon you," he warned them. "You are not heeding it at all and you are playing around with all kinds of tomfoolery which does not amount to anything."[14]

Luther obviously had Carlstadt, Zwilling, and the Zwickau prophets in mind when he spoke of tomfoolery. What infuriated Luther was their attempt to quote Scripture in their favor, be it on the gifts of the Holy Spirit or, as in Müntzer's case, on the need for rebellious behavior. Those who have vision and speak like biblical prophets, Luther contended, must also endure suffering and persecution like the prophets and apostles. He advised Melanchthon, "Therefore examine (them), and do not even listen if they speak of the glorified Jesus unless you have first heard of the crucified Jesus."[15] Luther himself refused to become involved in a debate concerning the proper use of Scripture by the "prophets." He simply used his influence against them: Zwilling became an obedient disciple; Carlstadt was forbidden to preach in Wittenberg and went to nearby Orlamünde, where he continued his experimental "evangelical" reform; two of the Zwickau prophets met Luther sometime in the spring of 1522, but quickly disappeared again when Luther refused to take them seriously.[16]

Luther summarized his position on the lay chalice in a widely circulated treatise entitled "Receiving Both Kinds of the Sacrament."[17] Repeating his call for moderation and patience in matters of liturgical change, Luther suggested ten steps to teach the simple people:[18] (1) continue the old practice but teach rigorously why change is necessary; (2) avoid every reference to "sacrifice" in the celebration of the Mass so as not to imply that the priest is the only mediator of Christ's presence and power; (3) preach on the meaning of the Lord's Supper, especially the words "This is my body and blood given for you"; (4) do not force the distribution of both bread and wine if it causes serious offense and try to teach that love supersedes law; (5) celebrate the sacrament only when it is needed, even though no Sunday Mass should be without a Lord's Supper; (6) abolish private masses; (7) continue the practice of private confession; (8) keep images as long as they are not worshiped; (9) allow priests to marry and monks to leave the monasteries in accordance with their conscience; and (10) do not impose fasting as a "good work" which appeases God. All these steps should disclose the relationship between the sacrament and Christian unity rather than Christian division.

You should never say: I am a Lutheran, or a Papist. For neither of them died for you, or is your master. Christ alone died for you, he alone is your master, and you should confess yourself a Christian. But if you are convinced that Luther's teaching is in accord with the gospel and that the pope's is not, then you should not discard Luther so completely, lest with him you discard also his teaching, which you nevertheless recognize as Christ's teaching. You should rather say: whether Luther is a rascal or saint I do not care; his teaching is not his, but Christ's.[19]

With peace restored in Wittenberg, Luther once again concentrated on the principal task of his life: the interpretation of the Bible in preaching and teaching. In 1522 he delivered 117 sermons on the prescribed biblical texts for that day (pericopes); in 1523, the number of sermons increased to 137.[20] From February 1523 until the spring of 1524 he lectured on Deuteronomy, following it with a lengthy series on the prophetic books.[21]

Life in the monastery had changed, since all the other friars except one had left. The Augustinian Order had agreed to donate Luther's services as professor at the university in return for Elector Frederick's upkeep of the monastery buildings, so Luther was now quite poor. He had free room and board at the monastery, but his only income was from preaching at the Town Church, which was not sufficient even to buy fabric for a new habit. But the elector sent him the best fabric available, and Luther had a tailor make him an elegant patrician coat instead of a habit. After October 1524, he wore "civilian" clothes and gave up the monastic habit altogether. However, Luther, though living alone at the monastery, was not lonely. Melanchthon and John Bugenhagen (pastor of the Town Church since 1523) became Luther's best friends, as did the artist Lucas Cranach, Nicholas Amsdorf (formerly one of his students and now a colleague on the faculty), and the lawyer Justus Jonas. Students from various parts of Germany and from other countries, especially Switzerland and France, came to Wittenberg. In fact, Wittenberg had become a tourist attraction if not a pilgrimage site, and Luther was frequently visited by a variety of European intellectuals and noblemen.[22]

Luther related the insights derived from his work on the Bible and his critical study of the Christian past to various aspects of congregational and public life. He went on a short preaching tour through nearby Saxon towns in April 1522 and discovered that marriage had become a chief issue for both clergy and laity. He therefore summarized what he had to say about marriage in two short treatises, "The Persons Related by Consanguinity and Affinity Who Are Forbidden to Marry According to the Scriptures, Leviticus 18" and "The Estate of Marriage," which were published in the summer and fall of 1522. The first treatise simply listed the persons who should not be married and followed much of Jewish and canon law. The second treatise rejected marriage as a sacrament and attempted to answer three questions: (1) Which persons may enter into marriage with one another? (2) Which persons may be divorced? (3) What is a Christian marriage?

Luther rejected the normative medieval view that only those people able to have children should marry. "Be fruitful and multiply" (Gen. 1:28) is a "divine ordinance" *(Werk)* rather than a "command" *(Gebot)*. "Just as God does not command anyone to be a man or a woman but creates them the way they have to be, so he does not command them to multiply but creates them so that they have to multiply."[23] Marriage is a "worldly undertaking" just like eating, drinking, sleeping, buying, selling, etc. Jews and Turks are married as are Christians.[24] He added that when marriage cannot function because of "bodily or natural deficiencies," such as adultery or refusal to do one's conjugal duty, it should be dissolved.[25] He insisted that a Christian marriage takes personhood before God seriously; therefore no partner should dominate or abuse the other even though sin tempts them to do so. God can even turn sin into "his work": "Intercourse is never without sin; but God excuses it by his grace because the estate of marriage is his work."[26]

Closely related to the question of marriage was the question of "temporal authority" *(Obrigkeit)*. The imperial mandate against innovations in Wittenberg and elsewhere, issued on 20 January 1522, raised various issues: Should Christians resist unjust authority? Should they submit to evil in accordance with the injunction of the Sermon on the Mount (Matt. 5:39)? Should they submit to "governing authorities" (Rom. 13:1)? Luther preached six sermons on the subject of political authority at Weimar in October 1522 at the request of the court chaplain Wolfgang Stein, who worried about the persecution of Luther's disciples in the Netherlands and the threat of persecutions in Germany as a result of the Edict of Worms.

Luther's sermons were summarized in a treatise entitled "Temporal Authority: To What Extent It Should be Obeyed" published in December 1522. This treatise offered the basic features of Luther's "two-kingdoms" ethic.[27] Since Christians belong to the kingdom of God through the gospel and to the kingdom of the world through the law, they have to discern the difference between the two kingdoms in each situation they face. "If all the world were composed of real Christians, that is, true believers, there would be no need for or benefits from prince, king, lord, sword, or law."[28] However, since there is sin and the threat of chaos, God instituted not only the ministry of the gospel but also the ministry of the sword. "Neither one is sufficient in the world without the other."[29] Moreover, there are always weak Christians and tyrannical rulers. That is why resistance to unbelief and to tyranny go hand in hand. A strong believer

> should be so disposed that he will suffer every evil and injustice without avenging himself. . . . On behalf of others, however, he may and should seek vengeance, justice, protection, and help, and do as much as he can to achieve it. . . . No Christian shall wield or invoke the sword for himself and his cause. In behalf of another, however, he may and should wield it and invoke it to restrain wickedness and to defend godliness.[30]

Luther advised his readers to practice passive resistance in the face of oppression by tyrants who wanted to confiscate Luther's translation of the New Testament. "Outrage is not to be resisted but endured; yet we should not sanction it, or lift a little finger to conform or obey."[31] Christian princes, on the other hand, should be devoted to their subjects, consider the counsel of others, and be just with evildoers. Above all, reason and justice should prevail in a society which considers itself Christian.

Having dealt with the problem of temporal authority, Luther turned to the question of ecclesiastical authority. In the spring of 1523, a delegation from the newly formed "evangelical" Saxon congregation at Leisnig visited Wittenberg to seek advice on how to care for the poor, how to call a pastor, and how to reform public worship. Like other towns, especially Wittenberg, they had drawn up an "Ordinance of the Common Chest" designed to help the poor in town. But since quarrels had arisen over its implementation, they turned to Luther who, after a visit to Leisnig, wrote a "Preface" to the ordinance containing "suggestions on how to deal with ecclesiastical property."[32] These suggestions were derived from his experience in Wittenberg where a "common chest" had been established successfully. Luther endorsed the Leisnig ordinance, but warned against the use of force and advised patient, careful, and just implementation; he reminded the congregation that one should not expect miracles. "The world must remain the world," he concluded, "and Satan its prince. I have done what I can, and what I am in duty bound to do."[33]

Regarding the calling of pastors, Luther penned a brief treatise entitled "That a Christian Assembly or Congregation Has the Right and Power to Judge All Teaching and to Call, Appoint, and Dismiss Teachers, Established and Proven by Scripture," which was published in May 1523.[34] After reaffirming the common priesthood of all the baptized, Luther ascribed to the local congregation the power held only by bishops in the Roman Church. He added that since bishops had abused their calling, every individual baptized member of a congregation is to be considered priest and bishop, "called and anointed by God from within" in an emergency. But once the emergency is over, a congregation or church should call certain of its members into the ministry of Word and sacrament.[35] Luther was still optimistic enough in 1523 to expect congregations like Leisnig to become models of a renewed church free of abuse.

This same kind of optimism was displayed in another treatise on the structure and function of ministry, published during the winter of 1523 at the request of Hussite leaders who wanted Luther's approval for an independent national church in what is now Czechoslovakia.[36] Afraid that the Hussites would compromise with Rome on the matter of priestly ordination, Luther advised them not to have any ordained ministers at all, because of the "Babylonian confusion" in their territory.[37] In such a situation as theirs, he said, the father of each household should function as priest since the public ministry is too high an office to be perverted by episcopal ordination. He added that when Christ instituted the Lord's Supper he had "enjoined the same ministry of the Word to them all equally"; as a result, all ministerial functions, including the celebration of the Lord's Supper, belong to all who are baptized. "If then that which is greatest, namely, Word and baptism, is conferred on all, then it can rightly be maintained that the lesser, the power to consecrate, is also so conferred, even if there be no direct authority of Scripture."[38] Nevertheless, "it is one thing to exercise a right publicly; another to use it in time of emergency. Publicly one may not exercise a right without consent of the whole body or of the church. In time of emergency each may use it as he deems best."[39] Unfortunately, the Hussites soon returned to episcopal ordination; Luther's views did not prevail.[40]

Although political rulers, including the Elector Frederick, exercised their legal right to install "evangelical" pastors, they frequently permitted congregations and/or town councils to elect their own pastors. That is how Bugenhagen became the pastor of the Town Church in the fall of 1523. When the monastic community objected, Luther simply mounted the pulpit and declared him elected!

Both Elector Frederick and the Wittenberg city council also accepted Luther's proposals for the reform of public worship. These proposals called for the abolition of daily full masses in favor of a liturgy consisting of Scripture lessons, sermons, prayers, and hymns, and reserving the full Mass for Sundays. Luther sought a middle way between radicals and defenders of the status quo. He therefore advocated that, instead of the "rattling and prattling" of priests, there should be aesthetic simplicity. "We can spare everything except the Word," he told the Wittenbergers. "Again, we profit by nothing as much as by the Word."[41] The Mass should not be abrogated, but it should nevertheless be cleansed of "everything that smacks of sacrifice," that is, all propitiatory words and gestures should be abolished in favor of giving thanks to God for his sacrifice in Jesus Christ. All else in the Mass is secondary and is to be arranged according to the best of tradition and the needs of the people.[42] Luther himself composed and rearranged several hymns, among them the one which celebrates the justification of the ungodly through Christ, "Dear Christians Let us Now Rejoice" (Nun freut euch liebe Christen gemein).[43]

Many people who supported Luther's cause were confused about the power of the common priesthood of all baptized believers. Wittenbergers had seen Dean Carlstadt renounce his academic titles and become a country pastor, ostensibly to devote himself to the "simple Christian life" propelled by the inspiration of the Holy Spirit rather than by human wisdom. Many monastic schools had been dissolved. Luther felt that he had to speak out in favor of education. His programmatic ideas on the subject are contained in the treatise addressed "To the Councilmen of All Cities in Germany That They Establish and Maintain Christian Schools" published early in 1524.[44] Luther pleaded for public schools because congregations as well as parents appeared to be too unconcerned about the education of the young. Education is an investment in the future, he insisted. History and classical languages, especially Latin and Greek, should be taught, because Germany needed young people who had learned to use their reason wisely. "We have been German beasts all too long," he told German city fathers. "Let us for once make use of our reason, that God may perceive our thankfulness for his benefits, and other nations see that we too are human beings."[45] He also recommended that public libraries be established to encourage citizens to become civilized and to learn more about the world. "No effort or expense should be spared to provide good libraries or book repositories, especially in the larger cities which can well afford it."[46] According to Luther, the renewal of the church catholic also calls for a renewal of the mind. All the children of God, young and old, are called to be faithful witnesses of Christ wherever they live.

DIVIDING LINES

After 1522, Luther, like a bishop, presided over a fast-moving reform movement. He was surrounded by loyal friends, was visited by numerous supporters, and was constantly responding to various requests for counsel and advice. His four closest friends helped him shape the movement which bore his name. Melanchthon had become a widely respected linguist in Greek and Hebrew; Bugenhagen, through his humor, was able to console Luther, and was his confessor in private confession; Justus Jonas translated many of Luther's writings from Latin into German; and Nicholas Amsdorf was a staunch supporter and later (in 1541) was "ordained" Bishop of Naumburg by Luther.[47] Spalatin and others helped spread the movement through diplomacy.

While Wittenberg was peaceful and serene, the rest of Germany was not. Both the newly elected pope, Hadrian VI (1522–23), and the Emperor Charles V tried to persuade German princes to enforce the Edict of Worms and to outlaw Lutheranism. But in 1522 the Diet of Nuremberg rejected these efforts in favor of calling for an ecumenical council to deal with matters of reform. Some noblemen, however, did not wait for a peaceful solution to the religious question. Francis of Sickingen, supported by some other German knights and by Humanists like Ulrich of Hutten, declared war on Rome, but they were defeated in 1523 by the Archbishop of Trier and his allies. Sickingen died shortly after the last battle, and Hutten retreated to Switzerland where he died that same year. Luther, who had corresponded

with both, refused to lend his support to the knights' uprising, associating
the attempt with Satan.[48]

When a majority of German princes again refused to enforce the Edict of
Worms at the 1524 Diet of Nuremberg, King Ferdinand of Austria, some
Bavarian princes, and some South German bishops covenanted at Re-
gensburg to resist Protestant German uprisings—by force if necessary.
Territorial lines were starting to be drawn.

The schisms in Christendom were widening. On the one hand, there were
Rome's strong diplomatic efforts to suppress the reform movements, led by
the late Pope Leo X's cousin, Pope Clement VII (1523–34), and his able
legate to German diets, Cardinal Campegio. Rome was strongly supported
by Bavarian princes. On the other hand, there were the radical left-wing
reformers like Carlstadt in Orlamünde and Müntzer in Allstedt. Luther
sensed a satanic connection between the papists and the "enthusiasts"
(Schwärmer, from "swarming about"), as he called them. When Müntzer
founded a "covenant of the elect" in 1523 to be the nucleus for a large-scale
rebellion against the authority of the princes, Luther felt sufficiently
provoked to ask the princes to move against these Schwärmer.[49] He criticized
Müntzer for avoiding open debate in defense of his stance, and urged the
princes—specifically the princes of Saxony—to suppress rebellion. He
contended that the issue between himself and the radicals was the issue of
proper distinction between ministry of the gospel and ministry of the sword.

> As far as doctrine is concerned, time will tell. For the present, your Graces
> ought not to stand in the way of the ministry of the Word. Let them preach as
> confidently and boldly as they are able, and against whomever they may wish.
> For, as I have said, there must be sects, and the Word of God must be under
> arms and fight. . . . But when they want to do more than fight with the Word,
> and begin to destroy and use force, then your Graces must intervene, whether it
> be ourselves or they who are guilty, and banish them from the country.[50]

The princes responded by asking Luther to travel through the region of
Thuringia, where minor uprisings of peasants had already occurred. He
preached in Jena on 22 August 1524, and attacked Carlstadt as a demonic
spirit who incited rebellion. Carlstadt, who had found support in Jena,
requested a meeting to defend himself against what he regarded as an unfair
attack. Luther met him at the "Black Bear," an inn crowded with Carlstadt
followers. The exchange ended with Luther's pledge—symbolized by his
giving a gulden and a toast—to engage only in literary feuds with Carlstadt.[51]
In a less humorous encounter between Luther and the leaders of the
Orlamünde parish, who defeated him in that debate, Luther was forced to
leave town accompanied by curses from an angry crowd.[52] The experience
convinced him that Carlstadt was a Schwärmer, and he urged Elector
Frederick to ban him from his territory. After his expulsion from Saxony,

Carlstadt found some support in Strassburg, and Luther again intervened by writing an open letter "to all Christians in Strassburg" in the fall of 1524.[53] "As I see his [Carlstadt's] course," Luther told Martin Bucer and other leaders of the Strassburg reform movement,

> he pounces on outward things with such violence, as though the whole strength of the Christian enterprise consisted in the destruction of images, the overthrow of the sacrament and the hindering of baptism. He would like with such smoke and mist to obscure altogether the sun and light of the gospel and the main articles of Christianity, so that the world might forget everything that we have hitherto taught.[54]

In January 1525, Luther fired off his most extensive polemical theological blast against Carlstadt and all those who held similar views, especially against their notion that there is no "bodily presence" of Christ in the Lord's Supper.[55] He admonished his readers to concentrate on the renewal of the church rather than on the peculiar theological interpretations offered by Carlstadt and others. Luther also summarized his earlier views on the validity of images, his perception of Carlstadt's activities in Saxony, and his own understanding of the Lord's Supper as the mystery of Christ's presence. He preferred the "middle way" between Rome and "Lutheran" radicals.

> Now when God sends forth his holy gospel he deals with us in a twofold manner, first outwardly, then inwardly. Outwardly he deals with us through the oral word of the gospel and through material signs, that is, baptism and the sacrament of the altar. Inwardly he deals with us through the Holy Spirit, faith, and other gifts. But whatever their measure or order *the outward factors should and must precede. The inward experience follows and is effected by the outward....* *Observe carefully, my brother, this order, for everything depends on it.*[56]

Since Carlstadt had denied any presence of Christ in the Lord's Supper in an extensive "dialogue" on the "blasphemous abuse" of this sacrament, Luther took him to task in extensive polemical arguments, showing how badly Carlstadt interpreted Christ's words at the Lord's Supper (Matt. 26:26–30; 1 Cor. 11:23–26). Carlstadt had claimed that the word "this" in the sentence "this is my body" referred to Jesus himself, his own body, rather than to the bread and wine. According to Carlstadt, Jesus had pointed to himself when he said "This is my body."[57] Luther declared that with such ideas Carlstadt "robs God of his honor, contradicts the truth, destroys the teaching of St. Paul, and makes the passion of Christ unnecessary."[58] Moreover, he said, Carlstadt, Müntzer, and all their disciples must be rejected because "they run about and teach without a call"; and they "are silent about the main points of Christian doctrine." They do not really teach "how we are to become free from our sins, obtain a good conscience, and win a peaceful and joyful heart before God."[59] Luther ignored Carlstadt's rebuttal; he had fired his last shot on this matter.[60]

Müntzer demonstrated the connection between radical theology and political rebellion. By the spring of 1525, Müntzer had associated himself with bands of peasants who were plundering towns in Thuringia in rebellion against their feudal landlords. Müntzer made it clear that he was the leader of a radical reformation which intended to realize the Christian freedom Luther had promised to those who were oppressed by the medieval feudal system. In one of his fiery treatises, written in 1524, Müntzer had called Luther the "soft-living flesh of Wittenberg" hiding behind biblical rhetoric and the political power of the German princes.[61] The peasants circulated their demands in the form of "Twelve Articles" and appealed to Luther for counsel; Luther advised conciliation between them and the princes, but at the same time accused them of using the gospel to justify violence and rebellion. He asked representatives of princes and city councilmen to mediate the conflict in order to avoid bloodshed. "If you do not follow this advice—God forbid!" He concluded his detailed commentary on the "Twelve Articles":

> I must let you come to blows. But I am innocent of your souls, your blood, or your property. The guilt is yours alone. I have told you that you are both [princes and peasants] wrong and that what you are fighting for is wrong. . . . I, however, will pray to my God that he will either reconcile you both and bring about an agreement between you, or else graciously prevent things from turning out as you intend.[62]

But Luther's advice appeared too late. Rebellious peasants were already on the march throughout Thuringia. On the way to Eisleben to establish a Christian school at the request of Count Albrecht of Mansfeld, Luther preached in Nordhausen and was heckled during the sermon. He angrily drafted the treatise which earned him the reputation of being an enemy of the oppressed, "Against the Robbing and Murdering Hordes of Peasants," which was published in May 1525.[63] "The peasants have taken upon themselves three terrible sins against God and man," he fumed. They have violated the oath of obedience to divinely instituted government, they have destroyed property which is not theirs, and they rebel in the name of the gospel. Princes, therefore, have no choice but to put down the rebellion in the name of God.

> Thus, anyone who is killed fighting on the side of the rulers may be a true martyr in the eyes of God, if he fights with the kind of conscience I have just described [to avoid sedition], for he acts in obedience to God's word. On the other hand, anyone who perishes on the peasants' side is an eternal firebrand of hell, for he bears the sword against God's word and is disobedient to him, and is a member of the devil.[64]

Encouraged by Luther, an army led by George of Saxony and Philip of Hesse killed several thousand peasants in a "battle" at Frankenhausen on 15

May 1525, losing only six men on their own side. Müntzer, who had fled before the battle began, was captured, tortured, and beheaded. Luther's friends urged Luther to retract his harsh condemnation of the peasants. He explained his position in sermons during the Pentecost season of 1525 and in another treatise shortly afterwards.[65] In the treatise, he accused both princes and peasants of inhuman behavior, but nevertheless defended his view that rebellion is wrong no matter what the reason.

> Rebellion is a crime that deserves neither a court trial nor mercy, whether it be among heathen, Jews, Turks, Christians, or any other people; the rebel has already been tried, judged, condemned, and sentenced to death, and everyone is authorized to execute him. Nothing more needs to be done than to give him his due and to execute him.[66]

Luther had seemingly lost interest in negotiations for the sake of reasonable compromise in the name of justice. He told Caspar Müller, the Chancellor of Mansfeld, to whom he wrote the letter,

> If anyone is not satisfied, let him remain, in God's name, wise and prudent, righteous and holy; and let me remain a fool and a sinner. I wish that they would leave me in peace. . . . If anyone wants to be peculiar, I, too, shall be peculiar, and we shall see who is right in the end.[67]

The peasants' uprising in 1525 led Luther to the conclusion that any attempt to transform the communication of the gospel into a political crusade was doomed to produce only misery for anyone involved. Moreover, he thought Germany was plagued by a general lack of law and order precipitated not only by peasants but also by rulers. "It is evident," he complained in his exposition of Psalm 118 a few years later,

> that at the present time there is not a single soul in Germany who would preserve law and order in the face of these lawless and robbing nobles or protect government from such faithless and thievish subjects. Robbery and stealing abound; assassins follow their singular practices; men plot and rage. Yet no one's conscience is pricked by these sins against God. . . . If human wisdom and the power of man were governing Germany today, she would be lying in ruins tomorrow.[68]

Luther, who was forty-two years old in 1525, married the twenty-six-year-old Catherine of Bora in the midst of the political unrest. He had met Katie, as he called her, and eight other apostate nuns during the Easter season of 1523. He tried to help them to survive and to find husbands for them. He succeeded in arranging marriages for the eight nuns, but Katie resisted all his attempts to match her with someone else. Luther rejected any notion of getting married himself. Since the Edict of Worms had made him subject to the death penalty, he had no wish to expose a spouse and children to his own danger. "I daily expect death and the punishment due to a heretic," he told

Spalatin, who had heard rumors about a possible wedding in November 1524.[69] But conversations with his parents, the biblical ideal of marriage, the death of Elector Frederick on 5 May 1525, and the consequent reminder that life seems so short when surrounded by death finally convinced Luther. Following tradition, he and Catherine exchanged vows in a private ceremony in the monastery on 13 June 1525. Five of Luther's friends witnessed the ceremony, among them Justus Jonas and Lucas Cranach, with whose family Katie had resided. The public wedding took place on 27 June and included a festive procession to the Town Church and a banquet for fifteen guests including Luther's parents. Elector John, the successor to and brother of Frederick, presented the young couple with one hundred gulden, the monastery as a parsonage, and a monthly salary of two hundred gulden for the bridegroom.

Katie became treasurer and manager of the household, which included a garden and farm animals such as chickens and pigs. A year after the wedding, Luther fell deeply in love with his wife. He told a friend how happy he was with Katie, his "rib." "She is . . . obedient and obliging to me, more than I had ever dared to hope (thank God), so that I would not want to exchange my poverty for the riches of Croesus."[70] Eventually six children were born: Hans, born in 1526; Elizabeth, 1527; Magdalena, 1529; Martin, 1531; Paul, 1533; and Margaretha, 1534. The Luthers also raised four others, children of relatives who had been left orphaned. In addition, they frequently boarded students and entertained numerous guests.[71] Katie tended the animals and the garden, brewed beer, and treated Luther's illnesses with the expertise of a physician. She transformed the Black Cloister (the name for the new parsonage and old monastery) into a home filled with children, friends, guests, and good "table talks" despite a constant lack of funds.[72]

Not even during his first year of marriage could Luther concentrate on domesticity. The year was dominated by a controversy which Luther regarded as the most significant encounter in his life: his literary debate with Europe's most famous philosopher, Erasmus of Rotterdam, on the question of whether or not the human creature has the freedom to accept or to refuse divine grace. Erasmus had initially supported Luther's efforts to reform the church, but had become fearful of the divisions thus created within Christendom. In an elegantly argued "Diatribe," he pleaded for a compromise between two extreme positions which had already arisen in Western theology during the fifth-century debate between the North African bishop Augustine and the British monk Pelagius, and which he saw as the issue between Rome and Luther—the view of a deterministic God who predestines his creatures whether they like it or not, and the view of the human creature who, even in the face of God's power to save or condemn, is endowed with the image of God and thus has free choice. According to Erasmus, neither the abuse of indulgences, which encourages common folk to try to earn salvation through financial good works, nor Luther's radical denial of human cooperation with the will of God for salvation, which tempts people to become amoral, reflected the true intent of Scripture and Christian tradition. There is clear evidence even in Scripture, Erasmus asserted, that the human creature has the freedom to accept or to refuse divine grace. Otherwise it would truly be nonsense to assert both the justice and the mercy of God. God is neither a tyrant requiring the sacrifice of human intellect and freedom nor a Creator ruled by the whims of his creatures. Erasmus viewed God as the wise Creator who wants his creatures to exercise the basic freedom he gave them when they were created "in his own image" (Gen. 1:27).

Luther's response was vehement and elaborate, unequivocally asserting "The Bondage of the Will."[73] Attempting to refute the Erasmian arguments point by point, Luther attacked a "theology of observation," as it were, with the theologian Erasmus observing God from a neutral corner. In contrast, Luther defended a "theology of the Word," with the theologian already drawn into the struggle between God's "good news" in Christ and Satan's "bad news" in the temptation to become God (Gen. 3:5).

> Thus the human will is placed between the two like a beast of burden. If God rides it, it wills and goes where God wills. . . . If Satan rides it, it wills and goes where Satan wills; nor can it choose to run to either of the two riders or to seek him out, but the riders themselves contend for the possession and control of it.[74]

According to Luther, there is no neutral ground between the gospel and Satan, between God's revelation in Christ and the mysterious opposition to it by "hardened hearts" like that of Pharaoh (Exod. 7:13). The *Christian* theologian must concentrate on what God has disclosed rather than on what he has mysteriously hidden.

> We have to argue in one way about God or the will of God as preached, revealed, offered, and worshiped, and in another way about God as he is not preached, not revealed, not offered, not worshiped. To the extent, therefore, that God hides himself and wills to be unknown to us, it is no business of ours. . . . God must therefore be left to himself in his own majesty, for in this regard we have nothing to do with him, nor has he willed that we should have anything to do with him. But we have something to do with him insofar as he is clothed and set forth in his Word, through which he offers himself to us.[75]

The real issue between Luther and Erasmus was methodological. Whereas Erasmus viewed God from the viewpoint of a speculating observer, Luther saw God as both hidden and revealed: hidden as the almighty Creator of the universe full of paradoxical mysteries, and revealed as the Redeemer of human creatures in the suffering, death, and resurrection of Jesus.

> God does many things that he does not disclose to us in his word; he also wills

many things which he does not disclose himself as willing in his word. Thus he does not will the death of a sinner, according to his word; but he wills it according to that inscrutable will of his. It is our business, however, to pay attention to the word and leave that inscrutable will alone, for we must be guided by the word and not by that inscrutable will.[76]

Erasmus responded to Luther's attack in 1527 with "Defense,"[77] but Luther decided not to reply. A reconciliation was impossible as long as their theological positions reflected the radical differences disclosed in their debate on the freedom of the will.

The subsequent controversy between the Swiss reformer Ulrich Zwingli and Luther on the Lord's Supper revealed similar differences. Zwingli had adopted and elaborated the interpretation of the Dutch Humanist Cornelius Hoen (known as Honius), who had argued that the Lord's Supper is basically a memorial at which "spiritual," not "material," eating and drinking takes place. Therefore the words of Jesus "This is my body" mean "This *signifies* my body," and the celebration of the Lord's Supper is an affirmation of personal faith and commitment to Christ rather than an event of Christ's "bodily presence" as taught by Roman theologians and by Luther.[78]

The controversy began in the fall of 1525 with literary skirmishes between Zwingli supporters, especially the Basel reformer John Oecolampadius and the Strassburg reformer Martin Bucer, and Luther supporters like pastor John Bugenhagen and the Schwäbisch Hall reformer John Brenz. Luther had no choice but to get involved, and he did so with three major publications: (1) a sermon preached in the spring of 1526 and published in the fall, entitled "The Sacrament of the Body and Blood of Christ—Against the Fanatics";[79] (2) a highly polemical treatise published in 1527 entitled "That These Words of Christ, 'This is My Body' etc., Still Stand Firm Against the Fanatics";[80] and (3) a final summation published in 1528 entitled "Confession Concerning Christ's Supper."[81]

These writings on the meaning of the Lord's Supper disclose Luther's unconditional commitment to God's incarnation in Christ communicated through the "audible word" of speech and the "visible word" of sacraments.[82] Luther rejected the Zwinglian distinction between the human and divine natures of Christ in the Lord's Supper, a distinction asserting that there is a "spiritual" presence of the divine nature at the expense of the human nature, which is material. Luther argued that God and Christ, as well as Christ's two natures, cannot be divided according to the dogma of the Trinity affirmed in the creeds. "My grounds, on which I rest on this matter, are as follows," he declared.

> The first is this article of our faith, that Jesus Christ is essential, natural, true, complete God and man in one person, undivided and inseparable. The second, that the right hand of God is everywhere. The third, that the Word of God is not

false or deceitful. The fourth, that God has and knows various ways to be present at a certain place.[83]

Luther could not concede that God as "body" must be limited to realities determined by Greek logic or physics. Christ can be "seated at the right hand of the Father" and also be in bread and wine. God's "ubiquity" is unlimited, and since he promised in the gospel to be present in the Lord's Supper, that promise is a better source of what is true and real than the speculations of a Greek mind. On the other hand, Luther insisted, if God is truly incarnate, then Christ can be everywhere, because he is also God who breaks through all modes of existence. Thus Luther contended that Zwingli not only did not trust the promise of the gospel, he did not reason well either. "They understand the matter as little as an ass does the Psalter, except that they may wrench a little piece from it and abuse and mutilate it, as an excuse for ignoring and skipping over the main subjects."[84] To give up the view of Christ's "bodily (real) presence" in the Lord's Supper, Luther argued, means to abandon faith in God's incarnation. That is why the doctrine of the Lord's Supper is part of a confession of faith which begins with the praise of the Triune, incarnate God and ends with the hope of the resurrection.[85]

It is possible that Luther's most famous hymn, "A Mighty Fortress is our God" (Ein feste Burg ist unser Gott)—written between 1527 and 1528 and based on Psalm 46—was composed because of this controversy, although a contributing factor was the outbreak of the plague which struck Wittenberg in August 1527. Elector John Frederick evacuated the university to Jena until the spring of 1528, but Luther refused to leave Wittenberg, where he kept himself busy by tending the sick and the dying.[86]

THE TERRITORIAL IMPERATIVE

After 1525, theological differences continued to shape political decisions. German-speaking Swiss rallied around Zwingli, who had persuaded the Zurich city fathers to accept his reforms. Luther's reform movement conquered Prussia by 1526, with the help of the Knights of the Teutonic Order, and Denmark adopted Lutheranism by legislative action in 1527.[87] The Zwinglian reform movement made headway in German territories near the Swiss and French borders, with the city of Strassburg as the center. German Roman Catholic princes formed a military alliance in Dessau in the summer of 1525 led by Luther's opponents Duke George of Saxony and Archbishop Albrecht of Mainz. In response to the Dessau alliance, Elector John Frederick and Philip of Hesse established the League of Torgau (Bund) in February 1526; it was supported by a number of northern cities, including Magdeburg. The 1526 Diet of Speyer made another compromise concerning the enforcement of the Edict of Worms: each territorial prince had the right to treat the matter in such manner as he thought "is responsible towards God and His Imperial Majesty."[88] This compromise was interpreted as a license to fuse religion and territorial politics.

Electoral Saxony used this political compromise to strengthen Lutheranism in its territory. Luther and Melanchthon, with the help of the city council of Wittenberg and the electoral court, moved to link reform of public worship with educational reforms. Luther devised a plan of "visitations" in order to discern what needed to be done in the Saxon countryside. Teams of four "visitors" toured the territory, two of them to examine the economic situation, and the other two to evaluate parish life. Melanchthon composed a guidebook of "Instructions" based on Luther's suggestions; Luther wrote a "Preface" to it. The guidebook appeared at the beginning of 1528 after the first visitation resulted in suggestions for improvements. Luther was convinced that this effort to reform Saxony was similar to the cooperation of church and state at the Council of Nicaea in A.D. 325 which had, under Emperor Constantine, established orthodoxy.

> While His Electoral Grace is not obligated to teach and to rule in spiritual affairs, he is obligated as temporal sovereign to so order things that strife, rioting, and rebellion do not arise among his subjects; even as the Emperor Constantine summoned the bishops to Nicaea since he did not want to tolerate the dissension which Arius had stirred up among the Christians in the empire.[89]

Each visitation team had the duty to investigate eighteen matters: doctrine (the difference between Roman and Lutheran assertions); Decalogue; prayer life; morality ("tribulation"); baptism; Lord's Supper; penance; private confession; satisfaction for sin; human order in the church (compared to order in government); marriage; free will; Christian freedom: the Turks; worship; the ban (excommunication); the office of bishop (called "superintendent"); and schools (elementary, grammar, and liberal arts). The team's main concern was the competence of pastors.[90]

Under the impact of the first visitations he helped to conduct, Luther immediately detected the need for catechetical instruction. Consequently he composed a "German" or Large Catechism, using the materials from catechetical sermons he had preached during Lent of 1528. This Catechism consisted of a preface and five parts: Decalogue, Creed, Lord's Prayer, Baptism, and Lord's Supper, concluding with "A Brief Exhortation to Confession." A Small Catechism in the form of posters which could easily be attached to walls appeared together with the Large Catechism; it was illustrated with woodcuts and was designed so it could be easily memorized. It was taught by a question-and-answer method to initiate the young into Christian life after baptism. An appendix included morning, evening, and table prayers.[91]

Worship and catechetics were to Luther the twin pillars of Christian life.

He urged everyone, especially pastors, to use the catechisms as the bridge from false security and vanity to proper conflict with the world's evil.

> Let all Christians exercise themselves in the Catechism daily, and constantly put it into practice, guarding themselves with the greatest care and diligence against the poisonous infection of . . . security and vanity. Let them continue to read and teach, to learn and meditate and ponder. Let them never stop until they have proved by experience that they have taught the devil to death and have become wiser than God himself and all his saints. If they show such diligence, then I promise them—and their experience will bear me out—that they will gain much fruit and God will make excellent men of them. [92]

The Roman Catholic and Lutheran military alliances as well as several small wars between European territories and the invasion of the Turks were the motivation for Luther to address the question of war. A nobleman had shared his concern with Luther about "whether soldiers, too, can be saved," so Luther responded in 1526 with a treatise so entitled. [93] He asserted that since the world is an evil place, the ministry of the sword is needed to prevent lawlessness and rebellion. Thus a soldier's vocation is quite legitimate provided he understands that military violence is used to establish justice. War, then, is justified when it is defensive, that is, when a prince under attack defends himself. "Whoever starts a war is in the wrong." [94] Pacifism is utopian, and ideological crusades are evil; only "just wars" are legitimate.

> No war is just, even if it is a war between equals, unless one has such a good reason for fighting and such a good conscience that he can say, "My neighbor compels and forces me to fight, though I would rather avoid it." [95]

Luther was aware that professional soldiers frequently faced moral dilemmas. Does a soldier have to fight for a feudal landlord because he is a vassal? Must he engage in a war which is not a defensive one? Can he serve more than one lord as a mercenary? May he fight for the sake of pride? Luther advised that soldiers should discern when to fear God rather than men (Acts 5:29) and then follow their conscience. "In every other occupation we are also exposed to the danger that the rulers will compel us to act wrongly; but since God will have us leave even father and mother for his sake, we must certainly leave lords for his sake." [96]

Luther dealt in similar fashion with the question "Of the War against the Turks" in April 1529 [97] when urged by friends and princes to speak out on the subject. He separated himself from any notion of a religious crusade against the Muslim threat from the south: "This is absolutely contrary to Christ's doctrine and name . . . because he says that Christians shall not resist evil, fight, or quarrel, nor take revenge or insist on rights (Matt. 5:39)." [98] He did say that if attacked by Turks, or anyone else for that matter, Christians have to

defend themselves as the guardians of just government. But "this fight must
be begun with repentance, and we must reform our lives, or we shall fight in
vain."[99] Turks are as human as Christians, and war against them must take
that into account. He added that it is best to fight against them only in the
name of the emperor in order to avoid unnecessary battles and bloodshed.

> If our kings and princes were to agree and stand by one another and help each
> other, and the Christian man were to pray for them, I should be undismayed and
> of good hope. The Turk would stop his raging and find his equal in Emperor
> Charles. . . . What do our dear lords do? They treat it as just a joke. . . . [They]
> consult about how they can harass Luther and the gospel. . . . What devil
> commands you to deal so vehemently with spiritual things concerning God and
> matters of conscience which are not committed to you, and to be so lax and
> slothful in things that God has committed to you? [100]

When Luther accused princes of confusing the "two kingdoms"—the
ministry of the Word and the ministry of the sword—he had the 1529 Diet of
Speyer in mind. It was at that diet that the Emperor Charles V succeeded,
with the help of Roman Catholic princes, in ending the toleration of
"Lutherans" and in enforcing the Edict of Worms. Five princes and fourteen
cities delivered a "Protestation" to the emperor in response, thus becoming
known as "Protestants."[101] Territorial lines were again being drawn.

Meanwhile, political efforts to bring Lutherans and Zwinglians together
also failed. Whereas Zwingli and his supporters felt that agreement about the
Lord's Supper was not essential to Protestant unity, Luther thought it was.
When the Protestant prince Philip of Hesse insisted on a colloquy between
the factions in Marburg in 1529, Luther reluctantly agreed to attend with a
delegation. "Your Sovereign Grace can easily see," he wrote Landgrave
Philip in a letter dated 23 June 1529,

> that all discussions are futile and the meeting vain, if both parties come with the
> intention of conceding nothing. Thus far I have found nothing other than that
> they want to insist on their position, though they have become very familiar
> with the basis of our position. On the other hand, having also become familiar
> with the basis of their position, I certainly know that I am unable to yield, just as
> I know that they are wrong.[102]

Luther and his Wittenberg colleagues prepared themselves for the
meeting in Marburg by drawing up a consensus statement known as the
"Schwabach Articles." After a private meeting between Luther and
Oecolampadius on the one hand and Melanchthon and Zwingli on the other,
both delegations, each consisting of probably five members, met at Marburg
Castle on 2 and 3 October 1529, in the presence of Landgrave Philip and
other guests.[103] Luther drew up fifteen articles, later known as the "Marburg
Articles," and the Zwinglian delegation agreed with fourteen of them. The
articles dealt with the dogma of the Trinity, sin, faith, justification,

proclamation, baptism, confession, good works, and the role of government. Concerning Article 15 on the Lord's Supper, the signers declared that

> although at this time, we have not reached an agreement as to whether the true body and blood of Christ are bodily present in the bread and wine, nevertheless, each side should show Christian love to the other side insofar as conscience will permit, and both sides should diligently pray to Almighty God that through his Spirit he might confirm us in the right understanding.[104]

An epidemic of a disease known as "English sweat" (because of the high fever) struck Marburg, and Landgrave Philip speeded up the discussions originally scheduled to last a week. But agreement would not have been achieved regardless of how long the colloquy had lasted. Luther and Zwingli parted without bitterness, but Luther later called the Swiss reformer a heretic. When he heard of Zwingli's death in a battle between Swiss Protestants and Catholics in 1531, he told some guests at table that heretics like Zwingli, Müntzer, and the pope eventually end up being driven to the sword.[105] He was convinced that no theological concessions should be made for the sake of political alliances, since such alliances tend to pervert rather than to further the gospel.

Emperor Charles V finally agreed to give the Lutheran party a hearing at the Diet of Augsburg in 1530. Luther consented to have Melanchthon write the Augsburg Confession. "I have read through Master Philip's *Apologia,* which pleases me much," he wrote to Elector John from the Castle Coburg, where John had advised him to stay during the Augsburg proceedings.

> I know nothing to improve or change in it, nor would this be appropriate, since I cannot step so softly and quietly. May Christ, our Lord, help to bear much and great fruit, as we hope and pray.[106]

During his stay at Castle Coburg—he called it "the wilderness"—Luther once again enjoyed the more leisurely pace of exile just as he had at the Wartburg. But his pen never rested. Reflections on ecclesiastical authority, a commentary on Psalm 118, musings on biblical translation, and a call for good schooling streamed to the printers. In addition, he wrote many letters, especially to Katie, and sent forth a kind of Augsburg Confession of his own entitled "Exhortation to All the Clergy Assembled at Augsburg."[107]

Though quite different in tone and content from Melanchthon's Augsburg Confession, Luther's summary of significant issues and their interpretation is quite impressive. Beginning with "indulgences," Luther summed up his theological reflections on the sacrament of penance, excommunication, the Lord's Supper, and the episcopacy, and finally listed the things which he felt characterize the "Christian church" and "the things which have been practice and custom in the pretended church."[108] Again reminding his readers that gospel and bloodshed do not mix, Luther appealed to the diet not to dismiss Lutherans as heretics:

I maintain that you will not very well be able to do without the Lutherans, the pious heretics, least of all their prayers, if you want to achieve anything lasting. . . . We are and want to be innocent of your blood and damnation, since we pointed out to you sufficiently your wrongs, faithfully admonished to repentance, prayed sincerely, and offered to the uttermost all that could serve the cause of peace.[109]

The Augsburg Confession was rejected and the Edict of Worms was reendorsed at the diet, which increased Luther's suspicion that Rome would fight rather than compromise.[110] "We will never again get as close together as we did at Augsburg," he was heard to say sometime in the 1530s.[111] Saxon jurists convinced him that the Protestant territories would have to engage in armed resistance against the imperial forces if attacked, and that this would not violate his "just war" theory. In a "Warning to His Dear German People," published in April 1531, Luther agreed that Protestant territorial self-defense did not constitute sedition or rebellion even if the enemy was the emperor. He was never theologically comfortable with the notion of defending the gospel with the sword, yet he condoned the formation of the military League of Smalcald in February 1531.[112] "I want to make a distinction between sedition and other acts and to deprive the bloodhounds of the pretext of boasting that they are warring against rebellious people," he wrote in justification of his support of armed resistance to the emperor by Protestant territories.[113]

Luther only reluctantly accepted the alliance of the reform movement with political territorial power, but his loyalty to what he considered to be divinely instituted government proved stronger than his obedience to the church that had ordained him. He reminded his critics of his vow to be faithful to Holy Scripture, then told them that the movement he had begun was bigger than any man.

In God's name and call I shall walk on the lion and the adder, and tread on the young lion and dragon with my feet [Ps. 91:13]. And this which has begun during my lifetime will be completed after my death. St. John Huss prophesied of me when he wrote from his prison in Bohemia, "They will roast a goose now (for 'Huss' means 'a goose'), but after a hundred years they will hear a swan sing, and him they will endure." And that is the way it will be, if God wills.[114]

Protestant territories once again prevented emperor and pope from successfully implementing or enforcing the Edict of Worms. Luther had too many powerful political friends and allies, especially the successors to Elector Frederick—his brother John (1525–32) and his nephew John Frederick (1532–47). Afraid of losing the much-needed support of the German princes for the struggle against the Turkish threat from the south, Emperor Charles V agreed to a truce between Protestant and Catholic territories in Nuremberg in 1532. The agreement stated that legal and military actions waged between Catholic and Lutheran territories would be avoided until the convening of a free, universal council which would have to deal with the schism.[115] Thus the Lutheran movement was, for the first time, officially tolerated and could enjoy a place in the political sun of the Holy Roman Empire.

4

BEGGARS CANNOT
BE CHOOSERS

Pray for me, miserable and despised worm that I am, vexed with a spirit of sadness by the good will of the Father of mercies to whom be glory even in my misery. My only glory is that I handed on God's work purely and have not adulterated it because of any striving for glory and wealth. I hope that he who made a beginning will be merciful to the end. For I seek and thirst only for a gracious God who offers himself and asks to be so received even by those who hold him in contempt and are his enemies. (Letter to Melanchthon, 27 October 1527, no. 1162. WA.BR 4:272.27–33)

ENDURING ISSUES

The Nuremberg truce of 1532 enabled the Lutheran reform movement to establish a number of territorial churches adhering to the Augsburg Confession and under the protection of the Smalcald League. But nascent Lutheranism faced opposition, often from within its own ranks, from a variety of radical groups later known as the "left wing of the Reformation" or "radical Reformation."[1] One such group was the "Swiss Brethren," nicknamed "Anabaptists" (from the Greek *anabaptizein*, "to baptize again"). Originally dissenters from the Zwinglian movement in Zurich in the 1520s, they were almost immediately declared heretics and persecuted; the practice of baptizing twice had been condemned by imperial law since the time of Justinian I (527–65).[2]

When Luther heard that some groups rejected the practice of infant baptism in favor of an adult "believers' baptism" after a personal confession of faith, he tried to expose such teaching as contrary to Holy Scripture and church tradition. Since faith is always laced by doubt, Luther argued, the church must follow Christ's mandate to "baptize all nations" (Matt. 28:19) rather than wait until individuals make a commitment to Christ. The command to baptize is therefore more important than an adult's profession of faith. "Were we to follow their [the Anabaptists'] reasoning, we would have to be baptizing all the time," Luther declared in the treatise "Concerning Rebaptism" (1528).[3] He heard rumors of Anabaptists appearing in his hometown of Eisenach and denounced them angrily as clandestine messengers of Satan and disciples of the notorious *Schwärmer* Thomas Müntzer. "Since these infiltrators are sent by the devil to preach nothing but poison and lies," he wrote to an official in the electoral court of Saxony,

> and the devil is not only a liar but a murderer [John 8:44], it can only be that he intends through these emissaries to create rebellion and murder (even if for a while he carries on peacefully), and to overthrow both spiritual and temporal government against the will of God.[4]

For the most part, Luther relied on rumors about Anabaptist behavior, and so did not investigate what the Swiss Brethren and their disciples really taught. Consequently, he never realized that most Anabaptists were pacifists committed to suffering persecution without resistance, in imitation of the attitude of first-century Christians toward the Roman government.[5] However, his assessment of Anabaptist *Schwärmer* was apparently confirmed in 1534 when a small Dutch group of fanatic Anabaptists succeeded in persuading the authorities in Münster, Westphalia, to transform the town into what they considered to be the political realization of the kingdom of God on earth. They abolished Sunday worship in favor of "love feasts"; they instituted polygamy, in accordance with Old Testament practice; and they executed in the marketplace all citizens who resisted them.[6] Popular accounts of the Münster events linked them to Thomas Müntzer, who had been executed in 1525 for teaching similar ideas. Most people, therefore, approved of the military action in 1535 against the Münster Anabaptists, undertaken jointly by the Catholic Bishop Francis of Walde and the Lutheran Landgrave Philip of Hesse. The Anabaptists were massacred and their leaders were caged on the church tower and left to rot. When the Wittenberg theologians were asked by several German authorities to draft a theological justification for punishing Anabaptists, they wrote an "opinion" in 1536 in which they advocated the death penalty. Luther signed that statement, but in an appended sentence admonished the authorities to show mercy, particularly to heretics who were not seditious.[7]

Luther had no use for Anabaptists, but he was willing to support Melanchthon's efforts to achieve unity with the Swiss and German Zwinglians who had become estranged because of disagreements on the Lord's Supper. These efforts were due to Rome's announcement in 1533 that a general council would be convened at Mantua in 1537 to deal with the schismatic reform movements. Luther himself met briefly on 7 November 1535 with a papal emissary, Vergerio, and insisted that his cause be reviewed by a "free, general, not a papal council."[8] Thus, when the Strassburg reformer Martin Bucer urged a meeting with the Wittenberg reformers to

work towards a compromise between Luther and Zwingli, Luther invited
Bucer and other moderate Zwinglians to Wittenberg to discuss the Lord's
Supper and additional issues. Luther was impressed by Bucer's polemics
against the Anabaptists as well as by his rejection of Zwingli's radical notion
that the Lord's Supper is only a "memorial" of Christ's death rather than a
celebration of Christ's "bodily" or "real" presence. It was therefore no
surprise that a meeting of the Bucer delegation with Luther and his
Wittenberg friends in May 1536 succeeded in removing the principal
theological obstacles to unity which had plagued the Marburg colloquy of
1529. The "Wittenberg Concord" claimed that the breach had been healed
between Wittenberg and the southwestern territories. Concerning the
Lord's Supper, Bucer and his delegation agreed

> that with the bread and wine the body and blood of Christ are truly and
> essentially present, distributed, and received . . . and that it [the validity of the
> sacrament] does not depend on the worthiness or unworthiness of the minister
> who distributes the sacrament or of him who receives it.[9]

Since this agreement echoed Luther's as well as the Augsburg Confession's
stance, there was great exultation in Wittenberg. The Bucerians attended a
festive worship service with Holy Communion, sealing the theological
concord between Wittenberg and Zurich. A united Protestant German front
against Rome seemed assured, and its exclusion of radical Zwinglians and
Anabaptists demonstrated that the Protestant reform movement remained in
the "catholic" tradition by affirming infant baptism and the doctrine of
Christ's bodily presence in the Eucharist.

But the "Wittenberg Concord" did not last long. Zwinglians in Zurich and
elsewhere refused to abide by the Wittenberg agreement; by the early 1540s
the eucharistic controversy flared up again. Luther charged that the
Zwinglians and others rejected Christ's bodily presence in the Lord's Supper
and were therefore "slanderers of the sacrament."[10]

Though increasingly plagued by illness, particularly by nasty kidney-stone
attacks and spells of dizziness, Luther nevertheless adhered to a busy
schedule of writing, teaching, preaching, and receiving visitors, and still
found time to spend with his family and friends. He summarized much of his
basic theological thought in a series of public disputations at the University of
Wittenberg during the last two decades of his life. The new statutes of the
university, drafted by Melanchthon in 1533, instituted festive public debates
in connection with the awarding of doctoral degrees. The Saxon court
encouraged and supported these public academic events, and in 1536
Elector John Frederick provided a generous endowment to be used for four
academic disputations each academic year. A committee of twelve professors
representing the various faculties asked Luther to arrange such disputations
whenever he could to sharpen intellectual skills in the conduct of theological
controversies.[11]

In September 1535, Luther prepared, arranged, and supervised the first of several doctoral disputations on the central theme of his theology: justification by faith through grace without the works of law (Rom. 3:28). The disputation dealt with "theses concerning faith and law." He procured scholarship money for the two doctoral candidates who would debate— Hieronymous Weller, a frequent houseguest and friend, and Nikolaus Medler, a recorder of Luther's table talks. He hosted a dinner at which he served game provided by Elector John Frederick at his request. He invited well-known reformers, and many of them, including an English delegation led by Robert Barnes, one of Luther's supporters at Cambridge, attended this premiere of the Wittenberg disputations. Luther also drafted the theses, as was the custom, and he even wrote candidate Weller's oration.

Seventy-one theses described "true faith" and eighty-seven theses defined "works of the law." The audience was urged to make proper distinctions between faith and law. Faith is the gift of the Holy Spirit, which enables believers to have a relationship with the God who, in the person of Jesus, wooed his creatures to love him again. True faith, therefore, is complete trust; indeed, it is abandonment to Jesus, the son of God "who loved me and gave himself for me" (Gal. 2:20). "Accordingly, that 'for me' or 'for us,' if it is believed, creates that true faith and distinguishes it from all other faith, which merely hears the things done."[12] Hearing without trusting is "acquired faith" which "stands like a lazy man concealing his hand under his armpit and says, 'That is nothing to me.' "[13]

The basic function of the law, on the other hand, is to reveal sin rather than to earn salvation. Since everyone is a sinner, incapable of fulfilling God's law, no one can be saved by the law. Only Christ fulfilled the law, because he was without sin. "Through the obedience of this one man many are made righteous, Romans 5 [:12–19]."[14] The foundation of Christian life is forgiveness rather than merit. Those who think that they can earn the favor of God by good works are only victims of a satanic illusion.

Luther continued to deal with the theme of justification in another public disputation "On Man" (de homine) in January 1536. Whether he debated personally or had one of his students defend the theses is not known.[15] The theses argued for a proper distinction between a "philosophical" anthropology grounded in the confidence of the intellect to define human persons through introspection and a "theological" anthropology which views persons as creatures in need of being reconciled with God. To be truly human means to be "justified by faith," that is, to be related to God in the complete trust that Jesus Christ is the only source of this relationship. Only those who are hooked to the story of Jesus, as it were, understand what it means to be truly human. It means to be pursued by God's love intending to restore the harmony between Creator and creature which was destroyed by the fall of Adam. This divine love shapes Christian life on earth. "Therefore, man in

this life is the simple material of God for the form of his future life."[16] A truly
Christian anthropology must make the proper distinction between God's
grace and love, and human sin and pride. The point was reiterated that true
humanity is based on forgiveness rather than merit; and forgiveness is the
gift of constant renewal. Man's destiny is with God, who will transform and
perfect the human creature so that sin, death, and evil will be no more.
Meanwhile, however, life in this old world is a struggle between the purity of
divine love and the pollution of human sin.[17] Thus Luther rejected much of
medieval Christian anthropology because it shares the classical Greek-
Roman assumption that human reason has the power to reach and indeed
even comprehend God as the "final cause of everything." "Philosophers and
Aristotle are not able to understand or to define what the theological man is,
but by the grace of God we are able to do it, because we have the Bible."[18]
Luther made it quite clear that he did not intend to downgrade human
reason, but rather to assign it its proper place. He contended that philosophy
as well as Holy Scripture praise reason as the power to organize and maintain
life in the world, even after the fall of Adam. But reason has no redemptive
power. That is why "he [man] can be freed and given eternal life only through
the Son of God, Jesus Christ (if he believes in him)."[19]

Luther summarized his views in a third round of disputations on
justification in October 1536.[20] "As you have often heard, most excellent
brothers," he declared in the preface,

> because that one article concerning justification even by itself creates true
> theologians, therefore it is indispensable in the church and just as we must often
> recall it, so we must frequently work on it.[21]

To "work on it" means, according to Luther, that the doctrine of justification
must not be understood as one doctrine among other doctrines. Rather, this
Pauline doctrine must be the norm of theological discourse itself. One cannot
speak of God unless one speaks of him as the one who made the unrighteous
righteous through Christ. There is, then, a radical difference between divine
and human righteousness: God accounts complete faith in Christ as
righteousness, whereas human beings view righteousness as a reward for
good works. Justification of the ungodly, therefore, "is a mystery of God, who
exalts his saints, because it is not only impossible to comprehend for the
godless, but marvelous and hard to believe even for the pious themselves."[22]
In argument after argument, Luther defended the basic thesis that the life of
a Christian is linked to the lifeline of mercy which God established in Christ.
Thus the Christian truly lives by faith alone rather than by the merit of good
works aimed at pacifying God. Again, Luther wanted to make it quite clear
that he did not reject good works. Rather, there must be a proper distinction
between faith and works. Works do not justify the sinner, they only reveal
faith active in love towards the neighbor in need.

I say, therefore, that works justify, that is, they show that we have been justified, just as his fruits show that a man is a Christian and believes in Christ, since he does not have a feigned faith and life before men. For the works indicate whether I have faith. I conclude, therefore, that he is righteous when I see that he does good works. In God's eyes that distinction is not necessary, for he is not deceived by hypocrisy. But it is necessary among men, so that they may correctly understand where faith is and where it is not.[23]

When this distinction is clearly understood, "faith" stands for the relationship which God, through Christ, established between himself and his creatures. Luther called the awareness of this relationship "inward righteousness," that is, the knowledge that in Christ my sins are forgiven in the sight of God. From "inward righteousness" proceeds an "outward righteousness," that is, love for my fellow-creatures, especially those in need.

This [outward] righteousness follows, the former precedes, since the order is a priori, that is, from the efficient cause of justification. I am really bound to view the works of man from the effective cause, so that he may show by his works that he has faith. . . . For Christ proclaimed both kinds of righteousness, those who are righteous secretly before God in spirit and those who are righteous openly before men. . . . Before God, faith is necessary, not works. Before men works and love are necessary, which reveal us to be righteous in our own eyes and before the world.[24]

Luther planned to write an extensive treatise on justification but never had the time to do so.[25] Nevertheless, the article of justification did become the centerpiece of his public theological testament, the Smalcald Articles. In a letter dated 11 December 1536, Elector John Frederick asked Luther to draw up a list of articles summarizing his theological position and indicating where Lutherans were willing to make compromises with Rome, and where they would stand pat.[26] Quite ill at the time with heart and kidney disorders, Luther nevertheless went to work and finished the Smalcald Articles in January 1537. "I have decided to publish these articles," he wrote in the preface,

so that, if I should die before a council meets (which I fully expect, for those knaves who shun the light and flee from the day take such wretched pains to postpone and prevent the council), those who live after me may have my testimony and confession . . . to show where I have stood until now and where, by God's grace, I will continue to stand.[27]

In the first section, Luther affirmed the doctrine of the Trinity, which neither Lutherans nor Catholics disputed. The second section treated "the articles which pertain to the office and work of Jesus Christ," centering in the article of justification, and was entitled "Christ and Faith." This "chief article" declared that Christ "was put to death for our trespasses and raised again for our justification (Rom. 4:25)." Only such faith in Christ justifies.

> Nothing in this article can be given up or compromised, even if heaven and earth and things temporal should be destroyed. . . . On this article rests all that we teach and practice against the pope, the devil, and the world. Therefore we must be quite certain and have no doubts about it. Otherwise all is lost, and the pope, the devil, and all our adversaries will gain the victory.[28]

This affirmation of Christ's absolute lordship as the source of human redemption before God was for Luther the article on which the church stands or falls.[29] Its essential thrust was both doxological and polemical: it was to lead to joyful and grateful worship of God who poured out his love for humankind in Christ; and it was to serve as the battle cry against the idolatrous hierarchical structure of the Roman Church, especially against the Mass, the great symbol of institutional self-righteousness. The medieval practice of priests celebrating Mass for themselves, without offering God's promise of salvation in Christ to others, embodied for Luther "the greatest and most horrible abomination because it runs into direct and violent conflict with this fundamental article."[30]

The third section dealt with "matters which we may discuss with learned and sensible men, or even among ourselves": sin, law, repentance, gospel communication, baptism, the Lord's Supper, ecclesiastical authority ("the power of the keys"), confession, excommunication, ordination and vocation, clerical marriage, the church, good works, monastic vows, and human traditions.[31] Luther's polemical tone, however, cast a dark shadow over the possibility of fruitful dialogue on these matters. He saw the church too plagued with "the pope's bag of magic tricks" to facilitate any rapprochement with Rome.[32]

Luther undertook the three-week-long journey from Wittenberg to Smalcald, despite severe pain from kidney- and gallstone attacks, because he wanted to make sure that nothing would be compromised through diplomacy. But, since he remained bedridden with illness during his stay of almost three weeks, Melanchthon had to replace him at the negotiations after all.[33] He and a number of other theologians and churchmen joined Luther in signing the Smalcald Articles; but he added the written reservation that a papacy may exist "by human right" for the sake of peace and unity, and explained his position in a "Treatise on the Power and Primacy of the Pope" which was signed by the Smalcald delegates.[34] Luther was either too ill to sign that document or refused to do so. The Smalcald Articles were not endorsed by the League but did become part of the collection of Lutheran confessions contained in the *Book of Concord* in 1580, fifty years after the writing of the Augsburg Confession.

In anticipation of the impending ecumenical council, which would deal

with the reform movement, Luther in 1539 published a massive treatise
entitled "On the Councils and the Church."[35] After reminding his readers
that Rome did not really want a reform council, he presented a threefold
critique of papal and conciliar authority. First, he argued that papal decrees
and councils had served institutional self-interests rather than advanced the
cause of the gospel. Then he discussed the historical significance of the first
four ecumenical councils dealing with the formation of the trinitarian dogma:
Nicaea (325), Constantinople (381), Ephesus (431), and Chalcedon (451).
Finally, he presented a view of the church which, based upon the biblical
witness, should be known in the world by seven characteristics: the Word of
God, baptism, the Lord's Supper, the power of penance and forgiveness, the
office of the ministry, worship, and suffering. The whole treatise discloses
Luther's skill in historical research and theological argumentation. Luther
concluded that ecumenical councils should have a limited role in the life of
the church.

> A council, then, is nothing but a consistory, a royal court, a supreme court, or
> the like, in which the judges, after hearing the parties, pronounce sentence. . . .
> Thus a council condemns a heretic, not according to its own discretion, but
> according to the law of the empire, that is, according to Holy Scripture. . . . This
> law is God's word, the empire is God's church; the judge is the official or servant
> of both.[36]

Luther's model was the council of apostles in Jerusalem (Acts 15) where Paul
persuaded the other apostles to approve his mission to the Gentiles and to
excuse Gentiles from having to observe Jewish law before becoming
Christians.

Frequently talking about his own end as well as that of the world, the
aging Luther still seemed intent on steering a middle course between
extreme Catholic and Protestant positions. He rejected both the notion of a
divinely instituted papacy and the denial of sacraments as means of grace.
But by 1539 it had become doubtful whether Luther could truthfully claim
what Melanchthon had stated in the Augsburg Confession, that he had
"introduced nothing, either in doctrine or in ceremonies, that is contrary to
Holy Scripture or the universal Christian church."[37] Some leaders in the
Lutheran reform movement, for example, had difficulties with the way
Luther tried to balance the relationship between the principle of justification
by faith and the authority of Christian tradition. One particular issue, the
relationship between faith and moral discipline, had surfaced as early as the
1520s, when Luther had presented the basic features of his theology and
reform program. If one is justified by faith *alone*, as Luther insisted, does
one still need moral exhortations? Would not one do voluntarily, indeed
naturally, whatever moral law requires? Would not one love one's neighbor,
work for justice in the world, endure suffering, and pursue all the other

virtues associated with the name "Christian"? Had not Luther himself said, when he talked about Christian freedom, "A Christian has no need of any work or law in order to be saved, since through faith he is free from every law and does everything out of pure liberty and freely"?[38]

In 1539 the question of whether or not "justified" Christians needed the preaching of the law as well as the preaching of the gospel became the issue in a hot debate. John Agricola, one of Luther's friends and colleagues, who headed the Latin school in Eisleben, argued—first against local Catholics, and then against both Luther and Melanchthon—in theses prepared for disputation that there is no need at all for the preaching of the law. He asserted that once one was converted by the gospel, penance and moral discipline were the natural fruits of faith. Neither the Decalogue nor any other biblical law plays a role in Christian life since the gospel is the only source of moral behavior.

Luther followed his usual pattern of responding when attacked. First he preached sermons, reminding his congregation that justification is never completed in this life, and thus the need for exhortation to move from faith to good works remains. Then he conducted three "antinomian disputations." Unfortunately, the controversy flared up just at the time Agricola was being proposed as a candidate for the position of dean of the liberal arts faculty at Wittenberg University. Perhaps that is why Agricola decided not to attend the first disputation and, when he appeared at the second one, told Luther that he was not completely opposed to the preaching of the law. When he failed to appear for the third disputation, Luther angrily requested a public recantation. Embarrassed by the whole affair, Agricola agreed to recant and asked Luther to draft a document to that end. To Agricola's surprise, Luther published the recantation as part of an open letter to Caspar Güttel, a friend of his in Eisleben and one of Agricola's most ardent opponents.

Entitled "Against the Antinomians," the letter reveals Luther's biting satire and harsh polemics:

> Master John Eisleben [Agricola] wishes to withdraw what he taught or wrote against the law or the Ten Commandments and to stand with us here in Wittenberg, as the [Augsburg] *Confession* and the *Apology* did before the Emperor at Augsburg; and if he should later depart from this or teach otherwise it [what he taught and wrote on the law] will be worthless and will stand condemned. I would like to praise him for humbling himself in this way.[39]

Luther then proceeded to state his own position on the matter of law and gospel. He declared that both are necessary because Christians have to live in the conflict between sin and grace as long as they are pilgrims in the world. "How can one know what sin is without the law and conscience?" he asked,

> and how will we learn what Christ is, what he did for us, if we do not know what

the law is that he fulfilled for us and what sin is for which he has made satisfaction? . . . Therefore the law must be preached wherever Christ is to be preached, even if the word "law" is not mentioned, so that the conscience is nevertheless frightened by the law when it hears that Christ had to fulfill the law for us at so great a price.[40]

Luther's public humiliation of Agricola embarrassed some of his friends, who rallied around Agricola and requested he be appointed dean at the university. But Luther's will prevailed; Agricola was not appointed. When Agricola appealed to the rector of the university and to Elector John Frederick asking for an impartial investigation, Luther countered with another open letter, "Against the Eislebener," in the spring of 1540.[41] He angrily depicted Agricola as a potential destroyer of all ethical order, the ultimate result of antinomianism. In the summer of 1540, when the elector ordered Agricola confined to Wittenberg until a hearing could settle the controversy, Agricola fled—frightened by Luther's vindictiveness—and went to Berlin, where he became the court preacher to Elector Joachim II of Brandenburg. Melanchthon later persuaded him to become reconciled with Luther and the Saxon court, but he never really recovered from that confrontation. He did recant once more, and he withdrew all complaints against Wittenberg, but he stayed away from Luther. And Luther never really did defeat the antimonians; the controversy was to flare up again after his death.[42]

FRUSTRATING POLEMICS

Luther still enjoyed a good fight, but he felt increasingly tired and mortally ill. Kidney- and gallstones, stomach disorders, increasing deafness, shortness of breath, and severe headaches frequently left him exhausted. "I have worked with all my might," he commented at table on 2 April 1539.

> For one person I've done enough. All that's left is to sink into my grave. I am done for, except for tweaking the pope's nose a little now and then.[43]

Nevertheless, Luther carried on in an odd mixture of happy home life and frustration about seemingly useless battles with both the defenders of the old and the radicals of the new religion. Since Pope Paul III constantly postponed the convening of the announced general council, Emperor Charles V hoped to settle the religious schism by quiet negotiations. A Catholic delegation of theologians, led by Luther's old enemy John Eck, and a Protestant team under the leadership of Melanchthon held several meetings in 1540 and 1541 and reached some doctrinal agreements at Regensburg. But Rome refused to endorse these results, and Luther rejected their widely publicized consensus on the doctrine of justification as an attempt to "glue together" (zusammenleimen) what really needed to be kept apart, unless Rome were willing to recant its treason against the gospel.[44] Wittenberg and Rome remained at odds.

An incident unfortunate for the Protestants allowed Charles V to gain the upper hand in his political struggle with the Protestant princes led by the head of the Smalcald League, Philip of Hesse. The unhappily married Philip had entered a bigamous marriage with a young lady at his court, Margaret von der Saale, after intensive negotiations with lawyers and theologians, including Luther. Canon law permitted bigamy under certain circumstances linked to an intricate network of moral and legal casuistry. Luther himself favored bigamy over divorce, as he had told the English theologian Robert Barnes in 1531 when asked for advice in the matter of King Henry VIII's divorce. "Before I would approve of such a divorce," he had told Barnes, "I would rather permit the King to marry still another woman and to have, according to the examples of the patriarchs and kings [of Israel], two women or queens at the same time."[45] Thus when Philip of Hesse asked for advice on the matter, Luther and Melanchthon advised him in a special memorandum that bigamy was acceptable to God as a "Turkish marriage" (since Turks allowed marriage to more than one woman); but Philip was also advised to keep the second marriage a secret since Luther and Melanchthon viewed the advice to contract a bigamous marriage as being under the seal of confession. However, when Philip's shrewd new mother-in-law asked for all the details of his negotiations, he gave her a copy of the Wittenberg memorandum, thus violating his oath of secrecy; of course the story spread. Informed of Philip's violation of the seal of confession, Luther felt betrayed, especially since he then discovered that Philip had concealed from him the existence of a concubine and of venereal disease. He admitted that, "Had I known that, indeed no angel should have persuaded me to give such advice."[46]

Since Philip's sister and second mother-in-law had made the bigamous marriage known, Philip wanted Luther to agree to authorize the legality of the second marriage. At this point Luther used his medieval training in casuistry and advised the prince to deny the existence of the second marriage. His rationale for such advice was the rule of medieval moral casuistry that a father confessor should advise a "lie of expediency" (*Nutzlüge*) rather than divulge the content of a private confession. But Philip refused to lie about the affair.

His behavior caused an uproar in Germany, particularly among the members of the Smalcald League. Since bigamy was a civil crime punishable by territorial and imperial laws, Philip was forced to bargain with Emperor Charles V in the summer of 1540. The emperor agreed to be gracious in return for Philip's promise not to increase the power of the Smalcald League through alliances with friendly territories. With its most powerful leader neutralized, the Smalcald League was doomed to be defeated in the

Smalcald War of 1546 and 1547. Philip, who nevertheless fought in the war, was captured and became the emperor's prisoner for five years (1547–52), and the Protestant territories were forced to negotiate the Peace of Augsburg in 1555.[47]

Luther vented his frustration about all politicians in a violently polemical treatise against one of the worst enemies of the Lutherans, Duke Henry of Braunschweig/Wolfenbüttel, who had called Elector John Frederick Luther's "Hanswurst"—a German carnival figure of a fool, who carries a leather sausage around his neck and wears a clown costume. Luther entitled the treatise "Against Hanswurst" and displayed his masterful use of medieval abusive language and wit to expound the distinctions he made between the true church of the gospel and the false church of Rome.[48] He addressed the duke as "Hanswurst Harry," then accused the Roman Church of being the "devil's whore" who prostitutes the gospel in the world. He called Duke Henry, Albrecht of Mainz, and the pope the evil pillars of this false church, persecuting those who try to be faithful to Christ—Elector Frederick and Luther himself. Luther then solemnly exhorted:

> I first ask all pious Christians and honorable hearts who read or hear this to remember most earnestly that the Lord God (as is right) has, through so many legal examinations and judgments, condemned this Harry as a murderer, bloodhound, and arch-assassin to the fires of hell, since he cannot be overcome by fire here. And I ask that every man do God this service: glorify and praise his divine judgment wherever he can, both in public and in private; spit on the ground, to the glory of God, wherever he sees Harry; and hold his ears closed whenever he hears him named, just as he would do against the devil himself.[49]

Duke Henry did not fare well in his controversy with Luther: bad political moves, scandalous affairs with women, and tyrannical behavior ruined his reputation as a defender of orthodox religion. In 1542 he fled to France; after Luther's death, he returned, somewhat chastened, to his territory.

Luther was convinced that there was an intimate relationship between the turmoils within his reform movement and the end of the world. "I think the last day is not far off," he commented at table.

> My reason is that a last great effort is now being made to advance the gospel. It's like a candle. Just before it burns out it makes a last great spurt, as if it would continue to burn for a long time, and then it goes out. . . . That's how it is with a sick person too. When he's about to die he generally seems to be very alert, as if he might recover, and then in a jiffy he's gone.[50]

In January 1542, Luther drafted a will, making minimal legal arrangements for bequeathing his worldly possessions to Katie, whom he made his executrix. He excused his neglect of legal formulations and terminology with the reminder that he was a public figure "known both in heaven and on earth, as well as in hell, having respect or authority enough that one can trust or believe more than any notary."[51]

The Black Cloister was not spared suffering at this time. Katie had been seriously ill in 1540, and on 20 September 1542 thirteen-year-old Magdalena died after a painful illness. Luther grieved long and hard, finally struggling through to the conviction that heaven would be a better place for her than this troubled world. When the Wittenbergers tried to comfort him during the funeral, he replied, "Flesh is flesh, and blood is blood. I'm happy that she's safely out of it. There is no sorrow except that of the flesh."[52] Magdalena's death, the political events in Germany, and the burdens of his own illness made Luther aware of how close he himself was to death. "For myself I desire a good hour of passing on to God. I am content, I am tired, and nothing more is in me," he told a friend in a letter dated 20 June 1543.[53]

And yet when he heard rumors of Jews trying to convert some Christians, he vented his frustration against the Jews in the most controversial treatise of his later years—"On the Jews and Their Lies" (1543).[54] He accused Jews of using Holy Scripture to pervert Christianity and attempted to refute existing Hebrew Bible studies which denied that Jesus was the Messiah. The refutation is not the kind of biblical work one expects from Luther. Crude polemics, allegorical methods, and a kind of self-righteousness permeate his exegesis. Quite aware of the fact that neither refutation nor conversion were any longer options in Christian-Jewish relations, Luther succumbed to the temptation of urging a kind of final, Christian solution of the Jewish problem:[55] synagogues and schools should be burned; Jews should not be allowed to keep their books or to teach their doctrines; they should not be given safe conduct on highways; they should not be permitted to have money, since they practice usury; and they should be made to work on farms under guard by Christians. He declared that both church and state have an obligation to keep Jews in check.

> Burn down their synagogues . . . force them to work, and deal harshly with them, as Moses did in the wilderness, slaying three thousand lest the whole people perish. . . . If God were to give me no other Messiah than such as the Jews wish and hope for, I would much, much rather be a sow than a human being.[56]

Although these words may have been penned by a Luther plagued with the excruciating pain of a kidney-stone attack, they are nevertheless an unforgivably harsh judgment for a scholar who had shown so much love for the people of Israel in his work as an Old Testament expert.

Jews, Turks, the pope, *Schwärmer*, pestilence, disease, and an increasing deterioration of moral life in Wittenberg, especially among students—all of these *Anfechtungen* were indeed potent clues in Luther's mind that the world was approaching the end. "I am fed up with the world," he told Katie during the winter of 1542/43, and it is fed up with me. I'm quite content with that. . . . I am like a ripe stool, and the world's like a gigantic anus, and so we're about to let go of each other. I thank thee, dear God, that thou dost allow me to stay in thy little flock that suffers persecution for the sake of thy Word.[57]

But in the summer of 1544 Luther engaged in one more battle against his old enemies, the "sacramentarians" and the pope. He published a "Brief Confession Concerning the Holy Sacrament," once again refuting the view, this time of Caspar Schwenckfeld, a Silesian theologian, that only the divine nature of Christ was present in the Lord's Supper.[58] "Since my death is imminent," he wrote in the preface,

I want to take this testimony and this honor along with me . . . that I have earnestly condemned and rejected the fanatics and enemies of the sacrament—Carlstadt, Zwingli, Oecolampadius, Stenckefeld, and their disciples at Zurich and wherever they are.[59]

Recalling his long struggle with the "sacramentarians," he appealed to his readers to hold fast to the doctrine of Christ's bodily presence in the Lord's Supper as testimony to the incarnate God who was bodily present in Jesus of Nazareth in accordance with the ancient trinitarian and christological creeds.

When Luther received the news that Pope Paul III had finally announced that the long overdue general council would be convened in March 1545 in Trent, Italy—it convened in December—he decided to deliver a final blast against the papacy's political ambitions. The result was the treatise "Against the Roman Papacy, an Institution of the Devil."[60] It raised one more time the old questions debated at Leipzig and elsewhere: whether there should be a pope lording it over Scripture and tradition; whether a pope can be judged or even deposed; and whether the pope has the right and power to crown kings and emperors.

By now, Luther had nothing good to say about the "Most Hellish Father," the pope. Employing abusive and violent language, Luther denied that Christ gave Peter the keys to the kingdom to be handed on to successors in Rome (Matt. 16:18). Fury, wit, and a preoccupation with Satan dominate this treatise.

If I should die meanwhile, may God grant that someone else make it a thousand times worse, for this devilish popery is the last misfortune on earth, nearest to that which all the devils can do with all their might. God help us.[61]

Luther now felt that his work was finished. Others could carry on. They could always make use of his collected writings, which had been published in both a Latin and a German edition.[62] Moreover, Wittenberg had become like a prison to Luther. People had changed over the years. The spirit of the Italian Renaissance in fashions and morals had invaded even this far corner of the empire. There were new dances, with women baring more and more of their body; there was more and more drinking and carousing on the part of students and townspeople; and Luther's own household had been invaded by a loose woman who had concealed the fact that she was pregnant with an illegitimate child and fooled him into hiring her as chief maid. She stole from him and cheated him, so Luther fired her. But he saw in her a reflection of what the world was coming to, and he felt that he had to get away from all this devilish confusion.

Therefore, in the company of his friend Caspar Cruciger, his eldest son Hans, who had just turned nineteen, and another young student-boarder from the Black Cloister, he journeyed by coach to nearby Zeitz and Merseburg to attend an ordination and a wedding. Elector John Frederick also wished Luther to visit him at his vacation home in Torgau. Despite the enthusiasm which his preaching aroused and the good food and wine he was served, Luther remained depressed. He wrote to Katie on 28 July 1545 to tell her he would not return to Wittenberg, "this Sodom"; he advised her to sell everything so that they could move to their little country estate in Zölsdorf, south of Leipzig, which they had bought in 1540 from Katie's brother John.[63]

Both town and gown reacted to the news with shock and dismay. Elector John Frederick commissioned Matthias Ratzeberger, his personal physician who also treated Luther, to persuade Luther to return, and added his personal wishes in writing.[64] Luther did return on 18 August 1545, but at the beginning of October he left again for three weeks, accompanied by the worried Melanchthon, to help settle a feud in Mansfeld between the two Mansfeld dukes, Philip and John George. On 17 November 1545, Luther finally finished his gigantic lecture series on Genesis, a work he had begun in March 1535.[65]

THE FINAL *ANFECHTUNG*

In March 1545, immediately following Luther's final attack on the papacy, Landgrave Philip of Hesse sent him an Italian pamphlet, along with a German translation, entitled "An Italian Lie Concerning Dr. Martin Luther's Death."[66] An anonymous author had recorded "a terrible and unheard of miraculous sign which the blessed God has shown in the shameful death of Martin Luther."[67] The "sign" depicted Luther's request to have his body placed upon an altar and worshiped after his death. The request, however, could not be granted, argued the author, because Christ himself intervened, handing Luther's body over to the devil in an awful and noisy ceremony. Only "a sulfurous smell" remained near the empty tomb where Luther had been laid.

Luther had the pamphlet published with a brief comment that he had enjoyed reading the lie about his death. He expressed his hope that pope and papists might still be turned away from the devil, but left the matter in God's hands.

> If, however, it has been decided that my prayer for their sin unto death is in vain, well then, God grant that they fill their cup to the brim and write nothing but such pamphlets for their consolation and joy. Let them go to hell, they have deserved it! They wanted it that way! Meanwhile, I want to observe how they intend to be saved or how they can make amends for and recant all their lies and blasphemies, with which they fill the world.[68]

Luther anticipated his own death with a clear head and with the certainty that he had been faithful to the Word of God. His last days have been meticulously recorded by the friends who accompanied him on his final journey of eighty miles to his birthplace, Eisleben, 3 January to 18 February 1546.[69] Luther had been asked to help settle a family feud between the two counts of Mansfeld over the proper division of rights, privileges, and responsibilities in their domain. Luther had been unsuccessful in his previous attempts to negotiate a settlement, both in October and during the Christmas holidays of 1545.

The sixty-two-year-old professor was not feeling well, but he was determined to do his duty as a friend of the families involved in the feud; he was accompanied by his three sons (Hans, nineteen; Martin, fourteen; and Paul, thirteen), his secretary John Aurifaber, and Justus Jonas. The journey was difficult: a bitter winter cold plagued both men and horses; the Saale river flooded, delaying Luther for three days in Halle; and Luther suffered a severe attack of dizziness during the official welcoming ceremony at the border of the Mansfeld territory on 29 January 1546.

Luther wrote to Katie and to Melanchthon whenever he could, keeping them informed about his health and his activities. His three sons spent their time on a farm in nearby Mansfeld, and he himself enjoyed the comforts of the town clerk's house in Eisleben, where the negotiations took place. He loved the good company of friends and local dignitaries. He preached several times at the church and, for one or two hours every day, he led the delicate negotiations with lawyers. But he was becoming increasingly weak and frail, often unable to walk because of an open sore on his leg, and virtually blind in one eye. A physician tended him as best he could, but an angina attack increased the pain he was already suffering from stomach disorder, stones, insomnia, and headaches.

On 14 February 1546, the feud between the Mansfeld counts was settled amicably. Luther wrote to his wife on that day that he would be home soon, "God willing," and he sent her a trout given to him by the Countess Anna, Count Albrecht's wife. "We are well cared for," he added, "even too well, so that we might easily forget about you people in Wittenberg."[70]

On 15 February Luther preached his last sermon, on the meaning of bearing the yoke for Christ's sake (Matt. 11:25–30). Telling the large crowd of people that God does not want "wiseacres" but simple, faithful Christians, Luther again warned them against papal sophists and Protestant sacramentarians who avoid both the joys of faith and the cruciform life. However, physical weakness prevented him from finishing the sermon.[71]

During the evening of 17 February, Luther complained of severe chest pains and went to his temporary study on the second floor of the town clerk's house. The pain did not ease. Luther's sons, Count Albrecht, his friends and others crowded in. The physician covered him with warm blankets and, when all the other remedies he tried brought no relief, he agreed to give Luther a dose of "unicorn horn," a last medical resort. "Unicorn horn" consisted of pulverized scrapings from the horn of a narwhale, an arctic whale with a protruding nose resembling a unicorn's horn.[72] It was the closest medieval doctors could come to the healing powers attributed to the legendary unicorn. Luther drank it with wine. He was given massages, his limbs were rubbed with water and other liquids, and he was wrapped in warm blankets. He tried to keep awake, but he dozed off frequently. Sometime after midnight, when he had been quiet for a while, Justus Jonas called to him, "Reverend Father, do you wish to die standing up for Christ and for the teaching you have preached?" Luther answered clearly, "Yes." Then he turned onto his right side and seemingly fell asleep. During the early hours of 18 February, the physician approached his bed and discovered that Luther had died, apparently of a heart attack. Friends later found a slip of paper on Luther's desk, dated 16 February, on which were the last words to flow from his industrious pen:

> Nobody can understand Vergil in his *Bucolics* and *Georgics* unless he has first been a shepherd or a farmer for five years. Nobody understands Cicero in his letters unless he has been engaged in public affairs of some consequence for twenty years. Let nobody suppose that he has tasted the Holy Scriptures sufficiently unless he has ruled over the churches with the prophets for a hundred years. Therefore there is something wonderful, first, about John the Baptist; second, about Christ; third, about the apostles. "Lay not your hand on this divine Aeneid, but bow before it, adore its every trace." *We are beggars. That is true.*[73]

These words, written by the sick and very tired sixty-two-year-old priest-professor, disclose the basic lesson he had learned during the long years of attempting to fathom the depth of wisdom flowing from the Bible and from the classic authors of the Greek-Roman world: a life spent struggling for the proper understanding of their wisdom is, at best, the life of a beggar. But beggars are known to be persistent, proud, humble, frustrated, impatient, and at times even filled with the wish to die. Luther was all these, especially during the final years of his career as reformer of the church catholic.

With Luther's body in a pewter coffin, a memorial service was held at Eisleben's St. Andrew's Church on the afternoon of 19 February 1546. Justus Jonas delivered a stirring oration to a large crowd, calling on Germany to repent. While Eisleben waited for official instructions from the Saxon court concerning Luther's interment in Wittenberg, a second memorial service was held on 20 February, with Luther's coffin guarded by citizens in the choir of St. Andrew's Church. The local pastor, Coelius, also called for repentance at such a time when God took a great man from the world.

Luther's body was then transported to Wittenberg with an honor guard and was accompanied by large crowds along the whole route. On 22 February it arrived in Wittenberg; there was a long funeral procession, with Katie and her three sons in a carriage behind the coffin, from the Elster Gate to the Castle Church, where Luther was interred directly in front of the pulpit. Bugenhagen and Melanchthon were the eulogists at the service. They declared Luther a national German hero and compared him to Moses, saying that Luther had reluctantly led his people from the wilderness to the holy land. A stone tablet marks his final resting place.[74]

What did Luther look like? Although there are various portraits of him, from etchings by Lucas Cranach to various impressions of him on coins, two verbal portraits convey as much as any of the paintings.[75] The first comes from the Leipzig professor Peter Mosellanus, who saw and described the thirty-five-year-old Luther at the Leipzig Debate in 1519:

> Martinus is of medium height, haggard, and so emaciated with care and much study that one can almost count all the bones in his body. Nevertheless, he is still in the vigor of manhood. His voice rings clear and distinct. . . . In his manner and social intercourse he is cultivated and affable, not at all gloomy or arrogant, always in good humor, in company agreeable, cheerful, and jocose. No matter how hard his opponent threatens him, he is always confident and joyous.[76]

The second describes Luther during one of his biblical lectures sometime between 1518 and 1523. A young student from Lübeck, George Beneducti, wrote into his personal Bible:

> He was a man of medium height, with a voice that combined sharpness and softness: its tone was soft, but it sounded sharp in the pronunciation of syllables, words, and sentences. He spoke neither too fast nor too slow, but with medium speed, without getting stuck or being unclear. One statement smoothly led to another. He did not produce a labyrinth of words when he interpreted individual passages. At times he interpreted single words, at other times paragraphs, so that one realized that the content of the interpretation originated and flowed from the text. . . . He also used a book with his own notes as a source for what he talked about: conclusions, derivations, moral teachings as well as logical contrasts. Thus he never lectured on anything unless it was to the point.[77]

Before his condemnation as a heretic in 1521, Luther was thin and appeared nervous; after the Diet of Augsburg in 1530, he gained weight and seemed much more relaxed. Friends and contemporaries were impressed by his sparkling dark brown eyes. It is difficult to separate fact and legend in matters of physical details, but it is clear that Luther enjoyed the good life in his later years. He had a personal barber to dress his hair and shave him before any important appearance, be it on the pulpit, the cathedra, or before dignitaries. He liked to wear a coat lined with fox fur; he often wore a gold medallion around his neck, customary for Renaissance men; and he made conscious efforts not to appear as crude as he thought his fellow Germans were. [78]

Luther himself enjoyed the symbol of his reform of the church catholic embodied in the signet ring Elector John Frederick gave him in 1530 at the Coburg Castle. The seal became known as the Luther Rose: a blue ground on which is a white rose within a golden circle; a red, glowing heart in the rose, with a black cross embedded in it. The cross signifies faith which makes the heart glow; the rose signifies peace and joy; the blue ground signifies hope; and the golden ring depicts eternity. All are consequences of the Christ event which, to Luther, was the focus of his life and work. [79]

Luther's direct descendants continued through his fifth child, Paul (1533–93), to Martin Gottlieb Luther, who died in 1759. Martin Gottlieb was the last to bear the name Luther. After 1759, the family tree continued through the descendants of Luther's brother Jacob. [80]

PART 2

NEURALGIC HERITAGE

5

SCRIPTURE AND TRADITION

We do not condemn human teachings just because they are human teachings; for we would gladly put up with them. But we condemn them because they are contrary to the gospel and Scripture. While Scripture liberates consciences and forbids that they be taken captive by human teachings, these human teachings nevertheless trap consciences. This conflict between Scripture and human teachings we cannot reconcile. ("Avoiding Human Teachings." 1522. *WA* 10 / 2:91.21–26. *LW* 35:153. Author's translation)

THE PRIMACY OF THE WORD OF GOD

Luther struck a neuralgic theme when he called for a critical distinction between the authority of the Word of God and the power of the church in his exposure of the "Babylonian captivity" of the church in 1520.

The church has no power to make new divine promises of grace, as some prate, who hold that what is decreed by the church is of no less authority than what is decreed by God, since the church is under the guidance of the Holy Spirit. For the church was born by the word of promise through faith, and by this same word is nourished and preserved. That is to say, it is the promises of God that make the church, and not the church that makes the promise of God. For the Word of God is incomparably superior to the church, and in this Word the church, being a creature, has nothing to decree, ordain, or make, but only to be decreed, ordained, and made. For who begets his own parent? Who first brings forth his own maker? This one thing indeed the church can do: It can distinguish the Word of God from the words of men.[1]

This call for a critical distinction between divine revelation and ecclesiastical communication opened up a Pandora's box of issues related to the Christian perception of authority. If, for example, "authority" means "origin" (from the Latin *auctoritas*), what is the most faithful interpretation and communication of scriptural authority? The church through its teaching offices staffed by pope and bishops? A remnant of the faithful, or even a single individual, when the organized church becomes apostate? How are the trinitarian creeds related to the authority of Scripture and teaching office? The ancient church had perceived authority to be derived from biblical canon, trinitarian creed, and episcopal office, bulwarks against heresy; later, there was a gradual shift towards the authority of the episcopacy, headed by the papacy, as the only authentic interpreter of canon and creed. In his address "To the Christian Nobility of the German Nation" (1520), Luther attacked this shift in the perception of authority and described three "walls" behind which the "Romanists" were barricaded: the concept that the spiritual office of bishops is higher than the temporal office of princes; the conviction that only the papacy has the right to interpret Scripture; and the claim that the pope has authority over church councils.[2] Luther considered these claims to be manifestations of ecclesiastical arrogance, and he delineated the proper relationships between the Word of God and Scripture on the one hand, and the Word of God and tradition on the other.

Luther, of course, dealt with the question of authority as a biblical theologian who was guided by the unshakable conviction he stated succinctly at the Diet of Worms in 1521 that his conscience was "captive to the Word of God."[3] In more than three decades of work as an expositor of Scripture, Luther made it clear that captivity to the Word of God means complete trust in Christ, and that trust in Christ must be properly distinguished from any other trust. He discovered that Paul was his best guide in making the proper distinction between faith in Christ's righteousness and self-righteousness. In struggling with his own anxiety concerning the biblical understanding of righteousness, Luther eventually concluded that the medieval understanding of conscience as an independent inner voice, part of the immortal soul which would function as a barometer of spiritual and moral health, was wrong. He came to consider conscience as the most sensitive point of creaturely existence, addressed and challenged by the external communication of a Word which may be either a threat or a promise.[4]

When Luther turned to the study of Paul's Epistle to the Romans (1515–16), after a thorough exposition of Psalms (1513–15), he became aware of the fact that the Word of God in Scripture is both law and gospel. As the communication of divine law demanding more from sinful humans than they can do, the Word of God threatens judgment and damnation. But as gospel, the communication of the "good news" which promises forgiveness of sin through complete trust in Christ's substitutionary atonement, the Word of God assures eternal fellowship with God. God communicates both law and gospel to his creatures through prophets and apostles, whose witness constitutes the truth of Holy Scripture in both the Old and the New Testaments. Further work on Paul's Epistle to the Galatians (1517, 1531, 1535) and the Epistle to the Hebrews (1517–18) reinforced Luther's view that the proper distinction between law and gospel is the best way to celebrate Christ as the sole mediator of God's grace and as the source of sanctified Christian life. Luther used his own sermons to describe God as a preacher who preached two significant sermons to humankind: a mighty and splendid sermon on the law, beginning with Moses and Israel and culminating in the Decalogue (Exodus 19—20); and a sermon on the gospel culminating with the proclamation of Christ's apostles when they received the Holy Spirit on Pentecost (Acts 2:2–4).

> The law commands and requires us to do certain things. The law is thus directed solely to our behavior and consists in making requirements. For God speaks through the law, saying, "Do this, avoid that, this is what I expect of you." The gospel, however, does not preach what we are to do or to avoid. It sets up no requirements but reverses the approach of the law, does the very opposite, and says "This is what God has done for you; he has let his Son be made flesh for you, has let him be put to death for your sake." So, then, there are two kinds of doctrine and two kinds of works, those of God and those of men. Just as we and God are separated from one another, so also these two doctrines are widely separated from one another.[5]

If one lives by the law, one can rely only on what one can do to fulfill the law. In this sense, the law becomes a human word disclosing the radical distance between God and his human creatures. Luther knew the *Anfechtung* of trying to please God by making radical efforts of piety and self-righteousness. In the end, however, these efforts lead to the awareness that God is merciless in his judgment and anger. To Luther, the God of wrath is the truly hidden God. Since the law only discloses the unbridgeable gulf between God and the human creature, it reveals sin. This is its true function.

> Thus the Law is a prison both politically and theologically. In the first place, it restrains and confines the wicked politically, so that they are not carried headlong by their passions into all sorts of crime. Secondly, it shows us our sin spiritually, terrifying us and humbling us, so that when we have been frightened this way, we acknowledge our misery and our damnation. And this latter is the true and proper use of the Law, even though it is not permanent; for this confining and custody under the Law must not last any longer than until the arrival of faith; and when this [faith] comes, this theological prison of the Law comes to an end.[6]

Whereas the law functions as the "custodian" of sin (Gal. 3:24), the gospel promises liberation from prison through Christ. Instead of demanding human righteousness expressed in good works, the gospel evokes faithful trust (*fiducia*). In its purest form, therefore, the gospel is the gift of faith. It is the marvelous experience of trusting the God who will love me forever once I am wooed into believing that Jesus Christ died so that my sins may be forgiven. This experience of unconditional trust is born in the encounter between myself and the story of Christ which is communicated—live, as it were—through the spoken word, and is the "true (*eigentlich*) function of the

Gospel."[7] Adhering to the earliest Christian tradition, Luther regarded the Old Testament as Scripture, that is, as something written down. But he considered the true gospel a living word which is preached and heard, a "living voice" (*viva vox*).

> The gospel should really not be something written, but a spoken word which brought forth the Scriptures, as Christ and the apostles have done. This is why Christ himself did not write anything but only spoke. He called his teaching not Scripture but gospel, meaning good news or a proclamation that is spread not by pen but by word of mouth.[8]

Luther repeatedly asserted that the good news of salvation means that one receives something which cannot be earned: a "passive righteousness" alien to human "active" self-righteousness. Thus Paul's conviction that man's justification before God comes through faith (Rom. 3:28) became Luther's basic stance in his conflict with Rome. To him the gospel in its purest form is the divine promise that only the righteousness of faith saves, a promise he had also found in the Old Testament when he turned from his study of Psalms to an exposition of the Minor Prophets (1524–26).[9] But Luther's theological taskmaster was Paul's Epistle to the Galatians, the epistle to which he was married, "my Katie von Bora."[10] Nowhere else did Luther find his own *Anfechtungen* and breakthroughs so well reflected than in this epistle. It taught him "that in the terrors of conscience and in the danger of death we look at nothing except our own works, our worthiness, and the Law."[11] Despair drives the sinner to the illusion that salvation is attainable by ever greater efforts to fulfill divine law. "For it is impossible for the human mind to conceive any comfort of itself, or to look only at grace amid its consciousness and terror of sin, or consistently to reject all discussions of works."[12] That is why salvation is a free gift of God. "As the dry earth of itself does not produce rain and is unable to acquire it, that much can we men accomplish by our own strength and works to obtain that divine, heavenly, and eternal righteousness."[13] True preachers and theologians, therefore, must know that law and gospel are the taskmasters of the human conscience in the world.

> The flesh is accused, exercised, saddened, and crushed by the active righteousness of the Law. But the spirit rules, rejoices, and is saved by passive righteousness, because it knows that it has a Lord sitting in heaven at the right hand of the Father, who has abolished the Law, sin, and death, and has trodden all evils underfoot, has led them captive and triumphed over them in Himself (Col. 2:15).[14]

According to Luther, then, theology and churchly proclamation must concentrate on the gospel, on "passive righteousness," that is, on the cheering news that life with God is grounded in the "alien righteousness" of

Christ who, as the only Mediator between God and sinful creatures, is to be completely trusted. This christocentric view of life with God is what Luther wanted to secure through the doctrine of justification by faith alone. "For if the doctrine of justification is lost, the whole of Christian doctrine is lost."[15] Luther simply refused to see any middle ground between God's Word embodied in the distinction between law and gospel and the human word of self-righteousness. One either trusts Christ or one is doomed to fall into trusting one's own good works as the precondition of God's acceptance. Luther admonished future preachers, the "instructors of consciences," to practice finding the distinction between law and gospel through study and prayer, because life's *Anfechtungen* always threaten to confuse this distinction, particularly in the hour of death.

> Give no more to the Law than it has coming, and say to it: "Law, you want to ascend into the realm of conscience and rule there. . . . Stay within your limits, and exercise your dominion over the flesh. You shall not touch my conscience. . . . In my conscience not the Law will reign, that hard tyrant and cruel disciplinarian, but Christ, the Son of God, the King of peace and righteousness, the sweet Savior and Mediator. He will preserve my conscience happy and peaceful in the sound and pure doctrine of the Gospel and in the knowledge of this passive righteousness.[16]

Luther traced the history of God's Word, the distinction between law and gospel, throughout the "history of salvation" (*Heilsgeschichte*) of God's dealings with his people in Scripture. In the lectures on Genesis he reminded his students that the Word of God created the world out of nothing, that is, God spoke and acted according to the meaning of the Hebrew term for "word" (*dabar*). "It [Gen. 1:3, "Let there be light . . . "] says that God is, so to speak, the Speaker who creates; nevertheless, He does not make use of matter, but He makes heaven and earth out of nothing solely by the Word which He utters."[17] Luther repeatedly pondered the relationship between the Word of God which created the world and the Word of God which was flesh in Christ (John 1:10). His view of God was as a man who converses with himself, part of himself being the "son of God." "It is an invisible and incomprehensible conversation."[18] Nevertheless, God decided to enter the world of time and space, on special occasions speaking and acting redemptively. He did so with the Old Testament people of Israel in various ways, but never did he reveal himself completely. Not even Moses was permitted to see God's face when he was given the Decalogue; he only saw the divine back (Exod. 33:23). Luther viewed this as God's graciousness and mercy and as a christological promise. "I will be gracious to whom I will be gracious" (Exod. 33:19) means that Moses is in agreement with the New Testament in so far as "Jesus Christ Jehovah is God and man, and was the preacher to the people of Israel." In this sense, Moses is a Christian.

In this way the Lord shows us the proper method of interpreting Moses and all the prophets. He teaches us that Moses points and refers to Christ in all his stories and illustrations. His purpose is to show that Christ is the point at the center of a circle, with all eyes inside the circle focused on Him. Whoever turns his eyes on Him finds his proper place in the circle of which Christ is the center. All the stories of Holy Writ, if viewed aright, point to Christ.[19]

What had been witnessed in the Old Testament as the redemptive Word of God became, in the New Testament, the ultimate divine Word and deed. This Word and deed is Christ, disclosed in both the Old Testament Scriptures and in the New Testament record of his own and his apostles' proclamation. Holy Scripture, as the Word of God, is "the spiritual body of Christ."[20] His crucifixion and resurrection are the center of the "good news." Luther developed a canon within the canon, as it were, when he rated the New Testament books according to the way in which they witness to justification by faith through grace without the works of law. Consequently the Epistle to the Romans "is really the chief part of the New Testament, and is truly the purest gospel."[21]

In this epistle we thus find most abundantly the things that a Christian ought to know, namely, what is law, gospel, sin, punishment, grace, faith, righteousness, Christ, God, good works, love, hope, and the cross; and also how we are to conduct ourselves toward everyone—be he righteous or sinner, strong or weak, friend or foe—and even toward our own selves. Moreover this is all ably supported with Scripture and proved by St. Paul's own example and that of the prophets, so that one could not wish for anything more. Therefore it appears that he wanted in this one epistle to sum up briefly the whole Christian and evangelical doctrine, and to prepare an introduction to the entire Old Testament. For, without doubt, whoever has this epistle well in his heart, has with him the light and power of the Old Testament.[22]

Luther considered the Gospel of John and 1 Peter close companions to Paul's Epistle to the Romans. They depict "in masterly fashion how faith in Christ overcomes sin, death, and hell, and gives life, righteousness, and salvation."[23] What makes Holy Scripture the Word of God is the proclamation that salvation comes through Christ by faith alone through grace.

All the genuine sacred books agree in this, that all of them preach and inculcate (treiben) Christ. And that is the true test by which to judge all books, when we see whether or not they inculcate Christ. . . . Whatever does not teach Christ is not yet apostolic, even though St. Peter or St. Paul does the teaching. Again, whatever preaches Christ would be apostolic, even if Judas, Annas, Pilate, and Herod were doing it.[24]

Luther stressed the relationship between the Word of God in Holy Scripture and the Word of God in the church, especially its oral communication. Since Christ is the Lord of the past, the present, and the future, his proclamation continues in his body, the church. Thus the proclamation of God's Word is a means of grace which calls, gathers, and redeems the people of God, the body of Christ, the church. That is why Luther insisted that the church ought to be "a mouth-house" rather than a "pen-house."[25] Why Luther emphasized the oral communication of preaching as opposed to the "sacramental Word" is not clear. He may have been influenced by the medieval emphasis on an almost magical use of sacraments, especially of the Lord's Supper, as well as by his own fascination with language and oral communication.[26]

In any case, Luther insisted that all preaching be normed by Holy Scripture, the unique record of the Word of God among the people of Israel and the church, the "new Israel." He changed his own style of preaching in 1521 from thematic to expository. His aim of preaching now was the communication of God's love in Christ who transcended any and all conditions of life, and who even overcame death, and in whom one should place total trust. Such preaching was quite different from traditional medieval preaching which favored the unfolding of a theme of Christian life.[27] At the same time, his concern was to preserve Christian proclamation from error. Since the church is always tempted to confuse law and gospel or to elevate human over divine authority, Scripture must be the spring, and the tradition of the church fathers is the brook flowing from that spring. When Scripture is no longer master and judge of tradition, teachings "lose themselves in the salty sea, as happened under the papacy."[28] The church is therefore normed by Holy Scripture, the vessel of the Word of God, which constantly renews the church in its pilgrimage on earth. Nothing is higher for Luther than the faithful proclamation of God's Word, even if only a few— or indeed only one individual—proclaim it. "If I were the only one in the entire world to adhere to the Word," he told his students in a lecture on Gen. 7:17–24, "I alone would be the church and would properly judge about the rest of the world that it is not the church."[29]

BIBLE AND HISTORY

To Luther, the God of the Bible was the omnipotent Lord of time. Whatever happened, happened as a result of God's will. When Erasmus objected to Luther's deterministic image of God, Luther insisted that to be omnipotent is God's business. There is simply a vast difference between God and the human creature, between the ability of human reason and the power of the divine will. God's will "is itself the rule of all things," he told Erasmus in 1525. "For if there were any rule or standard for it, either as cause or reason, it could no longer be the will of God."[30] God remains in charge, even though it may appear that evil is gaining the upper hand.

Luther linked this insistence on divine omnipotence with his view that the world is the playground of God who, as its Creator, is fully in charge of it. Nations rise and fall, natural disasters come and go, and the course of history appears, at least on the surface, to be without meaning. But to the believer God is not a capricious God; he merely hides "under the contrariness" (*sub contrario*) of events. On the one hand, he is the omnipotent Lord who appears to use his power arbitrarily; on the other hand, God is Christ who appears weak and who seems destined to succumb to the powers of this world. But both are viewpoints of an observer accustomed to solving the puzzle of an incarnate God by using traditional rules of logic and a concern for the proper relationship between cause and effect. Luther, however, argued that history only makes sense when seen in the light of the history of God's people, which is the record of God's promise to establish an everlasting covenant with humankind. Viewed as the scene of God's covenant with his people, history becomes pregnant with meaning and salvific power. Luther saw this power revealed throughout the Bible. He thus followed in the footsteps of Augustine when he made a basic distinction between temporal, chronological history and spiritual, salvific history. Augustine had linked the biblical prophecies to the notion of a struggle between satanic, temporal powers and divine, spiritual powers, between the "city of God" and the "earthly city" of the devil.

Although Luther used the humanistic historical-critical skills of his time, he was always guided by the Augustinian assertion that history must be viewed as a divine scheme, the center of which is the fulfillment of time in Christ's first and second coming. "Histories are nothing else than a demonstration, recollection, and sign of divine action and judgment," Luther wrote in the preface to the works of the historian Galeatius Cappela in 1538,

> ... how He [God] upholds, rules, obstructs, prospers, punishes, and honors the world, and especially men, each according to his just desert, evil or good. . . . The historians, therefore, are the most useful people and the best teachers, so that one can never honor, praise, and thank them enough.[31]

But historians are to be honored and praised only when their record of history is based on the presupposition that the God of the Bible controls every move of time. Any other historiography is incapable of communicating the real meaning of time. Luther later elaborated, in his final lectures on Genesis in 1543 / 44:

> But what are the histories of the heathen written by Vergil, Homer, Livy, or others, no matter how much they are decked out with words? They are histories of the Greeks, of Alexander, and of Hannibal. But they lack the magnificence, the glory, and the crown of the Word and promise of God. This diadem they do not have. Therefore they are records of things that have no value, rather than

actual histories. For what is history without the Word of God when the Lord says, "This is my will, My glory; this is pleasing to Me; with this I am delighted: I dwell here"? Accordingly, no matter how puerile and sordid these things are, yet they have immense and unlimited weight, namely, the Word of God. Although the histories of Alexander, Julius Caesar, etc. are outstanding and very splendid, they lack the true adornment. Therefore they are like chaff scattered by the wind and destitute of true weight; they are glory only of the belly and the flesh.[32]

Luther himself devised chronological computations in his "Reckoning Years of the World" (*Supputatio annorum mundi*) by following a traditional medieval scheme of viewing world history as a succession of millennia analogous to the seven days of creation.[33] His "Reckoning" envisioned the six ages preceding the endtime as the ages of Adam, Noah, Abraham, David, Christ, and the pope. He based his scheme on an ancient Jewish prophecy attributed to the prophet Elijah:

> The world is six thousand years old, and thereafter it will break apart. Two thousand years it will be empty, two thousand years it will have law, and two thousand years it will have the Messiah.[34]

The seventh millennium will be "the day of the eternal Sabbath," that is, the beginning of eternal life.[35] By coordinating biblical chronology with the available chronologies of classical antiquity, Luther criticized existing and frequently legendary accounts of the origins and development of the Christian church. Comparing, for example, biblical statements about Peter and Paul with the length of the Roman emperors' reigns, Luther concluded with obvious pride "that the first Roman saints who went to heaven had never seen either St. Peter or St. Paul."[36] Like Augustine and his disciples, Luther saw the sixth-millennium world divided between believers and unbelievers, with many unbelievers belonging to the Church of Rome. This world is composed of heroes and villains, endowed either with the power of God or the might of Satan; this struggle between good and evil affects everyone, believers and unbelievers alike. According to Luther, God selects certain people to do his bidding. For example, the Roman leader Hannibal was not just a military genius, but "one created by God Himself to be the master of this art, neither trained nor made by other people." He was one of God's "miracle men" (*Wundermänner*). On the other hand, there are those he called "Master Smart Aleck, that infamous, dangerous man who can do everything better and still is not a man." One can be a Goliath and still lose in the struggle with David.[37] For every Elector Frederick the Wise there is a Duke George of Saxony who persecutes the gospel; and the pope is the great manifestation of satanic power.

Thus the Bible was Luther's best source for ascertaining the meaning of history, the struggle between God and Satan, between belief and unbelief.

Read as the earthen vessel which contains the Word of God best embodied and yet still hidden in Jesus Christ, the Bible reveals the basic difference between God's will and human tradition. Luther loved to cite the "Magnificat" in the New Testament (Luke 1:46–55) as a basic clue for discerning the meaning of political power in history. God revealed his intentions when he "put down the mighty" and "exalted those of low degree," especially the Virgin Mary:

> We see in all the histories and in experience that He puts down one kingdom and exalts another, lifts up one principality and casts down another, increases one people and destroys another; as He did with Assyria, Babylon, Persia, Greece, and Rome, though they thought they would sit in their seats forever. Nor does He destroy reason, wisdom, and right; for if the world is to go on, these things must remain. But He does destroy pride and the proud, who use these things for selfish ends, enjoy them, do not fear God, but persecute the godly and the divine right by means of them, and thus abuse the fair gifts of God and turn them against Him.[38]

Luther also viewed history as the record of conflict between the true church, consisting of those who are faithful to Christ and Scripture, and the false church of those who, like the pope, use Christ and Scripture to serve their own ends and thus succumb to the ancient temptation to be like God (Gen. 3:5). Recalling the traditional notion preserved in canon law that there always will be a holy remnant preserving the true faith, Luther rejected Rome's claim to be the true church until the end of time. "We should rather believe a layman, if he has plain Scripture and clear reason on his side, than a pope or a council."[39] But Luther did not defend the idea of a true, hidden church at the expense of the visible, organized church he experienced. Rather, he was committed to combining both the visible and invisible components of the church. For just as God is hidden under the mask of history, so are true believers hidden in the organized church, the body of Christ.

By maintaining a dialectic, as it were, between the visible and invisible aspects of the church, Luther refused to ascribe infallibility to any organized gathering of Christians, be it the Church of Rome or his own reform movement. Unlike other anti-Roman theologians, such as Thomas Müntzer and the Anabaptist Jacob Huter, Luther did not develop a theology of history marked by a "fall" and a "golden age" (the theory that the true church existed before the fusion of church and state under Emperor Constantine in the third century but was corrupt afterwards until the time of the Reformation). He was convinced that the church is a participant in the conflict between God and Satan, good and evil, faithfulness and apostasy. Thus he could say that, on the one hand, "God does not want the world to know when he sleeps with his bride"; and that, on the other hand, "the assembly of the church is visible for the sake of the confession of faith" (Rom. 10:10).[40]

Luther learned from the Bible that the true church is a suffering church modeled after Christ. The history of this church begins with Adam, who already embodied both belief and unbelief and thus foreshadowed the history of humanity. Yet God never completely condemns either Adam or all his children. They are instead given signs of promise and hope, beginning with the messianic prophecy that the serpent's head and heel will be crushed (Gen. 3:15).

> This very clear promise remained dark until Mary had given birth. . . . But what is born from Mary was conceived by the Holy Spirit and is the true Seed of Mary, just as the other promises given to Abraham and David testify, according to which Christ is called the Son of Abraham and the Son of David.[41]

There is, then, a tradition of God's Word in the Bible and in history—a "handing on" (from the Latin *traditio*) of the basic meaning of time as God's time culminating in the first and second coming of Christ. The church, as the body of Christ, is charged with guarding the tradition of God's Word in the interim between Christ's resurrection and the end of time, when Christ will return as the Lord of a new world. Luther saw himself as the guardian of this tradition in his own time. Thus he did not oppose tradition, if this means the church's responsibility to communicate God's Word in proclamation and sacramental celebration. Rather, he wanted to make a proper distinction between this authentic tradition of Word and sacrament and other traditions used by rival authorities to enhance their own power at the expense of God's Word.[42]

Researching the Greek and Latin church fathers of the first five centuries, Luther discovered that many of the fathers identified God's Word—even in Scripture—with legalism and moralism. Moreover, his own experiences as a monk convinced him that asceticism and celibacy were distortions of what Scripture meant by the kingdom of God. When moralism and legalism were then combined with rationalism, especially the Aristotelianism of medieval scholastic theology, the gospel was totally perverted. Thus the best tradition was the faithful exposition of Holy Scripture in the light of the historical situation in which the church found itself at any one time. For the true church fathers "most certainly considered Scripture the principal light and the greatest clarity and certainty to which they appealed and upon which they relied as upon the most obvious and clearest teaching to judge and to test all teaching."[43] Luther therefore called into question the traditional medieval appeals to extra-biblical authorities, such as pope and council, to preserve the church from error.

Since his first encounter with papal authority, at the hearing before Cajetan in Augsburg in 1518, Luther had realized that the battle for church renewal was intimately linked to proper distinctions between Scripture and tradition. Church renewal therefore meant the liberation of Scripture from

Roman traditionalism, which was the worst example of the "word of man." That is why Luther moved ever closer to the principle that the church should be normed by "Scripture alone" (*sola scriptura*). But this did not lead Luther to embrace a biblicism rejecting the authority of Christian tradition in post-biblical history. Rather, he wanted tradition to be tested by Scripture, since Scripture is the vessel which best preserves the gospel's promise that the human creature is justified "by faith alone" (*sola fide*), "by grace alone" (*sola gratia*), and "by Christ alone" (*solo Christo*). This *sola* tradition, as it were, stemmed from the discovery Luther made during his study of Paul's Epistle to the Romans that the power of Scripture is directed to those whose consciences are terrified by the question of whether or not God accepts them as ungodly sinners.

That God "justifies" the ungodly was to Luther the heart of the Word of God. This insight made Luther review his position as a biblical theologian in the church catholic. The chief result of this review was a deep awareness, hardened into a firm conviction by the pressure of papal ban and imperial edict, that the church exists to celebrate the freedom of the Word of God and that theology must guard this freedom against the perduring human desire to domesticate God. The more Luther pondered the power of God's Word, the more he became aware of the fact that the pain and joy of discovery transport the biblical theologian from his own preoccupations to the strange and wonderful world of God's dealings with his creatures. He told his students:

> This is the reason why our theology is certain: it snatches us away from ourselves and places us outside ourselves, so that we do not depend on our own strength, conscience, experience, person, or works but depend on that which is outside ourselves, that is, on the promise and truth of God, which cannot deceive.[44]

PROTESTANT PRINCIPLE AND CATHOLIC SUBSTANCE

Luther's attempt to reform the church catholic by subjecting its teachings to what he understood to be Christian gospel and the authority of the Bible has been called the "Protestant principle"—"the divine and human protest against any absolute claim made for a relative reality."[45] So defined, this principle judges any Christian tradition claiming to represent the absolute reality of God captured in an infallible "catholic substance"—"the body of tradition, liturgy, dogma, and churchmanship developed chiefly by the ancient church and embodied, but not exhausted, in the Roman Catholic Church of his [Luther's] day."[46] Whereas Luther did not use such terms in his critique of Roman hierarchical authority, he did in fact insist that ecclesiastical tradition must be tested by the Word of God in Holy Scripture. When accused of rejecting tradition altogether, Luther appealed to tradition, especially to the great fathers of the Western church, to make his point. Since nothing human is ever safe from error, no teacher of the church can claim to communicate the pure Word of God at all times; this is why Augustine and Jerome, the most revered fathers of the Western church, agreed with Paul's injunction to "test everything" and to "hold fast what is good" (1 Thess. 5:21). "Holy Scripture must necessarily be clearer, simpler, and more reliable than any other writings," Luther declared in his defense against Rome's attacks.

> Especially since all teachers verify their own statements through the Scriptures as clearer and more reliable writings, and desire their own writings to be confirmed and explained by them. But nobody can ever substantiate an obscure saying by one that is more obscure; therefore, necessity forces us to run to the Bible with the writings of all teachers, and to obtain there a verdict and judgment upon them. *Scripture alone is the true lord and master of all writings and doctrine on earth.* If that is not granted, what is Scripture good for? The more we reject it, the more we become satisfied with men's books and human teachers.[47]

Luther's principle of "Scripture alone" did not entrap him in the proof-text syndrome, even though he frequently succumbed. When a specific biblical text is used to test ecclesiastical teachings, "We are guided by two [rules]," he told Latomus in 1521 during their quarrel over the proper interpretation of Isa. 64:6, ("We have all become like one who is unclean, and all our righteous deeds are like filthy rags").

> [We assume figurative speech if the result would otherwise lead to] absurdity of meaning, and the circumstances in which the words are spoken. Thus in the case of the "sword upon the thigh," in Ps. 45[:3], and the two swords of the disciples in Luke 20 [22:38], the context more forcefully shows that they are not made of iron than does the absurdity [of such an interpretation]—though that also holds. On the other hand, when it is said that he who has left a wife shall receive a hundredfold in this life [Matt. 19:29], it is the absurdity of the [literal meaning] which compels us to understand that this does not refer to physical leaving and receiving.
>
> Thus in the present case, it is not enough for my Latomus to say that "all" can be figuratively understood as "some." *I will tolerate no figure as long as it is not required by an absurdity or by the necessity of circumstances.* I shall urge upon him that he ought to understand the simple, proper, and primary meaning of "All our righteousness is unclean." He ought to do this, I say, because there is here no absurdity nor opposition to what is found in Scripture.[48]

Latomus used figurative interpretations of the Bible, which were based on the consensus of ecclesiastical authorities, but Luther insisted that the literal sense of Scripture is to be preferred unless a passage appears totally absurd. The literal sense, then, is what leads to the true understanding of the Bible as the earthen vessel for the divine truth that God acts in a history of salvation which has its focus on Christ. To discern this truth as "scriptural" is the task of the biblical theologian. As such a theologian, Luther discovered that "Scripture interprets itself," contrary to the traditional rule that only the church can interpret Scripture.[49] Its prophetic witness in the Old Testament and its apostolic witness in the New Testament are constitutive for the church. Since most prophets and apostles, with some exceptions like Paul, were common people, Luther was convinced that common people with common sense should be able to understand the good news of Scripture that God saves humankind through Christ. Luther consequently accused the church of having made the understanding of Scripture more complicated than it is so as to increase ecclesiastical power and, in the face of such power, he insisted on the polemical principle of "Scripture alone."

Whereas Luther consistently applied the principle of *sola scriptura* in his critique of the Roman Church, he made strong appeals to ecclesiastical tradition when struggling with the *Schwärmer*—especially Zwingli and the Anabaptists, who used literal and figurative biblical interpretations to denigrate the sacraments of Holy Baptism and the Lord's Supper. When he heard that the Swiss Anabaptists rejected infant baptism on the basis of a literal interpretation of Mark 16:16 ("He who believes and is baptized will be saved") and that they contended that adult confession of faith must precede baptism, Luther used tradition to defend the practice of infant baptism. Arguing that Scripture commands baptism without stipulating age, according to Matt. 28:19 ("Go therefore and make disciples of all nations, baptizing them in the name of the Father, and of the Son, and of the Holy Spirit"), he offered a controversial conclusion:

> If the first, or child, baptism were not right, it would follow that for more than a thousand years there was no baptism or any Christendom, which is impossible. For in that case the article of the creed, I believe in one holy Christian church, would be false. For over a thousand years there were hardly any other but child baptisms. If this baptism is wrong, then for that long period Christendom would have been without baptism, and if it were without baptism it would not be Christendom. . . . If, indeed, child baptism were not common throughout the world, but (like the papacy) were accepted only by some, then the Anabaptists might seem to have a case. . . . But the fact that child baptism has spread throughout all the Christian world to this day gives rise to no probability that it is wrong, but rather to a strong indication that it is right.[50]

In his fierce battle against Zwinglians, Luther even used traditional medieval scholastic speculations to defend the bodily presence of Christ in the Lord's Supper. Accordingly, Christ used a "corporeal mode of presence" when he walked on earth, a "spiritual mode of presence" when he passed through everything created (like a sound travels through air), and a "divine, heavenly mode" of presence which gives him God's power to be wherever he wills. Comparing Christ's "divine mode" to the voice of a preacher reaching thousands of ears, Luther concluded:

> If God can do this with a physical voice, why should he not be able to do it far more easily with the body of Christ, even if it were at a particular place, as they say, and yet at the same time be truly in the bread and wine at many places, as it were, in two ears? For his body is much quicker and lighter than any voice, and all creation is more permeable to him than the air is to the voice, as he proved in the ease of the gravestone, inasmuch as no voice can pass through a stone as easily as Christ's body does.[51]

Luther used these speculations and analogies to defend the validity of the literal meaning of the words "This is my body" (Matt. 26:26) against Zwingli's translation "This signifies (*significat*) my body." The real issue, of course, was whether or not the mystery of Christ's "real" or "bodily" presence can be unraveled by the clever use of Greek metaphysical tradition with its dualism of matter and spirit. Zwingli's attempt to explain the sacrament of the Lord's Supper either as remembrance of Christ's last supper or as a ritual in which the faithful perceive Christ to be "spiritually" present was to Luther a *Schwärmerei* bordering on heresy. The end result of such a line of reasoning, he thought, could only be the denial of God's incarnation in Christ, the second person of the Trinity embodying the full interpenetration of human and divine natures which the Council of Chalcedon had affirmed in 451. By adhering to the doctrine of Christ's bodily presence in the Lord's Supper, Luther could claim to be in harmony with a fifteen-hundred-year-long tradition, including the tradition of the Roman Church.[52]

Luther wanted to be known as a reformer who used the authority of Scripture to preserve the best of catholic substance, that is, the tradition of communicating the gospel's salvific thrust in various places and at various times. Luther felt that he was in agreement with the great fathers of the church when declaring that articles of faith, namely, doctrines concerning salvation, must not be established without clear scriptural evidence even though human tradition not concerned with salvation may be tolerated as a matter of Christian liberty at specific times and places.[53]

True "catholic substance," therefore, is God's Word, which promises salvation in Jesus Christ and is summarized in Scripture in various historical contexts. Luther shared the view of his time that the ancient ecumenical creeds represented such a summary of Scripture. Consequently he considered his reform movement to be clearly grounded in the catholic substance of the trinitarian and christological doctrines of the ancient church, which had formulated these doctrines in order to delineate clearly the difference between orthodoxy and heresy on the one hand and between divine revelation and human authority on the other. According to Luther, the three trinitarian creeds (Apostles', Nicene, and Athanasian) express the real thrust of God's Word as witnessed in Scripture, "that Jesus Christ is true God and man, that he died and has risen again for us" and that he is the "base, ground, and the whole sum, around and under which everything is gathered and found."[54] Yet whereas the medieval church taught the creeds as objective information about God, Luther in his catechisms emphasized the existential and soteriological dimensions: the dogma of the Trinity proclaims that God was incarnate in Christ "for me" (pro me), that is, for the sake of my salvation. That is why the creeds are recited in the liturgy; they are the doxology of the faithful, showing "how much it cost Christ and what he paid and risked in order to win us and bring us under his dominion."[55]

Luther distinguished between the catholic substance formulated by the ancient church in its struggle against heresy and the human traditions which had obscured and even perverted catholic substance. On the basis of his own study of church history, he concluded that the first four hundred years were not as much polluted by human traditions as the last four hundred years (1100–1500). Thus he saw the church of his time, the Roman Church, as both instigator and victim of a millennium of self-righteous human authority which had denigrated and indeed perverted the power of God's Word. Luther, of course, felt God had called him to expose the satanic power of human traditions and to reform the church by recalling it to faithfulness to God's Word. The last four hundred years were, he said, dominated by "the very feeble decrees of the Roman pontiffs" who claimed "that the Roman Church is superior to all others." In 1519, in his thirteenth thesis at the Leipzig Debate, Luther declared, "Against them stand the history of eleven hundred years, the text of divine Scripture, and the decree of the Council of Nicaea, the most sacred of all councils" (A.D. 325).[56] Thus Luther rejected the traditional interpretation of Matt. 16:18 ("You are Peter, and on this rock I will build my church") that Christ had founded the papacy with Peter, leading to a succession of Roman bishops. Instead, he affirmed the authority of the Council of Nicaea, which was chaired by Emperor Constantine the Great rather than by a Roman bishop.

What infuriated John Eck and other opponents was Luther's proposal that the authentic meaning of Scripture could be established without the approval of the Roman Church and its pope, which considered itself the representative of Christ's authority on earth. By separating divine revelation in Scripture from ecclesiastical authority, Luther rejected the official doctrine formulated by Vincent of Lerins in the fifth century. According to this doctrine, the truth of the Christian faith is established only by the principles of universality, antiquity, and consent (that "which has been believed everywhere, always, and by all men").[57] These principles also determined the church's interpretation of Scripture. And since the church existed in and through the episcopal hierarchy, any biblical interpretation had to have the approval of this hierarchy. Thus the real issue between

Luther and his opponents was that of biblical versus ecclesiastical authority. Luther contended that Scripture interprets itself; Rome insisted that Scripture must be interpreted by the teaching office of the church, the *magisterium* of bishops headed by the bishop of Rome.

According to Luther, the church must be faithful first to Scripture and then to tradition tested by Scripture, because the Word of God in Scripture preceded the church. To this extent, the church is always the creature of God's Word, whose center is Christ; and the Holy Spirit is always given through faith in Christ.

> But the Holy Spirit is not given except in, with, and by faith in Jesus Christ, as St. Paul says in the introduction [to Romans]. Faith, moreover, comes only through God's Word or gospel, which preaches Christ, saying that he is God's Son and a man, and has died and risen again for our sakes, as he says in chapters 3[:25], 4[:25], and 10[:9]. So it happens that faith alone makes a person righteous and fulfils the law. For out of the merit of Christ it brings forth the Spirit. And the Spirit makes the heart glad and free, as the law requires that it shall be. Thus good works emerge from faith itself.[58]

If the church is to have the Holy Spirit, it must be normed by Scripture. Scripture is the vessel God himself chose to communicate his Spirit. That is why Luther never tired of reminding his students to cherish the study of the Bible. He demanded they be well-versed in Hebrew and Greek, able to distinguish between clear and obscure passages, and ready to wrestle with the text through hard study and prayer. For "the languages are the sheath in which the sword of the Spirit is contained" (Eph. 6:7); and when necessary, the Holy Spirit can bring the languages down from heaven, as the apostles experienced at Pentecost (Acts 2:4). "The Holy Spirit is no fool."[59] Luther came close to theories of verbal or plenary inspiration with this enthusiastic praise of biblical authority, but the basic distinction he made between the Bible as external word and God's Word as a word of salvation coming alive in interpersonal communication "for me" prevented him from drawing dangerous conclusions.[60] Luther contended that the true biblical theologian must simultaneously be a preacher of God's Word at all times. For the Word of God by itself "is not as fruitful and powerful as it is through a public preacher whom God has ordained to say and preach this."[61]

Luther's distinctions between Scripture and tradition are not always as clear as they could be, at least according to Luther interpreters who strive for a systematic arrangement of his views and who frequently have modern questions in mind. After all, Luther lived and worked before the time of the Enlightenment, when philosophical reflections on the nature of time and historical-critical evaluation of biblical texts became commonplace. What is clear, however, is Luther's opposition to a traditionalism which he associated with the Roman Church's claim to have more authority than Holy Scripture.

If true Christian tradition, "catholic substance," always communicates the gospel of salvation through Christ alone, then Luther cannot be said to have opposed tradition. He opposed a traditionalism which moves away from the gospel or impedes its freedom. "Our dear fathers wanted to lead us to the Scriptures by their writings," Luther told the German nobility in 1520, "but we use their works to get away from the Scriptures."[62] He saw papal teaching authority as the issue which would make or break the church of his time. That is why he called the pope the Antichrist, following a tradition of criticism dating from the twelfth century.[63] When Rome refused to heed his call to return to Scripture as the highest authority and was indeed unwilling even to debate it, Luther became convinced that the Holy Spirit would no longer dwell in the Roman Church but would instead make its home in the Lutheran movement which did submit itself to the sole authority of Scripture.

However, Luther's stance on the authority of God's Word found in Scripture reveals two trends which seem to contradict each other. On the one hand, his almost exclusive reliance on the literal sense of the Bible makes Luther sound like an American fundamentalist.[64] On the other hand, his criticism of specific biblical texts, and even of entire books like the Epistle of James, makes him appear guilty of establishing a new tradition, namely, a canon within the canon of the Bible. Luther, after all, based his biblical criticism on what he understood to be the Pauline gospel of justification by faith alone. How then did Luther reconcile these two trends? When he himself wrestled with the question of the unity of Scripture, especially the relation of the Old and the New Testaments, he discovered a simple truth:

> From the very beginning the word has come to us in various ways. It is not enough simply to look and see whether this is God's word, whether God has said it; rather, we must look and see to whom it is spoken, whether it fits us. . . . The word in Scripture is of two kinds: the first does not pertain or apply to me, the other kind does. And upon that word which does pertain to me I can boldly trust and rely, as upon a strong rock. But if it does not pertain to me, then I should stand still.[65]

In other words, if my life has become meaningless under the *Anfechtung* of total despair, my encounter with Scripture can be the liberation from meaninglessness—not because it is the inspired, written Word of God, but because it proclaims in its prophetic and apostolic witness the destiny of the human creature: to be with God through Christ despite sin, death, and devil. As such, Scripture is precisely what I need in my despair over the destiny of my life. For as the record of the history of both the fall and the salvation of humanity, Scripture also addresses my fall and my salvation. That is why Luther insisted on a continual and regular exposure to Scripture. One never knows when the Word of God will strike at the human heart, turning it towards God.

In the context of critical hindsight, what makes Luther's views on authority neuralgic is their intimate link to a vision of Christendom in which feudal political authorities like princes functioned as "emergency bishops" and exercised supreme authority over Lutheran congregations in their territories. Luther certainly did not intend to align the *sola* character of faith in Christ with temporal political power, but he feared the power of Rome more than the power of feudal princes. Moreover, the 1525 uprising of the peasants in the name of the gospel disclosed to him the failure of the common people to exercise proper teaching authority.[66] Is this Luther's weakness—a medieval man bound by nurture and environment to fear any breakdown of law and order and consider it a betrayal of the Word of God? Did Luther believe that, on the basis of Scripture and tradition, there is a mysterious correlation between an order of creation disclosed in temporal government and an order of redemption revealed in the biblical history of salvation? Clear answers to these questions are difficult—if not impossible—since Luther's works always address specific situations rather than offer a systematic theology.

What made Luther cherish the Bible, especially the Old Testament, was the link between God's Word of law and gospel and human suffering. Not to be able to see God's love is the height and depth of suffering for those who cannot conceive reality without God. Luther lived at a time when there were hardly any agnostics; even Jews and Turks believed in God. To find despair over the love of God among the people of God in the Bible was a great comfort to Luther. He could identify with them, particularly with the authors of Psalms; that is why David was his model theologian. Luther saw in the life and work of this biblical hero the almost perfect embodiment of the struggle between divine love and human despair. God never let David be consumed by suffering; he turned suffering into an *Anfechtung* which became the bridge between sin and salvation. True theologians, biblical theologians, find themselves on that bridge, following the "rules of David" laid down in Psalm 119: prayer, meditation, and *Anfechtung* (*oratio, meditatio, tentatio*). David too had to face various enemies, false spirits, and factions, just as Luther did. "I myself (if you will permit me, mere mouse-dirt, to be mingled with pepper) am deeply indebted to my papists," he told his readers in the Preface to the German edition of his works in 1539, "that through the devil's raging they have beaten, oppressed, and distressed me so much. That is to say, they have made a fairly good theologian out of me."[67] Bad theologians, according to Luther, are those who think they serve God with fine books, beautiful sermons, and flattering praise. "If you are of that stripe, dear friend, then take yourself by the ears, and if you do this in the right way you will find a beautiful pair of big, long, shaggy donkey ears. . . . The honor is God's alone," not the theologian's.[68]

6

CHRIST AND CAESAR

You must know that since the beginning of the world a wise prince is a mighty rare bird, and an upright prince even rarer. They are generally the biggest fools or the worst scoundrels on earth; therefore, one must constantly expect the worst from them and look for little good, especially in divine matters which concern the salvation of souls. They are God's executioners and hangmen; his divine wrath uses them to punish the wicked and to maintain outward peace. Our God is a great lord and ruler; this is why he must also have such noble, highborn, and rich hangmen and constables. He desires that everyone shall copiously accord them riches, honor, and fear in abundance. . . . If a prince should happen to be wise, upright, or a Christian, that is one of the great miracles, the most precious token of divine grace upon that land. ("Temporal Authority: To What Extent It Should be Obeyed," 1523. *WA* 11:267.30–268.14. *LW* 45:113)

LIFE IN TWO REALMS

Luther's utterances on the relationship between Christian faith and political life have been widely and hotly debated. The various theories of church and state before and since the Reformation, Germany's rise and fall as a military superpower in two world wars, and Luther's unguarded statements on what has been dubbed the "two-kingdoms ethic" have contributed much towards making Luther's political ethic one of the most neuralgic topics in Luther research. Both expert and popular opinion alike are divided in their assessments of Luther's attitude toward political authority (*Obrigkeit*, in Luther's German). Karl Holl, the father of the German Luther research renaissance at the time of the Weimar Republic, saw Luther as the influential advocate of a cultural community (*Kulturstaat*) based on sound Christian moral principles and constitutional laws which aim for the common good.[1]

Ernst Troeltsch, the influential historian of Christian social ethics, criticized Luther for having created a disjunction between private and public morality which culminated with the demand to be obedient to the state even in the face of tyranny. He accused Luther of being unable to provide a clear rationale for a state grounded in both natural law and Christian sacrificial love, thus rendering his idea of the state "super-idealistic, almost Utopian in a Christian sense."[2]

When World War II began, the prominent Swiss theologian Karl Barth blasted Luther's ideas on political authority for being the source of Hitler's tyranny, "the bad dream of the German pagan who has been Christianized in Lutheran fashion."[3] Almost at the same time, in 1941, the Norwegian Lutheran bishop Eivind Berggrav urged his constituents to practice passive resistance against Nazi occupation forces in the name of Luther.[4] During the same period, another opponent of Nazi Germany, Dietrich Bonhoeffer, accused Luther of a fundamental misinterpretation of the New Testament. He asserted that Luther had confirmed "Constantine's covenant with the church" (A.D. 313), which resulted in a "minimal ethic of inner-worldliness."[5]

American Luther critics were even more adamant. Reinhold Niebuhr, the well-known scholar and churchman, spoke of Luther's "curiously perverse morality" centered in a "perfectionistic private ethic in juxtaposition to a realistic, not to say cynical, official ethic," a distinction which encourages tyranny.[6] In 1960, William L. Shirer's best-selling history of Germany under Hitler pictured Luther as "a passionate anti-Semite and ferocious believer in absolute obedience to political authority."[7]

These and other samples of interpretative judgments concerning Luther's attitude towards political order and disorder reveal not only the neuralgia, but also the nostalgia and even paranoia rampant among Luther interpreters. Yet even though there is no easy way out of the labyrinth of views on Luther's two-kingdoms ethic, a sober reading of Luther's principal utterances on the subject in light of his own historical circumstances should yield some basic insights.[8]

Luther's views on the relationship between the realm of Christ and the realm of Caesar were guided by his discernment that, on the whole, sixteenth-century princes ruled more justly than did ecclesiastical rulers. "It seems plain to me," he told his students during his lectures on Rom. 13:1 ("Let every person be subject to the governing authorities"),

> that in our day the secular powers are carrying on their duties more successfully and better than the ecclesiastical rulers are doing. For they are strict in their punishment of thefts and murders, except to the extent that they are corrupted by insidious privileges. But the ecclesiastical rulers, except for those who invade the liberties, privileges, and rights of the church, whom they condemn to excessive punishments, actually nourish pride, ambitions, prodigality, and contentions rather than punish them (so much so that perhaps it would be safer if the temporal affairs also of the clergy were placed under the secular power).[9]

Luther had learned from Augustine to view life as a struggle between two "cities" or commonwealths of people: the "city of God," consisting of those who love God and are obedient to him; and the "city of the earth" (*civitas terrena*), consisting of those who love themselves and are dominated by the sin of pride. Cain and Abel are the chief figures of these two cities (Gen. 4:1–8). But whereas Augustine stressed the dichotomy between the temporal and the eternal realms, as manifested in the individual by the spiritual soul and the carnal body, Luther emphasized the personal and social dimensions of the struggle between the two cities. He was deeply aware of the struggle between spiritual authority embodied in the priest and temporal authority embodied in the prince. On the one hand, both priest and prince participate in the struggle between God and Satan, as Augustine had described it. On the other hand, the individual Christian had to live in both the spiritual and the temporal realms, a believing member of the church and an obedient citizen of the state. Luther therefore wrestled with the question of how both realms are related, since both are the means by which God sustains and redeems the world in the face of sin, death, and evil.[10]

Luther's earliest utterances on "two kingdoms" echoed the Augustinian distinction between the realm of God and the realm of Satan. In a 1517 Lenten sermon, Luther preached on the second petition of the Lord's Prayer ("Your kingdom come") and told the Wittenberg congregation that Christians have to live in both kingdoms. "All of us dwell in the devil's kingdom until the coming of the kingdom of God."[11] But he differentiated between the godly and the ungodly in the kingdom of the devil; this kingdom is a paradise for the ungodly, but a vast prison of misery for the godly. Its citizens pretend to be godly by displaying a false, external righteousness, but yield to the devil; many of them are members in the church. "They are like lead organ pipes which fairly drawl or shout out their sounds in church, yet lack both words and meaning."[12] In contrast to the kingdom of the devil, the kingdom of God is a kingdom of truth and righteousness "ruled not by sin, but only by Christ and His grace."[13] Luther admonished his congregation to become aware of the difference between the two kingdoms, since they struggle with each other within every Christian.

> Now let everyone test himself to see whether he is inclined in this or in that direction, and he will know to which kingdom he belongs. There is, of course, no one who will not find some trace of the devil's kingdom in himself. Therefore he must pray, "Thy kingdom come." For God's kingdom does indeed begin and grow here, but it will be perfected in yonder life.[14]

Luther alerted his audience to two grave temptations which befall Christians in the two kingdoms. One temptation is the desire to become outwardly righteous in order to enter the kingdom of God. Such righteousness leads people to perform "outward works"—build chapels, do good, and produce a lot of glitter, albeit without inner commitment. These people go far afield in order to reach the kingdom of God, unable to perceive it where they are. Another temptation is to look only for joy, happiness, and eternal bliss—to strive always from earth toward heaven, unaware that "Christ came to us from heaven to earth; we did not ascend from earth into heaven to him."[15]

When the two kingdoms are properly distinguished, self-righteousness is clearly differentiated from "alien righteousness," that is, from a divine righteousness which is given by God without merit, by grace alone. This alien righteousness gives believers the power to do good and to fight evil. "Christ daily drives out the old Adam more and more, in accordance with the extent to which faith and knowledge of Christ grow," Luther declared in his Palm Sunday sermon on Phil. 2:5–6.[16] Thus the alien righteousness of grace creates "proper righteousness" in the believer, who must constantly slay self-love, must love the neighbor, and must live in fear of God. When evil, lawlessness, and chaos threaten the world, as Luther was convinced they did in his own time, secular government must exercise its divinely ordained function "to punish and judge evil men, to vindicate and defend the oppressed, because it is not they but God who does this."[17] This is the function of "public individuals" who in this fashion exercise their Christian love for the neighbor. "Private individuals," that is, the citizens of a political territory, must rely on their rulers for justice. They must follow the rule of Christ given in the Sermon on the Mount: suffer injustice if necessary without revenge (Matt. 5:44).

Luther soon discovered, particularly after the Diet of Worms in 1521, that the proper distinction between public and private Christians was a very complicated matter. Should adherents of the Lutheran movement, declared seditious at the diet, remain loyal to princes who issued this unjust edict? When citizens of Bavaria and of the territory of George of Saxony were prohibited from reading any of Luther's writings, including his translation of the New Testament, Luther was asked to give advice. Should Lutherans live by the injunctions of the Sermon on the Mount and Paul's mandate to be and to remain subject to secular government, or should they resist? Luther summarized his advice in the treatise "Temporal Authority: To What Extent It Should Be Obeyed" in 1523. These were Luther's salient points:

1. There is an essential and undeniable difference between the internal stance of a Christian heart and the external order of Christian life. Contrary to official ecclesiastical teaching, there is no distinction between "perfect" Christians who obey the special teachings of the Sermon on the Mount through some sort of ascetic life, as the monks claim, and "imperfect" Christians who live with compromises in a world filled with temptations.

> Perfection and imperfection do not consist in works, and do not establish any distinct external order among Christians. They exist in the heart, in faith and

love, so that those who believe and love the most are the perfect ones, whether they be outwardly male or female, prince or peasant, monk or layman. For love and faith produce no sects or outward differences.[18]

Real, perfect Christians belong to the kingdom of God. They do of their own accord what others are forced to do by the laws of government. "If all the world were composed of real Christians, that is, true believers, there would be no need for or benefits from prince, king, lord, sword, or law."[19]

2. The inability of Christians to create a Christian external order, be it ecclesiastical or secular, is because Adam infested the world with rebellion against God. That is why the world needs secular government and the preaching of the law in addition to the proclamation of the gospel. Secular government is the embodiment of God's law for the restraining and curbing of massive political sin which leads to tyranny and chaos, and Christian preaching of the law is the constant reminder that sin is always present and that Christians are therefore in constant need of returning in faith to the grace of God in Christ. It is impossible to fill the world with real Christians who do not need the law's restraint. "This you will never accomplish; for the world and the masses are and always will be un-Christian, even if they are all baptized and Christian in name."[20] The question is not whether the world will be Christian or un-Christian. Rather, the issue is the correct and careful distinction of God's two governments, the spiritual which produces inward righteousness and the temporal which creates external order.

Neither one is sufficient in the world without the other. No one can become righteous in the sight of God by means of the temporal government, without Christ's spiritual government. Christ's government does not extend over all men; rather, Christians are always a minority in the midst of non-Christians. Now where temporal government or law alone prevails, there sheer hypocrisy is inevitable, even though the commandments be God's very own. For without the Holy Spirit in the heart no one becomes truly righteous, no matter how fine the works he does. On the other hand, where the spiritual government alone prevails over land and people, there wickedness is given free rein and the door is open for all manner of rascality, for the world as a whole cannot receive or comprehend it.[21]

3. Even though real Christians do not need secular government, they nevertheless should serve in such a government to express their love for their neighbor.

In such a case you would be entering entirely into the service and work of others, which would be of advantage neither to yourself nor your property of honor, but only to your neighbor and to others. You would be doing it not with the purpose of avenging yourself or returning evil for evil, but for the good of your neighbor and for the maintenance of the safety and peace of others. For yourself, you would abide by the gospel and govern yourself according to

Christ's word (Matt. 5:39–40), gladly turning the other cheek and letting the cloak go with the coat when the matter concerned you and your cause.[22]

The best way to live in the two realms of sin and grace, law and gospel, good and evil is to move away from one's own—always egotistical—concerns and to serve those who are in need of love and justice. That is the way in which the Sermon on the Mount and obedience to secular government are creatively joined.

> A Christian should be so disposed that he will suffer every evil and injustice without avenging himself; neither will he seek legal redress in the courts but have utterly no need of temporal authority and law for his own sake. On behalf of others, however, he may and should seek vengeance, justice, protection, and help, and do as much as he can to achieve it.[23]

Thus Christians may confidently take positions in secular government, including the function of punishing malefactors with the sword.

> No Christian shall wield or invoke the sword for himself and his cause. In behalf of another, however, he may and should wield it and invoke it to restrain wickedness and to defend godliness.[24]

4. The realm of secular government and the realm of faith must be properly distinguished, albeit not separated. How people believe and what they believe is a matter for the individual conscience. Princes should be content with that, and they should not enforce this or that belief. "For faith is a free act, to which no one can be forced."[25] When rulers become tyrannical and claim authority over souls, they must be met with passive resistance. A Christian should respond:

> Gracious sir, I owe you obedience in body and property; command me within the limits of your authority on earth, and I will obey. But if you command me to believe or get rid of certain books, I will not obey; for then you are a tyrant and overreach yourself, commanding where you have neither the right nor the authority.[26]

The proper Christian stance is endurance without violence in the face of tyranny and persecution. The only weapon of resistance is the Word of God which reminds tyrants and heretics that God will prevail in his good time. "Heresy is a spiritual matter which you cannot hack to pieces with iron, consume with fire, or drown in water. God's word alone prevails here."[27] That is why it is best to have Christian princes who know the difference between the two realms and whose wise government is based on love and natural law. Luther considered Duke Charles of Burgundy, who ruled from 1467 to 1477, such a wise ruler, and cited an example:

> A certain nobleman took an enemy prisoner. The prisoner's wife came to ransom her husband. The nobleman promised to give back the husband on condition

that she would lie with him. The woman was virtuous, yet wished to set her husband free; so she goes and asks her husband whether she should do this thing in order to set him free. The husband wished to be set free and to save his life, so he gives his wife permission. After the nobleman had lain with the wife, he had the husband beheaded the next day and gave him to her as a corpse. She laid the whole case before Duke Charles. He summoned the nobleman and commanded him to marry the woman. When the wedding day was over he had the nobleman beheaded, gave the woman possession of his property, and restored her to honor. Thus he punished the crime in a princely way. Observe: No pope, no jurist, no lawbook could have given him such a decision. It sprang from untrammeled reason, above the law in all the books, and is so excellent that everyone must approve of it and find the justice of it written in his own heart.[28]

Scripture had taught Luther that God ordained secular government to prevent the world from falling into chaos. Ever since the fall of Adam and Eve, every human being has had a basic drive to rule and to dominate, "to be like God" (Gen. 3:5), and therefore everyone lives in violation of the first commandment of the Decalogue, "I am the Lord your God . . . You shall have no other gods before me" (Deut. 5:6–7). Thus princes are ministers of God's law and order, generating repentance and punishing the lawless with the sword. In this sense, then, secular government builds a bridge to spiritual government, which guides the people of God towards eternal life; the church, as the "body of Christ," is its spearhead, as it were. God has provided secular government to all people, even non-Christians, but he has given his spiritual government only to his own people, the people of Israel in the Old Testament and the people of the new Israel in the New Testament.

In 1523 Luther was quite optimistic about the relationship between God's secular and spiritual governments. He contended that Christians should be able to live by the apostolic injunction to obey secular authorities (Rom. 13:1, 1 Pet. 2:13–14) as well as living according to the will of Christ stated in the Sermon on the Mount. Christians should be able to endure the tensions between God and his creation. On the one hand, there is the universal power of God's kingdom, wooing his creatures back from Adam's original sin to eternal fellowship with himself. On the other hand, there is the cosmic force of Satan offering the continual temptation to become idolatrous. Both are intersected, as it were, by God's two specific governments, secular and spiritual. The secular government battles the kingdom of Satan with law and order; the spiritual government nourishes Christians with Word and sacrament.

But this view of life—two kingdoms and two governments—was severely tested after 1523. One of Luther's political allies, Francis of Sickingen, interpreted the reformer's view to justify German nationalism and thus rid Germany of papal influence. Sickingen hoped to achieve his goals by restoring the Estate of German Knights, whose influence had been eroded by the emperor, the pope, and the bishops. But when Sickingen and the German Knights staged an uprising against the Archbishop of Trier in the spring of 1523, they were defeated easily, and Sickingen lost his life in the final battle. Luther had been pleased by Sickingen's support of the reform movement, but after 1523 he denounced him as one of the *Schwärmer* who tend to become heretics or rebels and thus succumb to Satan.[29]

The uprising of the peasants in 1525 angered Luther even more. Initially, he warned both princes and peasants not to seek justice by either tyrannical oppression or political rebellion, but he soon confined his attack to the cause of the peasants because they called themselves a "Christian Association" (*Christliche Vereinigung*).[30]

> You may do anything that God does not prevent. However, leave the name Christian out of it. Leave the name Christian out of it, I say, and do not use it to cover up your impatient, disorderly, un-Christian undertaking. I shall not let you have that name, but so long as there is a heartbeat in my body, I shall do all I can, through speaking and writing, to take that name away from you.[31]

Too prejudiced and too angry to do otherwise, Luther finally called upon the princes to put down the rebellion by force. After the rebellion was put down, Luther declared:

> I was writing only for rulers who might wish to deal in a Christian or otherwise honest way with their people, to instruct their consciences concerning this matter to the effect that they ought to take immediate action against the bands of rebels both innocent and guilty. And if they struck the innocent, they were not to let their consciences trouble them, since they were by the very act confessing that they were bound to do their duty to God. Afterward, however, if they won, they were to show grace, not only to those whom they considered innocent, but to the guilty as well.[32]

The rulers, of course, did not show grace. Many innocent people were tortured and killed for the glory of feudal law and order. Luther had to learn the tragic lesson that it is very difficult, if not impossible, to achieve the proper distinction between God's two governments during a clash involving different political rights.

After 1525, in a world plagued by political unrest in church and state and by the military drive of the Turks towards the north, Luther became increasingly concerned with the problem of order. He stressed the preservation of law and order through the government of the sword which restrains sin and the government of the Word which promises eternal spiritual righteousness; yet his preoccupation with the Bible occasionally led him into interesting speculations. When he lectured on the Book of Zechariah in 1526, he discovered "four regimens" of God:[33] (1) God's work without any means, that is, God's actions as Creator when he creates, multiplies, and endows his creatures with powers and skills; (2) God's work through angels who inspire human creatures with good ideas and thus preserve people from significant disasters like fires, floods, and pestilence; (3) God's work through apostles and preachers who exercise the ministry of the gospel; and (4) God's work through secular government, which includes the home and family. These four governments represent the three realms of sword, Word, and reason which cooperate with each other as a wedge against the wiles of Satan, who uses heretics and rebels to upset the divine order. Luther emphasized the cooperation between secular government and preaching of the gospel in this view of divine order. Although the government of the sword is the lowest of the four, it serves the gospel by preserving the peace which is the necessary condition for proclaiming the gospel. The gospel ministry, in turn, serves the sword by teaching obedience to secular government.

> The sword and the Word, in turn, serve the angels; for they create opportunities and through peace and prosperity prepare the people so that the angels may all the better approach them and promote their rule. For in the midst of strife and error the angels find it difficult to rule through their reason.[34]

In his later years, Luther stressed reason and common sense (*Vernunft*) as the means of holding the world together against chaos and rebellion. To him marriage, family, natural and civil laws were blessed by God and were the pillars of an orderly creation; parents, educators, businessmen, jurists, and politicians were meant to exercise their calling for the sake of justice and equity in a world destined to be transformed into a new creation at the end of time. That is why Luther could offer the blunt advice to parents that bright students should become lawyers rather than preachers. "For in the preaching office Christ does the whole thing, by his Spirit, but in the worldly kingdom men must act on the basis of reason—wherein the laws also have their origin—for God has subjected temporal rule and all of physical life to reason (Gen. 2[:15])."[35] Luther no longer saw secular government as just a divinely instituted restraint on sin and evil. Instead, he regarded it as part of God's creation, like marriage. Using King David as an example, in his 1534 exposition of Ps. 101:5 ("I destroy him who secretly maligns his neighbor"), Luther stated:

> The spiritual government or authority should direct the people vertically toward God that they may do right and be saved; just so the secular government should direct the people horizontally toward one another, seeing to it that body, property, honor, wife, child, house, home, and all manner of goods remain in peace and security and are blessed on earth. God wants the government of the world to be a symbol of true salvation and of His kingdom of heaven, like a pantomime or a mask.[36]

In this connection, Luther could even speak of three regimens or hierarchies: the family, secular government, and the church, "God's own home and city."[37]

According to Luther, there is a natural connection between God's creation of the world and its redemption through Christ. There is a kind of law and order in nature from which sinful human beings can learn since people, not animals or plants, are the real problem in creation.[38] The descendants of Adam have to learn again and again that it is better to do unto others as they wish others would do unto them. In this sense, the golden rule of the Sermon on the Mount is in agreement with natural law, which demands that tyrants be punished by just rulers as part of God's will to preserve law and order in the world.[39] God holds the world together by disclosing his will through both secular and spiritual governments. These two ways of disclosure are "masks" (larvae) behind which God remains hidden, since total disclosure would terrify his creatures. Christians find themselves "facing God" (coram Deo) even when they are "facing the world" (coram mundo), because the Redeemer of the world is also its Creator.[40]

Discernment of the difference between God's secular and spiritual government is part of the discernment of the difference between law and gospel. What God demands in the Decalogue, in natural law, and through secular government must be carefully distinguished from what he offers as salvation from the sin of Adam in Word, sacrament, and response to prayer. The discernment of the difference between Christ and Caesar, in particular, belongs to the foundation of Christian ethics. Luther had dealt with the subject as early as 1517, but returned to it in a variety of contexts. How to be a disciple of Christ and a citizen of Caesar—that is an enduring problem. Luther told his congregation, in a sermon on the Sermon on the Mount (Matt. 5:38ff. "An eye for an eye . . ."):

> There is no getting around it, a Christian has to be a secular person of some sort.
> As regards his own person, according to his life as a Christian, he is in subjection
> to no one but Christ, without any obligation either to the emperor or to any
> other man. But at least outwardly, according to his body and property, he is
> related by subjection and obligation to the emperor, inasmuch as he occupies
> some office or station in life or has a house and home, a wife and children; for all
> these are things that pertain to the emperor.[41]

THE ROLE OF SECULAR GOVERNMENT

What Luther called "secular authority" (Obrigkeit) encompassed the personal authority of princes, whom Luther regarded as the guardians and embodiments of divinely instituted government for the sake of peace and order in God's creation. His view of politics was significantly influenced by his experiences with the rulers of Electoral Saxony: Frederick (1486–1525), whom Luther never met but with whom he frequently corresponded, using the court chaplain George Spalatin as go-between; Frederick's brother John (1525–32), who was a committed friend of Luther's reform movement; and his son John Frederick (1532–47), who regarded Luther as his "spiritual father."[42] Luther was quite aware of abuses perpetrated by secular authority elsewhere in Europe, but based his picture of a Christian ruler on Elector Frederick "the Wise."

In 1523, Luther listed four basic characteristics of a wise ruler: (1) "he must give consideration and attention to his subjects, and really devote himself to it";[43] (2) "he must be aware of the high and mighty (the "big wheels," *grosse Hansen*) and of his counselors, and so conduct himself toward them that he despises none, but also trusts none enough to leave everything to him";[44] (3) "he must take care to deal justly with evildoers";[45] and (4) "a prince must act in a Christian way toward his God also; that is, he must subject himself to Him in entire confidence and pray for wisdom to rule well."[46]

Luther was convinced that good and just government is anchored in the biblical view that both those who rule and those who are ruled belong together, forming God's "community" (*Gemeinde*) on earth. "For He has made, and makes, all communities," he stated in his commentary on Ps. 82:1 ("God has taken His place in the divine council; in the midst of the gods He holds judgment").

> He still brings them together, feeds them, lets them grow, blesses and preserves them, gives them fields and meadows, cattle, water, air, sun and moon, and everything they have, even body and life, as it is written (Gen. 1:29). For what have we, and what has all the world, that does not come unceasingly from Him?[47]

When a ruler is aware of his dependence upon God, he is a jewel and a treasure, enriching the ministry of the gospel which is God's most essential work on earth. In this sense, the Bible calls just rulers "gods" because they are "partakers of His divine majesty and help Him to do divine and superhuman works."[48] God has endowed some of these rulers with special gifts so that they become clearly visible embodiments of his wisdom and grace. Such people can be found throughout the history of the world and include Christians, Jews, pagans, and even politicians, who are generally not very trustworthy. They have "a special star before God," as Luther explained in his commentary on Ps. 101:1 ("I will sing of mercy and justice and sing praises to Thee, O Lord").

> These He teaches Himself and raises them up as He would have them. They are also the ones who have smooth sailing on earth and so-called good luck and success. Whatever they undertake prospers, and even if all the world were to work against it, it would still be accomplished without hindrance. For God, who puts it into their heart and stimulates their intelligence and courage, also puts it

into their hands that it must come to pass and must be carried out; that was the case with Samson, David, Jehoiada, and others. He occasionally provides such men not only among His own people but also among the godless and the heathen. . . . In Persia He raised up King Cyrus; in Greece, the nobleman Themistocles and Alexander the Great; among the Romans, Augustus, Vespasian, and others.[49]

Rulers generally represent God on earth by keeping the peace which is constantly threatened by the "original sin" of rebellion against God. That is why Luther instructed his people to view their rulers as "fathers" who embody the paternal authority of God on earth. To him this is the essential meaning of the Fourth Commandment ("You shall honor your father and mother"). "Because this commandment is disregarded," he wrote in his Large Catechism, "God terribly punishes the world; hence there is no longer any civil order, peace, or respect for authority."[50]

Luther favored the political status quo, that is, medieval feudal territorialism in the context of a monarchy, so he made no proposals concerning the best form of secular government; whatever is the most reasonable way to govern is the best way. "For this reason nothing is taught in the Gospel about how it [secular government] is to be maintained and regulated," he declared in his commentary on Ps. 101:5 ("I destroy him who secretly maligns his neighbor"),

> except that the Gospel bids people honor it and not oppose it. Therefore the heathen can speak and teach about this very well, as they have done. And, to tell the truth, they are far more skillful in such matters than the Christians.[51]

Ultimately, however, Luther favored rulers whose reasonable government was enlightened by faith. While reason is able to provide a just administration of wise laws, faith adds a healthy distrust of merely human power. Luther's commentary on Ps. 127:1 ("Unless the Lord builds the house, those who build it labor in vain") stressed this difference. Faith in God shields a statesman against the arrogance of power as well as against despair when human policies fail.[52] That is why, Luther argued, rulers ought to be Christians, although he was quite skeptical about a purely Christian government exemplified in the territorial rule of bishops. He nevertheless favored Christians in government, since they ought to know the limitations of secular power rather than being preoccupied with themselves and their own authority. Christians should be able to discern better than anyone else the differences between legalism and justice as well as between law and love. For example, Luther was angry with the princes for continuing their persecution of peasants after the uprising in 1525. He told them that noblemen who shed innocent blood and robbed the defeated were crude Germans behaving like swine and senseless beasts. "The law ought to yield, and justice should take its place," he wrote in his treatise on the salvation of soldiers in 1526:

For the law matter of factly says, "Rebellion is punishable with death; it is the *crimen lese maiestatis,* a sin against the rulers [in Roman and feudal law]." But justice says, "Yes, dear law, it is as you say; but it can happen that two men do similar acts with differing motives in their hearts. Judas, for example, kissed Christ in the garden. Outwardly this was a good work, but his heart was evil. . . . Peter sat down by the fire with the servants of Annas and warmed himself with the godless, and that was not good. Now if we were to apply the law strictly, Judas would have to be a good man and Peter a rascal; but Judas' heart was evil and Peter's was good; therefore justice in this case must correct the law.[53]

The same wisdom is to be applied in the case of war. No one should start a war; war is justified only when it is lawful self-defense:

We must distinguish between wars that someone begins because that is what he wants to do and does before anyone else attacks him, and those wars that are provoked when an attack is made by someone else. The first kind can be called wars of desire; the second, wars of necessity. The first kind are of the devil; God does not give good fortune to the man who wages that kind of war. The second kind are human disasters; God help in them![54]

Luther added that since all wars are disastrous, it is better to seek peace by negotiation, in accordance with Deut. 20:10–20; and pastors must always admonish rulers to seek peace by all means before waging war, since a ruler's primary duty is to protect his subjects from destruction. In his treatise "On War Against the Turk," which was addressed to Philip of Hesse, Luther wrote:

We must . . . urge them with continual preaching and exhortation, and lay it heavily upon their consciences that it is their duty to God not to let their subjects perish so terribly, and that they commit serious sin when they are not mindful of their office and do not use all their power to bring counsel and help to those who should live, with body and goods, under their protection and who are bound to them by oaths of homage.[55]

Should negotiations fail or be totally impossible, as was the case with the Turks, then princes must wage defensive wars. However, if they fight merely for personal gain, as was the case in the feud between Elector John Frederick and Duke Maurice of Saxony in 1542, they must be warned that God does not condone such violence; and Luther solemnly summoned these princes to maintain the peace in a letter dated 7 April 1542.[56] Luther asserted that ministers of the gospel must sometimes remind ministers of the sword of the limitations of their power.

Faithful preaching of the gospel creates appropriate attitudes towards secular government, be it a call to be obedient or a call to be critical, which is why Luther admonished parents to have their children trained well for the difficult tasks of administering both the Word of God and the power of the sword. "Peace, the greatest of earthly goods, in which all other temporal goods are included, is really a fruit of true preaching," Luther declared in his sermon on schooling in 1530:

> For where the preaching is right, there war and discord and bloodshed do not come; but where the preaching is not right, it is no wonder that there is war, or at least constant unrest and the desire to fight and to shed blood.[57]

Luther's biblical model of a wise prince was King David, who combined most extraordinarily the ministries of the Word and of the sword. In his commentary on Psalm 101, he wrote:

> Let anyone who can, follow David's example, and do his best with the ability that the grace of God gives him. Nobody will be able to do it as well as David anyway. He easily has the advantage over all kings and lords, because he did it so well. But everyone can at least be careful not to join that group to which the murderous kings and princes, or, as Psalm 2:2 calls them, the enemies of God and of Christ belong, and not to help or support the schismatic spirits in seducing souls and shedding the innocent blood of righteous teachers and Christians. He will also have toil and trouble enough preserving the preachers and the Word of God in the land, especially in our times.[58]

RESISTANCE

Although Luther has been depicted as a staunch defender of the political status quo, if not a "princely hireling," there is sufficient evidence to show that he did exercise and teach what has been called "the right to resist secular government" (*Widerstandsrecht*).[59] For example, he offended Elector Frederick when he publicly condemned the salvific power of indulgences associated with the veneration of relics. The Ninety-five Theses were posted on the eve of All Saints Day 1517, while Frederick was exhibiting his impressive collection of more than seventeen thousand relics, the prayerful viewing of which by visitors would earn them nearly one hundred twenty-eight thousand years relief from purgatory.[60] Frederick was wise enough to neither renounce his respect for traditions like the veneration of relics nor commit himself openly to Luther's cause—even though his actions seem to indicate his support.[61] Luther himself made it quite clear that he and his cause did not seek the protection of his prince. He disobeyed orders to stay at the Wartburg and rode to Wittenberg—in disguise—to assess the damage done by the fanatic "Zwickau prophets," writing to Frederick on 5 March 1522:

> I am going to Wittenberg under a far higher protection than the Elector's. I have no intention of asking Your Electoral Grace for protection. Indeed I think I shall protect Your Electoral Grace more than you are able to protect me. And if I thought that Your Electoral Grace could and would protect me, I should not go.

The sword ought not and cannot help a matter of this kind. God alone must do it—and without the solicitude and co-operation of men. . . . And since I have the impression that Your Electoral Grace is still quite weak in faith, I can by no means regard Your Electoral Grace as the man to protect and save me.[62]

Banned by the church and declared seditious by the imperial diet, Luther nevertheless asserted the right of freedom of faith and of conscience. Even "heresy can never be restrained by force," he declared in his first systematic treatment of the limitations of secular government in 1523:

One will have to tackle the problem in some other way, for heresy must be opposed and dealt with otherwise than with the sword. Here God's Word must do the fighting. If it does not succeed, certainly the temporal power will not succeed either, even if it were to drench the world in blood.[63]

In any clash between freedom of faith and the tyranny of a ruler, a Christian is bound by the apostolic injunction in Acts 5:29—"We must obey God rather than men." However, Luther held that the result of such obedience to God is suffering rather than violent resistance.

Should he [the ruler] seize your property on account of this and punish such disobedience, then blessed are you; thank God that you are worthy to suffer for the sake of the divine word. Let him rage, fool that he is; he will meet his judge. For I tell you, if you fail to withstand him, if you give in to him and let him take away your faith and your books, you have truly denied God.[64]

Ultimately, the question of resistance to tyrannical government is the question of the proper distinction between the First Commandment and the Fourth. As Luther put it, in a lecture on Gen. 27:5–10 (the conflict between Esau and Jacob):

If the government tolerates me when I teach the Word, I hold it in honor and regard it with all respect as my superior. But if it says: "Deny God; cast the Word aside," then I no longer acknowledge it as the government. In the same way one must render obedience to one's parents . . . . God wants us to deny ourselves and our life in the Second Table if it is contrary to the First. But if they are in agreement, then reverence for parents is reverence for God. If, on the other hand, they conflict with each other, then an exception is necessary.[65]

Luther, however, opposed any revolution against government. He was convinced that when either Christians or non-Christians use rebellion as a means to advance their cause—as the rebellious peasants did in 1525—they confuse the internal freedom of conscience with the external order which secular government is to uphold in God's stead. In such a case rulers are obliged to use the sword in order to eliminate sedition.[66] Luther advised Christians to emigrate rather than fight when threatened by persecution. He told the restless peasants, "Thus you permit men to wrong you and drive you away; and yet, at the same time, you do not permit men to take the gospel from you or keep it from you."[67] Heretics like the Anabaptists should be treated the same way; rulers should banish them from their lands, even though they could be put to death if they remained obstinate.[68]

After the Diet of Augsburg in 1530, Luther had to confront the question of armed resistance to Catholics on the part of Lutheran princes who feared imperial and territorial moves against them. When Elector John Frederick asked for Luther's reactions to the formation of the Lutheran Smalcald League, Luther advised against allying the gospel to weapons. "The devil would like such a development," he wrote to the elector on 6 March 1530, "but may God preserve us from it and graciously help us."[69] At the same time, however, Luther seemed open to the idea of armed resistance, telling his "dear German people" in a "Warning" published in April 1531 that the injunction "We must obey God rather than men" may justify a defensive war waged by territorial princes against the emperor. But he was not yet ready to advocate such a war.

> I do not wish to incite or spur anyone to war or rebellion or even self-defense, but solely to peace. But if the papists—our devil—refuse to keep the peace and, impenitently raging against the Holy Spirit with their persistent abominations, insist on war, and thereby get their heads bloodied or even perish, I want to witness publicly here that this was not my doing, nor did I give any cause for it.[70]

Although Luther stuck to his basic position that the gospel did not need to be defended by military means, he and his Wittenberg colleagues did not object when Saxon jurists concluded that armed resistance against the emperor is justified when there is evidence beyond reasonable doubt that he has exceeded the limits of his power. A memorandum the jurists prepared for Elector John Frederick in late October 1530 argued: (1) that any secular authority may be resisted if that authority is exercised with manifest injustice or mixes into questions of faith; and (2) that proper juridical procedure requires the execution of a sentence to be postponed if there is an appeal to a higher court, but Emperor Charles V had attempted to restore the old religion by force and disregarded the Protestant appeal for a general council to debate matters of faith. Therefore he had exceeded the limits of his authority and violated just laws, and armed resistance against him was justified.[71]

At a special meeting in Torgau, 26-28 October 1530, Luther and his Wittenberg colleagues at least expanded their earlier position regarding obedience to secular government when, in their response to the memorandum, they stated:

> Since we have always taught that one should acknowledge civil laws, submit to them, and respect their authority, inasmuch as the gospel does not militate against civil laws, we cannot invalidate from Scripture the right of men to defend

themselves even against the emperor in person, or anyone acting in his name. . . . In previously teaching that resistance to governmental authorities is altogether forbidden, we were unaware that this right has been granted by the government's own laws, which we have diligently taught are to be obeyed at all times.[72]

Thus Luther's "just war" theory, based on the idea that self-defense belongs to creaturely existence, seems suddenly to have encompassed theories of legal justice derived from existing statutes of criminal and civil law.

Relations between Protestants and Catholics continued to deteriorate, and war between them seemed inevitable. In 1538, Luther and the Wittenberg theologians told the leaders of the Protestant Smalcald League, Philip of Hesse and Elector John Frederick, that armed resistance against the emperor is a clear case of self-defense. In an "Opinion" (*Gutachten*), the Wittenbergers declared:

This is our answer: if there is an [imperial] interdict [*Acht*] against one or more allies in the [Smalcald] League, then the enemy has begun a war and those who are attacked may engage in a defensive war, according to natural and written laws. The gospel confirms this office of secular government and their natural law.[73]

Luther himself summarized his position on armed resistance during a public disputation at Wittenberg University on 9 May 1539. Using Matt. 19:21 ("If you would be perfect, go, sell what you possess and give to the poor") as his text, Luther subtitled the disputation:

Concerning the three divine hierarchies or arch-powers, namely the Christian church, secular government or the policing power, and the civil or family regimen [*Haushaltung*]—that the papacy cannot be found among any of these divine orders and is a public enemy and persecutor of these divine orders.[74]

After repeating his position that one must distinguish properly between spiritual and secular government, Luther admonished private citizens to endure political persecution without resistance in obedience to the injunction "sell what you possess"; but he reminded public citizens, the princes, to exercise their God-given right to defend themselves against unlawful attacks. Just as one is permitted to use violence in repelling a murderer attacking one's neighbor, so are princes justified in using armed resistance to repel the emperor, who has gone beyond the limitations of his office by threatening to enforce the pope's wishes in Germany. The emperor's confusion of secular with spiritual government reflects the rule of Satan, the apocalyptic tyrant of the endtime.

If the pope wants to incite people to wage war, he must be resisted as a raging and mad changeling [*Wechselbalg*] or a bear-wolf [*Bärwolf*]. For he is not a bishop, heretic, prince, or tyrant, but the animal of abomination, in accordance with Daniel 1 [11:31]. That is why no one should be fooled when seeing princes, kings, or emperors on the pope's side, and think that he persuaded them to serve the Christian church by fighting for him. . . . He who defends robbers and murderers by fighting on their side should know that such fighting deserves eternal damnation.[75]

Yet Luther made it clear that he was not calling for a crusade against Rome as the enemy of Christendom. Rather, he wanted secular authority to check the power of the pope. "I take the sword from the pope, not from the emperor," he remarked at table, "for the pope should be neither a prince nor a tyrant."[76] He became increasingly convinced that the confusing constellation of events in Germany was a sign of God's anger and foreshadowed the end of the world. He therefore admonished the clergy to pray hard and not expect political miracles. "The devil does not sleep, the Turks do not wait, and the papists do not repent."[77] Luther was growing old and could no longer be sure that God was taking sides, that is, favoring Protestants over Catholics. There was so much confusion that only God could know what would be best for the life of the gospel in Germany.

Luther was not always consistent in his views of the proper distinction between Christ and Caesar, between spiritual and secular government. Nevertheless, in his role as pastor he always tried to proclaim the sovereignty of God over against all earthly authority and power. He reiterated that while Christians are on earth they must recognize the divine institution of secular government as the principal guardian of law and order in God's creation; when persecuted, Christians are called to live a cruciform life without rebelling against tyranny. Only a divinely instituted secular government may legitimately check tyrants by armed resistance. Thus "lower estates" like territorial princes may wage war against the tyranny of "higher estates" like the emperor. Luther saw no justification whatsoever for a revolution of the common people against their rulers. He did not share the political convictions of a later time when democratic ideals made every citizen a "prince," thus endowing every citizen of a given territory with public political responsibilities.

To this extent, any debate about the "two-kingdoms ethic" must take into account the radical difference between the sixteenth century and later periods. Only later was political revolution justified for the sake of justice.[78] In the final analysis, Luther was consistent in saying no to any attempt to identify the secular with the divine. In his desire to preserve his own creation, God sees to it that law and order are preserved in the face of injustice by rulers and rebellion by subjects. One must let God be God and pray for *his* peace.

For where there is no government, or where government is not held in honor, there can be no peace. Where there is no peace, no one can keep his life or anything else, in the face of another's outrage, thievery, robbery, violence, and wickedness. Much less will there be room to teach God's Word and to rear children in the fear of God and His discipline (Eph. 6:4). . . . But God Himself will punish wicked rulers and impose statutes and laws upon them. He will be Judge and Master over them. He will find them out, better than anyone else can, as indeed He has done since the beginning of the world.[79]

7

THE GOSPEL AND ISRAEL

I wish and ask that our rulers who have Jewish subjects exercise a sharp mercy toward these wretched people . . . to see whether this might not help (though it is doubtful). They must act like a good physician who, when gangrene has set in, proceeds without mercy to cut, saw, and burn flesh, veins, bone, and marrow. Such a procedure must also be followed in this instance. Burn down their synagogues . . . force them to work, and deal harshly with them, as Moses did in the wilderness, slaying three thousand lest the whole people perish. They surely do not know what they are doing; moreover, as people possessed, they do not wish to know it, hear it, or learn it. Therefore it would be wrong to be merciful and confirm them in their conduct. If this does not help we must drive them out like mad dogs, so that we do not become partakers of their abominable blasphemy and all their other vices and thus merit God's wrath and be damned with them. ("On the Jews and Their Lies," 1543. WA 53:541.24–542.2. LW 47:292)

STRUGGLE WITH HARDENED HEARTS

When you lay eyes on or think of a Jew you must say to yourself: Alas, that mouth which I there behold has cursed and execrated and maligned every Saturday my dear Lord Jesus Christ, who has redeemed me with His precious blood. . . . If I were to eat, drink, or talk with such a devilish mouth, I would eat or drink myself full of devils by the dish or cupful; just as I surely make myself a cohort of all the devils that dwell in the Jews and that deride the precious blood of Christ. May God preserve me from this![1]

Outbursts such as this one, combined with his demand to rid Germany of Jews, give credence to the notion that Luther was the father of German anti-Semitism—the anti-Semitism which produced Hitler's policies and led to the extermination of over six million European Jews during the Nazi era. When confronted with Luther's violent attacks on the Jews as the most stubborn enemies of the Christian gospel, especially with the 1543 treatise "On the Jews and Their Lies," even the most apologetic Luther interpreters wince. "One could wish that Luther had died before ever this tract was written."[2]

Some historians of modern Germany excoriate Luther, "this towering but erratic genius, this savage anti-Semite and hater of Rome, who combined in his tempestuous character so many of the best and worst qualities of the German."[3]

Was the anti-Semitic Luther the same Luther who had found so much consolation in the Old Testament when he yearned for peace with God during the early years of his career as a priest-professor? Had he changed his mind? Or were these violent outbursts against the Jews part and parcel of a theology which vehemently rejected any kind of attempt to denigrate the unrivaled lordship of Christ as the one and only Mediator between God and his sinful creature? Luther also attacked papists and *Schwärmer* as traitors to the gospel which proclaims access to God through Christ alone. When he moved on to the Jews, one could argue, Luther combined his theological reflections with the anti-Semitism prevalent in his day.

The roots of anti-Semitism reach far back into time. One of the most revered fathers of the Western church, Augustine, had argued that the murderous clash between Cain and Abel foreshadowed the perduring enmity between Christians and Jews. Jews had become the scapegoats for many cultural sins: ritual murder, kidnaping of children, contamination of water, and many other atrocities vividly portrayed in popular history books.[4] Anti-Jewish legislation led to the expulsion of Jews from many regions in the Holy Roman Empire, and the Spanish Inquisition initiated a cruel persecution of Jews at the end of the fourteenth century.[5] German territories were no exception: Jews were massacred in 350 places and 140 communities during an outburst of anti-Semitism in 1348 and 1349.[6] Both friends and foes of Luther seemed agreed that, since they had refused to become Christians, Jews were enemies of society, "cunning, false, perjured, thievish, vindictive, and traitorous."[7] Yet why did Luther concur with this attitude towards the Jews when he so vehemently differed from prevailing attitudes in matters of Christian faith and morals? Was the old reformer more critical and less patient than the young professor? How did Luther view the relationship between the gospel and Israel?

Luther's view of Israel was guided by basic distinctions between the Old Testament as the Holy Scripture of the "faithful synagogue," the primitive church of Christ's apostles, and the Judaism which embodies the "hardened heart of Pharaoh" (Exod. 14:4).[8] As early as 1513–15, in the first lectures on Psalms, Luther identified the Jews as self-righteous people who have treacherous tongues and do mischief against the godly. They are the ones whom "God will break . . . down forever" (Ps. 52:5). He listed four kinds of destruction:

> So also the Jews were destroyed: For the synagogue came to an end and fell, never to rise again in a way that it would be a synagogue. Second, they were

plucked from their land and scattered throughout every land. Third, they were removed, namely, from this life, through various forms of death. Fourth, they were uprooted from the olive tree and the church, from faith and a true understanding of Scripture.[9]

According to Luther, the true understanding of Scripture, especially of the unity between the Old and the New Testaments, is given when the interpreter believes that the Old Testament prophecies about a Messiah are fulfilled in the New Testament testimonies regarding Jesus as the Christ. In this sense, the Old Testament is a "prefiguration" (*figura*) and "foreshadowing" (*umbra*) of the New Testament.[10] As Luther put it in his exposition of Ps. 77:1 ("I cry aloud to God"):

So when this Psalm is spoken in the person of the faithful synagogue or the primitive church, the church confesses the works of the Lord Christ, by means of which He led it out of the spiritual Egypt, out of the rule of sin and world and devil. Hence the spiritual crucifixion and the plagues of Egypt in a moral sense are here beautifully depicted. First the moral Egypt must be stung and humbled and destroyed, and then, finally, follows the change of the right hand of the Most High. . . . The whole psalm has what the book of Exodus has from the beginning [the liberation from the yoke of self-righteousness].[11]

Luther's polemics against the Jews were grounded in this christological interpretation of the Old Testament. Whenever the Psalms speak of "liars" and "bloodthirsty people," Luther thought of the Jews. Accordingly, he literally applied Ps. 5:6 ("The Lord abhors bloodthirsty and deceitful men") to the Jews:

who called down upon themselves Christ's blood and also killed Him, and are abominable in his blood still. . . . To the present day they pour Christ's blood on themselves while they disparage Him.[12]

Luther sided with Paul, who regarded self-righteousness as the principal reason why God "hardened the heart" of Israel. His lectures on Romans viewed Jews as the primary examples of the universal drive to find pleasure in egotistic pride. In his commentary on Rom. 2:11 ("For God shows no partiality"), he wrote:

The Jews wanted God to act in such a way that He would bestow the good on the Jews only and the evil on the Gentiles only, as if because they were the seed of Abraham, they should automatically be like Abraham in merits. Thus the Jews always strive to make of God a judge who considers the persons.[13]

He asserted that this attitude is shared by heretics and "spiritually conceited people" who feel chosen by God without being ready to pay the price of suffering and tribulation. Yet, he insisted, there is no love of neighbor unless there is the willingness to let the neighbor be equal, if not superior. "Then we will have fulfilled total humility both against God and against man, that is, complete and perfect righteousness."[14]

Luther, therefore, distinguished between a "historical" and a "spiritual" Israel, thereby following Augustine's differentiation between the "letter" and the "spirit" in the interpretation of Scripture. The patriarchs Abraham, Jacob, and Isaac were prime examples of a spiritual Israel which prefigured faith in Christ. They received the promise of becoming the new Israel to be ruled by Jesus, "the seed of Abraham" born of the Virgin Mary. "We ought, therefore, not treat the Jews in so unkindly a spirit," Luther told the young prince John Frederick of Saxony in the "Magnificat" in 1521,

> For there are future Christians among them, and they are turning every day. Moreover, they alone, and not we Gentiles, have this promise, that there shall always be Christians among Abraham's seed, who acknowledge the blessed Seed, who knows how or when?[15]

There was, then, a curious mixture of praise and vituperation in Luther's early reflections on the relationship between the gospel and Israel. Despite the constant pressure of anti-Semitism, he pleaded for toleration of Jews as a first step towards their conversion, for they were, after all, the first people to receive God's promise of salvation. Luther therefore sided with the well-known Hebraist John Reuchlin when he was attacked by a converted Jew, John Pfefferkorn, for his Humanist endeavor to use Hebrew literature, including the Talmud, to achieve a better understanding of the Bible. When in 1514 the Dominicans in Cologne supported Pfefferkorn's call for a burning of Jewish literature, Luther let it be known at the Saxon court, through George Spalatin, that he favored the Humanists' critical scholarship over the Dominicans' prejudices. He declared that ultimately the conversion of the Jews is in the hands of God, and the Roman Inquisition should turn to sinful Christians rather than coerce Jews to convert.[16]

Whereas Luther hoped for a conversion of the Jews during his early days as priest-professor in Wittenberg, he also continued his attacks on them for their obstinate refusal to accept Jesus as the Messiah promised in the Old Testament. For a while, it seemed that the young interpreter of Scripture could live with Paul's view that the "hardening" of Israel was a divine mystery somehow connected with the conversion of the Gentiles (Rom. 11:25). Israel was like a human body under the impact of God's promise. "For just as the members of the flesh are crucified to sin in order that they might thus live to righteousness, so also the Jews had to die with Christ to the law of sin in order that they might rise with Him to the life of grace."[17]

In 1522, Luther became aware of rumors, originating at the Diet of Nuremberg, that he had denied the virgin birth of Jesus and considered Jesus to have been conceived by Joseph. He defended his orthodoxy in a treatise on Jesus Christ as Jew in 1523. Strongly arguing the messiahship of

Jesus on the basis of Scripture, Luther chided the church for being a bad example to the Jews.

> They have dealt with the Jews as if they were dogs rather than human beings; they have done little else than deride them and seize their property. When they baptize them they show them nothing of Christian doctrine or life, but only subject them to popishness and monkery. When the Jews then see that Judaism has such strong support in Scripture, and that Christianity has become a mere babble without reliance on Scripture, how can they possibly compose themselves and become right good Christians?[18]

Luther hoped that fair treatment and good Christian example based on sound biblical teaching would convert many Jews, and to this end he offered arguments from Scripture to show that Jesus was the Messiah the Old Testament had prophesied.

1. Jacob's prophecy to his sons about "the scepter of Judah" belonging to a future king had been fulfilled in the person of Jesus (Gen. 49:10–12). Between the destruction of Jerusalem by the Romans in A.D. 70 and Luther's own time, there had never been a Jewish state ruled by a king. Yet the prophecy referred to a king who would rule over both Jews and Gentiles: Jesus Christ, born a Jew and destined to restore the broken covenant between God and Israel in a new and everlasting covenant ushering in eternal righteousness. Luther found it amazing that Jewish interpreters of Scripture would not agree with such an interpretation.[19]

2. Daniel's prophecy, inspired by the angel Gabriel, about "seventy weeks of years" before the final desolation of Israel also points to the person of Jesus (Dan. 9:24–27). Using the popular year-week interpretation, Luther calculated the resulting 490 years to be the period between the Persian king Cambyses (529–522 B.C.) and the appearance of Christ in his thirtieth year (Luke 3:23). Although these calculations were neither consistent nor precise, Luther found sufficient agreement between Scripture and history to conclude that Daniel spoke of Jesus rather than of anyone else.[20]

3. Still clearer to him were the prophecies of Hag. 2:9 ("The latter splendor of this house shall be greater than the former") and Zech. 8:23 ("In those days ten men of all languages of the Gentiles shall take hold of the robe of a Jew saying, 'We want to go with you'"). These sayings clearly indicated to Luther the greater power of the new Israel, which includes Gentiles under the lordship of Christ.[21]

Luther was convinced that argumentative dialogues between Christians and Jews were better than political decrees ordering their surrender to Christianity or their confinement in ghettos. First they must learn to agree that Jesus was the expected Messiah; then they might be led to believe that Jesus was also the Son of God. "Let them first be suckled with milk, and begin by recognizing this man Jesus as the true Messiah; after that they may drink wine, and learn also that he is true God."[22] He closed the treatise with this advice:

> If we really want to help them, we must be guided in our dealings with them not by papal law but by the law of Christian love. We must receive them cordially, and permit them to trade and work with us, . . . hear our Christian teaching, and witness our Christian life. If some of them should prove stiff-necked, what of it? After all, we ourselves are not all good Christians either.[23]

Luther's own attempts to convert visiting Jews in Wittenberg were not successful. Dialogues based on Old Testament texts about the coming of the Messiah proved to be quite frustrating to both sides. Luther's paternal attitude and Jewish visitors' insistence on the validity of their own interpretations did not mix well. In about the year 1526, three rabbis visited Luther and discussed the messianic passage in Jer. 23:6 ("This is the name by which he will be called: 'The Lord is our righteousness'"). The rabbis refused to apply the passage to Jesus. In a sermon preached later on the same text, Luther said, "They did not stick to the text but tried to escape from it"; the encounter, according to Luther's recollection, ended with the expressed hope for mutual conversion.[24]

There were rumors of Jewish conspiracies and plots to kill Luther, which only increased his suspicion that Jews were afflicted with hardened hearts.[25] Moreover, the news reached Wittenberg of Jewish agitation and efforts to convert Christians in Bohemia and Moravia, which increased Luther's anger. The final straw was his discovery that supporters of his own cause espoused the restoration of the Sabbath rather than Sunday as well as a revival of Jewish laws to improve Christian morality; he attacked these "Sabbatarians" who were "apes of the Jews."[26] By 1537, he changed his mind about the wisdom of tolerating Jews; he supported John Frederick's decree in 1536 prohibiting Jews from settling in Electoral Saxony. In 1537, he refused the request of the most famous leader of German Jews, Rabbi Josel of Rosheim, for support in an effort to gain permission for safe passage through Electoral Saxony. In a letter dated 11 June 1537, Luther told Rabbi Josel that he still favored kind treatment of Jews, "but not so that through my good will and influence they might be strengthened in their error and become more bothersome."[27] A remark he made at table dating from this same period disclosed Luther's anger over Jewish conversion of Christians in Moravia. "Why should these rascals, who injure people in body and property and who withdraw many Christians to their superstitions, be given permission? . . . I'll write this Jew not to return."[28]

Luther summarized his views in an "open letter to a good friend," the Moravian Count Wolfgang Schlick of Falkenau. The letter was published in March of 1538 and responded to two questions: Why is it so difficult to convert Jews? Why should Jewish laws be valid for Christians? Luther answered the first question with a lengthy argument to show that Jews cling to a divine promise which denies Jesus as the Messiah; thus Jews have clung to a lie which has become their abominable sin. Instead of believing the divine promise that the Messiah would come while Israel was still a nation, before the destruction of Jerusalem in A.D. 70, they still expected a Messiah—even though there had not been a Jewish state for fifteen hundred years. Thus, added Luther, "the Jews are slandering God and deceiving themselves when they accuse God of breaking faith and trust with David because he did not send the Messiah in the manner they would have liked and as they prescribe and imagine him to be."[29] Regarding the question of the validity of Jewish laws for Christians, Luther contended that these laws were no longer needed after the coming of the Messiah Jesus. Moreover, he said, Jewish laws died with the priesthood, the Temple, the kingdom, and the worship—all of which require a Jewish state that no longer exists.[30] Only the Decalogue had validity for Luther because of its universality as "natural law," a view he shared with many contemporary theologians. "For even if a Moses had never appeared and Abraham had never been born, the Ten Commandments would have had to rule in all men from the very beginning, as they indeed did and still do."[31] Luther concluded his diatribe with the judgment that the conversion of Jews may have become a hopeless enterprise.

> Since these fifteen hundred years of exile, of which there is no end in sight, nor can there be, do not humble the Jews or bring them to awareness, you may with a good conscience despair of them. For it is impossible that God would leave his people, if they truly were his people, without comfort and prophecy so long.[32]

Since Luther's earlier calls for patience with the Jews had been motivated by the anticipation of increasing numbers of Jewish converts in Reformation territories, the lack of interest on their part to convert convinced him that the reconciliation of Israel with the gospel was God's affair rather than the church's obligation. Luther's hopes for his own kind of improved Jewish-Christian relations had died by 1538. Jews, together with papists and *Schwärmer*, embodied the hardened hearts which God seemingly permitted in order to disclose the enduring struggle between good and evil in the world. The rise of Christian radicals who denied biblical authority and dispensed with sacraments, the revolt of peasants, and the conversions of Christians to Judaism convinced Luther that Satan had invaded the world to do final battle before the endtime. He therefore decided to confine himself to a struggle with the "Judaizers" among Christians—the papists and *Schwärmer* who praised self-righteousness as the means to salvation—rather than dealing with the Jews, who seemed hopelessly entangled in a satanic web of mischief against the Christian gospel. Why add the problem of hardened hearts in the synagogue to the struggle with the "Judaizers" in the church?

SHARP MERCY

But another report from his friend Count Schlick that Jews were still trying to convert Christians in Moravia so incensed Luther that he vented his anger in the treatise which advocated a "final solution" of the Jewish question: "On the Jews and Their Lies." Published in January 1543, the treatise was a response to an allegedly Jewish pamphlet trying to refute Christian claims concerning the Old Testament.[33] The treatise deals with four major concerns:

1. Luther wanted to refute Jewish arguments favoring "Zionism," that is, an emphasis on ethnic pride based on the righteousness of covenantal law and the promise that all Jews would assemble in Israel in anticipation of the Messiah. All this is a "false boasting," according to Luther. Jerusalem was destroyed in A.D. 70, the Jews were dispersed, and Palestine was lost to them. If God had loved them, he would have restored their pride. Instead, he let them suffer, thus showing his wrath against a people who rejected Christ, in fulfillment of Hosea's prophecy, "Call his name Not my people, for you are not my people and I am not your God" (Hos. 1:9). "It sends a shudder of fear through body and soul," Luther said, "for I ask, What will the eternal wrath of God in hell be like toward false Christians and all unbelievers?"[34] He advised his readers not to be surprised at the stubbornness of the Jews, for they had been under God's wrath for too long to be able to comprehend such Christian teachings as the Trinity and the virgin birth. "No human reason nor any human heart will ever grant these things, much less the embittered, venomous, blind heart of the Jews."[35]

Yet, at the same time, Jews want to convince Christians that they are a special people because of their lineage and because of circumcision. Luther labeled such pride the height of self-righteousness. The Jews, he said, are just like the Italians who "fancy themselves the only human beings; they imagine that all other people in the world are non-humans, mere ducks or mice by comparison."[36] According to Luther, it was this ethnic self-righteousness which angered God and made him commission prophets to promise punishment, as Jeremiah did when he announced divine punishment for those "uncircumcised in the heart" (Jer. 9:25–26).[37] But the Jews interpret it to mean that they have divine sanction to punish uncircumcised Gentiles, as the Book of Esther suggests. "The sun has never shone on a more bloodthirsty and vengeful people than they are, who imagine that they are God's people who have been commissioned and commanded to murder and to slay the Gentiles."[38] Again and again Luther cited biblical passages showing the stubbornness and disobedience of Israel.

> A defiled bride, yes, an incorrigible whore and most evil slut with whom God ever had to wrangle, scuffle, and fight. If He chastised and struck them with His Word through the prophets, they contradicted him, killed his prophets, or, like a mad dog, bit the stick with which they were struck.[39]

The Jews, therefore, are an accursed people, surviving only as living examples of God's wrath. They violate their own laws by practicing usury; and they persecute those who try to lead them back to the righteousness of God.[40] To Luther, the Jews were the most vivid examples of a works-righteousness which denies the unmerited grace of God in Christ. Such sinful behavior puts them in the company of Turks, papists, and *Schwärmer,* all of whom "claim to be the church and God's people in accord with their conceit and boast, regardless of the one true faith and the obedience to God's commandments through which alone people become and remain God's children."[41]

2. Luther offered a christological interpretation of the Old Testament in opposition to the Jewish claims based on Scripture that the Messiah had not yet come. Here Luther relied on traditional methods of interpretation, especially those developed by Nicholas of Lyra (1270–1349) and by Paul of Burgos (1351–1435), a Spanish rabbi who had converted to Christianity and had become an archbishop. Both had used rabbinical methods in their Old Testament interpretations to show that Christ was the Messiah foretold in the Jewish Bible. Luther followed their example and cited four passages of the Old Testament as proof texts for the coming of the Messiah: Gen. 49:10 ("the scepter shall not depart from Judah . . . until he comes to whom it belongs"); 2 Sam. 7:12–16 (Nathan's prophecy to David about an offspring whose throne will be established forever); Hag. 2:6–9 (the promise to reconcile all nations, presumably through the Messiah); and Dan. 9:24 (the prophecy concerning seventy weeks, following which an everlasting righteousness would come). Luther used lengthy exegetical arguments to show that all of these texts "prove" that Jesus was the Messiah. He also related his impressions of the work of the three rabbis who had visited him in 1526. He complained that even though he had written letters of recommendation for them, asking "the authorities" (Saxon princes?) to grant them freedom of movement, they had later betrayed his trust by slandering Christ. "Therefore I do not wish to have anything more to do with any Jew," he concluded.[42]

Since the Jews pervert Scripture by denying Jesus as the promised Messiah, they cannot be trusted, according to Luther; therefore whatever is said of them may be true: they contaminate wells, kidnap children, and are in league with the devil.[43] Luther repeatedly used detailed exegetical work to refute the "lie" that the Messiah was still to be expected. This lie is anchored in a confusion of what is divine and what is human, he asserted. True followers of Moses—that is, Christians—are able to make proper distinctions between "human ordinances" and the divine grace disclosed in Christ, but the Jews are unable to do so.

> In brief, all their life and all their deeds, whether they eat, drink, sleep, wake, stand, walk, dress, undress, fast, bathe, pray, or praise, are so sullied with

rabbinical, foul ordinances and unbelief, that Moses can no longer be recognized among them. This corresponds to the situation of the papacy in our day, in which Christ and his Word can hardly be recognized because of the great vermin of human ordinances.[44]

3. Luther vented his anger against what he conceived to be Jewish polemics against Christianity, especially "lies against persons" like Jesus, Mary, and believers in general. When Jews and papists are unable to refute the gospel, he contended, they charge that Christ was a devilish sorcerer whose mother Mary was a whore.[45] They use plays on words to make their point:

> When a Christian hears them utter the word "Jesu," as will happen occasionally when they are obliged to speak to us, he assumes that they are using the name Jesus. But in reality they have the numeral letters Jesu in mind, that is, the numeral 316 in the blasphemous word *Vorik*. And when they utter the word "Jesu" in their prayer, they spit on the ground three times in honor of our Lord and of all Christians, moved by their great love and devotion. But when they are conversing with one another they say, *Deleatur nomen eius*, which means in plain words, "May God exterminate his name," or "May all the devils take him."[46]

Luther made use of a popular collection of anti-Semitic polemics, compiled by Anthony Margaritha and published in Augsburg under the title *The Whole Jewish Faith (Der ganze jüdische Glaube)* in 1530. Margaritha was a Jew who had converted to Lutheranism in 1522, leaving his prominent rabbinic family. Much of what he reported to be anti-Christian Jewish polemics turned out to be false; he was jailed and eventually expelled from Augsburg when the Jewish community complained about his slanderous statements. Nevertheless, Luther enjoyed reading Margaritha's stories at table and cited them whenever he dealt with the Jewish question.[47] One of these items was that Jews considered Jesus the product of adultery—the whore Mary had relations with a blacksmith—and therefore Luther called for stern measures against the people who so abused the toleration extended to them by Christians. Since Jews had slandered the holiest of holy in Christendom, Jesus, Mary, and the Trinity, they should be deprived of Christian mercy.

> We are at fault in not slaying them. Rather we allow them to live freely in our midst despite all their murdering, cursing, blaspheming, lying, and defaming; we protect and shield their synagogues, houses, life, and property. In this way we make them lazy and secure and encourage them to fleece us boldly or our money and goods, as well as to mock and deride us, with a view to overcoming us, killing us all for such a great sin, and robbing us of all our property (as they daily pray and hope).[48]

4. Luther offered this "sincere advice" to political leaders, although most

princes who heard of the advice did not heed it. His call for seven moves to be undertaken against the Jews disclosed a strong alliance between medieval anti-Semitism and his own views. He had concluded that since conversion was no longer possible, "sharp mercy" (*scharfe Barmherzigkeit*) must be practiced.

> Since they live among us, we dare not tolerate their conduct, now that we are aware of their lying and reviling and blaspheming. If we do, we become sharers in their lies, cursing, and blasphemy. Thus we cannot extinguish the unquenchable fire of divine wrath, of which the prophets speak, nor can we convert the Jews. With prayer and the fear of God we must practice a sharp mercy to see whether we might save at least a few from the glowing flames. We dare not avenge ourselves. Vengeance a thousand times worse than we could wish them already has them by the throat.[49]

Luther then advised that: (1) synagogues and schools be burned down and eradicated; (2) private Jewish homes be torn down in favor of communal, supervised settlements; (3) all Jewish religious literature be confiscated in order to punish blasphemy; (4) rabbis be forbidden to teach on pain of losing their lives; (5) safe conduct be denied to all so that Judaism cannot spread; (6) expropriated Jewish funds be used for a common treasure from which converted Jews would receive support, otherwise usury would flourish; and (7) Jews be put to work in order to cure their laziness and their temptation to earn a living without "the sweat of their brow" (Gen. 3:19). In sum, Luther wanted to make certain that contact between Jews and Christians be kept at a minimum, if there were to be any at all. It would be best, Luther concluded his lengthy advice, if Jews were expelled from Christian countries as was done in France, England, Spain, and in several German regions. "For, as we have heard, God's anger with them is so intense that gentle mercy [*sanfte Barmherzigkeit*] will only tend to make them worse and worse, while sharp mercy will reform them but little. Therefore, in any case, away with them!"[50]

His advice to pastors and congregations was similar: they should segregate themselves from Jews because Jews endanger Christian teaching and life; pastors should remind political authorities of their obligation "to force the Jews to work, to forbid usury, and to check their blasphemy and cursing."[51] If such a reminder should go unheeded, Christ's advice is to be followed by shaking the dust off one's shoes and saying, "We are innocent of your blood." [Matt. 10:14][52] On the whole, he recommended that ecclesiastical authorities should act in concert with secular government in implementing these four steps: (1) pastors and congregations should cooperate in the burning down of synagogues; (2) they should make certain that Jewish religious literature is destroyed, including the Jewish Bible; (3) they should deny public worship to Jews; and (4) Jews should "be forbidden to utter the name of God within our hearing" because they speak only blasphemy.[53]

If I had power of them, I would assemble their scholars and their leaders and order them, on pain of losing their tongues down to the root, to convince us Christians within eight days of the truth of their assertions and to prove this blasphemous lie against us to the effect that we worship more than the one true God [alleged polemics against the Trinity]. If they succeeded, we would all on the self-same day become Jews and be circumcised. If they failed, they should stand ready to receive the punishment they deserve for such shameful, malicious, pernicious, and venomous lies.[54]

Contemporary Jews as well as Christians were shocked by these anti-Semitic outbursts. Rabbi Josel of Rosheim sadly declared, after reading the treatise, "Never before has a *Gelehrter,* a scholar, advocated such tyrannical and outrageous treatment of our poor people."[55] Philip Melanchthon, Andreas Osiander, Henry Bullinger, and other reformers who respected Luther's leadership in the reform movement were dismayed.[56] But Luther continued his hate-filled outbursts.

AFTERSHOCKS

As an expert in Scripture, especially in Old Testament studies, Luther could not read rabbinical interpretations of the Bible without attempting to refute them. Immediately after his main blast against the Jews and their "lies," he composed two other treatises: one was against the rabbinical understanding of "the *Shem Hamphoras* and of the genealogy of Christ" published in March 1543, and the other was an exegesis of 2 Sam. 23:7, "the last words of David" published in August 1543.[57] Both treatises were intended to demonstrate the superiority of Christian interpretations of the Old Testament over rabbinical ones.

Shem Hamphoras ("The name of the Lord is exposed") was the legend of a secret formula inscribed on the stone supporting the ark of the covenant in the Temple of Jerusalem. Luther read the *Shem Hamphoras* legend in a fourteenth-century book, *Victory Against the Jews (Victoria adversus Hebraeos)*, compiled by Salvagus Porchetus, a Carthusian monk from Genoa who died around 1315. The book had been reprinted in Paris in 1520. Luther translated the eleventh chapter of part 1, a rendering of supposedly Jewish accounts relating how Jesus abused the formula in order to perform the miracles that made people believe he was the Messiah.[58] The story has all the features of polemical medieval legends: Jesus appears in Israel at the time of Helena, the mother of Constantine the Great (ca. A.D. 260–340 ?). When he came upon the secret formula in the Temple, knowing it would enable him to use divine powers, he copied it on a piece of paper and hid it inside his leg in a self-inflicted wound—which would heal immediately, of course, since he now knew the formula for healing. Temple priests had placed two bronze dogs on two pillars to guard the stone with the formula and to so scare intruders that they would forget the formula while trying to escape from the dogs. Although the dogs succeeded in making Jesus forget the formula when he escaped them, he had tricked them by hiding the formula in his leg, thus enabling him to use it again. Once in possession of the formula, Jesus assembled disciples, did miracles, and seduced many people into following him. When the rabbis complained to Queen Helena, she tried in vain to kill him. Finally, Jewish wise men hanged him on a stump of cabbage, and cabbages have grown in the sanctuary ever since.

Most scholars of his time would not have bothered to deal with this rather senseless legend, but Luther not only translated it, he commented on it. Verbosely repeating his disgust with rabbinical polemics against Christianity, Luther then offered his demythologized version of the *Shem Hamphoras* formula: he contended it was nothing but the anagram of seventy-two names of angels, based on a combination of Hebrew letters from Exod. 14:19–21 and using three letters for each name. Luther had simply invented this scheme, since he was obviously intrigued by the minimal knowledge of Hebrew he had acquired from his friend Melanchthon. The anagram suggested, at least to Luther, that God's name as well as his deeds are hidden in the names of angels; sometimes they mean "love," at other times "salvation," etc.[59] It was Luther's way of telling Jews that all of this was speculation which could be used either to edify or to put people down. Jews, for example, could be teased with another version of *Shem Hamphoras,* namely, *Shama Perez* ("there is the dirt"). Luther reminded his readers that "dirt" and "swine" are closely related in the popular mind, which is why there is a stone relief in a Wittenberg church (and in other German churches) depicting a sow with suckling piglets to represent Judaism and the Talmud. A rabbi stands behind the sow and is lifting her right rear leg to study her anus, which represents the Talmud. Luther thought this kind of anti-Semitic "art" was a way of illustrating the German proverb which satirizes people who pretend to be wise, "Where did he read it? In the ass of a sow."[60] He accused the Jews of trying to be clever with the "name" (*shem*) of God by using the mysterious tetragram JHWH (often spelled *Jehova*) instead of seeking honest communication with God. That, he said, is why God has imposed his wrath on them. Luther concluded his commentary on the *Shem Hamphoras* by saying, "I wish that they not only avoided the name 'Jehova' but any and all letters of Scripture. . . . For they only slander God, dishonor Scripture, and condemn themselves."[61]

In the second part of the treatise, Luther dealt with the question of the lineage of Jesus, basing his arguments on the different accounts in the Gospels of Matthew and Luke (Matt. 1:1–16 starts with Abraham and stresses the relation to David; Luke 3:23–38 begins with Adam and does not emphasize the Jewish heritage). Repeating some of the arguments he had made in the earlier treatise "On the Jews and Their Lies," Luther once again lashed out against the Jews' claim to be the only chosen people of God. Whether or not there is an Old Testament, he contended, Jews are known as the source of evil which has infiltrated the whole world. They are spies, they poison wells, commit arson, steal children, and do all kinds of evil; and all historical accounts agree that Jews are bad for the world.[62] Then Luther offered his own version of how Matthew and Luke could be harmonized: both trace Jesus to David, Matthew through Joseph, the "foster father" (*putativus pater, vermeinter Vater*), and Luke through Mary, who remained a virgin.[63]

Luther offered a lengthy defense of Mary's virginity, basing it on his interpretation of Isa. 7:14, "Behold, a virgin [young woman] shall conceive and bear a son, and shall call his name Immanuel." Whereas Jewish interpreters understood the Hebrew *alma* to mean "young woman," not "virgin," Luther defended the rendering of "virgin" and used other passages to prove his point.[64] His principal attack, however, was aimed at what he considered interpretations germinated by deceit:

> In sum: these desperate devilish liars think they own Holy Scripture like a piece of paper from which one can carve at will little figures of people, birds, houses, toys. And whatever they say Jews and Christians are to consider right. Let me give you my own judgment about these damned rabbis. First, Holy Scripture does not belong to the Jews nor the Gentiles, neither to angels nor even less to devils, but to God alone. He alone spoke it and wrote it, and He alone should interpret it, whenever necessary. Both devils and humans should be his students and hearers. Second, we Christians are not permitted, on pain of losing divine grace and eternal life, to believe and to accept as right the rabbis' glosses about Scripture. We may read them in order to see and to protect ourselves from the kind of devilish work they do.[65]

Luther told Hebrew scholars to cleanse Holy Scripture from the rabbinical pollution by using text-critical and other methods of interpretation in order to achieve harmony between the Old and the New Testaments.[66] "I am done with the Jews," he concluded. "I shall no longer write about or against them. . . . Those who want to convert, God may add His grace, so that they, together with us, acknowledge and praise God the Father, our Creator, together with our Lord Jesus Christ, and with the Holy Spirit unto eternity. Amen."[67]

The treatise "On the Last Words of David" was written in order to show that significant portions of the Old Testament can be viewed as christological prophecies. Luther translated 2 Sam. 23:1–7 from Hebrew into German as well as offering his own interpretation of this passage as a key to the understanding of Jesus as the Messiah. According to Luther, the passage points to Jesus as the descendant of David, "the anointed of the God of Jacob" (2 Sam. 23:1), through whom the Spirit of the Lord speaks (v. 2). He therefore viewed the passage as an Old Testament proof text for the Trinity

rather than just as a spiritual elevation of the house of David by the God of
Israel. Jews, Turks, and heretics misread Scripture when they deny the
Trinity.[68] They are thus totally under the dominion of the serpent, the
symbol of evil, which can only be overcome by the "seed of a woman," the
Virgin Mary (Gen. 3:15).[69] Luther's whole approach to the Old Testament
thus rested on the assumption that it can be truly understood only in light of
the New Testament.

> May God grant that our theologians continue to study Hebrew and save the
> Bible from these malicious thieves who want to do everything better than I have
> done. They should not be trapped by the rabbis' distorted grammar and false
> interpretation so that we are able to find and recognize the dear Lord and Savior
> clearly in Scripture. To him be praise and honor, together with the Father and
> the Holy Spirit unto eternity. Amen.[70]

Though more moderate in tone than the others, this treatise was still
considered a typical example of Luther's haughty approach to the Jews and to
the Old Testament. The Zurich reformer Henry Bullinger told the
Strassburg reformer Martin Bucer, in a letter dated 8 December 1543, that
Luther once again had exposed his proud and harsh personality; and Bucer
responded by praising the ironic approach to the Old Testament of the
Humanist Erasmus of Rotterdam. The Zurich city council issued a statement
in 1545 which branded Luther the crudest author with regard to matters of
faith, especially with regard to his *Shem Hamphoras* exposition. "If this had
been written by a swineherd, rather than by a celebrated shepherd of souls,
it might have some, but very little, justification."[71]

When Luther traveled to Eisleben in February 1546, he was annoyed to
see that regional political authorities had not heeded his advice to exile the
Jews and lashed out once more in his last sermon on 15 February 1546. He
proclaimed that besides papists, Turks, and *Schwärmer*, Jews are the most
dangerous enemies of the Christian faith; they should be either converted or
exiled.[72]

The story of how Luther arrived at his final solution to the Jewish problem
discloses the sad fact that even the best intentions to reform are not
completely unaffected by the temptation to find quick solutions to enduring
deformations. Luther scholars have debated extensively about whether or
not there was a significant change in Luther's attitude toward the Jews after
the 1520s, when he became increasingly frustrated by the opposition to his
reform movement on the part of Catholics, Humanists, peasants and
Schwärmer, and especially by the constant threat of a Turkish invasion.[73] But
the study of Luther's handling of the question of the relationship between the
gospel and Israel suggests that Luther's anti-Semitism was anchored in his
perception of human sin, which pits righteousness of self against God's

righteousness manifested in Jesus Christ. Luther saw this self-righteousness embodied in the defenders of the ecclesiastical status quo, the papists; in the dissenters from the externals of Word and sacrament, the *Schwärmer;* in the Turks, whose militant monotheism threatened trinitarian Christianity; and, of course, in the Jews. When viewed in the apocalyptic context of Luther's view of the world as the place of struggle between Christ and Antichrist— with the Antichrist represented by the pope, but also by other "false Christians"—his writings against the Jews can be seen as an integral part of a vehement no to any solidarity with the Antichrist, and as an emphatic yes to the gospel, which liberates people from the bondage of evil. [74]

Nevertheless, Luther's writings on the Jews are conspicuous in his extensive literary corpus because of their totally uncritical embrace of rampant and vicious Christian anti-Semitism. His love for the Old Testament as the Holy Scripture of Christians made him viciously jealous of the Jews, who claimed salvation through God without Jesus as their Messiah. This jealousy turned Luther into a harsh and cruel critic of Judaism, pronouncing it the manifestation of God's wrath—a view already argued with similar emotionalism by the apostle Paul, who told the Roman Gentiles, "As regards the gospel they (the Jews) are enemies of God, for your sake; but as regards election they are beloved for the sake of their forefathers" (Rom. 11:28). Yet the biblical theologian Luther enjoyed describing Jews as the "enemies of God" without honoring them at all as the "chosen people of God." This stance placed him among the worst and most fanatic anti-Semites of his age.

And yet it must be said that Luther forged a *theological* "anti-Judaism" rather than a *biological* "anti-Semitism." The biological, ethnic designation was disseminated in Germany during the financial panic following the Franco-Prussian War of 1870–71. [75] Luther was not therefore the real father of German anti-Semitism, with its mass murder of Jews efficiently executed by Hitler's bureaucratic henchmen.

But Luther was very much the son of medieval Christendom with its fear of religious pluralism and its cruel means of preserving cultural uniformity. Despite pioneering theological insights into the universality of God's love in Christ, Luther turned the "good news" of this love into "bad news" for the Jews.

This is why Luther cannot help post-Hitler Christians on the *via dolorosa* towards better Christian-Jewish relations. Only repentance and solidarity with people who have become rootless and persecuted can create the climate necessary for a dialogue on the question of the relationship between the gospel and Israel. [76]

8

RELIGION AND PSYCHE

I've heard no argument from men that persuaded me, but the bouts I've engaged in during the night have become much more bitter than those during the day. For my adversaries have only annoyed me, but the devil is able to confront me with arguments. Often he has offered an argument of such weight that I didn't know whether God exists or not. ("Table Talk," Spring 1533, no. 518. WA.TR 1:238.12–16. LW 54:93)

PSYCHO-HISTORICAL PITFALLS

Sigmund Freud's (1856–1939) introduction of psychoanalysis into the field of medicine created a long-distance interest, as it were, in Luther as a "patient." Roman Catholic interpreters of Luther, like the Dominican Heinrich Denifle and the Jesuit Hartmann Grisar, used Freudian psychology to arrive at their assessment that Luther was a monk obsessed with the lust of the flesh and a pathological manic-depressive personality. Their portraits of Luther were based on Luther's first and most hostile biographer, John Dobenick (1479–1552), who wrote under the pseudonym Cochlaeus and who regarded Luther as a creation of Satan.[1] These polemical portraits were corrected in the 1940s when an ecumenically oriented scholar, Joseph Lortz, rejected Freudian psycho-historical methods in favor of a more objective critical assessment to depict Luther as a faithful priest-professor who had succumbed to "subjectivism."[2]

Luther's many observations and evaluations of his own mental and physical problems provide fascinating source-material to psycho-historians. He talked freely about his childhood, his spiritual struggles in the monastery, his bouts with the devil, his stomach disorders and constipation, his insomnia, his headaches, his buzzing in the ears, his kidney- and gallstones, his intimacies with Katie—not to mention his *Anfechtungen* over such questions as whether or not God is an angry judge, a gracious father, or a fiction created by troubled minds. No wonder, then, that psychologists, physicians, and historians began to look for clues in Luther's own works concerning the relationship of faith to health! Their efforts to arrive at a psycho-historical diagnosis of Luther's personality seemed to be in line with Luther's own musings. After all, he had repeatedly observed how anxiety, melancholy, and a sense of sadness affected his physical well-being:

> Sadness (*tristitia*) causes disease. For when the heart is ill, the body becomes weak. The true diseases are those of the heart, such as sadness, grief, and temptation. I am a true Lazarus who is quite tempted by diseases.[3]

A detailed study of Luther's diseases and his reaction to them reveals that whenever he suffered from physical ailments he also experienced psychological depression. But these depressions only lasted a few days and hardly interfered with Luther's intensive schedule of teaching and writing. Even the severe kidney-stone attacks, which occurred sporadically between 1537 and 1546, did not impair his output, although he did suffer deep depression in their wake.[4]

Two psychologists, Ernst Kretschmer of Marburg and Hubert Rohracher of Vienna, analyzed the relationship between Luther's spiritual sensitivity and his seemingly robust physique in the context of a theory they had formed correlating character and body type. They concluded that Luther was physically "pyknic" (from the Greek *pyknos*, "fat, stocky") and emotionally "cyclothymic" (from the Greek *kyklos*, "curve, circle" and *thymos*, "spirit, temperament"), that is, that he was afflicted with a mild manic-depressive psychosis involving recurring cycles of exhilaration and depression.[5] The American historian Preserved Smith, author of widely known accounts of the Reformation and Luther's life, became fascinated with Freudian theories on the role of sex in personality development and applied them to Luther. In an essay about young Luther, he said:

> Luther is a thoroughly typical example of the neurotic quasi-hysterical sequence of an infantile sex-complex; so much so, indeed, that Sigismund [sic] Freud and his school could hardly have found a better example to illustrate the sounder part of their theory than him.[6]

The attempts to psychoanalyze Luther culminated in the work of the Danish psychiatrist Paul J. Reiter, who produced a massive study of Luther's "environment, character, and psychosis" in 1941.[7] He diagnosed Luther as a textbook case of psychopathology, that is, as a manic-depressive who, given a disturbed childhood and a peculiar environment, disclosed severe depressions and manic productivity, especially in his late thirties and early forties, and was consequently hardly ever himself despite a robust physical condition. What Luther had called *Anfechtungen*, especially the spiritual struggles he experienced during his early years in Erfurt and Wittenberg, Reiter associated with the "classic traits in the picture of most states of depression, especially the endogenous ones."[8] Reiter did not even rule out epilepsy caused by both biological and environmental factors when he read this diagnosis in a polemical Jesuit Luther biography.[9]

On the other hand, Luther may simply have been a true representative of the "waning of the Middle Ages," so aptly described by John Huizinga in a survey of late medieval literature and documentary art in France and the Netherlands: people weighed down by a somber melancholy; people who sense that history consists only of pride, violence, and death; people who believe that the end of the world is imminent.[10] A major pitfall of psycho-history is the disregard for the delicate balance between historical and psychological data. Besides, is it ever possible to psychoanalyze the dead?

Erik H. Erikson made a noble attempt to do so by using "young man Luther" as the subject for "a study in psychoanalysis and history."[11] He studied Luther undergoing "the major crisis of adolescence, the identity crisis": a decisive period in the cycle of life, when each youth must face the question of the meaning of life, "some central perspective and direction, some working unity . . . some meaningful resemblance between what he has come to see in himself and what his sharpened awareness tells him others judge and expect him to be."[12] In this sense, identity is linked to "ideology," which is an "unconscious tendency underlying religious and scientific as well as political thought." It is the tendency "to make facts amenable to ideas, and ideas to facts" in order to establish an individual and collective sense of identity.[13] Expressing sympathy and empathy for the young Luther, Erikson analyzed the way in which Martin wrestled with the relationship of identity and ideology. He concluded that:

1. Luther was severely handicapped in his struggle for identity by an unhappy childhood aggravated by a love/hate attitude toward his parents and brutal treatment by teachers. Basing his conclusions on evidence from two table talks and a few other fragments, Erikson created the portrait of a rather disturbed young Martin, whose later recollections reveal only the tip of a pathological iceberg:

> One ought not to flog children too hard. My father once whipped me so that I ran away and felt ugly toward him until he was at pains to win me back.[14]

> My parents kept me under very strict discipline, even to the point of making me timid. For the sake of a mere nut [stolen from the kitchen supply] my mother beat me until the blood flowed. By such strict discipline they finally forced me into the monastery.[15]

> I once was whipped fifteen times one morning in school.[16]

These table talks and whatever else is known about Luther's youth until he entered the Erfurt monastery at seventeen yield sufficient evidence, according to Erikson, to conclude that Martin's rebellion against medieval ecclesiastical authority can be traced to a rather pathological self-image: an awareness of being abused in a social structure which labeled the Luther family "dirty peasants"; a great fear of paternal punishment, be it from the natural father or God the heavenly Father; a sense of awe, if not terror, due to the belief in evil spirits which reveal themselves in evil thoughts about the function of reproductive and digestive human organs; and a deeply felt need to "convert" from an evil past to a good present and a promising future.[17]

2. Luther established his identity by successfully mastering certain basic psychological obstacles associated with Roman Catholic religious ideology. One such obstacle was ritual, particularly participation in and celebration of the Mass. Erikson made much of the psychological implications of young Luther's well-documented terror the first time he had to consecrate bread and wine in the Mass. "So terrified was I by those words! [*aeterno vivo vero Deo*, 'the eternal, living, and true God'] Already I had forebodings that something was wrong, but God didn't give me an understanding of this until later."[18] Since this incident occurred in the presence of Luther's father, Erikson viewed Luther's position at that moment as "the Great Divide of his life": facing the uncertain grace of the Eucharist and his father's wrath.[19] According to Erikson, Martin was not yet ready to change allegiance from his natural father to the Father in heaven. The legend of Luther's fit in the choir sometime during his twenties was to Erikson further proof that Luther was approaching a severe identity crisis. According to the legend, Luther, during the reading of the story describing Jesus healing a man possessed by a dumb spirit (Mark 9:17), screamed, "I am not, I am not (*Non sum*)!" The legend has been traced to Luther's enemies, especially to Cochlaeus, who propagated it widely and accused Luther of being possessed by demons.[20] Erikson used the incident as evidence of Luther's subconscious obedience to his father and his implied rebellion against the monastery, indeed "the crossroads of mental disease and religious creativity."[21] Luther's terror during the thunderstorm on 2 July 1505, when he vowed to become a monk, discloses the same psychological pattern. Young Martin had a "need for God to match Hans, within Martin, so that Martin would be able to disobey Hans and shift the whole matter of obedience and disavowal to a higher, and historically significant, plane."[22]

Luther's "tower experience," dated by Erikson around 1512, provided the "conversion" he needed to break away from his father. According to Erikson, psychological maturation requires the "internalization of the father-son relationship, the concomitant crystallization of conscience, the safe establishment of an identity as a worker and a man, and the concomitant reaffirmation of a basic trust."[23] In the tower, while reading how God makes believers right by their trust in him rather than by their merit through good works (Rom. 1:17), Luther experienced God as an internal force:[24]

> Instead of being like an earthly father whose mood-swings are incomprehensible to his small son, God is given the attribute of *ira misericordia*—a wrath which is really compassion. With this concept, Luther was at last able to forgive God for being a Father, and grant Him justification.[25]

3. Young Luther's road to maturity reveals the classic psychological pattern of the relationship between identity crisis and ideology. In *early infancy* the crisis is mastered by a basic trust in the mother. According to Erikson, Luther's mother provided him with such basic trust so that he was able to draw on it in his struggle for maturity. But Luther's father created a severe second crisis of *infancy* by driving young Martin out from "under his mother's skirts," that is, "making him precociously independent from women" and creating a strong longing for infantile trust later on. That is why Luther had to reformulate his faith, as evidenced in the "tower experience." The third stage of the identity crisis consists of the *struggle between initiative and guilt*, that is, the Oedipus complex. According to Freud,

> it involves a lasting unconscious association of sensual freedom with the body of the mother and the administrations received from her hand; a lasting association of cruel prohibition with the interference of the dangerous father; and the consequences of these associations for love and hate in reality and in phantasy. [26]

Luther revealed his initiative by disobeying his father, using his precocious mind in a constant search for liberation from a guilty conscience. What Freud called "the phallic stage of psychosexuality," which is manifested in fantasy, play, and work, became for Luther the drive to gaiety, the pleasure of conversation, and love for music and poetry. The struggle between initiative and guilt made Luther a theologian who pursued his own *Anfechtungen* as pathways to God while at the same time enjoying the liberating power of creativity. The fourth stage of the identity crisis consists of the *drive to learn and to integrate self and reality through reason*. In this stage, the young Luther became satisfactorily intimate with the source of his conversion, the Bible. That is why his stay at the Wartburg, where he began to translate the Bible into German, ended his prolonged identity crisis.

Luther was now ready to live with the final crisis of life, the *integrity crisis*. He now knew how to cope with "the question of how to escape corruption in living and how in death to give meaning to life." Jesus Christ was the source of the strength he needed to survive without fearing death as the enemy. [27]

Erikson's critics among Luther scholars have credited him with significant insights but, at the same time, they have pointed out the pitfalls of his psycho-history. [28] The pitfalls are rather obvious:

1. Erikson's thesis that Luther's Reformation is due to a personal identity crisis caused by an unhappy childhood lacks solid historical evidence. Three sayings from table talks and a legend (the "fit in the choir") simply do not provide sufficient material on which to build a case. Moreover, there is solid contradictory evidence that Luther's relationship with his parents was a good one. Luther's father tried hard to provide a good home and fine schools for Martin, and Martin found the relationship with his father warm and comforting. He later recalled that his father had opposed his entry into the

monastery because "he saw through the knavery of the monks very well."[29] When Hans Luther died on 29 May 1530, Luther wrote Melanchthon a letter recounting some fond memories of his father's love and care.[30] His memories of his mother were similar: he recalled her "sweet singing" in the home; he rejoiced at her presence at his wedding; he named a daughter after her; and he wrote a beautiful letter to her just before her death on 30 June 1531.[31] As for his story about the severe punishment he received from teachers, one must remember that caning was then common practice both in the home and in school. Besides, Luther recalled only one incident of caning, and the topic of conversation was the proper relationship between "the rod and the apple."[32] The caning Luther mentioned having received in school was for speaking German instead of Latin. Using Erikson's method, one could conclude from this scanty evidence of caning that Luther therefore loved German and hated Latin, thus leading him to translate the Bible.[33] But Luther loved Latin as much as he did German, and wrote in both. Nor were Luther's parents "dirty peasants" who abused their children; they belonged to the "middle class," and Hans Luther was a highly respected citizen.[34]

2. Erikson underestimated Luther's religious and theological competence. Luther did not enter the monastery because he rebelled against his father. Rather, as a faithful young Christian—better educated than most, but filled with the same fear of death as most of his contemporaries—he did what many young men did: he became a monk, just as many young men join the army in more modern times. Moreover, Luther's rebellion against the church was because he was a loyal Roman Catholic trained to be a biblical theologian; he was not so much caught in "a fanatic preoccupation with himself" as he was committed to the search for clarity in his relationship with God and with the church.[35] When the church finally declared Luther a heretic, he was far from rejoicing in his liberation from bondage to his father or to the church. Instead, he was plagued by doubt: "Are you the only wise man? Can it be that all the others are in error and have erred for so long a time?"[36] A detailed study of Luther's utterances about himself clearly shows that he was far more concerned about his work than about his person.[37] Most significantly, Luther did not project any love/hate relationship with his father onto God, but rather despaired of a God who is unjust and predestines people to suffering. Young Martin learned more from the Bible, from Paul, from Augustine, and from various Christian traditions than he did from introspection. In the end, he tended almost to believe in two gods, as it were: the God of wrath and the God of mercy revealed in Jesus Christ. In this sense, Luther was simply not a modern man and cannot be measured by Freudian or other psychological insights.[38]

Erikson misinterpreted Luther's verbosity about such matters as sex and digestion. In this regard, Luther was very much a child of his time. People like Ulrich von Hutten, John Eck, Thomas More, William Shakespeare,

Queen Elizabeth I—to mention only a few—all used anal and scatological language. Luther simply excelled as much in muck as he excelled in theological reflection! The composers of the Psalms talked about being lifted out of the "dunghill" (Ps. 113:7), and St. Paul also spoke of dung (Phil. 3:8). Medieval biblical interpreters used scatology, and it was commonplace to regard the latrine as the devil's peculiar seat of operations;[39] it was a way of describing the doctrine of sin as it affected human lives. Luther's preoccupation with sin, particularly with how it shapes individuals in their behavior and communication, must be balanced against his assessment of sin as the sphere of God's merciful action. When people recognize their sinfulness, their "dunghill," they begin to fathom the powerful work of divine grace which operates through Christ who identified with sin, death, and evil. Luther had a wholistic view of sin and grace. He contended that one must be just as realistic and accurate in describing the physical aspects of human existence as one ought to be in the description of spirituality. Viewed in their totality, Christians experience salvation with a sense of real, wholesome liberation from sin; at the same time, however, a Christian still knows the daily reality of sin in all its various aspects. Thus every believer is "simultaneously a righteous person and a sinner" (*simul iustus et peccator*)— a statement Luther regarded as the best expression of what it means to be "a whole person" (*totus homo*).

Uncovering these and other errors and distortions does not mean that psycho-historiography should be banned from Luther studies or from any other historical studies. Erikson and other psycho-historians have indeed provided some significant insights into Luther's personality. But psycho-historians must maintain the delicate balance between psychology and historical data. When this is done, the field of psychology will provide welcome assistance to historians, who are often trapped in a limited field of vision. Historiography is always faced with the lacunae still remaining after all the evidence is properly and critically analyzed. Thus there is the need for conjecture. Yet the warning given by one of Erikson's major critics must be heeded: "One who constructs a pyramid of conjectures may be compared to God who made the world out of nothing."[40]

FAITH AND HEALTH

Luther's diseases were caused by the way he lived rather than by genetic disposition. Years of malnutrition in the monastery, long days and nights of hard mental labor often accompanied by spiritual struggles, as well as his later thorough enjoyment of food, drink, and sex had their effect on Luther's health. During his exile at the Wartburg, Luther was plagued by stomach disorders and constipation. "The Lord has afflicted me with painful constipation," he told Melanchthon in a letter dated 12 May 1521, shortly after his arrival at the Wartburg.

> The elimination is so hard that I am forced to press with all my strength, even to the point of perspiration, and the longer I delay the worse it gets. Yesterday on the fourth day I could go once, but I did not sleep all night and still have no peace. Please pray for me.[41]

From 1526 on, he endured sporadic gall and kidney-stone attacks, which reminded him of death because of the excruciating pain. He frequently talked about these attacks, complaining about pain; he distrusted physicians and linked the experience to the kind of *Anfechtungen* sent by God to remind Christians that life is indeed a struggle with sin, death, and the devil. One of his worst kidney-stone attacks occurred when Luther attended the convention of the Smalcald League in 1537. He told his wife Katie, in a letter dated 27 February 1537:

> I had not been healthy there for more than three days, and from the first Sunday to this night [19-27 February?] not one little drop of water passed from me; I had no rest nor did I sleep, and I was unable to retain any drink or food. In summary, I was dead; I commended you, together with the little ones, to God and to my gracious Lord, since I thought that I would never again see you in this mortal life. . . . But many people prayed to God so hard on my behalf that their tears moved God to open my bladder this night, and in two hours about one *Stübig* [about 3 to 4 quarts] passed from me, and I feel as if I were born again.[42]

Those who were with Luther during this attack heard him grumbling about his wretched body which had become the target of the devil. "The devil hates me, and so he increases my pain," he said while sipping some almond broth.[43]

After 1530, Luther suffered from severe headaches which had begun during his stay at the Coburg and which often included a ringing or "buzzing" in the ears (*Ohrensausen*). After 1541, these headaches often forced Luther to interrupt his routine and even to avoid the bright light of a sunny day.[44] He was sometimes able to joke about them, describing them as the devil's ride through his brain; or, when they had ceased, as the devil's way of getting a vacation by traveling to a spa.[45]

After 1530 Luther also suffered from an open sore on his left leg, and doctors finally provided some relief in 1543 by keeping the sore open for drainage. Luther viewed all these physical ailments—as well as the epidemic diseases like the bubonic plague which struck Wittenberg in 1527[46]—as ways the devil used to persuade Christians to leave Christ and join his realm. "To be sure, Satan would gladly kill me if he could," Luther commented at table on 22 January 1532, with regard to his most recent attack of ringing ears and "faintness in the heart." "Every moment he is pressing me, is treading on my heels. Yet what he wishes will not be done, but what God wills."[47] Luther once admitted having touched victims of the plague. When confronted with the widespread fear of plague, he advised people to listen to the Word of God in church, to prepare for death through confession and Holy Communion, and to trust pastors and physicians as the experts in such times as the devil attacks the church.[48]

Throughout his life Luther cherished private confession as a special source of strength in times of *Anfechtung* such as illness. His first father confessor, Staupitz, and his friend and pastor, John Bugenhagen, heard his regular confessions and assured him of the comfort of the Word of God. "The devil would have slain me long ago," Luther told Wittenbergers in a sermon on private confession in the midst of turmoil over church practice in March 1522, "if the confession had not sustained me."[49]

Luther's consistent identification of illness with the devil's work was not just an odd residue of medieval superstition in his otherwise enlightened world of ideas. Rather, he considered the struggle with the devil, either through pain and disease or through violence and political rebellion, a necessary one to achieve clarity about the proper distinction between God's power and any other power. Ultimately, Luther viewed that struggle as the main road to the discovery of Christ, the source of all good news about salvation—real health, as it were—namely, the good news of a relationship with God, who will lead believers into a new life that excludes the devil.[50] He considered physicians and medical expertise an integral part of this struggle, even if many physicians failed to recognize that the devil was the cause of disease.[51] Luther consequently told the devil:

> If you can terrorize, Christ can strengthen me. If you can kill, Christ can give life. If you have poison in your fangs, Christ has far greater medicine. Should not my dear Christ, with his precepts, his kindness, and all his encouragement be more important in my spirit than you, roguish devil, with your false terrors in my weak flesh? God forbid![52]

According to Luther, medicine and faith belong together in the struggle for health. To be sure, Luther did not always obey the doctors' orders. In 1526, during his first attack of kidney stones, he defied his physician's order to avoid solid food, and instead persuaded Katie to cook one of his favorite meals of fried herring with mustard and cold peas. Shortly after the meal he passed a sizeable kidney stone, and he delighted in the surprise of his physicians and in telling the story.[53] It was this combination of faith, humor, and commitment to ministry which enabled Luther to endure what Paul called "the thorn in the flesh" (2 Cor. 12:7).

Yet despite all these physical ailments as well as the normal hazards of sixteenth-century living, Luther managed to do an extraordinary amount of work. The chronological statistics of his state of health and his accomplishments are simply astonishing.[54]

State of Health	Accomplishments
1521	sick with constipation (*Hartleibigkeit*) for seven months (April–October).	70 sermons, 100 letters, 30 tracts, work on the New Testament, trip to Worms, exile at the Wartburg.
1522	after medical attention at the Wartburg, relatively healthy.	138 sermons, 100 letters, 20 tracts, work on the Old Testament, return from Wartburg, trips to Zwickau, Leisnig, Erfurt, and Weimar.
1523	sick with fever for a month (April–May).	135 sermons, lectures, 90 letters, 40 tracts, work on Old Testament, hymns, brief journeys.
1524	sickly for one month (October).	120 sermons, lectures, 90 letters, 40 tracts, work on Old Testament, hymnal, trips to Kemberg and Orlamünde.
1525	sick for month of January, sore thigh treated with caustic substance to keep wound open for drainage, fainting spell.	100 sermons, lectures, 110 letters, 20 tracts, extended journey to Thuringia and Eisleben during peasant's rebellion.
1526	sick in June with kidney stones.	100 sermons, lectures, 80 letters, 20 tracts, brief trips.
1527	sickly for eight months (beginning January), dizzy spell during sermon on 22 April. Plague epidemic in Wittenberg.	60 sermons, lectures, 100 letters, 15 tracts, work on Old Testament, brief trips. Birth of daughter Elizabeth 10 December.
1528	rather healthy.	190 sermons, lectures, 150 letters, 20 tracts, work on Old Testament, trips to Torgau and Altenburg. Elizabeth died 3 August.
1529	sick for two months with colds (January, 14 April–7 May).	120 sermons, lectures, 120 letters, 20 tracts, catechisms, hymns, trip to Marburg for colloquy with Zwingli. Birth of Lenchen 4 May.

	State of Health	*Accomplishments*
1530	sick for ten months (beginning April) with stomach disorders, colds, sore on thigh, ringing in ears. Dizzy spell in pulpit 18 December.	60 sermons, during trip to Coburg, lectures, 170 letters, 30 tracts, work on Old Testament at the Coburg from April to October during Diet of Augsburg.
1531	sick for six months (exhaustion March–April, sickly and weak later).	180 sermons, lectures, 100 letters, 15 tracts, work on Old Testament, brief trips. Mother died in June.
1532	sick for six months (beginning January).	90 sermons, lectures, 70 letters, work on Old Testament, brief trips.
1533	sick in February with dizziness for one month.	75 sermons, lectures, 65 letters, 10 tracts, work on Old Testament, brief trips. Son Paul born 29 January.
1534	sick three months with colds (January, June, September).	80 sermons, lectures, 75 letters, 10 tracts, completion of Bible translation, brief trips.
1535	sick two months with headaches, diarrhea, colds (August and October).	60 sermons, 80 letters, 10 tracts, hymns, brief trips, lectures.
1536	sick eight months with colds, dizziness, pain in hip (January–March), kidney stones (May–June), exhaustion (October–December), severe chest pains at end of year.	50 sermons, lectures, 90 letters, 10 tracts, brief trips.
1537	sick two months with stones (February–April).	90 sermons, lectures, 55 letters, 25 tracts, hymns, trip to Smalcald (31 January–14 March). Trips to Lochau and Kemberg in October, to Torgau in December.

	State of Health	Accomplishments
1538	sick for six months with fever, stones, and dysentery (March–September).	100 sermons, lectures, 75 letters, 15 tracts, hymns, brief trips.
1539	sick with dizziness and stones (January–April).	70 sermons, lectures, 100 letters, 10 tracts, revision of Bible translation, trip to Leipzig in May.
1540	sick in February with rheumatism, fever in September shared by ten others at Cloister.	40 sermons, lectures, 90 letters, 10 tracts, Bible revision, trip to Eisenach in July. Katie's miscarriage in January.
1541	sick with sore throat (January), dizziness (February), middle ear infection (April–May), weakness in July and November.	7 sermons (5 in January), lectures, 80 letters, 10 tracts, Bible translation revision.
1542	sick in July, right eye blinded from cataract.	4 sermons, lectures, 100 letters, 10 tracts, hymnal, trips to Naumburg (January) and Dessau (September), Lenchen died 20 September.
1543	sickly for ten months (except September and October), problem with shinbone in November.	3 sermons, lectures, 85 letters, 10 tracts.
1544	sick in August and September with fatigue and stones.	40 sermons, lectures, 65 letters, 5 tracts, Bible translation revision, trips to Zeitz and Torgau.
1545	sick for ten months with stones, exhaustion and old age.	35 sermons, lectures, 80 letters, 15 tracts, trip to Eisleben (until January 1546) and other short trips.

State of Health	Accomplishments
1546 sick with cold during trip to Eisleben, problem with sore on thigh, died on 18 February of angina pectoris at age sixty-two.	8 sermons, 21 letters, 1 tract. Return to Eisleben.

Luther was certainly not a man who allowed himself to be severely impeded by physical and mental illness! On the contrary, he seemed to thrive under the impact of the various *Anfechtungen*, which is why he could say that Christians must view their sufferings as part of Christ's own sufferings and that Christ will also provide the strength to endure. He wrote to Elector Frederick in 1519, when the elector had become gravely ill:

> I cannot pretend that I do not hear the voice of Christ as it cries out to me out of your Lordship's body and flesh, saying, "Look, I am sick." Such evils as sickness and the like are borne not by us Christians, but by Christ himself, our Lord and Savior, in whom we live and who plainly testifies in the Gospel, "Whatever you have done unto the least of mine, you have done unto me" [Matt. 25:40].[55]

This statement clearly reflected his conviction that the lives and times of Christians are in God's hands, in accordance with Ps. 31:15, "My times are in thy hand." "I have now learned to understand this saying," Luther said in 1538:

> I had related it only to the hour of death. But it really means that all my life, every day, hour, and moment, living and dying, enjoying and mourning, misfortune and luck are in thy hands.[56]

SEX AND MARRIAGE

Luther's marriage on 13 June 1525 was a controversial event. There had been gossip about a possible marriage of the priest-professor since 1523 when he had assisted apostate nuns to find husbands. But Luther himself did not have marriage on his mind at this time. "The way I feel now, and have felt thus far, I will not marry," he told Spalatin in a letter dated 30 November 1524; after all, he was already forty-one years old.

> It is not that I do not feel my flesh or sex, since I am neither wood nor stone, but my mind is far removed from marriage, since I daily expect death and the punishment due to a heretic. Therefore I shall not limit God's work in me, nor shall I rely on my own heart. Yet I hope God does not let me live long.[57]

But only one year later, the forty-two-year-old Luther did marry a twenty-six-year-old apostate nun, one of nine who had deserted their nunneries in order to enjoy the Christian freedom Luther had so effectively proclaimed. Why? Because, Luther asserted, he had become convinced that getting married was one more testimony to the rediscovered gospel—the "good news" that God in Christ will triumph over sin, death, and the evil so strongly manifested in the papal church's self-righteousness.

Luther had somehow provided for the future of eight of the nine apostate nuns, and only Catherine remained unmarried; after she refused several offers and strongly hinted that she would rather marry Luther than anyone else, he decided to go ahead and marry her.[58] Besides, his father had recently remarked that he should preserve his name, and that seems to have had some influence on his decision. "Indeed, the rumor is true that I was suddenly married to Catherine," Luther wrote to his friend Nicholas von Amsdorf on 21 June 1525, at the same time inviting Nicholas to attend the public wedding banquet to be held 27 June.

> [I did this] to silence the evil mouths which are so used to complaining about me. For I still hope to live for a little while. In addition, I also did not want to reject this unique [opportunity to obey] my father's wish for progeny, which he so often expressed. At the same time, I also wanted to confirm what I have taught by practicing it; for I find so many timid people in spite of such great light from the gospel. God has willed and brought about this step. For I feel neither passionate love nor burning for my spouse, but I cherish her.[59]

Most of Luther's friends approved of his marriage, but some had apprehensions, which were probably best expressed by Luther's faculty colleague and legal advisor, Jerome Schurff. "If this monk marries," Schurff said when he heard of the wedding plans, "the whole world and the devil will laugh, so that everything he has accomplished will come to naught." When Luther heard of that remark, he advanced the wedding date![60]

Luther's foes were vitriolic. The Swiss poet Simon Lemnius composed nasty epigrams about Luther and circulated them in Wittenberg, and produced a Latin play depicting Luther and some of his friends as whoring monks.[61] The vice-chancellor of Leipzig University, John Hasenberg, wrote Luther a letter in which he called him the "most insane and libidinous of apostates" who, by sleeping with a nun, had transformed Wittenberg into Sodom and Gomorrah; he enclosed a vicious attack on Katie penned by a Leipzig University Fellow named Joachim von der Heyden, who threatened Katie with eternal punishment because she had left the nunnery and, "like a dancing girl," had cast her eyes "on that old spitfire Luther." Luther responded with a satirical fable, telling Hasenberg—among other things—that his servants had used the letters for toilet paper.[62]

Whatever others may have said or thought about Luther's marriage, then or later, Luther himself was a happy spouse; and so was Katie, though most of the evidence is transmitted only through Luther. Luther fell deeply in love with Katie after a few years of marriage. "I wouldn't give up my Katie for France or for Venice," he said in the summer or fall of 1531:

First, because God gave her to me and gave me to her; second, because I have often observed that other women have more shortcomings than my Katie (although she, too, has some shortcomings, they are outweighed by many great virtues); and third, because she keeps faith in marriage, that is, fidelity and respect.[63]

Luther was not the typical sixteenth-century spouse. He was paternalistic in his general behavior, but he admired Catherine's leadership in the difficult Black Cloister household where it was not unusual to have twenty or more people sitting down to a meal. Contrary to sixteenth-century German custom, Luther not only appointed Catherine executrix of his will but also tried to make sure she would not be legally impeded from carrying out these duties. Katie, who addressed Luther as *Herr Doktor* (at least in public!), strongly influenced Luther's daily life: she nursed him when he was ill, and he would not have lived as long as he did without her; and she taught him to say no when he was inclined to take on "just one more" chore for the kingdom of God or for the various people asking help and advice.

Psycho-historical accounts of Luther's sexuality and its influence on his work as a reformer run counter to Luther's own view of sex and marriage. Neither as a child nor as a monk did he seem to suffer from many sexual urges. He later recalled:

When I was a monk I did not feel much desire. I had nocturnal pollutions in response to bodily necessity. I didn't even look at the women when they made their confession, for I didn't wish to recognize the faces of those whose confessions I heard. In Erfurt I heard the confessions of no woman, in Wittenberg of only three women.[64]

Sexual temptations, however, seem to be the rule rather than the exception among members of religious orders and priests. Celibacy became a burden for even the most revered fathers in the church like Augustine, Jerome, Francis, and Bernard. When Luther read of the devil's assaults on them, he expressed amazement that "the holy fathers" fell for such "juvenile temptations." He thought that they should have been plagued by "loftier ones" like lack of faith, uncertainty about a gracious God, and self-righteousness—Luther's view of how God tests his saints.[65] Thus Luther could identify much more with Paul, whose conversion was from self-righteousness to selfless service with faith active in love. Whereas the devil allegedly appeared to the traditional saints in the form of an alluring woman, Luther encountered him when he despaired of God's gracious love for sinners.

Luther did not oppose celibacy, chastity, or religious vows. He conceded that some may want to dedicate themselves to such selfless service for God that their ministry excludes the joys of sex and marriage. But, he said, this does not mean that their chastity merits heaven. Christ praised eunuchs not because they castrated themselves, but because they did so for the sake of the kingdom of heaven (Matt. 19:12). To sacrifice sex may increase dedication to Christian witness in the world, but such sacrifice does not earn merit before God.

> It is therefore Christ's intent that chastity should be a servant of the kingdom of heaven, and a willing servant, not something which earns the kingdom, for it already possesses the kingdom. Such chastity labors in joyful service to bring the kingdom to others, or in any case to increase the kingdom for the kingdom's own sake. Such chastity is always ready to die and depart from this world for the sake of the kingdom.[66]

Luther thus clearly differentiated between a true and a false chastity. True chastity concentrates on faith in the God who loves sinners. False chastity relies on human merit and self-righteousness rather than on God's unconditional love for the ungodly in Christ. He insisted that if the church tempts people to join religious orders or to become priests so that they may earn God's love, then celibacy ought to be abandoned. Luther judged that the church of his day did tempt people to become self-righteous since it concentrated so hard on the "lusts of the flesh." Religious orders "make of their chastity merit, credit, and glory before God and the world," he contended in his commentary on 1 Cor. 7:6–7 (whether one should be married or chaste). "But St. Paul makes of it a technique and service for God's Word and faith."[67] Those who are not married to God's Word and to faith, as it were, ought to be married to a woman. They should not try to be celibate. When sexual drives are not controlled by true chastity, that is, by a true vocation for selfless ministry of and to the Word of God, these drives should be employed in marriage. "Because we have not been created for fornication but for marriage," he told his students in a lecture on Gen. 24:5–7 (part of the account of how Abraham got married), "it is not only permitted, but it is both godly and honorable to desire and to try to get a wife."[68]

In sum, Luther shared the traditional view of his time that sex should be located in the context of marriage, and that marriage is an estate divinely instituted for the propagation of humanity. But, in contrast to his time, Luther talked openly about the sex drive as something which, though constantly threatened by the perversion of original sin, God gave to his creatures to both guard and enjoy. If sexual activity is impeded for one reason or another, Luther nonchalantly advised, the suffering partner should find other outlets, as it were. If, for example, a woman's husband is impotent, she should, with the consent of her spouse, have intercourse with another man, preferably her brother-in-law. Under "divine law," Luther contended, she "cannot be compelled to remain continent."[69]

According to Luther, marriage is not a sacrament but "an external thing" like eating, drinking, and other activities designed by God to maintain life. As such, marriage is regulated by secular law; the church cannot legislate its features even though a Christian marriage (in contrast to a Mohammedan one) ought to be normed by a lifelong faithfulness to one partner. Luther never got tired of speaking of the mutual respect and love which ought to determine married life. In this sense, marriage is part of the paradise which was lost through the fall,[70] and this remnant of the original paradise is constantly threatened by various disasters. However, God always remains in charge. When Luther met a man whose wife has just died without previous warning of pain or illness, Luther commented, "Our Lord God is the worst adulterer. . . . This morning she slept with her husband, and tonight she sleeps with our Lord God."[71]

Remarks like these disclose a Luther at the brink of blasphemy, if judged by the propriety-conscious theological discourse of a church which neglects to reflect on the heights and depths of human experience. On the other hand, Luther's constant need to express himself—be it on sex and marriage or on any other aspects of life—made him the personality he was: a priest-professor who with theological sagacity studied every bone in the skeleton of Christendom to the degree that he no longer saw a difference between private and public life. Luther was one of the most wholistic personalities among the fathers of the church, and such a person is always controversial.

PART 3

ECUMENICAL LEGACY

9

A CHRISTOCENTRIC THEOLOGY

The proper subject of theology is man guilty of sin and condemned, and God the Justifier and Savior of man the sinner. Whatever is asked or discussed in theology outside this subject is error and poison. All Scripture points to this, that God commends His kindness to us and in His Son restores to righteousness and life the nature that has fallen into sin and condemnation. The issue here is not this physical life—what we should eat, what work we should undertake, how we should rule our family, how we should till the soil. . . . The issue here is the future and eternal life; the God who justifies, repairs, and makes alive; and man, who fell from righteousness and life into sin and eternal death. ("Commentary on Psalm 51," 1532. WA 40/2:328.17–24, 26–28. LW 12:311)

THE ORTHODOXY OF CONFLICT

Luther was not a systematic theologian who offered his views in the neat, orderly way one might expect of a German theologian. He was so intensively involved in the affairs of his sixteenth-century world that he had hardly any time to withdraw to the peace and quiet of a scholar's study. That is why Luther scholars have a hard time summarizing Luther's theological thought either by pursuing a single theme or by elaborating what appears to be the focus of his extensive reflections.[1] Nor did Luther perceive the task of theology to be that of offering a system of thought. Rather, he viewed the task of the theologian, particularly the biblical theologian, as being what he called "practical," not "speculative."

> True theology is practical, and its foundation is Christ, whose death is appropriated to us through faith. However, today all those who do not agree with us and do not share our teaching make theology speculative because they cannot free themselves from the notion that those who do good [will be rewarded].[2]

Theology is practical when it is related to the reality of life—with its struggles, suffering, joys, and frustrations—for, realistically seen, life is overshadowed by one's continual desire to be in charge, to dominate, "to be like God." The way of the serpent always seems more attractive than the way of Christ; the sin of pride is stronger than love of neighbor. This conflict between God the Creator and man/woman the creature was for Luther the cause for all other conflicts in life. Why this is so is a mystery. Theologians could speculate about the mystery of "original sin" in various ways, but such speculations, Luther contended, are futile because they attempt to penetrate the "hidden God," the God who is not disclosed to the human mind. He is only disclosed, albeit not totally, in his humanity, in Jesus Christ.

> But true Christian theology, as I often warn you, does not present God to us in His majesty, as Moses and other teachings do, but Christ born of the Virgin as our Mediator and High Priest. Therefore when we are embattled against the Law, sin, and death in the presence of God, nothing is more dangerous than to stray into heaven with our idle speculations, there to investigate God in His incomprehensible power, wisdom, and majesty, to ask how He created the world and how He governs it. If you attempt to comprehend God this way and want to make atonement to Him apart from Christ the Mediator, making your works, fasts, cowl, and tonsure the mediation between Him and yourself, you will inevitably fall, as Lucifer did (Isa. 14:12), and in horrible despair lose God and everything.[3]

Luther had learned the hard way, through the pain of spiritual *Anfechtung*, not to pursue a "speculative" theology. He was convinced that such a theology denigrated, if it did not abandon, the foundation of the Christian faith: God's clear promise, in Word and sacrament, that in his incarnation in Jesus Christ, the Second Adam, creation will be healed. That is why all theology is for Luther a lifelong undertaking to "learn Jesus Christ, 'and him crucified' (1 Cor. 2:2)."[4]

Such learning begins with infant baptism, which Luther viewed as the telling embodiment of God's promise of salvation through the Holy Spirit active in Word and water, strange as such a ritual may be. The "old Adam" is drowned and the "new Adam" is raised in baptism. Thus all of Christian life is nothing but a return to baptism, to the divine promise that only trust in God's incarnation will transform sinful creatures into joyful but nevertheless struggling children of God destined to eternal life. Luther told his Wittenberg congregation, in a sermon on baptism:

> I was a monk for fifteen years, yet I never found consolation through my baptism. I wondered, "When will you finally rejoice in having done enough so that you will get a gracious God?" I tortured and plagued myself; I did not eat; I did not drink; I did not wear warm clothes . . . I strictly followed all the rules.[5]

In his quest for a gracious God, Luther discovered through intensive study of Paul and Augustine the proper distinction between what theologians had come to call God's "active" and "passive" righteousness (*iustitia Dei activa et passiva*). God's active righteousness is disclosed in his anger against sin, his vindictive righteousness directed against sinners who vainly try to appease him with "good works." God's passive righteousness is revealed in his mercy towards sinners whose relationship with him is restored through Christ's atonement. This distinction had always been part of the catholic theological tradition, but late medieval theology "terrified consciences," as Luther put it, with its emphasis on God's active righteousness which requires that sinners do penance through good works before he grants forgiveness.[6]

If theology is to assist the church in communicating God's mercy, rather than his wrath, Luther argued, then all theological reflection had better start with what God wants to reveal and not succumb to the temptation to know God in his hidden majesty.

> I was troubled . . . by the thought of what God would do with me, but at length I repudiated such a thought and threw myself entirely on his revealed will. We can't do any better than that. The hidden will of God can't be searched out by man. . . . We have enough to learn about the humanity of Christ, in whom the Father revealed himself. But we are fools who neglect the revealed Word and the will of the Father in Christ and, instead, investigate mysteries which ought only to be worshiped. As a result many break their necks.[7]

Human ingenuity, the power to reason and to speculate, can easily be prostituted to the level of self-righteousness. Luther did not object to the use of reason, especially for building wise relationships in the world; but he did attack the claims of philosophers and theologians to have fathomed the mysteries of the hidden God. He was not against thinking; he was against certain thoughts and conclusions.[8] He insisted that making proper distinctions was better than forming assured conclusions on the basis of assumptions made in the context of Aristotelian logic.[9] That is why he turned against those theologians who seduced people into performing ascetic exercises, buying indulgences, and doing other things to please God by claiming that God's grace was both a reward and a bonus for fulfilling divine demands above and beyond the law. "It is plain insanity to say that man of his own powers can love God above all things," Luther told his students in his lectures on Romans,

> . . . and can perform the works of the Law according to the substance of the act, even if not according to the intentions of Him who gave the commandment, because he is not in a state of grace. O fools, O pig-theologians (*Sautheologen*)! By your line of reasoning grace was not necessary except because of some new demand above and beyond the Law. For if the Law can be fulfilled by our powers, as they say, then grace is not necessary for the fulfilling of the Law, but only for the fulfilling of some new exaction imposed by God above the Law. Who can endure these sacrilegious notions?[10]

Luther viewed the conflict between himself and the "pig-theologians" as part of a larger, indeed cosmic, conflict between sin and grace, good and evil,

God and Satan. This conflict may at times look like an irrelevant academic debate to people who care little for structures of thought and language. But when such structures either shape institutional power or are used to justify such power—be it the papacy or the sale of indulgences—they disclose the enduring conflict between the human and the divine. In the sixteenth century, that conflict was expressed in the sacrament of penance, which had become the chief instrument for aligning people with a particular institutional form of Christianity. Luther contended that such an alignment confused the real therapeutic conflict, as it were, between human desires and divine intentions and the issue of institutional authority and loyalty. Rome considered disloyalty to its tradition to be opposition to the Christian tradition itself. Luther could not subscribe to Rome's view, and therefore insisted on being heard in the church's traditional forum, the general council.

It was when the proper ecclesiastical authorities refused to heed Luther's demands to be heard and indeed tried to silence him with ban and edict that Luther sought help from the princes, whom he considered devout baptized Christians in positions of leadership. He thought that as "emergency bishops" they could be expected to initiate the reforms needed among the people of God. Luther based his arguments on what has been called "the common priesthood of all believers," a revolutionary concept in the sixteenth-century hierarchical and feudal arrangements of socio-political power and authority. The result of this practice of making princes "emergency" bishops was the territorial church. The Peace of Augsburg in 1555 granted to princes who adhered to the Augsburg Confession the right to practice their religion in their territories. Subjects who refused to subscribe to their rulers' religious choice were forced to emigrate or were banned from the land.[11] Luther and his movement had succeeded in gaining toleration with the help of secular government.

Luther had discovered that life on earth is never without conflict—a discovery he found confirmed in both Scripture and history. There had never been a consensus about the proper understanding of sin, evil, and salvation. Paul, for example, fought "Judaizers" over the question of the necessity to obey Jewish customs like circumcision when attempting to convert Gentiles to Christianity. Jewish defenders of the status quo insisted on the observance of Jewish law as a precondition for Gentile conversion, but Paul condemned those who preached a gospel contrary to the one he himself preached to the Gentiles (Gal. 1:8). Another example: Greek Christians insisted that the Christian gospel be preached according to rules of logic; but when Arius of Alexandria, on the basis of these rules, concluded that Christ was "not of one being with the Father" because he was the Son and thus must have come later, the Council of Nicaea condemned him in A.D. 325. The church has always needed to be recalled to the proper distinction between human authority and the Word of God, and Luther rediscovered that the very center and focus of the Word of God is Christ.

> Christ is the point at the center of a circle, with all eyes inside the circle focused on Him. Whoever turns his eyes on Him finds his proper place in the circle of which Christ is the center. All the stories of Holy Writ, if viewed aright, point to Christ.[12]

Christ alone is the Mediator in the cosmic conflict between God and his creation. He alone "justifies" before God, and in that sense is God himself, the God of mercy. "To seek God outside Jesus is the devil."[13] All conflict concerned with Christ as the source of salvation is therefore orthodox.

> Once this has been established, namely that God alone justifies us solely by His grace through Christ, we are willing not only to bear the pope aloft on our hands but also to kiss his feet. . . . In short, we can stand the loss of our possessions, our name, our life, and everything else; but we will not let ourselves be deprived of the Gospel, our faith, and Jesus Christ. And that is that.[14]

Good biblical theology, Luther contended, will always have to insist on the centrality of "Christ crucified." In that sense, theology is cruciform because it must be shaped by the event that intersected the history of the world, God's incarnation in Jesus of Israel. Law and gospel, faith and love are the four extensions of a cross which is the incarnation. No matter what the issue or the problem in life, the theologian must see it within the shadow of the cross. Thus theology must ultimately concentrate on Christ and not on the believer. True theology, therefore, always crucifies the theological ego.

> This is the reason why our theology is certain: it snatches us away from ourselves and places us outside ourselves, so that we do not depend on our own strength, conscience, experience, person, or works but depend on that which is outside ourselves, that is, on the promise and truth of God, which cannot deceive.[15]

JUSTIFICATION BY FAITH

Luther based Christian life on what he called "the chief and principal article of faith." He put it most succinctly in the Smalcald Articles, his theological testament:

> The first and chief article is this, that Jesus Christ, our God and Lord, "was put to death for our trespasses and raised again for our justification" (Rom. 4:25). He alone is "the Lamb of God, who takes away the sin of the world" (John 1:29). "God has laid upon him the iniquities of us all" (Isa. 53:6). . . .
>
> Inasmuch as this must be believed and cannot be obtained or apprehended by any work, law, or merit, it is clear and certain that such faith alone justifies us, as St. Paul says in Romans 3, "For we hold that a man is justified by faith apart from

works of law" (Rom. 3:28), and again, "that he [God] himself is righteous and that He justifies him who has faith in Jesus" (Rom. 3:26).

Nothing in this article can be given up or compromised, even if heaven and earth and things temporal should be destroyed. . . .[16]

This "chief article" expresses Luther's christocentric stance which is stated again in simple fashion, without even using the term "justification," in the Small Catechism:

I believe that Jesus Christ . . . is my Lord, who has redeemed me, a lost and condemned creature, delivered me and freed me from all sins, from death, and from the power of the devil, not with silver and gold but with his holy and precious blood and with his innocent sufferings and death, in order that I may be his, live under him in his kingdom, and serve him in everlasting righteousness, innocence, and blessedness, even as he is risen from the dead and lives and reigns to all eternity.[17]

To Luther, the theme of justification by faith alone was the "rhapsody" that determined all of Christian life and thought.

The article of justification is the master and prince, lord, guide and judge of all kinds of teaching. It preserves and rules over every teaching of the church and restores our consciences before God. Without this article the world is nothing but death and darkness.[18]

If this article stands, the church stands; if it falls, the church falls.[19]

Such formulations appear throughout his works and have led Lutheran theologians to call the article of justification "the article on which the church stands and falls."[20] Indeed, Luther's sharp distinction between "the Apostle's way of talking" about God (modus loquendi Apostoli) and "the metaphysical or moral way" of Luther's fellow theologians (modus metaphysicus seu moralis) has been called "a Copernican revolution" in the history of theology.[21]

Needless to say, there is hardly a consensus on the matter. Some post-Reformation Lutherans have contended that Luther's quest for a gracious God was typical of sixteenth-century Christians plagued by endless quarrels in the medieval church over the proper relationship between sin and grace. One could just as well ask the question, "How do I get a gracious neighbor?" or "How do I find meaning in my life?"[22] Whether or not Luther's article of justification in its various later formulations is or ought to be church-dividing is still an open question for some.[23]

It ought not to be an open question. With the doctrine of justification Luther did not construct a cornerstone of a theological system, as though Christian unity were dependent on dogmatic uniformity. Nor did he view the doctrine of justification as one doctrine among other doctrines. Rather, Luther used the language of "justification" he had found in Romans to console the "terrified conscience" plagued by the question of whether God cares for the individual at all or whether one's life is without value or meaning. This kind of existential crisis has plagued people throughout history; medieval Christendom with its repertoire of religious pacification seemed to exacerbate rather than to alleviate existential despair. Luther, who had experienced this terror and despair, felt victimized by the religion which was intended to help him. In one way he was encouraged—either in private confession or in the religious "system" itself—to "accept" God's salvation in Christ. Yet in another way the mandate to accept and "cooperate" with God at those times when he lacked trust in God only increased religious doubt and despair. Indeed, the notion that acceptance and cooperation are the work of God rather than the result of "free will" only made matters worse, for it is precisely God's power which is questioned by the terrified conscience.[24]

When religion becomes a matter of "doing something," there is always the fear that one cannot do enough; one feels that one must "justify" oneself before God "by the works of law." If God himself is the subject of one's doubt and despair, how then can one ever hope to do anything at all? Luther did not doubt the existence of God, but he did doubt whether God could ever be gracious to him. Thus the question of justification before God was rooted in the question of whether there is any justification for one's existence. Why live at all if one does not know whether God cares? Luther raised this radical question in the "forensic" context of a court of law, just as Paul had done.[25] At issue was the verdict on the value of life, a "last judgment."

Luther's despair over the meaninglessness of life led to the fundamental "Lutheran" insight that the value of life cannot be dependent on any effort of the self. For life to have any value at all means that it has to be unconditionally affirmed, without any "if." Any conditional affirmation—"if you do this, then . . . "—only increases despair in the face of what needs to be done to be liberated from despair. Luther discovered that if there is any meaning at all in what God did in Christ, it must be *unconditional* promise of salvation. The promise is unconditional because Jesus overcame death, the final condition of human existence, by his resurrection. Since Jesus lives *now*, the living Christ affirms my life by constantly addressing me. The communication-event of the gospel, the cheering news that Jesus has died for me and is living for me, affirms my life. My life has become addressed by the unconditional affirmation that not my self but my relationship to him constitutes the reason for living. I now live "by faith alone." Faith has become a mode of life, a constant listening to and benefitting from what Luther called Christ's "last will and testament."[26] The narrative of Christ's life, death, and resurrection becomes life's norm in a world filled with doubt, despair, and death. When communicated in Word and sacrament, the gospel knows no "ifs"—"if you do this, then God will fulfill your life." The gospel simply says, "Because Christ crucified lives, your life is good." And when despairing believers respond, "But I cannot believe," the gospel communicator retorts, "But it is precisely for people like you that Christ died and lives; for God justifies the ungodly" (Rom. 4:5).

That is why justification was for Luther the comprehensive term for a relationship of complete trust in the gospel, the cheering news of liberation from doubt and despair. As he put it, as early as 1516:

> Learn Christ and him crucified. Learn to praise him and, despairing of yourself, say, "Lord Jesus, you are my righteousness, just as I am your sin. You have taken upon yourself what is mine and have given to me what is yours. You have taken upon yourself what you were not and have given to me what I was not." Beware of aspiring to such purity that you will not wish to be looked upon as a sinner, or to be one. For Christ dwells only in sinners. On this account he descended from heaven, where he dwelt among the righteous, to dwell among sinners. Meditate on this love of his and you will see his sweet consolation.[27]

This is not an affirmation of mysticism, even though the young Luther appreciated that tradition. Rather, it is the affirmation of faith in the eschatological power of God who draws believers to himself no matter what obstacles stand in the way, and who does so through Christ alone.[28]

Luther viewed all theology as the continuous attempt to free the communication of God's unconditional promise, "the gospel," from every temptation to make that promise conditional through exhortations to do something, to fulfill "the law." He insisted that this distinction between "law" and "gospel" must be made at all levels of life, rationally as well as experientially.

> The knowledge of this topic, the distinction between the Law and the Gospel, is necessary to the highest degree; for it contains a summary of all Christian doctrine. Therefore let everyone learn diligently how to distinguish the Law from the Gospel, not only in words but in feeling and in experience; that is, let him distinguish well between these two in his heart and in his conscience. For so far as the words are concerned, the distinction is easy. But when it comes to experience, you will find the Gospel a rare guest but the Law a constant guest in your conscience, which is habituated to the Law and the sense of sin; reason, too, supports this sense.[29]

It is very important to understand what Luther meant by "distinction." He did not mean theoretical distinction in the sense of affirming something which already exists, as if God first issued "the law" and then "the gospel." Rather, Luther meant a continuing process, a constant, difficult sorting out of demands and promises which requires "the greatest skill in Christendom."[30] Life is filled with both: there is always some kind of demand made on me, and there is always some sort of promise given. The question is, "Which of the demands and promises come from the God who is the Father of Jesus Christ?" That God, Luther contended, is a God who says what he does and does what he says. His Word, be it law or gospel, is never communicated without doing what it says. But one must clearly distinguish between the divine Word and the human word. While the former does what it says, the latter does not do what it says. Only God is truly wholistic; fallen, sinful creatures are not, which is why they pervert God's Word when they try to make it completely their own.

The faithful communicators of the Word of God must remain passive, as it were, and be constantly aware of the temptation to identify their word with the Word of God. That is why the distinction between the divine and the human can be made only in the process of communicating—in preaching, according to Luther. "Preaching" means total dedication to the communication of what one has heard as liberating "gospel." Such dedication, however, always puts preachers in conflict with themselves because the self is always tempted to falsify the message by adding conditions to human life, rather than letting God be God. The act of communication itself is the only guard against the serpentine desire "to be God" and thus violate the First Commandment of the Decalogue, the original "law."

Luther was convinced that from the viewpoint of God both law and gospel ultimately have the same aim: to restore the original communion of trust, the "garden of Eden," which has been polluted—indeed, devastated—by sin. Sin remains a mystery, and any speculation as to why it occurred—whether it occurred with God's permission or was the work of Satan, "the fallen angel"—only leads to confusion, and confusion is always "diabolic" (from the Greek *diaballein*, "to throw things about," thus "to deceive"). What counts, according to Luther, is complete trust in God who, in his terrifying majesty, makes demands only in order to drive his creatures to his promise that in Christ sinners have their only chance to become once again his children. The law, Luther insisted, reveals sin (Rom. 3:20).

> For this reason, therefore, the Law is not against the promises of God: first, because the promise does not depend on the Law but on the truth of God; secondly, because in its highest and greatest use the Law humbles and by humbling makes men groan, sigh, and seek the hand of the Mediator. . . . Therefore the best use of the Law is to be able to employ it to the point that it produces humility and a thirst for Christ.[31]

The law, therefore, is God's way of causing despair in order to plow up the self-righteousness which is the typical human condition. Human beings are always tempted to appease God by fulfilling his law—"natural," "moral," or "spiritual." Yet its real function is to create genuine despair, an *Anfechtung* which discloses the total human inability to please God by assuming that sin can be eliminated by moral deeds. Moral deeds are the consequences of total trust in Christ's atoning death rather than the conditions for such trust. Thus the Law discloses the power of sin, which is the enduring human temptation to be self-righteous rather than to rely on the righteousness of God in Christ.

The gospel, not the law, is the ultimate "good word" which creates freedom and joy, true manifestations of a relationship with God. The gospel is the powerful divine beam of light which guides faithful Christians through the interim between Christ's first and second coming, an interim filled with the constant struggle between human sin and divine righteousness. The gospel is the explosive power of God ("dynamite," from the Greek *dynamos*, Rom. 1:16) which is "imputed" by faith; and faith is the mode through which Christ's righteousness becomes the righteousness of the believer, an "alien righteousness," as Luther liked to say.[32]

> The person who believes in Christ is righteous and holy through divine imputation. He already sees himself, and is, in heaven, being surrounded by the heaven of mercy. But while we are lifted up into the bosom of the Father, and are clad with the finest raiment, our feet reach out below the garment, and Satan bites them whenever he can. Then the child struggles and cries out, and realizes that he is still flesh and blood, and that the Devil is still there, and plagues him constantly, until the whole man grows holy and is lifted up out of this wicked and evil world. Thus we are saints and children [of God], but in the spirit, not in the flesh, and we dwell under the shadow of the wings of the mother hen, in the bosom of grace. But our feet must still be washed, and because they are unclean must go on being bitten and tortured by Satan, until they are clean. For you must draw your tiny feet with you under the garment, otherwise you will have no peace.[33]

Thus to live "by faith alone" means to trust the promise as the consoling and affirming address (*promissio* in Latin, *Zusage* in German), the proclamation that Christ's righteousness mediates salvation from sinful human disobedience. Believers partake of Christ's benefits by faith. These benefits are conferred by verbal, audible communication as well as by sacramental enactment in Holy Baptism—the rite which initiates infants into communion with Christ through the gift of his Holy Spirit—and in the Lord's Supper, the event which sustains believers in their struggles against sin, death, and the devil. The Word, be it audible in proclamation or visible in sacramental enactment, leads to faith; and faith ties the believer to Christ, who is the incarnate Word of God (John 1:14).

With the help of Paul and Augustine, Luther rediscovered that there is no way to argue oneself into a faith in God who justifies the ungodly. Nor is there a way to appease God with moral deeds which might extinguish guilt about sin. Neither syllogism nor moralism have a place in Christianity. "Faith" is simply more than just "belief" in certain rational truths about God. Faith means being apprehended by God's Word that Christ is the meaning of life. "Faith makes the person, the person does good works, good works neither make the faith nor the person."[34]

Justification occurs in the "cheerful exchange" (*fröhlicher Wechsel*) of Christ's righteousness and human sin.[35] Thus Luther tied justification to the

dogma of the Trinity. The god who is revealed is the God who is Christ; and
Christ is the one who reconciles sinners with God, indeed he is the one who
"shares our sin" (2 Cor. 5:21).[36] When theology is normed by the stipulation
that sinners are "justified by faith alone," its enterprise is indeed essentially
doxological. By enabling believers to adhere to the communication of the
gospel and by distinguishing it from the law, theology lays the groundwork
for praise and thanksgiving, the only proper response to what God did in
Christ. A christocentric theology, therefore, will constantly guard the
mystery of the incarnation from rationalist explanations and moralistic
interpretations, be they anchored in legitimate Greek metaphysical tradition
or in honest attempts to please God by moral action.

A PROPOSAL OF DOGMA

It will not do to make articles of faith out of the holy Fathers' words or works.
Otherwise what they ate, how they dressed, and what kind of houses they lived
in would have to become articles of faith—as has happened in the case of relics.
This means that *the Word of God shall establish articles of faith* and no one else,
not even an angel [Gal. 1:8].[37]

With statements such as these, Luther opened up a Pandora's box of
questions related to the relationship between the authority of the Word of
God and "dogma" (from the Greek word for "philosophical norm" and/or
"public edict"). If God's Word reveals the justification of the ungodly by faith
alone, how does one move from existential confession to rational exposition
or from doxology, the praise of God, to orthodoxy, correct teaching?
Moreover, if the doctrine of justification functions as a stipulation for how the
Word of God is to be communicated, is it still possible to reflect about the
effects of the communication—how salvation through Christ alone affects life
in the struggle against sin, death, and evil? How does the article of
justification function as *dogma*—as a norm for theological reflection and as an
edict of the church concerning faith and morals?

Luther provided occasional hints of a "theory" of justification, but he did
not really expect the theory to be the article on which the church stands and
falls.[38] Nevertheless, Luther was the initiator of a proposal of dogma made to
the Roman Catholic Church by the Lutheran confessions, especially the
Augsburg Confession and its Apology. And this proposal of dogma was rooted
in his theme of justification and disclosed the results of certain basic
theological reflections:[39]

1. A serious confrontation with the power of the sin of idolatry—the desire
"to be like God." This desire is sheer nonsense when one considers the
absolute majesty and power of God who "is an inexpressible being, above
and beyond all that can be described or imagined."[40] Such a desire only

discloses the totally unrealistic understanding of human existence. For God alone can bridge the distance between himself and his creatures. He does so through the law, which reveals both the creature's distance from himself and the idolatry of trying to be God.

2. A recognition that one's relationship with God is a gift, given "by grace alone." Divine grace is revealed in the gospel of God's incarnation in Christ. But Christ's righteousness does not annul human sinfulness. As God's "alien righteousness," it is grasped "by faith alone" and thus coexists with human sin. Thus believers are simultaneously righteous and sinners: sinners "according to the way things are," but righteous by "imputation and promise."[41] While this may sound contradictory from the viewpoint of an ontological description of human nature and being, it is not contradictory when viewed within the dialectic of relationships. On the one hand, believers are related to God *(coram Deo)* and are righteous in God's view. On the other hand, believers are related to the world *(coram mundo)* and are sinners in their own view. Luther replaced medieval categories and those of classical antiquity with an analysis of the human condition *under the aspect of relationship.*[42] One's relationship to the God who justifies the ungodly in Christ creates the firm hope for total liberation at the end of time when God will create a new creation. The gospel already empowers one to overcome sin, to do good, and to transform oneself, albeit never completely. Trust in God creates hope and certainty about salvation since God does what he promises.

3. A complete faith that God's majestic power is linked to his unconditional love for his creatures. This faith is expressed in the confession that Christ is "for us" *(pro nobis)* rather than just "in us." Certainty comes through the Word of promise from the outside, not through concentration on internal feelings about God. The same God who is in charge of everything is also the God who justifies the ungodly. Divine predestination is the flip side of divine justification. That is why human will is in "bondage" to faith rather than "free" to decide whether or not to accept God's promise. God is also the God who predestines one for salvation. Christ, the revealed God, is also the hidden God, the Creator. If one is terrified by the hidden God, one must flee to the revealed God who has suffered, who died, and who was resurrected. Theology must concentrate on the communication of the gospel properly distinguished from law, so that terrified consciences may be consoled and not frightened.

> We could never come to recognize the Father's favor and grace were it not for the Lord Christ, who is a mirror of the Father's heart. Apart from him we see nothing but an angry and terrible Judge. But neither could we know anything of Christ, had it not been revealed by the Holy Spirit.[43]

The tragedy of the Reformation is that this christocentric way of speaking about God was proposed and argued in the polemical context of the relationship between faith and good works. Lutherans understood Catholics to insist that one could earn salvation by the merit of good works; and Catholics understood Lutherans to insist that justification by faith alone excludes good works altogether. As Philip Melanchthon put it in the Apology of the Augsburg Confession:

> They [the Roman opponents] condemn us both for denying that men receive the forgiveness of sins because of their merits, and for affirming that men receive the forgiveness of sins by faith and by faith in Christ are justified.
>
> In this controversy the main doctrine of Christianity is involved; when it is properly understood, it illumines and magnifies the honor of Christ and brings to pious consciences the abundant consolation that they need.[44]

Lutherans were unable to convince their opponents that the doctrine of justification was "the article of Christ" which did not exclude works, but rather viewed them as the fruits of faith in Christ alone rather than as a condition of salvation. So understood, the article of justification was a proposal of dogma to the church catholic *to return to christocentric theological reflection* and be christocentric rather than anthropocentric in all ecclesiastical endeavors. But Catholics did not view the matter in this fashion. The commission of Catholic theologians who had been appointed by Emperor Charles V to respond to the Augsburg Confession insisted that the Lutheran doctrine of justification was "diametrically opposed to the evangelical truth which does not exclude works."[45]

The Lutheran proposed dogma meant to be what could be called a "metalinguistic stipulation" for church proclamation rather than a theological doctrine.[46] What Lutherans proposed was a certain way of communicating, with or without using the word "justification." Simply put: "Speak in such a way that whatever is said is so understood that the merits of good works— self-righteousness—are excluded from any discourse about salvation." This does not mean that good works should not be done. But works should be part of faith rather than its condition. When the gospel is so communicated—and thus properly distinguished from law—God's love of his fallen creatures, revealed in his incarnation in Christ, will challenge hearers to ponder the meaning of their own lives as interpreted by the story of Jesus. No longer would they be guided by the conditions of law ("if . . . then") but by the pattern of promise ("because . . . therefore").

> The gospel tolerates no conditions. It is itself unconditional promise. And when it is rightly spoken, it takes the conditions we put on the value of our life as the very occasions of its promise. This is the first and fundamental Lutheran proposal of dogma.[47]

This proposal affects not only oral but also visible communication of the gospel. When Word and sacraments are so communicated that they disclose God's unconditional promise in the gospel of Jesus' life, death, and resurrection, they constitute the minimum requirement for Christian unity. "For the true unity of the church it is enough to agree concerning the teaching of the Gospel and the administration of the sacraments."[48]

The Lutheran proposal of dogma can be stated in various ways. Some post-Reformation Roman Catholic theologians no longer perceive Luther's article of justification as church-dividing; rather, they see it as the common basis for continuing the reformation of the universal church.[49] In this sense, Luther's proposal of dogma has finally found the hearing it deserves. In the words of Cardinal Jan Willebrands:

> It is good to remember a man to whom justification was the article on which the church stands and falls. He [Luther] may be our common teacher in that God must always remain in charge and that our most significant human answer must always be absolute trust in and adoration of God.[50]

10

A CRUCIFORM CHURCH

When Christians are not doing battle with the devil, or him who bites the heel, that is not a good sign, for it means that he who bites the heel is at peace and has his own way. But when he who bites the heel rages and has no peace, it is a sign that he, being under attack, shall be conquered, for it is Christ who is attacking his house. Therefore whoever desires to see the Christian Church existing in quiet peace, entirely without crosses, without heresy, and without factions, will never see it thus, or else he must view the false church of the devil as the real church. ("The Three Symbols or Creeds of the Christian Church," 1538. *WA* 50:272.30–273.1. *LW* 34:215)

CHRISTIAN FORMATION

Luther's liturgical, catechetical, and socio-economic reforms in Wittenberg and Electoral Saxony were designed to preserve the best of the ecclesiastical tradition and to honor common sense. His first steps towards revising public worship in 1523 took the basic liturgical rhythm of medieval Christendom for granted, provided the Word of God—the divine promise to justify the ungodly through Christ—was clearly communicated. Parishioners were encouraged to attend daily Matins and Vespers; the Roman Mass was celebrated in Latin and German on Sundays; and major festivals besides Christmas and Easter continued to be celebrated during the church year (including such mariological festivals as the Assumption of Mary, 15 August).[1] "We on our part confess that there is much that is Christian and good under the papacy," Luther asserted against the "left-wing" *Schwärmer* when he accused them of throwing the baby out with the bathwater in matters of liturgy and sacraments.[2]

Common sense, he said, should guide congregations in their efforts to eliminate begging, usury, and other economic injustices; no one should presume to have perfect solutions to problems resulting from ecclesiastical abuses. He gave advice where he could and encouraged others to find better solutions.[3]

Luther considered worship and Christian education the twin pillars supporting the church militant on earth. His catechetical reforms were intimately linked to his reform of worship and were built on the tradition emphasizing the Decalogue, the Lord's Prayer, and the creeds; he added instruction concerning Holy Baptism and the Lord's Supper.[4] Both liturgy and catechetics challenge Christians to move from Sunday worship to a Monday ministry firmly founded on a "liturgy of the mind," as it were, against the forces of sin, death, and evil. He warned Christians never to assume they have sufficient security against idolatry unless they are continuously fortified by worship and daily catechetical exercise. "Let them never stop until they have proved by experience that they have taught the devil to death and have become wiser than God Himself and all His saints."[5]

These admonitions were firmly grounded in Luther's view of Holy Baptism as the constitutive sacrament of the church. Baptism confers a "spiritual estate" (*geistlicher Stand*) on every Christian. As a result, "there is no true, basic difference between laymen and priests, princes and bishops, between religious and secular, except for the sake of office and work (*Amt*), but not for the sake of status (*Stand*)."[6]

Luther scholars have had intensive debates on the questions of how Luther distinguished the office of the ordained ministry from the common priesthood of all the baptized, and why he accepted without question the medieval feudal stratifications so evident in the segregation between the nobility and the common people.[7] But the ecumenical implications of Luther's insistence that worship and education are interrelated and are grounded in the doctrine of baptism have yet to be more fully appreciated. To Luther, all of Christian life was a return to baptism, the event in which the Holy Spirit begins the work of combating evil, "the unclean spirit."[8] From that moment on, even though baptized Christians have to struggle against the "old Adam" every day, they know that Christ has joined the fray.

> Therefore let everybody regard his Baptism as the daily garment which he is to wear all the time. Every day he should be found in faith and amid its fruits, every day he should be suppressing the old man and growing up in the new. . . . But if anybody falls away from his Baptism let him return to it. As Christ, the mercy seat [Rom. 3:25; Heb. 4:16], does not recede from us or forbid us to return to him even though we sin, so all his treasures and gifts remain. As we have once obtained forgiveness of sins in Baptism, so forgiveness remains day by day as long as we live, that is, as long as we carry the old Adam about our necks.[9]

Thus baptism was to Luther the initiation into a lifelong struggle between love of God and love of self, a struggle which causes suffering and which is the most significant mark of membership in the body of Christ. In this sense, Christian life is "formed" by a loving suffering with and for others. All of life is a return to baptism.[10] Baptism frees believers to turn away from themselves, and towards others, and so to do the good works of faith. In this sense, "penance" is the flip side of baptism: it is one's continual confession of the sin of desiring to compete with God and the continual assurance that God absolves one from sin and thus liberates one to a life of faith active in love.

> Confession consists of two parts. The first is my work and act, when I lament my sin and desire comfort and restoration of my soul. The second is a work which God does, when he absolves me of my sins through a word placed in the mouth of a man. This is the surpassingly grand and noble thing that makes confession so wonderful and comforting. . . . We should therefore take care to keep the two parts clearly separate. We should set little value on our work but exalt and magnify God's Word. We should not act as if we wanted to perform a magnificent work to present to him, but simply to accept and receive something from him.[11]

What is received is the "gospel" which, according to Luther,

> offers counsel and help against sin in more than one way, for God is surpassingly rich in His grace: First, through the spoken word, by which forgiveness of sin (the peculiar [*eigentlich*] office of the Gospel) is preached to the whole world; second, through Baptism; third, through the holy Sacrament of the Altar; fourth, through the power of keys [Matt. 16:19 confession]; and finally, through the mutual conversation and consolation of brethren [Matt. 18:20].[12]

"Liturgy" (from the Greek *leiturgia*, "the work of the people") is the audible and visible enactment of the Word of God in its proper distinction between demand and promise. Believers turn to God to receive forgiveness of sins for Christ's sake; after they have been received into grace, they turn from God to their neighbors to serve them in their needs. Stimulated by Christ's parable of the Pharisee and the tax collector (Luke 18:10), Luther defined worship as "going in to God" and service as "going out from God." In worship one submits to God's judgment and grace, receives forgiveness of sins, and is strengthened for the life in the world. One can now move from God to the neighbor and do the work which God has commanded: teachers serve by teaching well, princes by governing justly, the head of the family by working to support his family.[13] True worship, therefore, is like inhaling and exhaling. Members of Christ's body inhale by hearing and receiving Word and sacraments in appropriate liturgical enactment in the church; and they exhale by serving others with selfless, sacrificial love.

"Catechesis" (from the Greek *katechein*, "sounding back") is instruction in what God "wishes us to do or not to do" (Decalogue), a "setting forth all that we must expect and receive from God" (the Creed), and a demonstration of "how we are to pray" (the Lord's Prayer).[14] Luther added that Christ instituted two sacraments—Holy Baptism and the Eucharist—without which "no one can be a Christian."[15] Catechetical instruction, therefore, provides cognitive insights into the ways God chooses to deal with his creatures. Luther insisted that every baptized Christian must have a minimal theological understanding of what happens in worship as well as how worship relates to everyday life. Those who live with open eyes and ears will soon learn how much they need the assistance of God's Word and sacraments in their struggle against sin, death, and evil. That is why the Lord's Supper, for example, is given as a "daily food" to sustain the people of God in their painful exposure to the world.[16] Luther added that those who do not feel the need for frequent eucharistic nourishment should ask themselves if they are really living in the world.

> If you are in the world, do not think that there will be any lack of sins and needs. Just begin to act as if you want to become good and cling to the Gospel, and see whether you will not acquire enemies who harm, wrong, and injure you and give you occasion for sin and wrong-doing. If you have not experienced this, then take it from the Scriptures, which everywhere give this testimony about the world.[17]

Christian formation thus begins with the promise of salvation given in infant baptism; it continues in repeated exposure to the "audible" Word of God (preaching, teaching, confession and absolution) and to the "visible Word" of the Lord's Supper; and it ends with death, the transition from the church militant to the church triumphant. According to Luther, all of life is a preparing to die. "You must look at death while you are alive and see sin in the light of grace and hell in the light of heaven, permitting nothing to divert you from that view."[18]

Luther's views on worship and education provide a significant ecumenical platform from which to face the ancient and troublesome question, "What ought to happen between baptism and death?" From the very beginning, Christians have been concerned about the time after baptism, about the forgiveness of post-baptismal sins, and about life in the world. If baptism means initiation into the kingdom of God, why should one struggle with evil? Could one not move on to something better after having experienced a touch of the Holy Spirit as a token of what would later become a never-ending life with God? Why must a Christian's life be so filled with suffering, so cruciform? Luther's answer was the assertion that all of a Christian's life is a *return to baptism,* not a march forward to something else, whatever that may be—spiritual self-fulfillment or even growth into "perfection." How does one return to baptism? One returns to baptism by clinging to God's promise of love, given and sealed by the Holy Spirit in infant baptism. This promise of divine love is continually proffered by other Christians who have thus become the instrument of the gospel: the cheering news that salvation from evil and liberation from death comes through Jesus Christ who is God incarnate. The gospel instruments are means of wholistic human communication: the judging and consoling Word in preaching, teaching and absolution, both public and private; and the Lord's Supper, the meal in which Christ promised to be present. Every time the gospel is communicated in these ways, the old life of sin is renounced and the new life in Christ is affirmed, just as in baptism the old Adam was drowned so that new life could emerge. In this sense, Christian life is a continual dying and being reborn by being exposed to the gospel in Word and sacraments. To Luther this external body-side of God was the sole source of comfort to the terrified conscience. Christian life is therefore structured, nurtured, and shaped by the externals of Word and sacraments.

Such a view of Christian formation conflicts with Western culture's "natural" pedagogy of anthropological concepts of potentiality, development, and self-realization. "Education" (from the Latin *educare*, "to draw out") in the context of Greco-Roman philosophy meant programs and processes designed to nurture the continuous and progressive development of a given potential until the desired maturity is achieved—a development from the first, innate nucleus to its full realization in the person. Luther perceived such a pedagogy to be the greatest temptation to become self-righteous, to trust the ability of one's inner self rather than having faith in God's work. This natural pedagogy has dominated the church both before and after the time of Luther; the philosophy of the Enlightenment, in particular, revived Greco-Roman ideals of education.

The relationship between infant baptism and the Lord's Supper is a case in point. Many churches have determined that one's admission to the Lord's Supper is predicated on one's ability to confess one's sin. Consequently only children attaining the age of discretion (variously defined as age seven or older) are permitted to participate in the Lord's Supper. Sacramental nurture has thus become closely linked to natural pedagogy, and therefore depends on specific psychological insights.[19] But is anyone ever "ready" to understand the Christian faith? Luther himself encouraged the participation of children in the Lord's Supper: "Since they are baptized and received into the Christian church, they should also enjoy this fellowship of the sacrament so that they may serve us and be useful. For they must all help us to believe, to love, to pray, and to fight the devil."[20] Did Luther assume a natural progression from sacramental initiation to cognitive appreciation of ecclesiastical events? He could certainly be read that way. But he also contended that theological reflection must indeed follow or accompany one's initiation into a "sacramental culture."[21] But worship, catechetical knowledge, and theological reflection must all be normed by the affirmation that life with God is a gift offered through Christ crucified and cannot be achieved on one's own. To enjoy the gift, however, one has to struggle with the "old Adam"; one has to crucify much of the self in order to become free for others; one has to suffer change. "For where God's Word is preached, accepted or believed, and bears fruit, there the blessed holy cross will not be far away."[22]

SUFFERING SERVANTHOOD

In conformity with the prophetic and apostolic tradition, Luther affirmed that the church, like Christ, must suffer tribulation. What Isaiah and Paul had taught was true: "The more the church is oppressed and hemmed in, the more it rises up";[23] what happened to the "suffering servant," the Messiah, also happens to the church. Hence the church is afflicted, storm tossed, and known as "Miss Hopeless."[24] Every Christian must endure the pain of the struggle against evil—be it persecution or any other *Anfechtung*—but it is the ordained ministers of the church who are in the forefront of the struggle, which began with Christ and will end only when he comes again at the end of time.

When Luther found himself confronted by the power of the papacy, he stressed the ministry of all baptized, the "common priesthood." But in the 1520s, when *Schwärmer* began their opposition to ordination, to sacraments, and to ecclesiastical structures in general and claimed the Holy Spirit to be the only authority, Luther defended the ecumenical tradition of a divinely instituted office of the ministry. He declared that the ordained form one of the three "holy orders and true institutions" along with marriage and government.[25]

> I hope, indeed, that believers, those who want to be called Christians, know very well that the spiritual estate [clergy] has been established and instituted by God, not with gold or silver but with the precious blood and bitter death of his only Son, our Lord Jesus Christ [1 Pet. 1:18–19]. From his wounds indeed flow the sacraments. . . . He paid dearly that men might everywhere have this office of preaching, baptizing, loosing, binding, giving the sacrament, comforting, warning, and exhorting with God's word, and whatever else belongs to the pastoral office. . . . Indeed, it is only because of the spiritual estate that the world stands and abides at all; if it were not for this estate, the world would long since have gone down to destruction.[26]

As servants of the Word of God, pastors lead the church in its struggle against sin, death, and evil. The church cannot be truly recognized without "bishops, pastors, or preachers."[27] But to Luther they are neither a special holy order, as the medieval church taught, nor simply functionaries representing individual congregations, as some later Lutherans suggested.[28] They are called by the church at large and pledged to tend and to guard the gospel of God's unconditional love for his creatures through the work of Christ. They continue the first apostles' charge from Jesus to communicate the good word about God's incarnation in Christ. They are servants of the gospel who may have to suffer for the gospel, for its power can only be shared, never possessed. Christ alone is "master," Christians are "brethren" (Matt. 23:8, 10). No single individual can claim to have authority over others.

But for the sake of good order the Christian community chooses and calls one or more, if necessary, to be the public representatives of the gospel (1 Cor. 14:40). Luther therefore linked ordination to what he called "the community rights": the right of a congregation to choose, approve, and appoint one of their own to be their pastor. Each individual Christian is a minister by baptism and shares in a "common" ministry. The "special" or ordained ministry should not be exercised without the consent of the Christian community; in an emergency, Christians must do what they deem best.[29]

How are "common" and "special" ministries properly distinguished? Luther gave no totally satisfactory answer, but it could be said that he viewed all "lay" vocations as gospel ministries to the world—be they exercised by princes or by peasants. He assumed that the "ordained" shared this ministry to the world, but contended that their primary responsibility was to the gospel itself within the Christian gathering. They are ministers *of* the gospel *in* the church: *of* the gospel because they are to communicate it verbally and sacramentally; *in* the church because it is the gathering created by the gospel and is responsible for its communication. That is why Luther could say, "Outside the Christian church (that is, where the Gospel is not) there is no forgiveness, and hence no holiness."[30] But if it is faithful, the church will suffer in the world.

> But when you are condemned, cursed, reviled, slandered, and plagued because of Christ, you are sanctified [Matt. 5:11–12]. It mortifies the old Adam and teaches him patience, humility, gentleness, praise and thanks, and good cheer in suffering. That is what it means to be sanctified by the Holy Spirit and to be renewed to a new life in Christ; in that way we learn to believe in God, to trust Him, to love Him, and to place our hope in Him [Rom. 5:1–5].[31]

Luther's doctrine of the church could be summarized as a recall to suffering servanthood, for suffering has always been one of the principal aspects of being a Christian in the world. But not the kind of suffering which many Christians throughout the ages had "enjoyed": a life full of sacrifices made to earn God's favor. Luther was quite aware of the dangerous connection which has always existed between the desire to mortify the flesh, to suffer, and the temptation to be self-righteous. "False worship," idolatry, begins with a "conscience which seeks help, comfort, and salvation in its own works and presumes to wrest heaven from God."[32] Those who want to be "religious" usually succumb to self-righteousness, if "religion" means worship of God through selfish mystical introspection, rational speculation, or moral action.

To Luther, the church is the gathering of those who trust in God's Word alone as the means by which the Holy Spirit gives faith. Consequently the church, as an institution, must be so constituted as to serve the instrumentation of Word and sacrament. Since such instrumentation, according to Luther, is always fraught with the possibility, indeed the reality, of idolatry, the church must always be "reformed"—that is, changed—whenever necessary in both spirit and structure. There has to be clear discernment of the difference between "essentials" (things necessary for gospel communication) and "adiaphora" (things not necessary for tending the gospel). He made it quite clear that the communication-event of the gospel must never be confused with the means and ways which make this event possible. Bishops are good for the well-being of the church, as long as they serve—but do not dominate—the gospel. Elizabethan English may enhance gospel communication; but if it is no longer clearly understood, the prevalent vernacular is to be preferred. Thus the church must remain task-oriented, that is, it must undergo change whenever necessary for the sake of serving the gospel faithfully.

Luther's insistence that "the church must always be reformed" (*ecclesia semper reformanda est*) was closely linked with his view of the church as a "suffering servant," the cruciform body of Christ on earth. When the Word of God is tended with complete trust in its power, suffering cannot be far behind. Serving and suffering belong together. Luther was convinced that the church may have to suffer the loss of its status in order to become a better instrument of the gospel. Or the church may have to endure persecution from those who want to enforce their own ways of attaining salvation. Whatever the reason for their suffering, Christians will be reformed by the various tribulations; they are tests for knowing the difference between the true and the false church, although it takes a childlike faith to know the difference.

> Thank God, a seven-year-old child knows what the church is, namely, holy believers and sheep who hear the voice of their Shepherd. So children pray, "I believe in one holy Christian church." Its holiness does not consist of surplices, tonsures, albs, or other ceremonies of theirs [the papists] which they have invented over and above the Holy Scriptures, but it consists of the Word of God and true faith.[33]

THE COST OF UNITY

Luther lived at a time when the church's abuse of ecclesiastical power threatened the unity of Christendom. The competition for power between two popes, one in Rome and the other in Avignon, France (1378–1415), created a devastating schism. There were persistent anti-papal movements like the Hussites, particularly after the execution of John Hus during the Council of Constance in 1415. Neither "conciliarists," defenders of the authority of councils of bishops, nor the "curialists," advocates of papal control over councils, succeeded in reforming the church. Throughout the fifteenth century, the popular demand grew for a radical church reform—"a reformation in head and members."[34]

Luther viewed this power struggle within the church as a conflict between God and Satan, a conflict which would end only with the second coming of Christ—an event Luther expected during his own lifetime. He believed that this cosmic conflict between God and Satan manifested itself in a power struggle between the true and the false church; but he was at first reluctant to call the pope the head of the false church. Even during the controversy over indulgences, he wrote Pope Leo X on 30 May 1518:

> Holy Father, I am throwing myself at your feet, pleading with all I have and am. Give me life, kill me, revoke, permit, reject—whatever you wish to decide: I shall acknowledge your voice as the voice of Christ who leads through you and speaks through you. If I have deserved death, I shall not refuse to die.[35]

When, however, Luther discovered that the pope had condoned the indulgences traffic in order to help the bishop of Mainz pay for the title of archbishop, he regretted having been so humble and naive; he added the words "I cannot recant" on the other side of the letter.[36] Finally, when Rome threatened to excommunicate him, so he condemned the pope "in the name and on the basis of the power by which I have become in baptism a child of God and co-heir of Christ through baptism."[37] On the other hand, Luther addressed the dying John Tetzel as a member of the body of Christ and wrote that he was praying for him; he also advised Tetzel to be of good cheer and not to be too upset about their conflict in the matter of indulgences. Luther regarded Tetzel as a victim of circumstances rather than as an evil man deserving to be hated.[38]

Luther also detected the struggle between the true and false church within his own reform movement. He considered radical *Schwärmer* like Thomas Müntzer, who preached rebellion and sedition in the name of the gospel, to be members of the false church. At the same time, he was willing to negotiate with *Schwärmer* like Ulrich Zwingli of Zurich on the matter of the interpretation of the Lord's Supper.

Luther refused to identify the truth of the Christian faith with any one set of teachings or practices. What was at stake for him was a basic orientation grounded in the gospel that through faith in Christ one received God's promise to restore the relationship which had been lost through sin. Thus the church's existence depends entirely on the proclamation of God's promise of a future with Christ. This future is assured by faith alone rather than by reliance on dogma, good works, or other factors; and the true church is wherever such faith exists. Much of the true church is invisible, according to Luther, for God hides spiritual truth from people who do not understand (1 Cor. 2:7–15); thus faith is "the conviction of things not seen" (Heb. 11:1). On the other hand, the church becomes visible in Word, sacraments, and institutional structures "for the sake of the confession of faith" (Rom. 10:10).[39]

Once Luther was convinced that his own church had become the victim of a triumphalist abuse of papal power, he labeled it "false" and saw himself involved in a struggle between a truly ecumenical gospel movement striving for reform without schism and a papal church refusing to yield to the power of the gospel and thus betraying it. There were, then, according to Luther, two opposing traditions: the papal tradition which claimed that the bishop of Rome was superior to all other bishops and represented the power of Christ on earth and the apostolic tradition which claimed the apostolic succession of the gospel, independent of any ecclesiastical structures. Luther was nevertheless quite willing to regard the episcopal structure as the best and most experienced manifestation of ecclesiastical authority:

> The church cannot be better governed and maintained than by having all of us live under one head, Christ, and by having all the bishops equal in office . . . and diligently joined together in unity of doctrine, faith, sacraments, prayer, works of love, etc. . . . It becomes apparent that, at its best, the teaching of the pope has been taken from the imperial, pagan law and is a teaching concerning secular transactions and judgments, as the papal decretals show. [40]

If, therefore, the pope would understand his power to be derived only from "human law" (*de iure humano*) and not from "divine law" (*de iure divino*), Lutherans would be willing to accept papal authority "for the sake of peace and general unity."[41] Luther stressed the pastoral aspect of the episcopal office, and he insisted that the office abide by the priority of theological reflections, especially concerning doctrine and liturgy, over church polity.[42] Eventually, Lutherans created territorial dioceses headed by a *superintendens*, the Latin designation for the Greek *episcopos*, meaning "overseer."

Luther's doctrine of the church was guided by the norm that "the church is always in a state of becoming (*Kirche im Werden*)" because of the conflict between the Word of God and human traditions.[43] At its best, the church is not just an institution but a gathering around the Word of God, which moves from its struggles in the world to full union with Christ at the end of time. That is why Luther did not like the term "church" (*Kirche*), especially if it was associated with an organization or a building.

> The word *ecclesia* properly means an assembly. We, however, are accustomed to the term *Kirche*, "church," by which simple folk understand not a group of people but a consecrated house or building. But the house should not be called a church except for the single reason that the group of people assembles there. For we who assemble select a special place and then give the house its name by virtue of the assembly. [44]

Luther always liked the term "community" (*communio*) for church since this term connotes a live gathering of people. As God's people, Christians must struggle through life on earth with the help of the Holy Spirit:

Now we are only halfway pure and holy. The Holy Spirit must continue to work
in us through the Word, daily granting forgiveness until we attain to that life
where there will be no more forgiveness.[45]

The church, as the communion of saints with the "appearance of a
sinner,"[46] must bear the burden of caring for Christian unity. When one part
of the church succumbs to sin in the struggle for survival, another part of the
church must try to help those who fall. The church is a community of those
who bear each others' burden, and those members who refuse to do so are
not true members of the church. Luther therefore chided the Bohemian
Hussites for their apostasy from the Roman Catholic Church. He told them
they should have worked at reforming the church from within, by running
right to its center rather than away from it, for the law of Christ demands
suffering for the sake of unity.[47] Luther himself never abandoned the idea of
catholicity in his doctrine of the church, and he linked Christian unity with
the confession of Christ who, as the head of the church, calls Christians to
suffer for each other as well as together in the face of adversity in the world.[48]

> Yes, how much better it would be if the devil did not insist on biting Christ's
> heel, or if he were made to desist from doing that! Then a quiet, peaceful church
> could easily become a reality. But since the devil is at present Christ's enemy
> and never stops creating strife, sects, and rebellion in the church, one is doing
> violence to the dear church by blaming it for the discord and undisciplined state
> of affairs. *It does not cause them, but, on the contrary, is obliged to suffer
> them*.[49]

Luther bequeathed to subsequent generations his view of the church: a
dynamic happening rather than a static institution. For any ecumenical
dialogue, an understanding of the church as an interim embodiment
between Christ's ascension and his second coming is crucial. Just as Christ
suffered on earth, so must his body the church endure various crosses in its
ministry to the world. Again Luther insisted that the church's unity is closely
linked to its cruciformity: those who affirm one faith, one baptism, and one
Lord will have to pay a heavy price in a world in which any gathering of
people is at all times tempted to deify, in one way or another, the human—
whether it be ideas, deeds, or organizations. Egotism and narcissism are
more easily institutionalized than a cruciform life. But if the church is
faithful, the most significant sign of its unity is its willingness to suffer.

> The holy Christian people . . . must endure every misfortune and persecution,
> all kinds of trials and evil from the devil, the world, and the flesh (as the Lord's
> Prayer indicates) by inward sadness, timidity, fear, outward poverty, contempt,
> illness, and weakness, in order to become like their head, Christ. And the only
> reason they must suffer is that they steadfastly adhere to Christ and God's word,
> enduring this for the sake of Christ, Matthew 5 [:11], "Blessed are you when
> men persecute you on my account."[50]

Such thinking can affect the question of ecclesiastical authority today. If the gospel makes things happen between people, then the doors between various Christian groups must be kept open; it should be possible to share authority, including the magisterial or teaching authority. On the one hand, this is much easier today than it was in Luther's day, since the world has experienced a communication explosion. On the other hand, there is such great religious diversity in the modern world that it has become quite difficult for any one Christian community to relate to others. However, if the principle of cruciformity were to be taken seriously by the organized churches, various ecumenical doors could indeed be thrown open.

What a witness it would be if Christian church leaders from all nations would assemble in order to consider joint ways of supporting persecuted Christians in various parts of the world! Should suffering and persecution not be on the agenda of every ecumenical council? It would be comforting to those who suffer persecution to know that their suffering is recognized by an ecumenical fellowship of church leaders who take Christian martyrdom as seriously as they do schisms.

The forces of idolatry are always strongest where power is concentrated, and it is indeed very difficult to persuade people in positions of power to live by the principle of cruciformity. And yet the church is forced to live with the necessity, imposed by God, to sacrifice institutional structures when these impede the effective communication of the gospel in any way. No worldly power has control over the gospel: not the church, not the state, not any other institution.

> The whole Christian church, with all its high spiritual function and authority, must live by the injunction [1 Pet. 5:1–11] that no human being or any creatures are able to exist by virtue of their own ideas, wisdom, and power. There is no comfort in seeking and relying on the power and protection of the world. God alone is able to keep the church alive, as he has done so wonderfully since the beginning of the world, in the midst of great weakness, division caused by sects and heresies, and persecution by tyrants. He alone rules the church, although he commits and uses the ministry of people to administer His word and sacrament. . . . If the church were dependent on human wisdom, power, and will, the devil would soon subvert and overthrow it with his own power.[51]

11

A WHOLISTIC LIFE

Now since the being and nature of man cannot exist for an instant unless it is doing or not doing something, putting up with or running away from something (for as we know, life never stands still), well then, let him who wants to be holy and full of good works begin to exercise himself at all times in this faith in all his life and works. Let him learn to do and to leave undone all things in such continual faith. Then he will find how much work he has to do, and how completely all things are included in faith, and how he may never grow idle because his very idling must be the exercise and work of faith. ("Treatise on Good Works," 1520. WA 6:212.32–213.1. LW 44:34)

IN TUNE WITH CREATION

Luther viewed all of human existence as a two-faced Gemini existence. There is life "in the face of God" (*coram Deo*), and there is life "in the face of other human beings" (*coram hominibus*). When I face God, completely relying on his grace in Christ, I am righteous; when I face other human beings, trusting them instead of God, I am sinful. That is why I am "simultaneously a righteous person and a sinner" (*simul iustus et peccator*)—a phrase Luther liked to use to describe reality in time and space.[1] Everything depends on what I am facing and how I look to whatever I am facing. To be "seen" (*gesehen*) means to have a "face" (*Gesicht*), an identity. Christians find their identity in their faith.

> Faith is a living, daring confidence in God's grace, so sure and certain that the believer would stake his life on it a thousand times. This knowledge of and confidence in God's grace makes men glad and bold and happy in dealing with God and with all creatures. And this is the work which the Holy Spirit performs in faith.[2]

Luther's intensive work with the Bible had also made him aware that the Holy Spirit works through external means.

> Now when God sends forth His holy Gospel He deals with us in a twofold manner, first outwardly, then inwardly. Outwardly he deals with us through the

oral word of the gospel and through material signs, that is, baptism and the sacrament of the altar. Inwardly he deals with us through the Holy Spirit, faith, and other gifts. But whatever their measure or order, the outward factors should and must precede. The inward experience follows and is effected by the outward. . . . For He wants to give no one the Spirit or faith outside of the outward Word and sign instituted by Him. . . . Observe carefully, my brother, this order, for everything depends on it."[3]

This "order" is the perspective from which Luther viewed the complexity of human life. Whatever happens in this life, the God who justifies the ungodly on account of their faith in Christ is also the mighty Creator in charge of all life.[4] Luther stressed both aspects of the two-faced Gemini existence: the righteousness of faith and the persistence of sin. If, on the one hand, he emphasized *Anfechtung*, spiritual discipline, and Satan's power in the world, he also knew the reality of faith's freedom, joy, and inward peace. Confidence in the God who justifies the ungodly liberates us from anxiety and makes earthly life enjoyable.

Thus a Christian man who lives in this confidence toward God knows all things, can do all things, ventures everything that needs to be done, and does everything gladly and willingly. . . .[5]

One can thus find pleasure in observing the marvelous majesty of God the Creator who is everywhere and in everything. For although the whole creation is a "face or mask of God,"[6] and a masked God may frighten others, Christians know that behind every divine mask there is a gracious God.

Luther had a deep doxological sense of life; he was able to enjoy and praise God's creation and was often in tune with it—in music, in love for "birds, dogs, and babies."[7] When Luther's little dog "Klutz" (from the German *Tölpel*) begged at table and concentrated all his being on the meat, Luther exclaimed, "Oh, if I could only pray the way this dog watches the meat!"[8] He had a sharp eye to observe nature's gifts:

Our Lord God has made the best gifts most common. The pre-eminent gift given to all living things is the eye. Small birds have very bright eyes, like little stars, and can see a fly a room-length away. But we don't acknowledge such everyday gifts. We are stupid clods. In the future life we'll see them, however; there we ourselves will make birds with pretty, shining eyes.[9]

He challenged philosophers and scientists to explain the birth of a baby or the hatching of a chicken by means of their system of "first and secondary causes."

These are all miracles. God is in the creature, which he creates and in which he works. But we pay no heed, and meanwhile we look for secondary and philosophical causes. We'll never learn the article about creation rightly in this way.[10]

Going fishing with Katie reminded Luther of the differences between praising God for simple pleasures and caring only for oneself:

> Greed and ambition prevent us from enjoying things. Many a skinflint sits in the midst of the greatest luxuries and yet can't enjoy them with pleasure. It's said that the ungodly won't see the glory of God; in fact, they can't even recognize present gifts because God overwhelms us so much with them. If they were rare, we might esteem them more highly. But we can't reflect on the pleasure which the creatures give.[11]
>
> Since, through Christ, Christians are children of God, they should be glad rather than sad, no matter what life brings. For God does not desert His own. "We are sad by nature, and Satan is the spirit of sadness. But God is the spirit of gladness, and he preserves us."[12]

Luther considered music the medium which most effectively responds to what God has done as Creator, Redeemer, and Holy Spirit:

> Next to the Word of God, music deserves the highest praise. She is a mistress and governess of those human emotions—to pass over the animals—which as masters govern men or more often overwhelm them. No greater commendation than this can be found, at least not by us. For whether you wish to comfort the sad, to terrify the happy, to encourage the despairing, to humble the proud, to calm the passionate, or to appease those full of hate—and who could number all these masters of the human heart, namely the emotions, inclinations, and affections that impel men to evil or good?—what more effective means than music could you find? The Holy Ghost himself honors her as an instrument for his proper work when in his Holy Scriptures He asserts that through her his gifts were instilled in the prophets [2 Kings 3:15]. . . . On the other hand, she serves to cast out Satan, the instigator of all sins [1 Sam. 16:23].[13]

Luther claimed that when Christians sing and make music, they are truly in tune with God's creation. Music has been in all creatures, individually and collectively, from the beginning of the world. The human voice is such a marvelous instrument that it has baffled philosophers. "How can the air projected by a light movement of the tongue and an even lighter movement of the throat produce such an infinite variety and articulation of the voice and of words?"[14]

Luther bequeathed to later generations the view that theology and music belong together: "God-talk" must always be not only rational but also doxological, praising God for what he did.[15] John Walter, his musical advisor, declared that music was wrapped in theology, and whoever does theology will be touched by music.[16] Luther himself composed a poem entitled "Dame Musica" in which music declares, "God in me more pleasure finds than in all joys of earthly minds."[17] Though not an expert in music theory, he had a sense for the wholistic expression of praise and thanks of the word, both spoken and sung. In this sense, his interest in music was directly related to his conviction that God's grace in Christ mediated unconditional divine love for sinful creatures. The spoken word issues from and goes to the head; the sung word issues from and goes to the heart. The Psalms exemplify this difference:

> Note that there is a difference between singing and saying, as there is between chanting or saying a psalm and only knowing and teaching with the understanding. But by adding the voice it becomes a song, and the voice is the feeling. Therefore, as the word is the understanding, so the voice is its feeling.[18]

Proper worship, therefore, consists of both rational discourse and singing—illustrated in the Lutheran Sunday liturgies of the sixteenth century and later.

Moreover, Luther urged city councils to introduce music and singing in the school curriculum so that children could receive a wholistic education.

> I would have them study not only languages and history, but also singing and music, together with the whole of mathematics. For what is all this but mere child's play? The ancient Greeks trained their children in these disciplines, and they grew up to be people of wondrous ability, subsequently fit for everything.[19]

Luther's emphasis on the relationship between edification and education not only influenced but helped to create a Christian Humanism in Germany, represented by philosophers like Wilhelm Leibniz and musicians like Johann Sebastian Bach.[20] Without Luther, neither choral nor instrumental music would have become as popular as they did.[21] To this extent, Luther was not only the voice of past medieval Christendom but also the prophet of a new age, which the Humanists called "golden." This "golden age" rejoiced in the fact that Christians could be in tune with God's creation and therefore use their hearts and minds to praise him for creating a fascinating world.

> We are at the dawn of a new era, for we are beginning to recover the knowledge of the external world that we had lost through the fall of Adam. We now observe creatures properly. . . . Therefore we praise, bless, and give thanks to Him and see in His creatures the power of His word. He spoke and things stood fast. See that force displayed in the stone of a peach. It is very hard, and the germ it encloses is very tender; nevertheless, when the moment has come, the stone must open to let out the young plant that God calls into life.[22]

Luther's sense of wonder at God's creation is sorely needed among Christians, who are often blinded by the forces of anxiety, guilt, and self-righteousness. Luther helped later generations embrace a wholistic view of life contrary to the bifurcated view of theological and philosophical anthropologies dominated by dualistic separations of mind/body and flesh/spirit. He was a realist who saw life on earth as a pilgrimage from the *Anfechtung* of history to final liberation at the end of time.[23] He contended that this life ought to be lived with increasing awareness that one is but a tiny part of a cosmic whole in which all others have the rights and privileges enjoyed by the creatures of God.[24] Anyone who like Luther knows the pains of *Anfechtung* as well as the joy of being one of God's children cherishes being in tune with creation, and thus becomes whole.

THE SANCTITY OF WORK

To Luther life was most real in its daily rhythm of earthly responsibilities of being a faithful Christian—in preaching, teaching, parenting, governing, farming, trading—in whatever work was associated with "stations" or "estates" (*Stände*), "vocations" (*Berufe*), and "duties" (*Befehle*), which constitute the divine "orders" of human life in the interim between the creation of the world and the new creation at the end of time.[25] Luther rejected the traditional medieval notion of two distinct orders: an order of spiritual perfection, consisting of clergy; and a lower secular order, consisting of the laity. He declared that since everyone is sinful, God offers his salvation in Christ to all; whoever is baptized is of the same estate. Consequently, "all the estates and works of God are to be praised as highly as they can be, and none despised in favor of another."[26]

Christians may indeed take special vows as a matter of free choice for the sake of serving God and their neighbors with greater intensity. But such vows do not bring special favors from God; they only enhance faith active in love. When some Christians, for example, take the vow of chastity, they should do so only for the sake of greater joy in their ministry:

> It is therefore Christ's intent that chastity should be a servant of the kingdom of heaven, and a willing servant, not something which earns the kingdom, for it already possesses the kingdom. Such chastity labors in joyful service to bring the kingdom to others, or in any case to increase the kingdom for the kingdom's own sake. Such chastity is always ready to die and depart from this world for the sake of the kingdom.[27]

According to Luther, all of life is normed by a twofold order. There is the order of daily work, manifested in a great variety of callings; and there is the "common order of Christian love" which links people together by the many ways they care for each other, either through their vocations or through their response to particular needs. Having been born sinful, however, Christians can never claim perfection in what they do, for every good can be perverted into something evil. Otherwise there would be no need to preach the gospel, to have civil government, or to pray "Forgive us our sins. . . ." What makes daily work holy is the fact that it is anchored in faith in Christ:

> We are saved through Christ alone; but we become holy both through this faith and through these divine foundations and orders. Even the godless may have much about them that is holy without being saved thereby. For God wishes us to

perform such works to His praise and glory. And all who are saved in the faith of Christ surely do these works and maintain these orders.[28]

Luther viewed work as God's assignment to us to care for the world in his name. God designed the various stations in life to sustain the world:

Where such stations operate as they should, there things go well in the world, and there is the very righteousness of God. But where such stations are not maintained, it makes for unrighteousness. Now God declares concerning these stations that they must remain if the world is to stand, even though many oppose and rage against them.[29]

Whatever work Christians do in their various stations in life is intended to serve God and neighbor. In this sense, daily work establishes and maintains human relationships. Such work has no particular "Christian" characteristics. It is the doing of it that makes the difference.

If you are a manual laborer, you find that the Bible has been put into your workshop, into your hand, into your heart. It teaches and preaches how you should treat your neighbor. Just look at your tools—at your needle or thimble, your beer barrel, your goods, your scales or yardsticks or measure—and you will read this statement inscribed on them. Everywhere you look, it stares at you. Nothing that you handle every day is so tiny that it does not continually tell you this, if you will only listen. Indeed, there is no shortage of preaching. You have as many preachers as you have transactions, goods, tools, and other equipment in your house and home. All this is continually crying out to you: "Friend, use me in your relations with your neighbor just as you would want your neighbor to use his property in his relations with you."[30]

Luther urged people to stay in their assigned stations in life because all stations, vocations, and duties are equal in the sense of being divine callings.[31] Here Luther followed the Pauline injunction "Everyone should remain in the state in which he was called" (1 Cor. 7:20). Luther's catechetical "table of duties" provides congregations with biblical descriptions of the various vocations significant in medieval feudal society: pastors, princes, parents, landlords, and other figures of authority.[32] He insisted that the existing order of life must not be disturbed. For example, even if married people have difficulties in their relationship, they should not seek a divorce, for "God's forgiveness of their sins will be much greater if only they remain in their station and do not leave it."[33]

Luther can, of course, be criticized for tempting Christians to acquire a "good conscience" by staying in their assigned stations because they might otherwise lose their state of grace. Thus the commandment of love could become a holy duty to cling to the status quo. The result is an ethical stance which encourages uncritical obedience to existing orders, which can cause useless suffering imposed by unjust authorities. Such a stance may not be in concert with the Sermon on the Mount, which makes a distinction between the internal attitude of persons and their external obedience to the law. It may be possible to obey the commandment "You shall not kill," but it may not be possible to avoid hating a brother or sister. Jesus, however, called for a real change of heart and mind in addition to obedience to the law: "Everyone who is angry with his brother shall be liable to judgment" (Matt. 5:21–22).[34]

However, Luther's doctrine of orders, with its elimination of the differences between "spiritual" and "secular" vocations, has enduring significance for ethical reflections concerning the value of work and vocation:

1. The orders or stations in life were instituted by God for the sake of a responsible interrelationship between people, creatures of God. Christians are not permitted to be so individualistic as to strive for special status (as monks did, according to Luther) or to place themselves in opposition to the world. On the contrary, Christians are called to stay in the world, to face all its problems and seek to overcome them in solidarity with others. There are no preferred places or ways to be closer to God. Luther's view of life was anchored in the article of justification by faith which assumes that "there is no distinction; since all have sinned and fall short of the glory of God, they are justified by his grace as a gift, through the redemption which is in Christ Jesus" (Rom. 3:22–24). Accordingly, one's conduct in the various orders and vocations is normed by one's trust in God's grace through Christ rather than by one's obedience to "natural law" or some other norm. "Having been justified by grace in this way, we then do good works, yes, Christ himself does all in us."[35] Work and vocation are grateful responses to what God did in Christ; they can no longer be regarded as either a means of gaining wealth for the sake of selfish pride or as burdens imposed by God to punish sin. Labor is the discipline God imposed on a sinful world; only he can give it meaning.

> God wills that man should work, and without work He will give him nothing. Conversely, God will not give him anything because of his labor, but solely out of His own goodness and blessing. Man's labor is to be his discipline in this life, by which he may keep his flesh in subjection. To him who is obedient in this matter, God will give plenty, and sustain him well.[36]

2. Human labor, no matter how menial, is service to the neighbor in obedience to God's commandment of love. That is why one should labor with joy in the human community charged with the care of the earth. Christians honor God by serving and, whatever their vocation, they should demonstrate such service by working carefully. Work and vocation are the ministry through which God uses his people to extend his love. Human labor is the mask of God who, like St. Nicholas, brings his gifts to his faithful children:

> What else is all our work to God—whether in the fields, in the garden, in the city, in the house, in war, in government—but just such a child's performance, by which He wants to give His gifts in the fields, at home, and everywhere else?

These are the masks of God, behind which He wants to remain concealed and do all things. . . . He could give children without using men and women. But He does not want to do this. Instead, He joins man and woman so that it appears to be the work of man and woman, and yet He does it under the cover of such masks. . . . God gives all good gifts; but you must lend a hand and take the bull by the horns; that is, you must work and thus give God good cause and a mask.[37]

That is why Christians should not regard labor as a dull duty, but rather as an opportunity to assist God in his ministry to the world. Parents should see in their children the mask of God's ministry, and children should be raised with the awareness that their relationship to parents is part of the divine ministry. Any work and vocation is but an opportunity to become a partner in God's ministry. "Even though it [work] seems very trivial and contemptible, make sure that you regard it as great and precious, not on account of your worthiness but because it has its place within that jewel and holy treasure, the Word and commandment of God."[38]

3. The sanctity of labor is grounded in the very being of God who is active in the world. Just as God enjoys doing something rather than sitting still, so his people should be active to enjoy life with God. Moreover, the discipline of labor is part of a Christian's way of controlling the "old Adam," who tempts everyone to become lazy.[39] To work and to have a vocation means to have a bulwark against sin and evil.

Since human labor serves the neighbor, neither the ideal of poverty, especially if understood as a means of gaining favor with God, nor the attainment of selfish wealth, particularly capitalistic profiteering, should be the reasons for work and vocation. "In the sight of God it is really faith that makes a person holy; faith alone serves him, while our works serve the people."[40]

Luther viewed work, even the daily grind of it, as a part of life which is in its totality a gift of God. In a world which has since the time of Luther lost sight of life's wholistic aspects, the notion of labor as a part of the divine ministry on earth deserves to be reconsidered.

WIT AND WITNESS

In 1542, a pamphlet entitled *New Newspaper From the Rhine* appeared in Halle. The anonymous author alerted the public to the transfer of Archbishop Albrecht of Mainz's collection of relics from Halle to Mainz, where they would be exhibited at St. Martin's Church and, if solemnly viewed, would grant an indulgence. The writer added that part of the money collected at the exhibition would be used to provide new wrappings for the old relics so that they would not have to freeze in their old ones. In addition, newly discovered relics would be exhibited, with a special indulgence offered by Pope Paul III. The new relics included:

1. A nice section from Moses' left horn [Exod. 34:29, Vulgate: "his face was horned from the conversation with the Lord"];
2. Three flames from the burning bush on Mount Sinai [Exod. 3:3];
3. Two feathers and an egg from the Holy Spirit;
4. A remnant from the flag with which Christ opened hell;
5. A large lock of Beelzebub's beard, stuck on the same flag;
6. One-half of the archangel Gabriel's wing;
7. A whole pound of the wind which roared by Elijah in the cave on Mount Horeb [1 Kings 19:11];
8. Two ells [about ninety inches] of sound from the trumpets on Mount Sinai [Exod. 19:16];
9. Thirty blasts from the trumpets on Mount Sinai;
10. A large heavy piece of the shout with which the children of Israel tumbled the walls of Jericho [Josh. 6:20];
11. Five nice shiny strings from David's harp;
12. Three beautiful locks of Absalom's hair, which got caught in the oak and left him hanging [2 Sam. 18:9].

The author concluded by sharing a tip he had received from a friend in high places: Archbishop Albrecht had willed a trifle of his pious, loyal heart and a whole section of his truthful tongue to the existing collection; and whoever paid one guilder at the exhibition would receive a papal indulgence remitting all sins committed up to the time of payment and for ten more years, thus giving the people of the Rhineland a unique opportunity to attain a special state of grace.

The author was Martin Luther, of course. He revealed his identity after the pamphlet had been widely circulated.[41] The old issue of indulgences had once more cropped up, and this was his way of annoying Archbishop Albrecht, the most notorious advocate of the indulgences traffic, one more time.

Luther was a Saxon wit who was able to balance his bouts of depression and melancholy with a well-developed sense of humor.[42] His humor manifested itself in satire, a creative use of language, and self-deprecation. Even a cursory reading of Luther's massive works discloses his use of humor to deliver the message that God and no one else is in charge of the world. To him faith, love, and laughter were close kin. Christians, he declared, ought to be overjoyed by the fact that the almighty Creator of heaven and earth became a human baby in Bethlehem. Faith in a God like this should make Christians break out into song. If they should ever take their own miserable human existence too seriously, they should be taught to laugh at it. To be able to laugh at oneself is a sign of humility; and humility makes it easier to love others. But humor and wit are certainly not just Christian faculties;

there are many Christians who have no sense of humor at all, and there are many non-Christians who do.

> Ah, what wretched people we are! To think that we are so cold and slothful in our attitude toward this great joy which, after all, happened for us, this great benefaction which is far, far superior to all other works of creation! And yet how hard it is for us to believe, though the good news was preached and sung for us by angels, who are heavenly theologians and have rejoiced in our behalf! Their song is the most glorious. It contains the whole Christian faith. For the *gloria in excelsis* [Luke 2:14] is supreme worship. They wish us such worship and they bring it to us in Christ. [43]

Luther used his wit to alert himself and others to the proper distinction between the human and the divine. Certain aspects of being human deserve to be laughed at and indeed need to be exposed through satire—laziness, pride, self-righteousness, and the like—and Luther did use his humor against such sins. But he never laughed at matters of life and death—God's wrath, salvation through Christ, dying—for he contended that what is truly "holy" can never be the subject of laughter and derision. Humor can deal only with penultimate questions. [44]

He was able to create an emotional distance between himself and circumstances which would otherwise depress him. In 1530, when he was ill and forced to spend time alone at the Castle Coburg during the decisive Diet of Augsburg, he wrote letters to friends in order to overcome his loneliness. To George Spalatin he wrote:

> It is not you people alone . . . who are traveling to a diet, for we, too, arrived at a diet as soon as we had parted from you, and so we overtook you by far. Therefore our journey to the diet has not been prevented, but only changed. [45]

What was Luther talking about? He described in great detail the diet he had attended: an assembly of jackdaws who live under the open sky; who show contempt for foolish luxury; who act in unison, whether it is in a war against barley, wheat, and fruit, or in song; and who are much better at conducting a diet than the noble lords at Augsburg. The letter continues with a word game based on the Latin and German names for "jackdaw": *monedula, Dohle*.

> If they were to find a fair interpreter, they would derive sufficient glory and praise from the very name *Mon Edula*, if it were taken to mean *man Edel*, or *Edelman* [nobleman] if you turn the word around. However, at this point begins an affront to your diet, for your *Edelmoni* [Latinized plural for nobleman] excel too much at *monedulana* virtues [the thievish nature of jackdaws] . . . [46]

Luther concluded the letter with the remark that it was necessary for him to use such humor in order to chase away his anxiety, but that he was quite prepared to live in the "kingdom of the winged jackdaws" while his friends wrestled with the emperor at Augsburg.[47]

Luther also used his wit to correct what he thought was undesirable conduct in others. When his servant, Wolfgang Sieberger, took up the trapping of birds as a hobby, Luther sent him a pamphlet entitled "A Complaint of the Birds Addressed to Dr. Martin Luther Concerning His Servant Wolfgang Sieberger."[48] The complaint was written in the legal language used at the Saxon court. The birds plead for their right to fly over Saxony without danger to life and limb; they ask Luther to intercede for them and to urge Wolfgang to cease trapping them, and they threaten to ask God to put a curse on Wolfgang if he does not comply.

> If he does not, but continues to go after us, we shall plead with God that He might direct him to trap frogs, grasshoppers, and gnats during the day and that he be covered at night with mice, fleas, lice, and bedbugs so that he forgets about us and no longer impedes our free flight.[49]

Luther could of course simply have ordered his servant to stop trapping birds. But he preferred this way of wooing him into giving up what he considered to be an unnecessary and somewhat cruel hobby.

Luther also used his wit in dealing with the Saxon court. When the plague struck Saxony in 1535 and Elector John Frederick urged Luther to move to Jena for the duration, Luther refused—even though the whole Wittenberg University moved its program to Jena. He wrote the prince that the plague would not strike Wittenberg.

> My weathervane is district Governor Hans Metzsch [the representative of the Elector] who has so far had a real buzzard-nose concerning the plague. Even if his nose were five ells under the earth, he would still smell it [the plague]. Since he is staying, I can't believe that the plague will come here.[50]

He did admit, however, that the plague had struck a few families in town, which pleased the students, because they liked to see their gear contaminated—their bags swollen, their books colicky, their pens with a rash, their papers rheumatic, and their ink moldy—and thus they could enjoy life. Luther recommended seeking expert medical help in case the plague should really strike, thus concluding the letter with a serious note.

Immediately after Luther's condemnation by pope and emperor in 1521, when his followers began to praise him as the great hero of the Reformation, he used his wit to defuse the situation. At the height of the Wittenberg unrest in the spring of 1522, he told the Wittenbergers, who had come to see and to hear their hero in the pulpit, that the Reformation was not his doing.

> And while I slept, or drank Wittenberg beer with my friends Philip [Melanchthon] and [Nicholas] Amsdorf, the Word so greatly weakened the papacy that no prince or emperor ever inflicted such losses upon it. I did

nothing; the Word did everything. Had I desired to foment trouble, I could have brought great bloodshed upon Germany; indeed, I could have started such a game that even the emperor would not have been safe. But what would it have been? Mere fool's play. I did nothing; I let the Word do its work.[51]

What others regarded as holy or taboo, Luther viewed realistically, using his wit and imagination to bring people around to his point of view. For example, many Wittenbergers could not adjust easily to the quick changes in public worship while Luther was exiled at the Wartburg in 1521/22. Carlstadt had celebrated an "evangelical" Mass, omitting the traditional vestments and declaring that all the baptized were priests too. When the illiterate folk were asked to take consecrated bread into their hands and to drink from the cup of the priest, they became confused. Some of them bragged about their new rights as baptized people of God, but others were afraid of doing something sacrilegious. So when Luther returned from the Wartburg during Lent 1522, he tried to remove as much offense over liturgical matters as he could and recommended a gradual transition from the old to the new:

But if there is anyone who is so smart that he must touch the sacrament with his hands, let him have it brought home to his house and there let him handle it to his heart's content. But in public let him abstain, since that will bring him no harm and the offense will be avoided which is caused to our brothers, sisters, and neighbors, who are now so angry with us that they are ready to kill us. I may say that of all my enemies who have opposed me up to this time none have brought me so much grief as you.[52]

On another occasion, Luther joked about liturgical customs which were too "Catholic." Elector Joachim II of Brandenburg had introduced a new Lutheran church order in 1539, in which almost all of the Roman ceremonies were retained. The new Lutheran pastor there, George Buchholzer, wrote to Luther to complain and to ask for advice, in particular about the rubric that the pastor wear eucharistic vestments and lead the worshiping congregation in procession around the church building every Sunday to carry and exhibit the consecrated eucharistic elements. Buchholzer was particularly upset about the procession and hoped that Luther would agree to have it abolished. Luther's response, however, was not quite what the pastor expected. He did criticize the procession in his letter to Elector Joachim II, but his response to Pastor Buchholzer—which he sent together with the letter to the prince—was quite different. Insisting that the main purpose of worship is the right proclamation of the gospel and the administration of the sacraments, Luther recommended the removal of the most offensive Roman facets of the liturgy, but added:

Why don't you, for heaven's sake, march around wearing a silver or gold cross, as well as a skull cap and a chasuble made of velvet, silk, or cotton? If your superior, the Elector, thinks that one cap or one chasuble is not enough, then put on two or three, like Aaron, the high priest, who wore three coats, one on top of the other, and they all looked wonderful [Lev. 8:7] . . .

If your Electoral Excellency thinks one procession is not enough, marching around with singing and with bells, then do it seven times, just as Joshua did in Jericho with the children of Israel. They shouted and blew their trumpets [Josh. 6:4–7]. Perhaps your Electoral Excellency might even jump around and dance in front of all the people with harps, drums, cymbals, and bells, just as David did before the ark of the covenant on its way to Jerusalem. I completely approve of such things, as long as they are not abused or steal the thunder from the gospel; and as long as they are not viewed as necessary for salvation, or as binding on consciences.[53]

Even when he was old and very sick, Luther did not lose his wit. During his last, dangerous journey in inclement weather from Wittenberg to Eisleben, Katie wrote him that she had sleepless nights worrying about him; Luther wrote her one letter after another to cheer her up. Some of these letters were written in the style of very formal "thank you" notes "To the holy lady, full of worries, Mrs. Catherine Luther, doctor, the lady of Zölsdorf, at Wittenberg, my gracious, dear mistress of the house."[54] He addressed her with the formal "you" (Sie) rather than the informal "thou" (Du) and thanked her for the great worry which robbed her of her sleep. He then claimed that her worries had almost killed him, since there had been a chimney fire in the inn where he stayed and big pieces of mortar had fallen from the ceiling and narrowly missed his head while he was sitting on the toilet. He bragged:

The stone was as big as a long pillow and as wide as a large hand; it intended to repay you for your holy worries, had the dear angels not protected [me]. I worry that if you do not stop worrying, the earth will finally swallow us up and all the elements will chase us. Is this the way you learned the Cathechism and the faith? Pray, and let God worry.[55]

Wit, humor, and imagination are significant components of Christian witness. A wooing ministry will seek to touch and to console others in a great variety of ways. Like people in love, Christians try to woo their neighbors into the relationship which God has promised. No aspect of life should be excluded from such a witness. There is ample room for laughter and for tears, for the whole range of human emotions. Luther himself was wholistic in his Christian witness. Having found a gracious God, he could sin boldly and rejoice boldly.

If you are a preacher of grace, then preach a true and not a fictitious grace; if grace is true, you must bear a true and not a fictitious sin. God does not save people who are only fictitious sinners. Be a sinner and sin boldly, but believe and rejoice in Christ even more boldly, for he is victorious over sin, death, and the world.[56]

12

GOD'S JESTER BEFORE THE COURT OF HISTORY

I ask that men make no reference to my name; let them call themselves Christians, not Lutherans. What is Luther? After all, the teaching is not mine [John 7:16], neither was I crucified for anyone [1 Cor. 1:13]. St. Paul, in 1 Corinthians 3 [:22; 1:12] would not allow Christians to call themselves Pauline or Petrine, but Christian. How then should I—poor stinking maggot-fodder that I am—come to have men call the children of Christ by my wretched name? Not so, my dear friends; abolish all party names and call yourselves Christians, after him whose teaching we hold. . . . I neither am nor want to be anyone's master. I hold, together with the universal church, the one universal teaching of Christ who is our only master (Matt. 23:8). ("A Sincere Admonition by Martin Luther to All Christians to Guard Against Insurrection and Rebellion," 1522. WA 8:685. 5–11. LW 45:70–71).

HERO AND VILLAIN

The historiographical assessment of Luther began in a morass of conflicting emotions. Melanchthon initiated the Lutheran history of uncritical praise of Luther when he declared, after hearing the news of Luther's death:

Oh my God! Gone is the charioteer of Israel [Elijah, 2 Kings 2:11] who has led the church during this last age of the world. God revealed through this man a doctrine which was not invented by human wisdom—the doctrine of the forgiveness of sins, and of faith in the Son of God.[1]

The first Lutheran biographers depicted a hero and saint who, like the prophets and apostles, was sent into the world to communicate the Word of God. John Matthesius is a case in point: he had been one of Luther's students and a participant in the "table talks." In 1565, he published a collection of seventeen sermons which he had preached in his parish, St. Joachimstal (now in Czechoslovakia), between 1562 and 1565. His reasons for preaching about Luther were clearly stated in the preface:

Since the eternal Son of God, the supreme archbishop of our souls, has deemed it right to relight and keep burning the obscured gospel through this miracle-man *(Wundermann)* who was liberated from the gruesome kingdom and doctrine of the Antichrist; since not too many people today know of the oppressed and bound state of the church fifty years ago; and since many ungrateful people want to forget the faithful diligence and work of this great man, I thought it advisable and useful to offer a thorough account—in honor of God and as a testimony to young people—of how God had begun this Reformation through a single man and has so graciously saved us in these last times and before the Last Day from the Babylonian prison and its abomination and idolatry, and has brought us again to the pure fountain of Israel, the prophetic and apostolic writings. Thus I want to remind my readers of this German prophet and blessed interpreter of Holy Scripture and to admonish them to adhere to him with joy and endurance.[2]

After a rather lively account of Luther's heroic and saintly life, Matthesius closed with a collection of Luther sayings about the mining industry, thus reminding his congregation and readers that Luther was as at home in their world of mining as he was in the "earthly mining" of God's Word.[3]

Matthesius's hagiography was a response to the Catholic vilification of Luther by one of Luther's first enemies, the theologian John Dobeneck—known as Cochlaeus—who published a popular Luther biography in 1549. Portraying Luther as a child of Satan, Cochlaeus concluded his detailed account of Luther's evil activities with a warning to the world:

> Just as he was a plague to Germany and the pope, so will he be a plague to those who believe him. He himself knows, without a doubt, how much of a plague he has been, dead or alive.[4]

Influenced by Cochlaeus, many Catholic biographers remained hostile to Luther until the beginning of the twentieth century.[5] After the Council of Trent (1545–63), Luther's works were listed on the "index" of prohibited books because he was judged to be one of the great arch-heretics of the church.[6] Catholic vilification of Luther climaxed with the judgment that Luther was responsible for making the German nation "sterile in holiness" and thus incapable of producing effective Catholic priests.[7] Catholic textbooks of history depicted Luther as a mentally unbalanced personality who managed to maneuver Germany into a schism. The popular nineteenth-century historian Ignaz Döllinger traced Luther's ideas of reform to a "vicious circle" of unresolved emotions:

> It is obvious how and why he could not find peace in his conscience: he could find no escape from the vicious circle in which he had become trapped. Prayer should have been his principal means to purify himself from sin and thus find a way to peace with God. But he thought that he could pray successfully only after he had become purified. He himself admitted that he was constantly plagued by distrust, doubt, despair, hatred and blasphemy. Overwhelmed by such a

gloomy, depressing state of mind, wildly confused by contradictory and destructive ideas about divine grace and human will, as well as about sin and faith, he gradually developed views which eventually would dominate his whole life and thought.[8]

There were a few Catholic historians who rejected Cochlaeus's interpretation that Luther was a child of Satan. They saw Luther as the victim of a Roman papacy which had lost interest in the worldwide church.[9] But even if they accepted Luther as a deeply religious man, they were not ready to grant him any "catholicity." Catholic "manuals" depicted his theology as the result of a subjectivist faith anchored in emotions rather than in objective Christian truths. Most of these Catholic textbooks, for example, expressed the judgment that Luther denied the objective efficacy of sacraments.

> They [the sacraments] have only a psychological importance for faith, to which alone effective power is ascribed. Consequently, the sacraments are the work God performs on us (opus operatum), but are effective only subjectively by means of the personal confidence which, according to Luther, is faith.[10]

Catholic biographers employed the best scholarly methods to produce the worst images of Luther. The popular and detailed analysis by the Jesuit scholar Hartmann Grisar portrayed Luther as a man who was a victim of stubbornness and pride. Grisar used the newly developed insights of psychology when in 1911 he wrote:

> With regard to his self-image, he is under the influence of ideas which disclose various pathological symptoms, all of which together raise serious questions as to the nature of his changing state of mind. Since he feels chosen by God to do great things, since he is not only "the prophet of the Germans" but also the restorer of the gospel for the whole Christian world, he thinks that he has been equipped by providence with faculties which hardly anyone else received. He frequently says so, even though he insists that God is behind it all. He likes to compare himself not only to his papistical opponents, but also to the most famous figures in the church of the past. In the same fashion, he likes to measure the opponents in his own camp against his own personal greatness. Thus it happens that he talks and sounds like a megalomaniac; and he likes himself so much in this role that he does not even notice how tasteless and offensive some of his exaggerations are.[11]

It was the German Catholic historian Joseph Lortz who provided the bridge from destructive criticism of Luther to a more ecumenical assessment of him by using the tools of historical-critical scholarship. He saw Luther as a "Catholic" who rediscovered the old Catholic doctrine of justification by faith, but saw it "one-sidedly."[12] "Within himself Luther wrestled and overthrew a Catholicism that was not Catholic."[13] Lortz asserted that, though given to overstatements and thus to "subjectivism," Luther nevertheless

needs to be seen in the light of the differences between his situation and that
of later Catholicism. As Lortz put it in 1964:

> Luther's "no" to the papal Church is both in content and intensity such that one
> could hardly imagine it more radical, but this "no" needs sober reexamination.
> For it was directed against a Church whose sub-Christian reality would deserve
> the strongest condemnation, if one took the sub-Christian elements as the
> essence of the Church. This is precisely what Luther did. His religious and
> pastoral zest seemed to leave him no other way. Here we have a special case of
> the influence of situations on Luther . . . and this should enter our analysis. [14]

Lortz and his "school" put an end to the Catholic vilification of Luther and
made it possible for Catholics to join Protestant and other Luther scholars in
a common effort to assess the ecumenical significance of the Wittenberg
reformer. [15]

Lutherans in particular, and Protestants in general, also took their time to
move from hagiographic portrayals to a more balanced, critical historiography. Seventeenth-century Lutheran Orthodoxy and eighteenth-century
Pietism continued to praise the life and work of Luther. It became
fashionable to think of him in connection with the image of an open Bible and
a lit candle, symbols of orthodoxy and moral piety. Coins appeared in
Germany with the inscription, "The Word of God and Luther's thought will
never ever come to naught" (*Gottes Wort und Luthers Lehr wird vergehen
nimmermehr*).[16] Lutheran dogmaticians like John Gerhard (1582–1637)
engaged in fierce literary debates with Catholic theologians like Robert
Bellarmini (1542–1621, sainted in 1930), the defender of the Council of
Trent, about the legitimacy of Luther's Reformation. The Lutherans
contended that the Reformation was a supernatural act of God, who had
founded the Lutheran Church as an example of unadulterated preaching of
the Word and dispensation of sacraments. Luther had now become an object
of faith rather than a subject for historical research. [17]

Lutheran Pietists, who advocated a "religion of the heart" over against the
orthodox "religion of the head," also claimed Luther for their cause. To
them, Luther was the defender of a heartfelt religion without the pomp and
circumstance of dogma and liturgy. As Philip J. Spener put it, in his Pietist
"Manifesto" of 1675:

> Compare the writings of our dear Luther, in which he expounds the Word of
> God or treats articles of the Christian faith, with the still extant works of many
> other theologians who lived in or shortly after his time, or with the majority of
> books being published today. To speak candidly, in the former one will assuredly
> encounter and experience great spiritual power, together with wisdom
> presented with the utmost simplicity, while the latter will seem to be quite
> empty in contrast, and in the newer books one will find more materials of showy
> human erudition, of artificial posturing, and of presumptuous subtleties in

matters in which we should not be wise beyond the Scriptures. I wonder if our sainted Luther, were he to be raised up today, would not find fault with one thing and another in our universities for which he vigorously upbraided the schools of his own time.[18]

Lutheran Enlightenment philosophers, such as Gottfried Leibniz (1646–1716) and John S. Semler (1725–91), tried to mediate between warring Protestants as well as between Protestants and Catholics. The Enlightenment revival of Greco-Roman ideas, especially those concerning the nature of humanity, contradicted Lutheran and Calvinist doctrines of sin, which rejected any notion of human choice in the matter of salvation. Leibniz hoped to achieve greater Christian unity by making theological compromises; Semler reinterpreted Luther to make of him the defender of freedom of conscience and of an inward spirituality uniting people of diverse external backgrounds.[19]

Under the influence of the Enlightenment, Luther had become the ideal "natural" man, no longer the saintly agent of God. The Lutheran historian John G. Walch (1693–1775) produced a German edition of many of Luther's works and wrote a biography which pictured Luther as a scholar, orator, and virtuous man struggling against Roman Catholic authoritarianism.[20] Dead was the myth of a divinely chosen reformer following in the footsteps of biblical miracle men.

The theologian and philosopher John G. Herder (1744–1803) spoke for a generation beginning to move from the Enlightenment to a romantic appreciation of nature and history which celebrated "genius" as the force holding the world together.

> Luther was a great patriot. He has long been recognized as the teacher of the German nation, indeed, as the one who helped reform all of enlightened Europe. Even those nations which do not accept his religious propositions enjoy the fruits of his Reformation. Like a true Hercules, he attacked the spiritual despotism which undermines or dissolves all free wholesome thinking; and he returned whole nations to the use of reason in religious matters, the most difficult feat of all. The power of his language and of his simple spirit became united with the sciences, which were revived by and with him.[21]

Some historians who criticized Luther were grinding their own axes at the same time. For example, Joseph Priestly (1733–1804), who had emigrated from England to Pennsylvania, rejected Luther's notion of predestination because, although he liked Luther's personality, he judged Luther's theology from the viewpoint of a Unitarian who loved chemistry.[22]

The seminal philosopher George F. Hegel (1770–1831) used his Lutheran background to identify "faith" with the subjective "spirit" (*Geist*) that is able to receive the divine spirit.[23] Hegel contended that once the divine and human spirits are united a person achieves true freedom; Luther pioneered this freedom by opposing a system which did not permit individuals to think for themselves. "Only with Luther did the nucleus of the freedom of the spirit emerge. The explication of this freedom occurred later, just as the formation of Christian doctrine occurred after the founding of the church."[24] Hegel of course believed that the full explication of freedom would occur in his own time.

Interpretations of Luther continued to vary according to the diverse climates of opinion in the nineteenth century. Inspired by the German Romantics, especially by Immanuel H. Fichte (1796–1879), the historian Leopold von Ranke celebrated Luther as the embodiment of a religion which, in its Christian form, releases the God-given powers of a humanity destined to be free from all bondage. In 1817, after the three hundredth anniversary of the "Ninety-five Theses," Ranke devoted much of his time to the writing of a "History of the Reformation in Germany" to show how Luther's genius shaped German culture.[25] Other philosophers and historians continued to use Luther for their own ideas and proposals. Arthur Schopenhauer (1788–1860) saw pantheistic tendencies in Luther, and Ludwig Feuerbach (1804–72) even managed to use Luther in support of atheism.[26]

The sociologically oriented historian Ernst Troeltsch tried to transcend all these nineteenth-century efforts to adapt Luther by relegating him to the Middle Ages. Luther's conservative and patriarchical political ideas, Troeltsch contended, only led to political absolutism and quietism in Germany. Luther, Troeltsch said, never managed to apply what he felt in his heart to the real issues of life in a different world; by urging Christians to tolerate injustice while preserving their "inward" freedom, Luther created a "super-idealistic" and "Utopian" idea of the state.[27]

Luther was also used by advocates of revolution, especially by Friedrich Engels (1820–95), the principal architect of political communism in Europe. Engels understood Luther's Reformation to have been an aborted bourgeois revolution—which could have succeeded if Luther had not rejected the uprising of the peasants in 1525.[28] As the 1983 propaganda pamphlet of the Academy of Sciences in the German Democratic Republic put it:

> The great tragedy of the great reformer lay in the conflict between his role as the initiator of a broad revolutionary movement embracing all progressive classes and groups in society, and the restricted nature of his own claims, which ultimately derived from his moderate bourgeois class-conscious position and its conditioned dependence on the feudal state in which he lived.[29]

Historians like Ranke, Jacob Burckhardt (1818–97), and Wilhelm Dilthey (1833–1911), by trying to view Luther and the Reformation in the broad context of the sixteenth century, especially in the context of the Renaissance,[30] opened up the way for a historical-critical assessment which avoids labeling him either hero or villain.

THE SCRUTINY OF SCHOLARSHIP

It could be said that a new era of Luther studies began when the first volume of the Weimar edition appeared in 1883, followed by Karl Holl's 1917 quadricentennial lecture "What Did Luther Understand by Religion?"[31] In essay after essay, Holl depicted Luther as a sagacious theologian and realistic reformer who was neither mentally unbalanced, as Catholic scholars had claimed, nor uncritically disposed toward the state, as Troeltsch had asserted. Holl, to be sure, disclosed some of his own presuppositions when he labeled Luther more progressive in matters of freedom than the *Schwärmer*—whom he viewed as the forerunners of what he called "Anglo-Americanism."[32] But Holl's thorough reading of Luther, combined with his keen sense for enduring theological issues, helped to create and sustain a renaissance in historical Luther research.

This "Luther renaissance" was soon involved in the theological debates precipitated by the "dialectical" theory of Karl Barth. Moreover, after World War I the rise of national socialism under the leadership of Adolf Hitler renewed the quest for Luther the "German Hercules" who opposed foreign tyranny. In 1933, on the occasion of Luther's 450th birthday, Barth once again rejected any notion of Luther as a "miracle man."[33] Some Luther scholars, however, did tip their scholarly hat in the direction of Hitler when they portrayed Luther as not only a great German, but as a great nationalist who considered faith and nation as the closest of kin.[34]

The bulk of new Luther studies, however, examined the central issues in Luther's thought like the two-kingdoms ethic, the centrality of Christ, the connection between the doctrines of creation and redemption in Christ, and the meaning of human life from an eschatological perspective—all of them enduring questions in systematic theology.

German and Scandinavian Luther research soon followed different paths and, at times, even conflicted. Led by the Swedish scholars Gustav Aulén and Anders Nygren, Scandinavian Luther researchers employed the method of "motif-research" (*motivforsking*) which traces certain basic ideas like "love" (*agape* and *eros* in Greek) as themes weaving through history, thus showing the consistency of tradition. As a result, Scandinavian Luther studies did not attempt to establish anything resembling a "system" in Luther's thought, as German Luther studies tended to do. Rather, the search for "motifs" produced detailed studies of specific ideas of Luther which have also appeared elsewhere in Christian tradition. Aulén, for example, contended that "atonement" is one of the most essential Christian categories describing salvation and that Luther affirmed a type of atonement which could be labeled "classic," since it views God as the Creator who defeats Satan's cosmic forces through love and shares this love with humanity in such a way that he creates an eternal relationship between himself and his creatures. This "classic" view of atonement can be traced to the early church fathers, especially to Irenaeus.[35] All in all, this kind of Luther research brought to bear what scholars thought to be the best of Luther on their own situation as Scandinavian churchmen without, however, neglecting the broad ecumenical context of Christian tradition as a whole.

The availability of an increasing number of Luther works text-critically edited in the Weimar edition, the impact of philosophical movements like existentialism, and the historical constellations created by two world wars— not to mention a growing interest in "historical science"—helped to proliferate Luther studies both quantitatively and qualitatively. One study called forth another, if for no other reason than to debate the previous findings. The German scholars Heinrich Boehmer and Otto Scheel did detailed research for a biography of the young Luther.[36] Other historians compared Luther with other Reformation figures. Karl Brandi, for example, saw Luther as the counterpart of Emperor Charles V.[37] Gerhard Ritter pictured Luther as a man of great sensitivity who echoed the hopes and dreams of a great multitude of his contemporaries both in Germany and throughout Europe.[38] Rudolf Thiel, who as a scientist was not a member of the guild of Luther scholars, nevertheless produced a lengthy biography which reads like a historical novel about a man who, by going through heaven and hell, becomes a teacher for everyone.[39] Historians, philosophers, theologians—all tried their hand at explaining Luther, with greatly varying results.[40]

Yet when Protestant scholars met in 1956 for their First International Congress for Luther Research, in Aarhus, Denmark, the German bishop Hanns Lilje told them that Luther still had not been fully rediscovered.[41] That first congress collected reports about the status of Luther research in Scandinavia, Italy, the United States, England, Germany, France, and Hungary. Scandinavian scholars were still heavily involved in "motif research," pursuing the themes of reconciliation, creation, and sanctification patterned on the dogma of the Trinity. They assured their colleagues, especially the Germans, that they opposed either a glorification of Luther by a Lutheran confessionalism or a Catholic traditionalism which disregarded the supremacy of Scripture.[42]

Italian scholars, far from numerous, had been working on the link between their own "forerunners of the Reformation"—the Waldensians[43]—and Luther, by researching hymnody and piety; they thus helped to increase knowledge about the virtually unknown Protestant tradition in Italy.[44] American scholars reported on their growing interest in Luther's life and thought, with special emphasis on questions of social ethics and hermeneutics.[45] British scholars described a growing interest in a truly transconfessional Luther.[46]

The large contingent of German scholars reported they were continuing the work of Karl Holl by concentrating on the question of Luther's transition from Catholicism to his "evangelical" stance and on the problem of Luther's doctrine of God. Walther von Loewenich declared three areas of research to be most significant: (1) Luther's ecumenical stance, particularly his relation to what is "catholic"; (2) his view of Scripture, particularly with respect to the unity and diversity of biblical statements; and (3) his relation to the modern world, be it the Enlightenment or other movements such as existentialism.[47]

French and Hungarian scholars reported minimal research but a growing interest in Luther in their Protestant churches; they were still relying heavily on the results of research from Germany and Scandinavia.[48]

Subsequent congresses dealt with Luther's relation to Melanchthon;[49] Luther's views on church, on mysticism, on sanctification, and on the "natural";[50] Luther's relation to the modern world[51] as well as to modern theology.[52] Roman Catholic scholars have participated in the congresses since 1966, and Luther scholars have formed working groups around specific themes since 1971. The main items for discussion are Luther's relation to late medieval thought and the question of his "breakthrough" to a Reformation stance, neither of which has yet been resolved satisfactorily. But the weight of precise ecumenical (rather than denominational) historical-critical scholarship can be clearly discerned in international Luther research.[53]

POSTHUMOUS REHABILITATION

On 18 June 1971, the Roman Catholic diocese of Cologne, Germany, requested the Holy Office in Rome to lift the ban on Luther in commemoration of the 450th anniversary of the Edict of Worms. This request echoed a similar plea made by a Hamburg jurist in 1963 to remove the 1054 ban on the leader of the Greek Orthodox Church, Patriarch Michael Cerularius, and thus to heal the schism between Rome and Constantinople. Cardinal Jan Willebrands, head of the Secretariat for Promoting Christian Unity, responded to Cologne that lifting the ban on Luther would be "essentially impossible" (sachlich nicht möglich) and would not serve to strengthen the already existing rapprochement between Catholics and Lutherans. For these reasons, Cardinal Willebrands suggested, it would be better to improve the relationship between Catholics and Lutherans through continual study, prayer, and other ecumenical means.[54]

Luther scholars tended to agree with this judgment. Both Catholic and Protestant experts on the matter of the ban have pointed out that it makes little sense to lift the ban on someone who is deceased. Lutheran church leaders agreed with Catholic authorities that Luther, once dead, is no longer under the jurisdiction of his church, but rather is subject to the judgment of God (1 Cor. 3:11–15). Lutherans were also concerned that the lifting of the ban would presume a solution to the problems still existing between Rome and the Lutheran churches.[55]

Still, Luther's rehabilitation seems to have progressed quietly and steadily through the intensive collaboration of Catholic and Protestant Luther scholars. There is now a plurality of Luther images derived from scholarly work rather than from church positions. Catholic and Protestant Luther scholars either agree or disagree with each other on the basis of their historical-critical work, so that the diversity of opinions about Luther can be traced through both confessional communities, not to either one alone.[56] On the Catholic side, Luther was first maligned, then explained, and finally praised, even though Catholic scholars must still face some thorny issues.[57] Even the most cautious Lutheran theologians agree that the very center of the Roman Catholic tradition, especially as affirmed at the Second Vatican Council (1962–64), is quite close to Luther's basic theological position.[58]

> Luther not only said things which are hardly perceived to be precarious today in the Catholic Church, but he also anticipated and expressed experiences of faith and of faithful existence which did not yet exist in the church's tradition before Luther. But these experiences are forced on us today from all directions in our confrontation with the reality of the world.[59]

Catholic theology has discovered, almost half a millennium after Luther's death, that there is a healthy tension between Scripture and tradition. Biblical theology has become the indispensable foundation for Catholic theological reflection today, so that theology as such is a "theology which must always be reformed" (theologia semper reformanda), just as the "church must always be reformed" (ecclesia semper reformanda). It was Luther who taught these lessons to succeeding generations of theologians;[60] accordingly, Catholics no longer need be hostile to Luther or to the Reformation. Both Catholic and Protestant scholars agree that Luther's reform movement aimed only to serve the gospel, and this is the lesson of history which Catholics now want to teach in their church. As a Catholic scholar put it in 1977:

> We have suddenly realized that Luther's Reformation was quite different than it is usually pictured. Given all its human, indeed its all too human, conditions, it ultimately served the gospel. That is why we, on our part, certainly must correct and newly evaluate the history of the Reformation. Once this is said, something else must finally be said: our church, which must proclaim the gospel to the world (evangelii nuntiandi) and Reformation Christianity—the evangelical church—belong together. It is doubtful whether either can survive in separation.[61]

Luther had indeed come a long way. After five hundred years, his "heresy" is hardly mentioned; he has become the subject of ecumenical attention in many parts of the world; cardinals have come to praise him, not to bury him:

Who could deny today [1970] that Martin Luther was a deeply religious personality who searched with honesty and commitment for the message of the gospel? Who could deny that he kept a significant proportion of the old Catholic faith, even though he pressured the Roman Catholic Church and the Apostolic See—for the sake of truth, one should not be silent about this. Indeed, did not the Second Vatican Council fulfill demands which were also expressed by Martin Luther, the fulfillment of which has given several aspects of the Christian faith and life better expression than they did before? Despite all the differences, to say this is reason for great joy and hope.[62]

The doctor of Holy Scripture, who fulfilled his oath in the guise of a fool (1 Cor. 3:18), a court jester,[63] is finally being heard before the court of history. Tried in absentia in 1521 in Rome, Luther has been posthumously acquitted—at least by ecumenical Luther research. Not that it would have mattered to him. Nevertheless, the court of history is where God does his peculiar work.

All of our experience with history should teach us, when we look back, how badly human wisdom is betrayed when it relies on itself. For hardly anything happens the way it is planned. But everything turns out differently, and the opposite happens from what one thought should happen.[64]

TIME CHART

The construction of this time chart has drawn on Lortz, *The Reformation in Germany*, 2:350–61 ("Chronological Table"); Haile, *Luther*, xi–xxx ("Important Events"); and Hendrix, *Luther and the Papacy* ("Chronology" preceding each chapter).

	Luther	*The World*
1483	Born 10 November in Eisleben.	Ambitious Charles VIII becomes king of France, Richard III starts reign in England with murder and intrigue. Renaissance and Humanism popular. Painter Raffael Santi is born. Printing press affects communication and banking.
1484	Family moves to Mansfeld.	Innocent VIII becomes pope, promulgates bull against witches. Zwingli is born.
1492	Attends school in Mansfeld.	Columbus discovers America. Alexander VI, father of Lucretia and Cesare Borgia, becomes pope. France invades Italy to secure Naples. Spanish Inquisition drives out Jews.
1497	Sent to school in Magdeburg.	Spanish crown receives papal title "Catholic Majesty." Melanchthon is born. Tobacco is introduced in Europe.

	Luther	*The World*
1498	Transfers to St. George School in Eisenach.	Albrecht Dürer paints *Apocalypse*. Hapsburg becomes superpower under Emperor Maximilian I (1493–1519).
1501	Enters Erfurt University.	
1502	Earns B.A. degree.	Frederick the Wise founds Wittenberg University. First pocket watches are made in Nuremberg.
1505	Earns M.A. degree in January. Begins law studies in May. Enters monastery 17 July.	Ivan III, the first Russian czar, dies. James Wimpfeling publishes first history of Germany (*Epitome*).
1506	Takes monastic vows.	Pope Julius II orders construction of St. Peter's in Rome. Columbus dies. Da Vinci paints *Mona Lisa*.
1507	Ordained.	Sigismund I becomes king of Poland. Tetzel sells indulgences in Germany.
1508	Sent to Wittenberg to lecture on moral philosophy.	Michelangelo begins painting Sistine Chapel ceiling.
1509	Earns Biblical Baccalaureate in March. Licensed to teach the *Sentences of Lombard* in the fall. Returns to Erfurt as *Sententiarius*.	Henry VIII becomes king of England. Philip of Hesse becomes ruler of Palatinate. Erasmus publishes *In Praise of Folly*. John Calvin is born.
1510	Sent to Rome in November by the Order.	
1511	Returns from Rome in April. Transferred to monastery in Wittenberg.	Humanist John Reuchlin and the Cologne Dominicans debate over the use of Hebrew in biblical studies.

	Luther	*The World*
1512	Earns doctorate, October. Joins theological faculty in Wittenberg.	Holy League is formed in Italy against France. Fifth Lateran Council convenes in Rome.
1513	Begins lectures on Psalms.	Leo X (Giovanni Medici) becomes pope. Balboa discovers the Pacific. Dürer paints *Knight, Death, and Devil*.
1514		Albrecht of Brandenburg becomes elector and Archbishop of Mainz. Dürer paints *Melancholia*. The Fugger Bank of Augsburg acquires control over sale of indulgences.
1515	Begins lectures on Romans. Reads John Tauler.	Francis I becomes king of France. Conquers Milan. Ulrich von Hutten and others publish *Letters of Obscure Men*.
1516	Begins lectures on Galatians.	Charles I becomes king of Spain. Erasmus publishes Greek New Testament. Thomas More writes *Utopia*.
1517	Begins lectures on Hebrews. Criticizes sale of indulgences. Attacks scholastic theology. Publicizes Ninety-five Theses, 31 October.	Pope Leo X increases number of cardinals. John Tetzel hired by Albrecht of Mainz to sell indulgences. Erasmus announces the dawn of a golden age.
1518	Defends his stance on indulgences. Summoned to Rome. Meets with Cardinal Cajetan in Augsburg, October. Asks to be heard by council.	Diet of Augsburg plans defense against Turks. Frederick the Wise rejects Cajetan's ultimatum to hand Luther over to Rome. Albrecht of Mainz becomes cardinal. Melanchthon joins Wittenberg faculty.

Luther	*The World*
1519	Meets with papal emissary Miltitz, January. Debates with John Eck at Leipzig. Condemned by universities of Cologne and Louvain.	Charles I of Spain becomes Emperor Charles V with help of Elector Frederick. Zwingli begins Swiss Reformation. Da Vinci dies. Magellan begins circumnavigation of the globe.
1520	Publishes major reform treatises, beginning with "To the Christian Nobility of the German Nation." Appeals to General Council. Burns papal bull in December.	Suliman II becomes Sultan of Turkey and starts drive to the north. Papal bull *Exsurge Domine* against Luther appears. Magellan reaches Cape Horn.
1521	Condemned by bull *Decet Romanum pontificem*, January. Appears before and is condemned by Imperial Diet of Worms. Hides at the Wartburg. Begins translation of New Testament.	Pope Leo X dies. Charles V begins war with France. Spain conquers Mexico. Radicals appear in Wittenberg. Henry VIII writes treatise against Luther defending seven sacraments. Pope calls him "defender of the faith."
1522	Returns to Wittenberg, March. Responds to Henry VIII. Publishes German translation of New Testament.	Cardinal Adrian of Utrecht becomes Pope Hadrian VI. Magellan completes circumnavigation of globe. Sickingen organizes German knights against emperor. Reuchlin dies.
1523	Initiates liturgical, educational, and social reforms in Wittenberg. Begins lectures on Deuteronomy.	Clement VII becomes pope. Diet of Nuremberg postpones resolution of religious conflict until Rome convenes a council. Emperor and pope form alliance against France. Zwingli's reforms are adopted in Zurich. German knights defeated. Hutten dies.

Luther	*The World*
1524	Begins lectures on Minor Prophets. Debates with Carlstadt on matters of social reform and the Lord's Supper.	Diet of Nuremberg fails to enforce Edict of Worms. South German Catholic princes form League of Regensburg. Popular expectations grow that the prophesied flood will end the world. Staupitz dies. Erasmus publishes *On the Freedom of the Will*. Peasants' War begins.
1525	Marries Catherine von Bora, 13 June. Writes against rebellious peasants and Carlstadt. Publishes "On the Bondage of the Will" against Erasmus.	Emperor defeats France and captures Francis I. Frederick the Wise dies. His brother John succeeds him. Thomas Müntzer is executed at end of Peasant's War. Anabaptist movement begins in Zurich and spreads to southern Germany.
1526	Becomes father of son Hans. Supports the organization of a Lutheran church in Saxony.	Philip of Hesse and Elector John form League of Torgau with North German Lutherans. Diet of Speyer postpones enforcement of Edict of Worms. Turks defeat Hungary at battle of Mohacs.
1527	Writes against Zwingli on Lord's Supper. Experiences first severe attacks of stones and heart problems. Becomes father of daughter Elizabeth.	Imperial troops plunder Rome ("*Sacco di Roma*"). Saxon visitations begin. Reformation spreads to Scandinavia. Macchiavelli dies.
1528	Grieves over death of Elizabeth. Writes seminal "Confession" on Lord's Supper.	Emperor Charles V wages war against France. Bern, Switzerland, becomes Protestant. Dürer dies. Marburg University is founded.
1529	Publishes Small and Large Catechisms. Becomes father of Magdalene (Lenchen). Travels to Marburg for colloquy with Zwingli.	Diet of Speyer decides to enforce Edict of Worms. Lutheran territories make formal "Protest." Turks besiege Vienna.

	Luther	*The World*
1530	Lives in Fortress Coburg in spring and summer. Meets Martin Bucer from Strassburg. Father dies.	Diet of Augsburg receives and rejects Augsburg Confession. Catholics draft "Confutation." Melanchthon responds with *Apology of the Augsburg Confession*.
1531	Becomes father of Martin. Writes "Warning" to his "Dear Germans." Mother dies.	Lutheran Smalcald League is formed. Zwingli is killed in battle against Catholics. Henry VIII breaks with Rome. Halley's comet appears and is linked to end of the world.
1532	Frequently ill. Meets with new elector who regards him as his "spiritual father."	Elector John dies and is succeeded by his son John Frederick. Diet of Regensburg and Peace of Nuremberg guarantee religious toleration in the face of Turkish threat. Pope and emperor begin negotiations for a council. Macchiavelli's *The Prince* is published.
1533	Becomes father of Paul. Writes on Mass and the priesthood.	Henry VIII becomes father of daughter Elizabeth (later Elizabeth I). Ivan "the Terrible" begins his rule in Russia.
1534	Becomes father of Margaret. Publishes German Bible.	Paul III becomes pope. Radical Anabaptists create "Kingdom of Münster." Henry VIII becomes supreme head of Church of England.
1535	Presides over doctoral disputations. Meets with papal emissary Vergerio regarding a future council.	Emperor forms a Catholic Defense League. Francis I of France makes pact with Suliman. Münster Anabaptists are defeated and executed. Thomas More is beheaded.

Luther	*The World*
1536	Agrees to "Wittenberg Concord" on the Lord's Supper after negotiations with South German Protestants.	Pope Paul III convenes council to meet in Mantua in 1537. Emperor starts war with France. Denmark becomes Lutheran. Erasmus dies.
1537	Travels to Smalcald. Has severe stone attacks. Publishes the "Smalcald Articles" as his theological testament.	Smalcald League rejects papal council. Charles V wages war against William of Jülich-Clevesberg over Dutch territories. Pope postpones council.
1539	Becomes involved in the antinomian controversies against John Agricola who claimed there is no need for law among Christians.	Frankfurt Truce is declared between Catholic and Lutheran territories. Duke Henry of Saxony dies.
1540	Agrees to Philip of Hesse's plan to commit bigamy.	Philip of Hesse's act of bigamy destroys effectiveness of Smalcald League. Catholics and Lutherans negotiate at Hagenau, Worms, and Regensburg; fail to agree. Pope ratifies Jesuit Order.
1541	Writes vitriolic treatises against pope and Duke Henry of Brunswick. Goes on preaching tour and consecrates Nicholas Amsdorf "bishop" of Naumburg.	Diet of Regensburg extends truce between Catholics and Protestants. Turks conquer Buda, Hungary. Carlstadt dies.
1542	Grieves over death of fourteen-year-old Lenchen. Drafts his will.	Diet of Speyer discusses Turkish threat. Pope convenes council to meet in Trent in 1543.
1543	Writes most offensive treatises against Jews.	Diet of Nuremberg discusses Turks. Emperor allies himself with England. The Lutheran Osiander publishes "On Revolutions" (*De revolutionibus*) by Copernicus. John Eck dies. Copernicus dies.

	Luther	*The World*
1544	Writes against Caspar Schwenckfeld's interpretation of the Lord's Supper.	Diet of Speyer makes concessions to Protestant territories which help fight the Turks. Pope Paul III protests, calls for a council to meet in Trent in 1545. Diet of Worms meets on the Turkish question. Emperor and Suliman conclude a truce of eighteen months. Protestants reject papal council.
1545	Makes final revisions on Bible translation. Writes pornographic treatise against the pope, and an autobiographical Preface to Latin edition of collected works.	Diet of Worms agrees to truce with Turks. Albrecht of Mainz dies. Council of Trent meets for first session (the last is in 1563).
1546	Dies in Eisleben, 18 February. Buried in Castle Church, 22 February.	Diet of Regensburg outlaws Smalcald League leaders John Frederick and Philip of Hesse. Smalcald War begins. Emperor invades Saxony.
1547		Emperor defeats Smalcald League. Cologne returns to Catholicism. Henry VIII dies. Francis I of France dies. John Frederick's cousin Maurice becomes Elector of Saxony. Michelangelo oversees construction of St. Peter's in Rome.
1548		Augsburg Interim between Catholics and Protestants grants some compromises (lay chalice and clerical marriage) until Council of Trent makes decisions.
1552	Catherine von Bora dies.	

	Luther	*The World*
1555		The Peace of Augsburg grants equal rights to Catholics and the adherents of the Augsburg Confession.

NOTES

PREFACE

1. Harley, *Little Journeys With Martin Luther,* 3.
2. Bornkamm, *Luther and the Old Testament,* 7.
3. Brandenburg and Gritsch, "Luther's Success and Failure."

CHAPTER 1

1. The encounter is suggested in "table talks" which, though not always reliable, provide significant evidence for piecing together Luther's early life. "Table Talk," 18 August–26 December 1531, no. 2255a. *WA.TR* 2:379, 7–19. (6–10 November 1538, no. 4091. *WA.TR* 4:129.30–131:1.). Summer 1540, no. 5371. *WA.TR* 5:98.21–28. See also Melanchthon, "Preface to the Second Edition of Luther's Complete Works" (*Prefatio Melanthonis in tomum secundum omnium Reverendi Doctori Martini Lutheri*), 1546. *CR* 6:160. *SML* 2:306.
2. "Infiltrating and Clandestine Preachers" (*Ein Brief M. Luthers von den Schleichern und Winkelpredigern*), 1532. *WA* 30/3:522.2–8. *LW* 40:387–88.
3. The story of family origins, childhood, and early education has been put together by Brecht, *Martin Luther,* chap. 1.
4. Luther biographers usually trace Luther's mother to the Ziegler family in Möhra with suggestions that *Ziegler* ("bricklayer" in German) was the profession of the head of the Lindemann family. But the case for Lindemann in Eisenach has been well argued by Siggins, *Luther and His Mother,* chaps. 1–2. *LW* editor Krodel held the same view before Siggins's work was published. See *LW* 48:329.
5. The beginnings were difficult in the foundry business, but Hans Luther was a successful "smelting master" (*Hüttenmeister*) by 1491, owning or renting foundries. See Brecht, *Martin Luther,* 16.
6. Luther's mother, known as "Hannah" in the family, remembered the day but not the year of Luther's birth. Melanchthon established the year. See his Preface to the Second Edition of Luther's Complete Works, *CR* 6:156. On Luther's brothers and sisters, see Siggins, *Luther and His Mother,* 14.
7. He was carried to school by a friend of the family, Nicholas Oehmler, probably at the age of four or five. See Melanchthon, "Preface to the Second Edition of Luther's Complete Works," *CR* 6:156–57.

8. There were also "sisters of the common life." Both orders were organized in Holland at the end of the fourteenth century. The best known member of the order was Thomas à Kempis (1380–1471), who wrote the devotional classic *The Imitation of Christ*. Whether or not Luther was greatly influenced by the Brethren is a matter of conjecture. For the story of the order, see Hyma, *Brethren of the Common Life*.

9. Since the Brethren of the Common Life did not have a school of their own, Luther may have attended the Cathedral School, where the Brethren taught. Music and singing were part of the curriculum. See Brecht, *Martin Luther*, 27–28.

10. "A Sermon on Keeping Children in School" (*Eine Predigt, dass man Kinder zur Schule halten soll*), 1530. WA 30/2:576.11–15. LW 46:250–51.

11. Ursula Cotta's maiden name was Schwalbe. There is a Cotta house in Eisenach, but there is little evidence to prove that Luther stayed there. See SD 211, and Brecht, *Martin Luther*, 30.

12. See Siggins, *Luther and His Mother*, chap. 5.

13. Luther corresponded with Braun until ca. 1516. See Brecht, *Martin Luther*, 31–32.

14. Melanchthon, "Preface to the Second Edition of Luther's Complete Works," 1546. CR 6:157.

15. Findings of Schwiebert, *Luther and His Times*, 128.

16. It is difficult to assess the importance of Luther's philosophical and theological studies in Erfurt. Methodology seems to have been stressed, especially logic. Theological reflection was influenced by a budding Humanism. See Brecht, *Martin Luther*, 42–53, and Zumkeller, "Martin Luther und sein Orden."

17. "Dedication of the Judgment of Martin Luther on Monastic Vows" (*De votis monasticis Martini Lutheri iudicium*) to his father, 21 November 1521. WA 8:573.23–24. LW 48:331. The treatise is in WA 8:573–669. LW 44:245–400.

18. Sources of *SML* 1, chap. 5. See also Rupp, *Luther's Progress*, 13–15; Schwiebert, *Luther and His Times*, 136–44; Brecht, *Martin Luther*, 55–58.

19. WA 8:573.30–574:2. LW 48:332.

20. "Table Talk" 15–16 July 1539, no. 4707. WA.TR 4:440.5–10, 12–19. See the translation in Schwiebert, *Luther and His Times*, 137–38. This account is corroborated by Crotus Rubeanus, Humanist and former roommate of Luther, based on a report by Justus Jonas from 28 January 1538. See SD 30. Another "Table Talk" tells the story of how Luther almost bled to death when his short sword struck his shin and cut an artery, probably on a trip home from Erfurt on 16 April 1503. "Table Talk," 9–30 November 1531, no. 119. WA.TR 1:46.18–19. LW 54:14. Some sources mention the murder of a friend; others know of an apparition from heaven. See SML 1:245–46; 321 n. 44. Staupitz and Luther may not have met before 1508. See Steinmetz, *Misericordia Dei*, 9–10. For a detailed comparison of Staupitz and Luther, see Steinmetz, *Luther and Staupitz*.

21. "Table Talk," 2 February 1538, no. 3722. WA.TR 3:564.6. LW 54:264.

22. "Table Talk," 21–28 March 1537, no. 3556a. WA.TR 3:410.42–43. LW 54:234.

23. Letter to his father, 21 November 1521. WA 8:574.2, 7–8. LW 48:332.

24. Luther's "monastic struggle" is well depicted by Schwiebert, *Luther and His Times*, chap. 5. Schwiebert's work is based on Strohl, *L'Évolution Religieuse de Luther*.

25. "Table Talk," spring 1533, no. 495. *WA.TR* 1:220.9–17. *LW* 54:85.

26. The evidence from various "Table Talks" is controversial. But Luther did immerse himself in intensive Bible study after his matriculation at Erfurt University in 1501. See Kooiman, *Luther and the Bible*, chap. 1.

27. "Lectures on Genesis" (*Genesisvorlesung*) 48:21, 1545. *WA* 44:716.22–27. *LW* 8:188.

28. "Table Talk," 9–30 November 1531, no. 116. *WA.TR* 1:44.31–32. *LW* 54:14.

29. *WA.BR* 1:133.31–34, 37–39. *LW* 48:53–54. Luther had known Spalatin since 1514. Spalatin was a counselor at the Saxon court, and court chaplain after 1522. After the death of Elector Frederick in 1525, he became pastor and "superintendent" (the Lutheran designation for bishop) in Altenburg, where he died in 1545. For his relationship with Luther, see Höss, "Georg Spalatins Verhältnis."

30. Especially his interpretation of Paul. See Grane, *Modus Loquendi Theologicus*, 60–62.

31. "Table Talk," 28 March–27 May 1537, no. 3582a. *WA.TR* 3:432.2–8. *LW* 54:237. How Luther concentrated on religion at the expense of Renaissance art is shown by Heinrich Boehmer, *Road to Reformation*, chap. 8, based on the author's *Luthers Romfahrt*.

32. Scheel, *SML* 2:311. Fifty guilders were worth about $470 in 1950. The Rhenish gulden of 1536 had a buying power of $13.40 in 1913 (based on the calculations of Schwiebert, *Luther and His Times*, 194, 258). Luther's annual salary at the university was $2,680 in 1525, and by 1546 had reached $5,360 (Ibid., 266–67). For the details of Luther's doctoral oath, see Scheurl, "Martin Luthers Doktoreid."

33. The date of Luther's first lecture is a matter of debate. My own interpretation follows Brecht, *Martin Luther*, 128. Staupitz appointed Luther preacher in the Augustinian monastery. Why, how, and when Luther received a call to preach at the Town Church is not known. Ibid., 150.

34. The glosses and scholia of the "First Lectures on the Psalms" (*Dictata super Psalterium*), 1513–15, in Luther's handwriting have been preserved. See *LW* 10:x. A chronological listing of Luther's lectures is available in Schubert and Meissinger, *Zu Luthers Vorlesungstätigkeit*.

35. Literally *Anfechtung* means "to be fought at," if not fenced at (from *fechten*, "fencing"), and is often rendered as "temptation," from the Latin term *tentatio* which Luther sometimes used. Bainton (*Here I Stand*, 42) thought of the German *Blitzkrieg* (lightning-war). Rupp (*The Righteousness of God*, 102) recalled John Bunyan's "bruised conscience." For a summary of *Anfechtung* in Luther, see Beintker, "Anfechtung."

36. "Table Talk," fall 1532, no. 352. *WA.TR* 1:146.12–14. *LW* 54:50.

37. "Table Talk," early November 1531, no. 94. *WA.TR* 1:35.17–20. *LW* 54:11. The reference to the "driven leaf" in Lev. 26:36 is found in a sermon for First Advent on Matt. 21:1–9, "Advent Postil" (*Adventspostille*), 1522. *WA* 10½:27.18. See also "Anfechtungen" in the "Index" (*Register*) of *WA* 58:57–61, and Rupp, *The Righteousness of God*, chap. 5.

38. "Table Talk," no. 94, *WA.TR* 1:35.17–20, *LW* 54:11.

39. *WA* 1:525.10–23. *LW* 48:65–66.

40. "Preface to the Incomplete Edition of the 'German Theology' " (*Vorrede zu*

der unvollständigen Ausgabe der "deutschen Theologie"), 1516. English translation of the longer 1518 edition with commentary by Hoffman, *The Theologia Germanica of Martin Luther.*

41. WA.BR 1:72.4–10, 11–13. LW 48:27–28.

42. "Table Talk," 9 June–July 1532, no. 3232c. WA.TR 3:228.31–32. LW 54:194. The variant no. 3232b mentions "cloaca." WA.TR 3:228.23. The other variants mention the "tower" (*Turm*). Evidence collected in *SML* 2:320, 435 n. 13; and *LW* 54:193 n. 65. Haile, "Great Martin Luther Spoof," has demonstrated how overrated the evidence has been in Luther research.

43. The search for a date for Luther's "breakthrough" to radically new insights has created a literary jungle. The debate discloses differences in methodology and philosophy of history. Some scholars prefer a genetic method and trace Luther's ideas to previous traditions. See, for example, Oberman, *Masters of the Reformation*, chap. 13. Others draw conclusions only from Luther's texts in historical contexts. See, for example, Grane, *Modus Loquendi Theologicus*, 192–99. Oberman and Grane have debated the question of whether Luther's Reformation is "epochal" or "episodal." See Oberman, "Reformation: Epoche oder Episode," *ARG* 68 (1977), 56–109, and Grane, "Lutherforschung und Geistesgeschichte," ibid., 302–15. For a summary of opinions, see Lohse, *Durchbruch der reformatorischen Erkenntnis*. A rather convincing approach is offered by Pesch, "Zur Frage nach Luthers reformatorischer Wende," ibid., 445–505, for Pesch distinguishes between a "tower experience" and a "Reformation breakthrough." That Luther may have experienced a decisive change between the fall of 1517 (after the "Ninety-five Theses") and before the summer of 1518 (when he spoke of a different understanding of penance) has been shown by Brecht, *Martin Luther*, 215–30. See also Pesch, *Hinführung zu Luther*, 99–100.

44. "Preface to the Complete Edition of Luther's Latin Writings" (*Vorrede Luthers zum ersten Band der Gesamtausgabe seiner lateinischen* Schriften), 1545. WA 54:185.13–186.16. LW 34:336–37. Italics mine.

45. Luther's glosses and scholia on the Psalms have been collected in WA 3. A new edition will appear in WA 55. The scholia have been translated in the "First Lectures on the Psalms," 1513–15. LW 10:11. The christological emphasis has been evaluated by Rupp, *The Righteousness of God*, chap. 7; by Ebeling, "Die Anfänge von Luthers Hermeneutik"; and by Maurer, "Die Anfänge von Luthers Theologie."

46. WA 3:424.10–14. LW 10:361.

47. The lectures are in WA 56–57. LW 25 and 29. Only the 1535 "Lectures on Galatians" are available in LW 26 and 27.

48. "Two Kinds of Righteousness" (*Sermo de duplici iustitia*), 1519. WA 2:145.9–12; 146.36–147.3. LW 31:297, 299.

49. "The Freedom of the Christian" (*Von der Freiheit eines Christenmenschen; Tractatus de libertate christiana*), 1520. WA 7:55.8–14, 24–27. German ibid., 25.34. LW 31:351–52.

50. "Disputation on the Question of Human Power and Will Without Grace" (*Quaestio de viribus et voluntate hominis sine gratia disputata*), 1516. WA 1:142–51. Bernhardi joined the Wittenberg faculty in 1518.

51. WA.BR 1:99.8–13. LW 48:42.

52. On Carlstadt's "conversion" to Augustine, see Grane, *Modus Loquendi Theologicus*, 130–37. On Luther's early years with Carlstadt, see Sider, *Andreas Bodenstein von Karlstadt*, chap. 1.

53. "Disputation Against Scholastic Theology" (*Disputatio contra scholasticam theologiam*), 1517. WA 1:228.34–36. LW 31:16.

54. For a historical sketch of the doctrine of indulgences, as well as of their use and abuse, see Todd, *Luther*, Appendix, 373–78.

55. On Matt. 11:25–30. WA 1:141.28–38. LW 51:31. Luther encountered the "edifice complex" of ecclesiastical authorities who issued a "jubilee indulgence," that is, forgiveness of sins for a trip to Rome and/or contribution to the building fund for a new basilica of St. Peter's in Rome. Pope Julius II had issued such an indulgence in 1510, and Pope Leo X revived the indulgence in 1515. See Benrath, "Ablass," *TRE* 1:347–64, and LW 31:21.

56. WA 1:233–38. LW 31:25–33. There is good evidence that the theses were not nailed to the door of the Castle Church. See Iserloh, *The Theses Were Not Posted*, and Bornkamm, *Thesen und Thesenanschlag Luthers*. The best source collection is in Aland, *Martin Luther's 95 Theses*.

57. Albrecht had to pay about $250,000 for his advancement to archbishop. Pope Leo X demanded $120,000 in cash immediately, the rest to be paid later through the sale of indulgences. The Fugger bank corporation was granted supervision of the collections of money by Rome. Tetzel was paid a monthly salary of about $1,000 with "bonuses" from the Fuggers. See Schwiebert, *Luther and His Times*, 309.

58. WA.BR 1:112.53–60. LW 48:48. Text of Albrecht's "Summary Instructions" (*Instructio summaria*) in Köhler, *Dokumente zum Ablasstreit*, 104–24.

59. "Introduction to the Theses." WA 1:233.1–2. LW 31:25.

60. Letter to Spalatin, 22 February 1518. WA.BR 1:149.6–9. LW 48:56.

61. For a blow-by-blow account of events, see Mackinnon, *Luther and the Reformation*, vol. 2, chap. 1.

62. "Lenten Sermon on John 9:1–38," 17 March 1518. WA 1:271.34–36. LW 51:42.

63. WA 1:529.30–530.8. LW 31:83.

64. WA 1:613.23–28, 33–37. LW 31:225–26.

65. For the first time in a letter to Spalatin in early November 1517. WA.BR 1:118.16. SJ 1:64.

66. "Heidelberg Disputation" (*Disputatio Heidelbergae habita*), 1518. WA 1:361.32–362.3. LW 31:40. Translation mine. The theses were crucial for Luther's entire theological thinking. See Loewenich, *Luther's Theology of the Cross*, Pt. 1.

67. Proof of thesis 20. "Heidelberg Disputation," 1518. WA 1:361.36; 362.5–13, 18–19. LW 31:52–53.

68. 9 May 1518. WA.BR 1:170.33–38. SJ 1:83–84.

69. "Sermon on the Virtue of Excommunication" (*Sermo de virtute excommunicationis*), 1518. WA 1:643.1–15. Translation mine.

70. See Tentler, *Sin and Confession*, 351–63.

CHAPTER 2

1. Extensive documentation for Luther's trial in Bäumer, ed., *Lutherprozess und Lutherbann*. See also Atkinson, *The Trial of Luther*; Olivier, *The Trial of Luther*; and Brecht, *Martin Luther*, chaps. 7, 11.

2. "A Response to the Dialogue of Sylvester Prierias on the Power of the Pope" (*Ad dialogum Silvestri Prieriatis de potesta papae responsio*), 1518. *WA* 1:686.28–33. Translation in *SJ* 1:101.

3. "Prierias's Response to Martin Luther" (*Replica F. Silvestri Prieritatis ad F. Martinum Luther*), 1518. *WA* 2:50.28–32.

4. "Table Talk," 6 April 1533, No. 491. *WA.TR* 1:216.3–4. *LW* 54:83.

5. The Hapsburg Holy Roman Emperor Maximilian I had married Mary of Burgundy in 1477, thus annexing territories in the Southwest, since Burgundy is in southeastern France, with Marseilles its large city; Mary also brought what is now the territory of the Netherlands to the marriage. Their only son, Philip, had married Johanna, the daughter of Ferdinand and Isabella of Spain, in 1496, thus bringing Spain under Hapsburg domination when the son of that marriage, Charles, inherited Spain upon the death in 1516 of Ferdinand and Isabella. Maximilian I had arranged to have Philip and Johanna's children Mary and Ferdinand marry the children of King Wladislaw II, Ludwig and Anna, in 1515. Since Henry VIII of England had married Catherine of Aragon—one of Ferdinand and Isabella's daughters—in 1509, Hapsburg also had some influence, though only indirectly, on England. It is therefore no wonder that Hapsburg was said to have lived by the proverb "When other nations make war, you, happy Austria, marry!" (*Si alii bella gerunt, tu felix Austria nube!*)

6. Frederick's relations to the church have been analyzed by Kirn, *Friedrich der Weise und die Kirche*. The "Golden Bull" of 1356 (so called because of its golden seal) decreed that the Holy Roman Emperor be elected by seven princes, four secular and three ecclesiastical: the king of Bohemia, the Count of the Palatinate, the Duke of Saxony-Wittenberg, the Margrave of Brandenburg; and the archbishops of Mainz, Trier, and Cologne. The designation "Holy Roman Empire of the German Nation" appeared under Emperor Frederick III (1440–93); it was used only for the German part of the empire, and did not refer to the entire empire.

7. Letter dated 8 August 1518. *WA.BR* 1:188.4–9. *LW* 48:71.

8. Both letters dated 25 September 1518. *EA var.* 2:362–63. Translation in Schwiebert, *Luther and His Times*, 362.

9. Maximilian I to Pope Leo X on 5 August 1518. *EA var.* 2:349. *SJ* 1:98–101. Leo X to Cajetan on 23 August 1518. "Proceedings at Augsburg" (*Acta Augustana*), 1518. *WA* 2:23–25. *LW* 31:286–89. Leo X to Elector Frederick on 23 August 1518. *EA var.* 2:352. *SJ* 1:105–6. The General of the Augustinian Hermits to Gerhard Hecker on 25 August 1518. Original text in Kolde, "Luther und sein Ordensgeneral in Rome." *SJ* 1:106–8.

10. The exact sequence of events is not entirely clear. See Bäumer, *Lutherprozess und Lutherbann*, 27. Luther's own account is in "Proceedings at Augsburg," 1518. *WA* 2:6–26. *LW* 31:259–92. See also Henning, *Cajetan und Luther*; and Hendrix, *Luther and the Papacy*, 52–70.

11. Explanation of thesis 7. *WA* 1:543.7–9. *LW* 31:104.

12. *WA* 1:236.22–23. *LW* 31:31. Text of *Unigenitus* in Mirbt-Aland I, 472–74.

13. *WA* 2:9.16–16.21. *LW* 31:264–75.

14. Evidence from Brecht, *Martin Luther*, 248.

15. "Martin Luther's Appeal to the Pope Through Cajetan" (*Appelatio M. Lutheri a Caietana ad Papam*), 1518. *WA* 2:28–33. Luther left Augsburg at night on horseback.

16. "Proceedings at Augsburg," 1518. *WA* 2:18.18–25. *LW* 31:278. For a summary of Cajetan's theology, see Wicks, *Cajetan Responds*.

17. 31 October 1518. *WA.BR* 1:225.25–26. *SJ* 1:129.

18. "Appeal of Friar Martin Luther to a Council" (*Appelatio F. Martini Lutheri ad concilum*), 1518. *WA* 2:40.9–20. For the origin and meaning of Luther's conciliarism see Johns, *Luthers Konzilsidee*, 137–43.

19. No exact date. *WA.BR* 1:267.4–5, 9–10.

20. Published as "Luther's Instructions Concerning Certain Articles Imposed and Ascribed to Him by His Detractors" (*Luthers Unterricht auf etliche Artikel, die ihm von seinen Abgönnern aufgelegt und zugemessen werden*), 1519. *WA* 2:66–73.

21. Letter dated 2 February 1519. *WA.BR* 1:373.17–18. *SJ* 1:160. Luther's conciliatory behavior during the negotiations has been shown by Leder, *Ausgleich mit dem Papst?*

22. *WA.BR* 1:365.20–31. *SJ* 1:172–73.

23. *WA.BR* 1:403.59–62. *SJ* 1:186.

24. On the beginnings of Melanchthon's career in Wittenberg, see Manschreck, *Melanchthon*, chap. 1; and Maurer, *Der junge Melanchthon*, vol. 2, chap. 1.

25. Eyewitness accounts of the debate are in "The Disputation of John Eck and Martin Luther Held at Leipzig" (*Disputatio Johannis Eccii et Martini Lutheri Lipsiae habita*), 1519. *WA* 2:250–383. Luther's own account ibid., 388–435. "The Leipzig Debate," 1519. *LW* 31:309–25. Good summary of issues in Selge, "Die Leipziger Disputation zwischen Luther und Eck"; and in Hendrix, *Luther and the Papacy*, 85–89.

26. *WA.BR* 1:359.28–32; 360.35–36. *LW* 48:114. For Luther's use of church history, see Headley, *Luther's View of Church History*, especially chap. 4 on the early church as "tentative norm."

27. "The Leipzig Debate," 1519. *WA* 2:161.35–38. *LW* 31:318. Detailed defense of the thesis in "Lutheran Resolution About Proposition 13 on the Power of the Pope" (*Resolutio Lutherania super propositione sua decima tertia de potestate papae*), 1519. *WA* 2:180–240.

28. How vital Elector Frederick's role was, in the election, has been shown by Brandi, *The Emperor Charles V*, 111.

29. The main source of the investigation was Luther's "The Babylonian Captivity," 1520. See Schwiebert, *Luther and His Times*, 433–34.

30. Ibid., 427–31. .

31. *WA.BR* 1:424.145–52. *LW* 31:325.

32. This designation appeared in an anonymous "preface" to the Basel edition of Luther's Works. See Todd, *Martin Luther*, 172–73. The 1518 edition was purchased by Cornell University. See Schwiebert, *Luther and His Times*, 427. How printing affected the spread of the Reformation has been described by Louise Holborn, "Printing and the Growth of a Protestant Movement." See also Bornkamm, "Luther als Schriftsteller."

33. For a chronological listing of publications and events between 30 October 1519 and 2 April 1521 see Buchwald, *Luther-Kalendarium*, 12–19. Summarized by Schwiebert, *Luther and His Times*, 438–39.

34. "A Sermon on Preparing to Die" (*Ein Sermon von der Bereitung zum Sterben*),

1519. WA 2:685–97. *LW* 42:97–115. "A Discussion on How Confession Should be Made" (*Confitendi ratio*), 1520. WA 6:157–69. *LW* 39:25–44. A Personal Prayerbook (*Betbüchlein*), 1522. WA 10/2:375–406. *LW* 43:5–45.

35. "Trade and Usury" (*Von Kaufhandlung und Wucher*), 1524. WA 6:58.13. *LW* 45:305. For a study of how Luther arrived at this compromise, see Schulze, "Luther und der Zins."

36. "On the Papacy in Rome" (*Von dem Papsttum zu Rom*), 1520. WA 6:309.16–310.8. *LW* 39:86–87. Luther had another feud about the papacy with the Leipzig theologian Jerome Emser. See "To the Goat in Leipzig" (*An den Bock zu Leipzig*), 1521. WA 7:262–65. *LW* 39:51–104; and "Answer to the Hyperchristian, Hyperspiritual, and Hyperlearned Book by Goat Emser in Leipzig" (*Auf das überchristlich, übergeistlich und überkünstlich Buch Bocks Emsers zu Leipzig Antwort*), 1521. WA 7:621–88. *LW* 39:139–228.

37. Sylvester Prierias's "Epitome of a Reply to Martin Luther" (*Epitome responsionis ad Lutherum*), 1519. WA 6:329.17–23. *LW* 44:118–19.

38. "Treatise on Good Works" (*Von den guten Werken*), 1520. WA 6:216.29–31. *LW* 44:38.

39. WA 6:249.2–6. *LW* 44:78.

40. WA 6:257.27–28. *LW* 44:90.

41. WA 6:276.1–4. *LW* 44:113.

42. WA 6:276.18–19. *LW* 44:114.

43. "To the Christian Nobility of the German Nation Concerning the Reform of the Christian Estate" (*An den christlichen Adel deutscher Nation von des christlichen Standes Besserung*), 1520. List of grievances in WA 6:415.19–427.29. *LW* 44:139–56. Such grievances had been submitted to German diets since 1456. Sources for 1521 in Strauss, *Manifestations of Discontent*, 52–63. For a general history of the gravamina, see Gebhardt, *Die Gravamina der deutschen Nation*.

44. WA 6:408.11–15. *LW* 44:129.

45. WA 6:435.3–4. *LW* 44:166.

46. WA 6:468.32–36; 469.13–17. *LW* 44:216–17.

47. "The Babylonian Captivity of the Church, A Prelude" (*De captivitate Babylonica ecclesiae praeludium*), 1520. WA 6:572.23–30. *LW* 36:124–25.

48. "The Freedom of the Christian," 1520. WA 7:65.32–36. *LW* 31:366.

49. Text of *Exsurge Domini* in Mirbt-Aland I, 504–13.

50. *EA var* 5:10. *SJ* 1:336.

51. *EA var* 2:351. *SJ* 1:338.

52. WA.BR 2:177.71–75. *LW* 48:178–79.

53. WA.BR 2:195. *SJ* 1:366.

54. "Against the Execrable Bull of the Antichrist" (*Adversus execrabilem Antichristi bullam, Wider die Bulle des Endchrists*), 1520. WA 6:595–629. "Dr. Martin Luther's Appeal to Leo X for a Council, Once Again Repeated and Renewed" (*Appelatio D. Martini Lutheri ad concilium a Leone X. denuo repetita et innovata*), 1520. WA 7:74–151. The appeal was accompanied by a defense of all the articles Rome had condemned.

55. "Why the Books of the Pope and His Disciples Were Burned" (*Warum des Papsts und seiner Jünger Bücher von Martin Luther verbrannt sind*), 1520. WA 7:181.1–8. *LW* 31:394–95.

56. Text of *Decet Romanum* in *MA.I*, 513–15.

57. Recorded proceedings with Luther in *DRTA.JR* 2:449–661. For an assessment of the Diet of Worms, see Reuter, *Der Reichstag zu Worms*. Illustrated source materials in Jensen, *Confrontation at Worms*. Some eyewitness accounts are in "Luther at the Diet of Worms" (*Verhandlungen mit Dr. Martin Luther auf dem Reichstage zu Worms*), 1521. WA 7:814–57. LW 32:103–31. Good account in Mackinnon, vol. 2, chap. 9.

58. Kalkoff, *Die Depeschen des Nuntius Aleander . . .*, 69. *SJ* 1:455–56; 61.

59. *WA.BR* 2:298.6–10. LW 48:198.

60. "Luther at the Diet of Worms," 1521. WA 7:838.4–9. LW 32:112–13. Luther's entire speech is in WA 7:832.1–835.18. LW 32:109–13. The account is from an unknown eyewitness. There is some doubt whether Luther said, "I cannot do otherwise, here I stand, God help me, Amen." I am persuaded by Bainton (*Here I Stand*, 185) who opted for the longer version because "the listeners at the moment may have been too moved to write." One eyewitness recorded only "May God help me" (*Das helf mir Gott*). *DRTA.JR* 2:587. But Luther himself recorded the words in his own account of the event.

61. The Teutonic Order (*Deutscher Orden*) was founded as a hospital order in 1198 and still exists today. In the sixteenth century, the order lost many of its land holdings and sided with Luther. See the historical sketch in LW 45:133–37.

62. The significance of these official negotiations between Luther and imperial officials has been neglected in Luther research. My account is based on Brecht, *Martin Luther*, 442–47.

63. Letter from Frankfurt am Main, 28 April 1521. *WA.BR* 2:305.5–8. LW 48:201.

64. *WA.BR* 2:309.111–13. LW 48:209.

65. Text in *DRTA.JR* 2:643–61. Jensen, *Confrontation at Worms*, 75–111.

66. *WA.BR* 2:354.22–27. LW 48:255.

67. One version of the story also has the devil throw the inkwell at Luther. The inkwell first appeared in 1650. On the demythologizing of the story, see Schwiebert, *Luther and His Times*, 518–19; and Bornkamm, *Luther in die Mitte seines Lebens*, 25.

68. "The Magnificat" (*Das Magnificat verdeutscht und ausgelegt*), 1521. WA 7:538–604. LW 21:297–358.

69. "To the People of Wittenberg," June 1521. WA 8:210–14. LW 48:248–53.

70. "Dr. Luther's Retraction of Error Falsely Forced Upon Him by the Most Highly Learned Priest of God, Sir Jerome Emser, vicar of Meissen" (*Ein Widerspruch D. Luthers seines Irrtums, erzwungen durch den allhochgelehrtesten Priester Gottes, Herrn Hieronymus Emser, Vicarien zu Meissen*), 1521. WA 8:247–54. LW 39:227–38.

71. "A Sincere Admonition to All Christians to Guard Against Insurrection and Rebellion" (*Eine treue Vermahnung zu allen Christen, sich zu hüten vor Aufruhr und Empörung*), 1522. WA 8:676–87. LW 45:53–74.

72. "Church Postil" (*Kirchenpostille*), 1522. WA 10¹/1.

73. Followed by the translation of the Old Testament in 1534. The Luther Bible of 1546 represents the final edition in Luther's lifetime. The gigantic work of translation encompasses twelve volumes. *WA.DB* 1–12. A selection of "prefaces" to various

biblical books has been translated in *LW* 35:227–411 (based on the 1546 edition). The German Bible has been analyzed by Reu, *Luther's German Bible*, and by Volz, *Martin Luthers deutsche Bibel*.

74. "On Confession, Whether the Pope Has the Power to Command It" (*Von der Beicht, ob die der Papst Macht habe zu gebieten*), 1521. *WA* 8:164.15–20.

75. *WA.BR* 2:407.66–69, 71–72. *LW* 48:34–42. The treatise "Against the Idol of Halle" (*Wider den Abgott zu Halle*) was probably never published. See Krodel, "Excursus" ibid., 344–50.

76. *WA.BR* 2:421.1–13. *SJ* 2:80.

77. "The Judgment of Martin Luther on Monastic Vows," 1521. *WA* 8:577.18–19. *LW* 44:251. See the careful analysis by Lohse, *Mönchtum und Reformation*, 356–79.

78. *WA* 8:605.15–18. *LW* 44:296.

79. *WA* 8:668.18–20. *LW* 44:399.

80. "The Misuse of the Mass" (*Vom Missbrauch der Messe*), 1521. *WA* 8:521.10–25. *LW* 36:179–80.

81. *WA* 8:537.25–34. *LW* 36:198.

82. "Against Latomus" (*Rationis Latomianae confutatio*), 1521. *WA* 8:103.35–107.12. *LW* 32:229.

83. See the exposition of Rom. 4:7 in "Lectures on Romans" (*Die Vorlesung über den Römerbrief*) 1515–16. *WA* 56:268.26–277.3, esp. 269.21–22. *LW* 25:257–77, esp. 258.

84. Luther was guided in his gigantic effort of translating by the way in which common people speak in the marketplace, "to look at the way in which they use their mouth" (*aufs Maul sehen*). "On Translating" (*Von Dolmetschen*), 1530. *WA* 30/2:637.21. *LW* 35:189. Luther focused on the German spoken at the Saxon court as well as on the dialects prevalent along trade routes and rivers, such as the Meissen German spoken along the river Main. See Reu, *Luther's German Bible*, 138–41; Kooiman, *Luther and the Bible*, chaps. 7, 9. How creative Luther was as a translator has been shown by Bluhm, *Martin Luther*. Luther used the Hebrew texts of the Bible, edited by the Humanist John Reuchlin and his school; and he used the Greek New Testament, edited by Erasmus in 1516. In 1521, Wittenberg University hired a professor of Hebrew, Matthias Aurogallus. Melanchthon taught Greek.

CHAPTER 3

1. "A Sincere Admonition by Martin Luther to All Christians to Guard Against Insurrection and Rebellion," 1522. *WA* 8:676–87. *LW* 45:57–74.

2. *WA* 8:679.4–8; 682.12–683.33. *LW* 45:61, 66–68. Like many of his contemporaries, Luther expected the end of the world to come soon, if not during his lifetime. Violence and the appearance of the Antichrist were signs of the end. How dominant this view was in Luther's life and work has been shown by Asendorf, *Eschatologie bei Luther*, 214–21 (on Luther's "eschatological self-consciousness"); 280–93 (on the "last day").

3. *WA* 8:685.5–11. LW 45:70–71.

4. On the "Wittenberg Movement" of 1521/22 see the collection of sources in Nikolaus Müller, *Die Wittenberger Bewegung*, and Rupp, *Patterns of Reformation*, chap. 6.

5. Müntzer became one of Luther's most violent opponents. On Luther's judgment, see Gritsch, *Reformer Without A Church*, 153–54, and Mühlhaupt, *Luther über Müntzer.* On Carlstadt and Müntzer, see Rupp, *Patterns of Reformation*, pts. 2, 3.

6. Based on Bornkamm, *Luther in der Mitte seines Lebens*, 68.

7. The text of the "ordinances" is in Lietzmann, *Die Wittenberger und Leisniger Kastenordnung.* See also James Preus, *Carlstadt's Ordinances and Luther's Liberty.*

8. See, for example, Luther's letter to Melanchthon dated 13 January 1522. *WA.BR* 2:424–27. *LW* 48:364–70.

9. *WA.BR* 2:456.89–96, 111–12. *LW* 48:391–92.

10. Letter of 7 or 8 March 1522. *WA.BR* 2:459–62. Quotation, 461.71–72. *LW* 48:393–99. Quotation, 397.

11. "Eight Sermons at Wittenberg" (*Acht Sermone D.M. Luthers von ihm gepredigt zu Wittenberg in der Fasten*), 1522. *WA* 10/3:1.1–10; 2.1–3. *LW* 51:70.

12. *WA* 10/3:2–20. *LW* 51:70–78.

13. *WA* 10/3:45.10–16; 46.1. *LW* 51:90.

14. *WA* 10/3:57.15–17; 58.4–5. *LW* 51:96.

15. Letter to Melanchthon dated 13 June 1522. *WA.BR* 2:425.39–40. *LW* 48:367.

16. See Luther's letter dated 12 April 1522 to Spalatin. *WA.BR* 2:493.17–30. In the spring of 1543, he ridiculed Mark in a "Table Talk," no. 5568. *WA.TR* 5:249.1–9. *LW* 54:455.

17. Published in April 1522. *WA* 10/2:11–41. *LW* 36:233–67.

18. *WA* 10/2:29.3–36.27. *LW* 36:254–62.

19. *WA* 10/2:40.5–12. *LW* 36:265.

20. Luther preferred to preach on whole biblical books, like Genesis, 2 Peter, and Jude, because he was always concerned about the unity of Holy Scripture. For the number of sermons preached in 1522, see *WA* 10/3: XL; for 1523, *WA* 11:L.

21. For a list of Luther's treatments of Old Testament books, see Bornkamm, *Luther and the Old Testament*, appendix, 269–83. Luther's work on the New Testament has been analyzed by Ebeling, *Evangelische Evangelienauslegung;* see especially the tabulations, 455–63.

22. On details of Luther's life in Wittenberg between 1522 and 1525, see Bornkamm, *Luther in der Mitte seines Lebens*, chap. 10.

23. "The Estate of Marriage" (*Vom ehelichen Leben*), 1522. *WA* 10/2:276.26–29. *LW* 45:18. The German title of the first treatise is *Welche Personen verboten sind zu ehelichen*, 1522. *WA* 10/2:265–66.

24. *WA* 10/2:283.1–16. *LW* 45:25.

25. *WA* 10/2:287.14–289.17. *LW* 45:30–34.

26. *WA* 10/2:304.9–10. *LW* 45:49.

27. *Von weltlicher Obrigkeit, wie weit man ihr Gehorsam schuldig sei.* *WA* 11:245–80. *LW* 45:77–129. See also Gritsch, "Luther and Violence."

28. *WA* 11:249.36–250.1. *LW* 45:89.

29. *WA* 11:252.14. *LW* 45:92.

30. *WA* 11:259.8–10, 11–13; 260.17–20. *LW* 45:101, 103.

31. *WA* 11:267.22–24. *LW* 45:112.

32. "Ordinance of a Common Chest" (*Ordnung eines gemeinsamen Kastens*), 1523. *WA* 12:11–30. *LW* 45:169–94.

33. WA 12:15.29–31. LW 45:176.

34. *Dass eine christliche Versammlung oder Gemeinde Recht oder Macht habe, alle Lehre zu urteilen und Lehrer zu berufen, ein-und abzusetzen, Grund und Ursach aus der Heiligen Schrift.* WA 11:408–16. LW 39:305–14.

35. WA 11:412.16–18, 30–33. LW 39:310.

36. WA 12:169–95. LW 40:4–44.

37. WA 12:171.3–7. LW 40:9.

38. WA 12:183.12–15. LW 40:25.

39. WA 12:189.25–27. LW 40:34.

40. The Hussites split over the question of reform. See Bornkamm, *Luther in der Mitte seines Lebens,* 121.

41. "Concerning the Order of Public Worship" (*Von Ordnung des Gottesdiensts in der Gemeinde*), 1523. WA 12:37.29. LW 53:14.

42. "An Order of Mass and Communion for the Church at Wittenberg" (*Formula Missae et Communionis pro Ecclesia Wittenbergiensis*), 1523. WA 12:211.20–22; 214.14–215.5. LW 53:26, 30–32.

43. WA 35:422–25. LW 53:217–20.

44. *An die Ratsherrn aller Städte, dazu sie christliche Schulen aufrichten und halten sollen.* WA 15:27–53. LW 45:341–78.

45. WA 15:48.27–30. LW 45:372.

46. WA 15:49.12–14. LW 45:373.

47. On Luther's role in the ordination, see Brunner, *Nicholaus von Amsdorf,* chap. 2. On Luther's Wittenberg team, see Tillmanns, *The World and Men Around Luther,* part 2, chap. 2. How influential this team was has been shown by Wolgast, *Die Wittenberger Theologie.* On the friendship with Cranach, see Ihlenfeld, "Luther und Lucas Cranach."

48. Letter to Philip of Hesse dated 23 June 1529. WA.BR 5:102.53–57. LW 49:231. On Hutten, see LW 48:163 n. 1; on Sickingen, ibid., 244–45.

49. "Letter to the Princes of Saxony Concerning the Rebellious Spirit" (*Ein Brief an die Fürsten zu Sachsen von dem aufrührerischen Geist*), 1524. WA 15:210–22. LW 40:47–59.

50. WA 15:218.17–21; 219.5–7. LW 40:57.

51. The encounter has been recorded by an anonymous eyewitness. See Sider, "Confrontation at the Black Bear," in *Karlstadt's Battle With Luther,* 36–48.

52. See "The Encounter of Dr. Martin Luther With the Council and Parish of the Town of Orlamünde" (*Die Handlung Dr. Martin Luthers mit dem Rat und der Gemeinde der Stadt Orlamünde*). WA 15:341–45. The encounter has been analyzed by Haendler, *Luther on Ministerial Office,* chap. 6.

53. "Letter to the Christians in Strassburg in Opposition to the Fanatic Spirit" (*Ein Brief an die Christen zu Strassburg wider den Schwärmergeist*), 1524. WA 15:391–97. LW 40:63–71.

54. WA 15:393.18–23. LW 40:67.

55. "Against the Heavenly Prophets in the Matter of Images and Sacraments" (*Wider die himmlischen Propheten*), 1525. WA 18:62–125, 134–214. LW 40:75–223.

56. WA 18:136.9–16, 24–25. LW 40:146. Emphasis mine.

57. See Sider, *Karlstadt's Battle with Luther,* 78 n. 11. Luther's reaction is in WA 18:149.26–165. 28. LW 40:159–76.

58. *WA* 18:191.27–29. *LW* 40:201.

59. *WA* 18:213.19–20, 29–30; 214.4–5. *LW* 40:222–23.

60. Carlstadt had tried to challenge Luther in "A Review of Some of the Chief Articles of Christian Doctrine in Which Dr. Luther Brings Andreas Carlstadt Under Suspicion Through False Accusation and Calumny," 1525. See Sider, *Karlstadt's Battle With Luther*, 126–38.

61. "Highly Necessary Defense and Answer to the Spiritless, Soft-Living Flesh of Wittenberg" (*Hoch verursachte Schutzrede wider das gottlose, sanftlebende Fleisch von Wittenberg*). Franz, *Thomas Müntzer*, no. 9. English text in Hillerbrand, "Thomas Müntzer's Last Tract Against Luther."

62. "Admonition to Peace: A Reply to the Twelve Articles of the Peasants" (*Ermahnung zum Frieden auf die zwölf Artikel der Bauernschaft in Schwaben*), 1525. *WA* 18:333.9–12; 334.3–5. *LW* 46:43. Text of the articles in Franz, *Quellen zur Geschichte des Bauernkrieges*, no. 43, 174–79. *LW* 46:8–16.

63. *Wider die räuberischen und mörderischen Rotten der Bauern*. *WA* 18:357–61. *LW* 46:47–55.

64. *WA* 18:357.21–358.32. *LW* 46:49–50. Quotation, *WA* 18:360.28–31. *LW* 46:53–54.

65. "An Open Letter on the Harsh Book Against the Peasants" (*Ein Sendbrief von dem harten Büchlein wider die Bauern*), 1525. *WA* 18:384–401. *LW* 46:63–85. On the "battle" of Mühlhausen, see Franz, *Der deutsche Bauernkrieg*, 268–70. Details in Bornkamm, *Luther in der Mitte seines Lebens*, chap. 14.

66. *WA* 18:398.34–399.2. *LW* 46:81–82.

67. *WA* 18:401.12–15, 17–18. *LW* 46:84–85.

68. "The Beautiful Confitemini" (*Das schöne Confitemini*), 1529. *WA* 31/1:83.7–12, 16–17. *LW* 14:54.

69. See below, chap. 8 no. 57, 253.

70. Letter to Michael Stiefel dated 11 August 1526. *WA.BR* 4:109.9–11. *LW* 49:154. On Luther's marriage, see Bornkamm, *Luther in der Mitte seines Lebens*, 360–62. On its influence on Protestantism, see Loewenich, "Luthers Heirat."

71. See Kooiman, "Luther at Home," 70–71.

72. Luther did not receive royalties for his publications. His annual salary in 1536 was ca. $4,000 (dollar value of 1950). See Schwiebert, *Luther and His Times*, 262.

73. *De servo arbitrio*, 1525. *WA* 18:600–787. *LW* 33:5–295. Erasmus, "Diatribe or Discourse Concerning Free Choice" (*De libero arbitrio diatribe sive collatio*). Rupp and Watson, *Luther and Erasmus*. For a detailed comparison, see Kohls, *Luther oder Erasmus*.

74. *WA* 18:635.17–22. *LW* 33:65–66.

75. *WA* 18:685.3–6, 14–16. *LW* 33:139.

76. *WA* 18:685.27–31. *LW* 33:140.

77. Latin title of Erasmus's defense: *Hyperaspistes diatribe*, 1526–1527. Luther viewed Erasmus as a defender of Rome after this time. See *LW* 33:11–13.

78. See the sketch of the Hoen-Zwingli interpretation, and the controversy with Luther, in *LW* 37:xii–xv.

79. *Sermon von dem Sakrament des Leibes and Blutes Christi, wider die Schwarmgeister*. *WA* 19:482–523. *LW* 36:331–61.

80. *Dass diese Worte, "Das ist mein Leib" noch fest stehen wider die Schwarmgeister.* WA 23:64–283. *LW* 37:5–150.

81. *Vom Abendmahl Christi, Bekenntnis.* WA 26:261–509. *LW* 37:153–372. See also the list of various writings attacking Luther, *LW* 37:8–11.

82. Augustine used the phrase "visible word" (*verbum visibile*). See his commentary on John 3 in Tract 80. Migne, *Patrologia, Series Latina,* 35, 1840.3. See also *BC,* 212.

83. WA 26:326.12–17. *LW* 37:214.

84. WA 26:341.21–24. *LW* 37:230.

85. Luther concluded his "Confession" with a list of principal articles of faith. WA 26:500.10–509.19. *LW* 37:360–72.

86. The date of the hymn has been debated. It was first found in an Erfurt hymnal in 1531, but was reported to have been in a Wittenberg hymnal of 1529. I agree with the *LW* editor's dating. See *LW* 53:283. Text ibid., 284–85.

87. On the Reformation in Prussia, see Bornkamm, *Luther in der Mitte seines Lebens,* chap. 12. Luther knew Grandmaster Albrecht of the Teutonic Order and urged the members to forgo celibacy. See "An Exhortation to the Knights of the Teutonic Order That They May Lay Aside False Chastity and Assume the True Chastity of Wedlock" (*An die Herren deutsch Ordens, dass sie falsche Keuschheit vermeiden und zur rechten ehelichen Keuschheit greifen*), 1523. WA 12:232–44. *LW* 45:133–58. The Danish King Frederick I tolerated Lutherans from 1527 on. His successor Christian III made Lutheranism the religion of the land in 1536.

88. Quoted in Bornkamm, *Luther in der Mitte seines Lebens,* 544. Based on the research of Friedensburg, "Die Reformation und der Reichstag zu Speyer 1526."

89. Preface to "Instructions for the Visitors of Parish Pastors in Electoral Saxony" (*Unterricht der Visitatoren an die Pfarrherrn im Kurfürstentum zu Sachsen*), 1528. WA 26:200.28–33. *LW* 40:273. Arius taught that Christ is not "of one being" with the Father, as the Nicene Creed later affirmed.

90. WA 26:201–40. *LW* 40:273–320.

91. Small Catechism, pts. 7–8. *BS* 521–23. *BC* 352–54. Extensive introduction and original texts in WA 30/1, 426–665. See also Gritsch, "Luther's Catechisms of 1529."

92. Large Catechism, preface, secs. 19–20. *BS* 552–53. *BC* 361.

93. *Ob Kriegsleute auch im seligen Stande sein können.* WA 19:623–62. *LW* 46:89–137.

94. WA 19:645.9. *LW* 46:118.

95. WA 19:647.28–31. *LW* 46:121.

96. WA 19:656.32–657.2. *LW* 46:130–31.

97. *Vom Kriege wider die Türken.* WA 30/2:107–48. *LW* 46:157–205. See also Forell, "Luther and the War Against the Turks."

98. WA 30/2:111.16–17. *LW* 46:165.

99. WA 30/2:117.21–22. *LW* 46:171.

100. WA 30/2:147.18–21; 148.1, 5–6, 9–11. *LW* 46:203; 204.

101. Text in *DRTA.JR* 7:1260–65. Partial English text in Kidd, *Documents Illustrative of the Reformation,* no. 107, 243–45.

102. WA.BR 5:102.37–43. *LW* 49:231.

103. Account in *LW* 38:8–14. *WA* 30/3:160–71. *LW* 38:15–89. Text edition and commentary by May, *Das Marburger Religionsgespräch 1529*. Text of the "Schwabach Articles" in *CR* 26:151–59. English in Reu, *The Augsburg Confession*, 40–44.

104. *WA* 30/3:170.6–14. *LW* 38:88–89.

105. "Table Talk," 28 June 1532, no. 291. *WA.TR* 1:121.22–23. *LW* 54:41.

106. Letter of 15 May 1530. *WA.BR* 5:319.6–9. *LW* 49:297–98. Luther was at Coburg from 23 April until 4 October. See Rupp, "Luther at the Castle Coburg."

107. *Vermahnung an die Geistlichen, versammelt auf dem Reichstag zu Augsburg, 1530*. *WA* 30/2:268–356. *LW* 34:5–61. Other writings: "On Translating" (*Sendbrief vom Dolmetschen*). *WA* 30/2:632–46. *LW* 35:177–202. "The Keys" (*Von den Schlüsseln*). *WA* 30/2:465–507. *LW* 40:323–77. "A Sermon on Keeping Children in School." *WA* 30/2:517–88. *LW* 46:209–58. "The Beautiful Confitemini" (Psalm 118). *WA* 3/1:65–182. *LW* 14:43–106.

108. *WA* 30/2:345.10–351.21. *LW* 34:53–58.

109. *WA* 30/2:355.7–9, 13–15. *LW* 34:60–61.

110. The diet adopted a "Confutation" of the Augsburg Confession written by a committee of Roman theologians. Text *CR* 27:6–244. English in Reu, *The Augsburg Confession*, 348–83.

111. "Table Talk," 1530s, no. 4780. *WA.TR* 4:495.7–9.

112. For the negotiations between Luther and the Saxon jurists on the question of armed resistance to the emperor, see *LW* 47:6–10, and Lohse, *Martin Luther*, 71–72. The Smalcald League united a number of territories and cities. See Fabian, *Die Entstehung des schmalkaldischen Bundes*.

113. "Dr. Martin Luther's Warning to His Dear German People" (*Warnung an seine lieben Deutschen*), 1530. *WA* 30/3:282.33–283.1. *LW* 47:19.

114. "Commentary on the Alleged Edict of Augsburg" (*Glosse auf das vermeinte kaiserliche Edikt*), 1531. *WA* 30/3:387.3–10. *LW* 34:103–4. The philological origins of the saying have been investigated by Hauffen, "Husz eine Gans," 21–22.

115. Text in Walch, *D. Martin Luthers sämtliche Schriften*, 16, no. 1202. See also Fischer-Galati, "Ottoman Imperialism and the Religious Peace of Nürnberg."

CHAPTER 4

1. Bainton, "The Left Wing of the Reformation," coined the term. Williams differentiated between "radical" and "magisterial" Reformation, the latter indicating an alliance between church reformers and their government. *Radical Reformation*, xxiv.

2. Detailed account ibid., chap. 6. Emperor Charles V enforced the Justinian Code against the Swiss Brethren in a mandate of 23 April 1529. Ibid., 238–39.

3. "Concerning Rebaptism" (*Von der Wiedertaufe*), 1528. *WA* 26:160.39–40. *LW* 40:247.

4. "Infiltrating and Clandestine Preachers," 1532. *WA* 30/3:519.37–520.4. *LW* 40:385.

5. Early Anabaptist teachings were summarized in the Schleitheim Confession of 1527. Text in Wenger, "The Schleitheim Confession of Faith." On Luther's polemics against the Anabaptists, see Oyer, *Lutheran Reformers Against Anabaptists*, chap. 4.

6. For almost a year they established a theocratic rule. Detailed account in Williams, *Radical Reformation,* chap. 13.

7. As early as 1531 Luther sided with Melanchthon who had supported the death penalty. See the opinion of the Wittenberg theologians, "Whether One Should Punish Anabaptists With the Sword" (*Bedenken der Theologen zu Wittenberg: ob man Wiedertäufer mit dem Schwert strafen muss*), 1531. *CR* 4:737–40. In another "opinion" in 1536, Luther agreed to the death penalty "according to the situation of cases" (*nach Gelegenheit der Fälle*). "Whether Christian Princes are Obliged to Resist the Anabaptist Sect With Bodily Punishment and the Sword" (*ob christiliche Fürsten schuldig sind, der Wiedertäufer unchristliche Sect mit leiblicher Strafe und mit dem Schwert zu wehren*), 1536. *WA* 50:15 (appended last sentence). In a "Table Talk" between 2 and 17 September 1540, Luther called for the execution of seditious Anabaptists and banishment of those who hold heretical views. No. 5232b. *WA.TR* 5:20.12–15.

8. *CR* 2:987. The meeting has been described in detail by Haile, *Luther,* chap. 1.

9. The Wittenberg Concord (*Wittenberger Konkordie*), 1536. *BS* 977.14—978.16. *BC* 571.13—572.16. For the origins and text of the document, see Bizer, *Zur Geschichte des Abendmahlsstreits,* chap. 1.

10. "Brief Confession Concerning the Holy Sacrament" (*Kurzes Bekenntnis D. Martin Luthers vom heiligen Sakrament*), 1544. *WA* 54:141.6. *LW* 38:287.

11. See *LW* 38:237, and Drews, *Die Disputationen Dr. Martin Luthers.*

12. "The Theses for the Doctoral Examination of Hieronymus Weller and Nikolaus Medler, 11 September 1535" (*Die Doktorpromotion von Hieronymus Weller und Nikolaus Medler. 11. und 14. September 1535*), thesis 24. *WA* 39/1:46.7–8. *LW* 34:111.

13. Ibid., thesis 21. *WA* 39/1:46.1–2. *LW* 34:110.

14. Ibid., theses 75–79. *WA* 39/1:52.20–30. *LW* 34:119. Quotation, thesis 79. *WA* 39/1:52.29–30. *LW* 34:119.

15. The theses were not found before 1546. Luther composed them for a disputation on 14 January 1536. They could have been part of the first disputation on justification. See the detailed commentary of Ebeling, *Disputatio de homine,* 6–8.

16. "Theses," thesis 35. *WA* 39/1:177.3–4. *LW* 34:139.

17. Ibid., theses 37–39. *WA* 39/1:177.7–12. *LW* 34:140.

18. Ibid., defense of thesis 22. *WA* 39/1:179.4–5. *LW* 34:142.

19. Ibid., thesis 23. *WA* 39/1:176.12–13. *LW* 34:138. On the praise of reason as the organizing power in the world, see theses 1–8. *WA* 39/1:175.3–19. *LW* 34:137.

20. The occasion was the licentiate examination of Jacob Schenk and Philip Motz, two preachers at the courts of princes who supported the Smalcald League, on Rom. 3:28. *WA* 39/1:82–126. *LW* 34:147–96.

21. *WA* 39/1:87.3–5. *LW* 34:157.

22. "Theses," thesis 5. *WA* 39/1:82.13–14. *LW* 34:151.

23. *WA* 39/1:92.4–12. *LW* 34:161.

24. *WA* 39/1:93.2–5, 6–8, 10–12. *LW* 34:162.

25. See the fragmentary outline of a treatise "On Justification" (*De iustificatione*), 1530. *WA* 30/2:657–76.

26. *WA.BR* 7:613.11–30.

27. *BS* 409.3. *BC* 289.3. Luther anticipated that the Smalcald Articles would be presented at the forthcoming general council. He therefore called them "Articles of Christian Doctrine which were to have been presented by our party at the Council of Mantua, or wherever else the council was to have been convened, and which were to indicate what we could or could not accept or yield." German and Latin texts in *BS* 407–68. *BC* 287–318.

28. "Smalcald Articles," pt. 2, I.5. *BS* 415–16. *BC* 292.

29. The designation "article on which the church stands and falls" (*articulus stantis et cadentis ecclesiae*) seems to have been first employed by the Lutheran theologian and bishop Valentin E. Löscher (1673–1749), a defender of Lutheran orthodoxy in its struggle against Pietists. See Loofs, "Articulus stantis," 345. Luther used a similar phrase in his exposition of Ps. 130:4, in 1532/33: "If this article stands, the church stands; if it falls, the church falls" (*quia isto articulo stante stat Ecclesia, ruente ruit Ecclesia*). *WA* 40/3:352.3.

30. Smalcald Articles, pt. 2, II.1. *BS* 416. *BC* 293.

31. Ibid., pt. 3. *BS* 433–62. *BC* 302–16.

32. Ibid., XV.4. *BS* 462. *BC* 316.

33. Luther stayed in Smalcald 7–26 February 1537. See Buchwald-Kawerau, *Luther-Kalendarium*, 111–12.

34. "*Von der Gewalt und Obrigkeit des Papsts*" (*De potestate et primatu Papae*), 1537. *BS* 471–98. *BC* 320–35.

35. *Von den Konzilien und Kirchen*, 1539. *WA* 50:509–653. *LW* 41:5–178.

36. *WA* 50:615.28–30; 616.2–4, 6–7. *LW* 41:133.

37. Augsburg Confession, conclusion of pt. 2. *BS* 134.5. *BC* 95.5.

38. "The Freedom of the Christian," 1520. *WA* 7:62.10–12. *LW* 31:361.

39. *Wider die Antinomer*, 1539. *WA* 50:470.1–6. *LW* 47:108–9. This was the last of four attacks on the Antinomians. The other three, from the years 1537–38, are in *WA* 39/1:360–584. Useful sketch of the controversy in Mackinnon, *Luther and the Reformation* 4:161–79.

40. *WA* 50:473.6–10, 15–19. *LW* 47:113.

41. *Wider den Eisleben*, 1540. *WA* 51:425–44.

42. For its further history, see the debates in the "Formula of Concord (Solid Declaration)," 1577, articles IV–VI on "good works" and on the distinction between law and gospel. *BS* 936–69. *BC* 551–68.

43. No. 4465. *WA.TR* 4:325.22–24. *LW* 54:343.

44. The meetings were held in Hagenau, June 1540; Worms, November 1540–January 1541; and Regensburg, April–May 1541. See Mackinnon, *Luther and the Reformation* 4:110–19. How conciliatory these negotiations were has been shown by Pfnür, *Die Einigung bei den Religionsgesprächen*. On Luther's reactions, especially to the most significant compromise in Regensburg, see von Loewenich, *Duplex Iustitia*, 23–55.

45. Letter of 3 September 1331. *WA.BR* 6:179.26–29. *LW* 50:33. Luther's negotiations about King Henry VIII's divorce have been analyzed by Heinrich Boehmer, *Luther and the Reformation*, 213–23.

46. Letter of June 1540 to Elector John Frederick. Quoted from and translated by Faulkner, "Luther and the Bigamous Marriage," 229. See also ibid. on the first printing of the letter in 1872.

47. Philip of Hesse died in 1567. The Protestant alliance was saved from complete destruction by the clever politics of Philip of Hesse's son-in-law, Maurice of Saxony. See the sketch of events in Elton, *Reformation Europe*, chap. 9.

48. *Wider Hans Wurst*, 1541. WA 51:469–572. LW 41:181–256.

49. WA 51:562.4–11. LW 41:250.

50. Summer or fall 1542, no. 5488. WA.TR 5:184.4–7, 10–12. LW 54:427–28.

51. "Luther's Will" (*Confessio et testamentum venerandi patris nostri* D. Lutheri), 1542. WA.BR 9:573.60–62. LW 34:297.

52. "Table Talk," September 1542, no. 5499. WA.TR 5:193.22–23. LW 54:433.

53. WA.BR 10:335.12–13. LW 50:242. The friend was Wenceslas Link, pastor in Nuremberg. Luther had known him since 1508; he was a fellow Augustinian. Before moving to Nuremberg, Link had been a member of the Wittenberg theological faculty (1511–16).

54. *Von den Juden und ihren Lügen*, 1543. WA 53:417–552. LW 47:123–306.

55. WA 53:523.1–526.16. LW 47:268–72.

56. WA 53:541.30–33; 542.5–7. LW 47:292.

57. No. 5537. WA.TR 5:222.14–15, 17–20. LW 54:448.

58. WA 54:141–67. LW 38:281–319. On Schwenckfeld's teaching, see Maier, *Caspar Schwenckfeld*, parts 2, 3.

59. WA 54:141.17–18, 19–20. LW 38:287–88.

60. *Wider das Papsttum zu Rom, vom Teufel gestiftet*, 1545. WA 54:206–99. LW 41:259–376.

61. WA 54:299.5–8. LW 41:376.

62. See Luther's prefaces to the German Wittenberg edition of his writings, and to the Latin writings, 1529 and 1545. WA 50:657–61. WA 54:179–87. LW 34:281–88, 325–38.

63. WA.BR 11:149.9–12; 150.1. LW 50:278–79. Luther was angered by a particular dance in the course of which women's skirts were lifted too high. Moreover, a woman named Rosina had become a maid in the Luther household by pretending that she needed help. She lied, stole, and became pregnant without benefit of a husband, and Luther was also incensed about this. The incident occurred in 1541. See LW 50:279 n. 48.

64. Letter of 5 August 1545. WA.BR 11:161–65.

65. "Lectures on Genesis," 1535–45. WA 42–44. LW 1–8. On the history and printing of the series, see Meinhold, *Die Genesisvorlesung Luthers*.

66. *Eine wälsche Lügenschrift von Doctoris Martini Luthers Tod*, 1545. WA 54:188–94. LW 34:363–66.

67. WA 54:191.8–9. LW 34:365.

68. WA 54:194.2–8. LW 34:366.

69. Two of the friends are named as authors of *Concerning the Christian Departure From this Mortal Life of the Reverend Dr. Martin Luther* (*Vom christlichen Abschied aus diesem tödlichen Leben des ehrwürdigen Herrn Dr. Martini Lutheri*), 1546: Justus Jonas, the Erfurt lawyer who had joined the Wittenberg theological faculty and had become bishop of Halle in 1541; and Michael Coelius, court preacher to Count Albrecht of Mansfeld.

70. WA.BR 11:300.17–19. LW 50:312. On the details of the settlement of the feud, see Kunst, *Evangelischer Glaube*, chap. 1.

71. The text was Matt. 11:25–30, with the famous saying of Jesus, "Come to me, all who labor and are heavy laden, and I will give you rest." The sermon was recorded by an anonymous eyewitness. *WA* 51:187–94. *LW* 51:383–92.

72. Until the seventeenth century, "unicorn" was used as a drug prescribed against plagues, poisons, fever, and pain. See Ebon, *Last Days of Martin Luther*, 29–30.

73. No. 5677. *WA.TR* 5:317.12–318.3. *LW* 54:476. Italics mine.

74. Details in Schwiebert, *Luther and His Times*, 751–52.

75. On the collections and reproductions of Luther pictures, see ibid., 571–76. The etchings of Lucas Cranach, as well as those of others, do not convey the real likeness of Luther. Perhaps closest is the drawing of Luther's face shortly after his death by the painter Furtenagel from Halle.

76. Boehmer, *Road to Reformation*, 282–83.

77. Bornkamm in Boehmer, *Der junge Luther*, 366–67.

78. Luther made special efforts to appear well-dressed for his visit with the papal emissary Vergerio in Wittenberg in November 1535. See Haile, *Luther*, chap. 1.

79. On the origins and history of the Luther rose, see Freund, "Zur Geschichte der Lutherrose."

80. For a complete listing of Luther's descendants until 1759, see Johannes Luther, "Die Nachkommenschaft Martin Luthers." On the descendants of Jacob Luther, numbering about 1,900 in 1960, see Clasen, *Luther-Nachkommenbuch*.

CHAPTER 5

1. "The Babylonian Captivity of the Church," 1520. *WA* 6:560.31–561.4. *LW* 36:107.

2. *WA* 6:406.21–29. *LW* 44:126. On the history of the shift from the authority of canon and creed to the authority of the episcopal office, see *LWC*, 72–74.

3. "Luther at the Diet of Worms," 1521. *WA* 7:838.7. *LW* 32:112. On Luther's understanding of the Word of God, see Bornkamm, "Das Wort Gottes bei Luther" and Watson, *Let God be God,* chap. 5. On the relationship between Word of God and Bible, see Pelikan, *LWC*, chap. 3.

4. How this view of conscience differs from medieval and modern anthropology has been shown by Lohse, "Conscience and Authority." The differences between late scholasticism and the young Luther are discussed by Baylor, *Action and Person*. For a summary, see Forell, "Luther and Conscience."

5. "How Christians Should Regard Moses" (*Eine Unterrichtung wie sich Christen in Mose sollen schicken*), 1525. *WA* 16:366.18–367.14. *LW* 35:162. For an incisive sketch of Luther's understanding of law and gospel, see Ebeling, *Luther*, chap. 7.

6. "Lectures on Galatians" (3:23), 1531. *WA* 40/1:520.17–24. *LW* 26:337. On Luther's twofold use of the law (political and theological), see Ebeling, *Luther*, chap. 8.

7. Smalcald Articles, 1537, pt. 3, IV. 45. *BS* 449.10. *BC* 310.

8. "A Brief Instruction on What to Look for and Expect in the Gospels" (*Ein klein Unterricht, was man in den Evangeliis suchen und gewarten soll*), 1521. *WA* 10¹/1:17.7–12. *LW* 35:123.

9. See, for example, "Lectures on the Minor Prophets" (*Praelectiones in prophetas minores*), Hab. 2:4 ("The righteous shall live by faith"), 1525. WA 13:433.25–434.26. *LW* 19:123–24.

10. "Table Talk," 14 December 1531–22 January 1532, no. 146. WA.TR 1:69.18–19. *LW* 54:20.

11. "Lectures on Galatians," 1535 (Summary of Paul's "Argument"). WA 40/1:41.27–29. *LW* 26:5.

12. WA 40/1:42.18–20. *LW* 26:5.

13. WA 40/1:43.18–20. *LW* 26:6.

14. WA 40/1:48.21–25. *LW* 26:9.

15. WA 40/1:48.28–29. *LW* 26:9.

16. WA 40/1:50.30–31, 33; 51.17–20. *LW* 26:11.

17. "Lectures on Genesis" (1:3), 1535. WA 42:13.32–33. *LW* 1:16.

18. "Sermons on the Gospel of St. John" (1:1), 1537. WA 46:545.10–11. *LW* 22:10.

19. WA 47:66.18–24. *LW* 22:339. This is the thrust of Luther's interpretation of Exodus 33—34. See "On the Last Words of David" (*Von den letzten Worten Davids*), 1543. WA 54:78.11–19. See also Bornkamm, *Luther and the Old Testament*, 103. On Moses as a Christian, ibid., 149–64.

20. "Defense and Explanation of All the Articles Which Were Unjustly Condemned by the Roman Bull," 1521. WA 7:315.24. *LW* 32:11. On Christ as Word of God, see Watson, *Let God Be God*, 149–52. How Luther used the Old Testament interpretation of Augustine and the Middle Ages in his first lectures on Psalms (1513–15) has been shown by James Preus, *From Shadow to Promise*, pt. 2.

21. "Preface to the Epistle of St. Paul to the Romans," 1546. WA.DB 7:3.3–4. *LW* 35:365.

22. WA.DB 7:27.15–25. *LW* 35:380.

23. WA.DB 6:10.16–18. *LW* 35:362.

24. "Preface to the Epistles of St. James and St. Jude," 1546 (1522). WA.DB 7:385.25–27, 29–32. *LW* 35:396.

25. "Sermon on the First Sunday in Advent," 1522 (on Matt. 21:1–9). "Advent Postil" (*Adventspostille*). WA 10½:48.5.

26. Pelikan in *LWC*, 64. For an illuminating analysis of Luther's significance to a Christian philosophy of language, see Meinhold, *Luthers Sprachphilosophie*.

27. Details in *LW* 51:xvi–xxi. On Luther's preaching, teaching, and rhetoric, see Nembach, *Predigt des Evangeliums*.

28. A simile borrowed from St. Bernard. "On the Councils and the Church," 1539. WA 50:520.9–10. *LW* 41:20.

29. WA 42:334.30–32. *LW* 2:102.

30. "The Bondage of the Will," 1525. WA 18:712.33–35. *LW* 33:181.

31. "Preface to Galeatius Capella's History" (*Vorrede zu Historia Galeatii Capellae*), 1538. WA 50:384.2–5, 15–17. *LW* 34:275–76. Luther introduced the translation into German by Wenceslas Link, the Nuremberg reformer, of Capella's (1487–1537) account of the conflict between Emperor Charles V and King Francis I of France.

32. WA 43:672.13–24. *LW* 5:353. How "secular" history and the "history of the people of God" in Genesis compare has been demonstrated by Pelikan. *LWC*, chap. 5.

33. This scheme had been suggested by the German bishop Otto von Freising, one of Augustine's disciples, in a "Chronicle or History of the Two Cities" (*Chronicon seu historia de duabus civitatibus*), 1143–46. His own time was the "sixth day," after which the world would end.

34. The motto at the beginning of the Reckoning, 1541. WA 53:22. The Reckoning was for the most part a biblical chronology, based on various sources, particularly the work of the mathematician John Clarion, who in 1532 had written a chronology of world history with the help of Melanchthon. Detailed evidence in WA 53:10–15. On Luther's division of church history, see Headly, *Luther's View of Church History,* chap. 3. The "seven days" scheme counted one day as equaling a thousand years, in accordance with Ps. 90:4, "For a thousand years in thy sight are but as yesterday . . . ." That is why the scheme has been called "millennial" (from the Latin *millennium,* "thousand"). Luther also summarized his chronological scheme in a "Table Talk" between 3 and 19 October 1540, no. 5300. WA.TR 5:50.27–51.4. LW 54:407. He saw in the reign of Gregory VII (1073–85) the beginnings of a dangerous political papacy, because Gregory had enforced ecclesiastical legislation requiring clerical celibacy and confronted Emperor Henry IV with papal power.

35. "Reckoning," 1541. WA 53:22.

36. "Against the Roman Papacy," 1545. WA 54:276.13–14. LW 41:348. See also "Reckoning," 1541. WA 53:127.

37. "Commentary on Psalm 101:1," 1534. WA 51:208.24–25, 28–30, 35–40.

38. "The Magnificat," 1521. WA 7:590.9–18. LW 21:344.

39. "Defense and Explanation of All the Articles," 1521. WA 7:430.10–11. LW 32:81.

40. "Sermon on Luke 19:1–10," 1527. WA 17/2:501.35–36. Thesis 12 of "The Doctoral Disputation of Johannes Macchabaeus Scotus" (*Die Promotionsdisputation von Johannes Macchabaeus Scotus*), 3 February 1542. WA 39/2:161.8–9. On the problem of the relationship between "visible" and "invisible" church in Luther, see Kattenbusch, *Die Doppelschichtigkeit;* Rupp, *The Righteousness of God,* chap. 15; and Bornkamm, "What is the Church?"

41. "Lectures on Genesis (3:15)," 1536. WA 42:144.35; 145.5–8. LW 1:193,194. See also "The Magnificat," 1521. WA 7:598.23–29. LW 21:352.

42. See Headly, *Luther's View of Church History,* 78. Useful sketch of Luther's "reformulation" of the concept of "tradition," ibid. 69–94.

43. "Answer to the Hyperchristian, Hyperspiritual, and Hyperlearned Book by Goat Emser," 1521. WA 7:640.32–35. LW 39:166.

44. "Lectures on Galatians," 1535. WA 40/1:589.25–28. LW 26:387.

45. Tillich, *The Protestant Era,* 163. Pelikan, *Obedient Rebels,* 13, used the term "Protestant principle" to describe Luther's Reformation.

46. Ibid., 13.

47. "Defense and Explanation of All the Articles Which Were Rejected by the Roman Bull," 1521. WA 7:317.1–9. LW 32:11–12. Italics mine. On the causes and contents of the classic debate concerning Luther's *sola scriptura* as it relates to tradition, see Pelikan, *LWC,* 83–134. Luther can be criticized for denigrating tradition (see Tavard, *Holy Writ and Holy Church,* chap. 6) or for being an optimistic Humanist who assumed that the knowledge of original sources authenticates them

(see Pesch, *Hinführung zu Luther,* 67). That Luther used the current humanistic scientific method has been argued by Junghans, "Luther als Bibelhumanist," esp. 9.

48. "Against Latomus," 1521. *WA* 8:64.10–22. *LW* 32:168. Italics mine. It is difficult to sort out all the implications of the controversy over biblical interpretations for Luther's relationship to scholasticism and Humanism. See the team research of the International Congress for Luther Research in Grane, "Luther und Latomus."

49. The principle that Scripture interprets itself is stated simultaneously with the rejection of papal power in "Defense of All the Articles of Martin Luther Condemned by the Latest Bull of Leo X" (*Assertio omnium articulorum Dr. Lutheri per bullam Leonis X novissimum damnatorum*), 1520. *WA* 7:97.20–24; 98.40–99.2. See also Holl, "Luthers Bedeutung," 559–60; and Mostert, *Scriptura sacra,* 66–69.

50. "Concerning Rebaptism," 1528. *WA* 26:168.27–33, 35–37, 40; 169.1–2. *LW* 40:256–57.

51. "Confession Concerning Christ's Supper," 1528. *WA* 26:338.2–9. *LW* 37:225. On the various "modes" of presence, see *WA* 26:327.2–338.8. *LW* 37:215–25.

52. "Brief Confession Concerning the Holy Sacrament," 1544. *WA* 54: 145.16–18. *LW* 38:292. See also the case study on Luther's interpretation of "This is my body" (Matt. 26:26) by Pelikan, *LWC,* chap. 7; and the succinct summary of Luther's view by Jenson, "Of Another Spirit."

53. "Against King Henry [VIII] of England" (*Contra Henricum Regem Angliae*), 1522. *WA* 10/2:192.1–21. This is Luther's response to Henry VIII's "Defense of Seven Sacraments" (*Assertio septem sacramentorum*).

54. "The Three Symbols or Creeds of the Christian Faith," 1538. *WA* 50:266.35–37, 39–267.1. *LW* 34:207. Luther always viewed the dogma of the Trinity from the perspective of salvation, that is, soteriologically. See Jansen, *Studien zu Luthers Trinitätslehre.*

55. Large Catechism, pt. 2.31 (the Creed), 1529. *BS* 652. *BC* 414. How Luther's stress on the soteriological aspect of the doctrine of the Trinity affects his Christology has been shown by Lienhard, *Luther: Witness to Jesus Christ;* and by Siggins, *Martin Luther's Doctrine of Christ.* This emphasis on the "God of the Gospel" underlies Luther's trinitarian logic. See Jenson, *The Triune Identity,* 27–28.

56. "The Leipzig Debate," 1519. *WA* 2:161.35–38. *LW* 31:318.

57. *Quod ubique, quod semper, quod ab omnibus creditum est.* "The Commonitory" (*Commonitorium*), 434 A.D. 2. Migne, *Patrologia Latina,* 50, 640. McCracken, *Early Medieval Theology,* 38.

58. "Preface to the Epistle of St. Paul to the Romans," 1546. *WA.DB* 7:6.15–23. *LW* 35:368–69. How Luther dealt with the tension between Scripture as inspired Word of God and as human book is analyzed by Kooiman, *Luther and the Bible,* chap. 19. On Luther's "canon" within Scripture, see Lönning, "Kanon im Kanon," 72–160.

59. "To the Councilmen of All Cities in Germany," 1524. *WA* 15:39.10. *LW* 45:361.

60. Some Luther interpreters speak of his "biblical inerrancy." See, for example, Wood, *Captive to the Word,* 145. But this interpretation does not take into account Luther's insistence on the significance of the Word of God as "*viva vox.*" See Kooiman, *Luther and the Bible,* chap. 17, and Østergaard-Nielson, *Scriptura sacra et viva vox.*

61. Sermon of 21 July 1532. *WA* 36:220.27–29. Quoted in *LWC,* 64 n. 66.

62. "To the Christian Nobility of the German Nation," 1520. WA 6:461.8–9. LW 44:205.

63. See Benrath, "Antichrist." TRE 3:26.

64. Wood, Captive to the Word, 148.

65. "How Christians Should Regard Moses," 1525. WA 16:385.7–16. LW 35, 170.

66. See Grane, "Luther und Luthertum," 43.

67. WA 50:660.10–14. LW 34:287.

68. WA 50:660.35–37; 661.1–6. LW 34:288.

CHAPTER 6

1. Holl, Cultural Significance of the Reformation, 53.

2. Troeltsch, Social Teachings, 552.

3. In a letter addressed in 1939 to a French pastor. Eine Schweizer Stimme, 113.

4. Berggrav, Man and State, 300–19.

5. Bonhoeffer, No Rusty Swords, 324.

6. Niebuhr, Nature and Destiny of Man, 2,194–95.

7. Shirer, Rise and Fall of the Third Reich, 236.

8. See the useful collection of Luther texts in Hertz, Two Kingdoms and One World, especially "Luther's Reception and Modification of the Medieval Teachings Concerning the Power and Estates," 53–66. Based on Duchrow and Hoffmann, Die Vorstellung von Zwei Reichen. Good summaries of Luther's views are presented by Althaus, Ethics of Martin Luther, chaps. 4, 8, 9; and Bornkamm, Luther's Doctrine of the Two Kingdoms. See also the illustrative collection of interpretations in Günther Wolf, Luther und die Obrigkeit, and the bibliography in Sauter, Zur Zwei-Reiche-Lehre Luthers, chap. 6.

9. "Lectures on Romans," 1515–16. WA 56:478.26–32. LW 25:471. See also Hillerdal, "Römer 13 und Luthers Lehre von den zwei Reichen."

10. Augustine described the basic differences between the realms of time and timeless eternity at a time when the differentiation between the medieval church and the state did not yet exist. For the differences between Luther and Augustine, see Bornkamm, Luther's Doctrine of the Two Kingdoms, 16–28. For the influence of medieval theories of church and state, especially those of William Occam and Gabriel Biel, see Junghans, "Das mittelalterliche Vorbild für Luthers Lehre von den zwei Reichen." Sources in Hertz, Two Kingdoms, 25–32, 43–66.

11. "An Exposition of the Lord's Prayer for Simple Laymen" (Auslegung deutsch des Vaterunsers für die einfältigen Laien), 1519. WA 2:96.27–29. LW 42:38.

12. WA 2:97.14–16. LW 42:39.

13. WA 2:97.28–29. LW 42:40.

14. WA 2:97.31–36. LW 42:40.

15. WA 2:98.27–28. LW 42:41.

16. "Two Kinds of Righteousness," 1519. WA 2:146.32–34. LW 31:299.

17. WA 2:151.3–4. LW 31:305.

18. WA 11:249.18–23. LW 45:88.

19. WA 11:249.36–250.1. LW 45:89.

20. WA 11:251.35–37. LW 45:91.

21. *WA* 11:252.14–23. *LW* 45:92.

22. *WA* 11:255.5–12. *LW* 45:95–96.

23. *WA* 11:259.9–13. *LW* 45:101.

24. *WA* 11:260.17–19. *LW* 45:103.

25. *WA* 11:264.19–20. *LW* 45:108.

26. *WA* 11:267.4–7. *LW* 45:112.

27. *WA* 11:268.27–29. *LW* 45:114.

28. *WA* 11:279.36–280.15. *LW* 45:128–29.

29. Letter to Philip of Hesse dated 23 June 1529. *WA.BR* 5:102.53–55. *LW* 49:231. In an earlier letter to Sickingen, dated June 1, 1521, Luther had addressed him as "Special Lord and Patron." *WA* 8:138.4. *LW* 48:245.

30. Organized by Swabian peasants in March 1525. Text in Franz, *Quellen zur Geschichte des Bauernkrieges*, 197–98. The peasants also listed Luther as one of several "judges" (*Richter*) asked to interpret the meaning of "divine law." For Luther's involvement, see Kirchner, *Luther and the Peasants' War*. On the uprising and its complex historiographical treatment, see the collected essays on the occasion of the 450th anniversary of the war in Oberman, *Deutscher Bauernkrieg 1525*. See also Maron, "Bauernkrieg." Representative interpretations and bibliography are offered in Scribner-Benecke, *German Peasant War*.

31. "Admonition to Peace," 1525. *WA* 18:314.12–17. *LW* 46:31–32.

32. "An Open Letter on the Harsh Book Against the Peasants," 1525. *WA* 18:400.16–23. *LW* 46:83–84.

33. "Lectures on the Minor Prophets." *WA* 23:511.34–514.31. *LW* 20:169–73.

34. *WA* 23:514.27–31. *LW* 20:172.

35. "A Sermon on Keeping Children in School." *WA* 30/2:562.27–29. *LW* 46:242.

36. *WA* 51:241.35–41. *LW* 13:197.

37. "On the Councils and the Church," 1539. *WA* 50:652.12–18. Quotation 652.16. *LW* 41:177. At times Luther called the hierarchies "orders" (*Ordnungen*), especially in the context of polemics against religious orders. See, for example, "Confession Concerning Christ's Supper," 1528. *WA* 26:504.30–31. *LW* 37:364. On the shifting of Luther's views, see Cranz, *Luther's Thought on Justice, Law and Society*, 173–78 on the "hierarchies."

38. Wingren, "Das Problem des Natürlichen," 157. See also the discussion of the "natural" by Ebeling, "Das Problem des Natürlichen," and Lazareth, "Luther on Civil Righteousness."

39. "Whether Soldiers, Too, Can Be Saved," 1526. *WA* 19:638.30–31. *LW* 46:114. See also Haikola, "Luther und das Naturrecht."

40. See Ebeling's treatment of "man as a Christian and man in the world" in *Luther*, chap. 12. For a detailed analysis of Luther's view of the interraction between the divine and human in every Christian, see Nilsson, *Simul*, esp. 413–33.

41. "Sermons on the Sermon on the Mount." *WA* 32:390.19–24. *LW* 21:109.

42. See his letter of 20 December 1520. *WA.BR* 2:237:2. For a detailed analysis of Luther as a political advisor to the three Electors, see Kunst, *Evangelischer Glaube*, chaps. 3–5. There are two useful sketches of Luther's views by Bornkamm, "The Nation" and "The State." See also Althaus, *Ethics of Martin Luther*, chaps. 8–9.

43. "Temporal Authority: To What Extent It Should Be Obeyed." *WA* 11:273.7–8. *LW* 45:120.

44. *WA* 11:274.7–9. *LW* 45:121.

45. *WA* 11:276.6. *LW* 45:123.

46. *WA* 11:278.14–15. *LW* 45:126.

47. *WA* 31/1:193.30–34. *LW* 13:46.

48. *WA* 31/1:201.24–25. *LW* 13:54–55.

49. "Commentary on Psalm 101," 1534. *WA* 51:207.22–33. *LW* 13:154–55.

50. Large Catechism, 1529, pt. 1.177 (Fourth Commandment). *BS* 605. *BC* 389. Princes and other superiors stand in the place of "fathers" and thus are "fathers of the country." Ibid., pt. 1.142. *BS* 596. *BC* 384–85.

51. *WA* 51:242.4–8. *LW* 13:198.

52. "Lectures on Psalm 127," 1532–33 (complete ed., 1540). *WA* 40/3:222.24–223.2.

53. "Whether Soldiers, Too, Can Be Saved," 1526. *WA* 19:631.14–25. *LW* 46:101–2.

54. *WA* 19:648.1–6. *LW* 46:121.

55. *WA* 30/2:131.24–31. *LW* 46:186–87.

56. *WA.BR* 10:35.140–36.165.

57. "A Sermon on Keeping Children in School," 1530. *WA* 30/2:538.20–23. *LW* 46:226.

58. *WA* 51:235.15–24. *LW* 13:189–90.

59. "Princely hireling" is a description used in Marxist historiography. See Friesen, *Reformation and Utopia*, 235. For a collection of primary and secondary sources on Luther's and other contemporaries' views on the right to resist secular government, see Scheible, *Das Widerstandsrecht*. For a summary of Luther's views, see Shoenberger, "Justification of Resistance."

60. This is the estimated value of 1518. Schwiebert, *Luther and His Times*, 312.

61. See Bornkamm, "Luther und sein Landesherr Kurfürst," 38.

62. *WA.BR* 2:455.76–456.85. *LW* 48:391.

63. "On Temporal Authority," 1523. *WA* 11:268.23–26. *LW* 45:114.

64. *WA* 11:267.8–13. *LW* 45:112. This was Luther's advice to those whose "Luther Bibles" had been confiscated in the territories of George of Saxony and in Bavaria.

65. "Lectures on Genesis," 1542. *WA* 43:507.13–23. *LW* 5:114–15.

66. "Admonition to Peace," 1525. *WA* 18:299.1–2. *LW* 46:22.

67. *WA* 18:323.26–28. *LW* 46:36.

68. This is the thrust of Melanchthon's memorandum which Luther signed in 1536. See above, chap. 4, n. 7. How Luther moved from a soft to a hard position on the matter of capital punishment has been shown by Bainton, "Luther's Attitudes on Religious Liberty," especially 40–42.

69. *WA.BR* 5:261.114–15. *LW* 49:280.

70. "Dr. Martin Luther's Warning to His Dear German People," 1530. *WA* 30/3:320.21–28. *LW* 47:55. On Luther's view of resistance after the Diet of Augsburg in 1530, see Wolgast, *Die Wittenberger Theologie*, esp. 173–88.

71. "Opinion of the Jurists of Electoral Saxony" (*Gutachten der kursächsischen Juristen*), October 1530. Scheible, *Das Widerstandsrecht*, 63–66 (no. 15). See also the Wittenberg response of 26–28 October 1530: "Declaration of Luther, Jonas, Melanchthon, Spalatin, and Other Theologians" (*Erklärung Luthers, Jonas', Melanchthons, Spalatins und anderer Theologen*). Ibid., 67–68 (no. 16).

248   NOTES (CHAP. 6)

72. Ibid., 67 (no. 16). Translation in *LW* 47:8.

73. Scheible, *Das Widerstandsrecht*, 94 (no. 21). Translation mine. The "Opinion" was signed by Luther, Melanchthon, Bucer, and Jonas on 13 or 14 November 1538.

74. "Disputation Concerning the Right to Resist the Emperor" (*Zirkulationsdisputation über das Recht des Widerstandes gegen den Kaiser*), 1539. *WA* 39/2:44.8–13. Translation mine.

75. Theses 66–69. *WA* 39/2:50.22–51.7. Translation mine.

76. "Table Talk," 3 March 1539, no. 4380. *WA.TR* 4:273.10.

77. "An Admonition to All Clergy" (*Eine Vermahnung an alle Pfarrherren*), 1546. *WA* 50:486.24–25. Composed in the spring of 1539, the "Admonition" was printed after Luther's death in 1546.

78. Luther researchers have been plagued by the question of what Luther might have to say about political developments in Germany before, during, and after World War II. See, for example, Ohlig, *Die Zwei-Reiche-Lehre Luthers*, and the 1977 discussion, "Luthers Lehre von den zwei Reichen" in Grane and Lohse, *Luther und die Theologie der Gegenwart*, 147–55. For an international debate among Lutherans on the topic, see Duchrow, *Two Kingdoms*.

79. "Commentary on Psalm 82," 1530. *WA* 31/1:192.21–25; 193.3–6. *LW* 13:44–45.

CHAPTER 7

1. "On the Jews and Their Lies," 1543. *WA* 53:528.5–7, 13–17. *LW* 47:274, 275.

2. Bainton, *Here I Stand*, 379.

3. Shirer, *Rise and Fall of the Third Reich*, 91. On this controversial interpretation, see Moellering, "Luther's Attitude Toward the Jews"; Montgomery, "In Defense of Martin Luther"; Matheson, "Luther and Hitler"; Bainton, "Luther, Begin, and the Jews."

4. See Trachtenberg, "The Jew as Sorcerer," pt. 2.

5. Bainton, *Travail of Christian Liberty*, chap. 1.

6. Roth, "Jews in the Middle Ages," 658.

7. John Eck, "Refutation of a Jew-Book" (*Ains Judenbuechleins Verlegung*), 1541. Quoted in *LW* 47:129. Eck attacked the Lutheran Andreas Osiander, who had defended Jews against the charge of ritual murder. For the history of the controversy between Osiander and Eck, see Oberman, *Wurzeln des Antisemitismus*, 45–47.

8. This distinction is the key to Luther's understanding of the Old Testament. See Bornkamm, *Luther and the Old Testament*, chap. 6.

9. "First Lectures on the Psalms," 1513–15. *WA* 3:296.13–17. *LW* 10:245.

10. How Luther used this christological hermeneutic is shown by Ebeling, "Die Anfänge Luthers Hermeneutik," esp. 42–51.

11. "First Lectures on the Psalms," 1513–15. *WA* 3:535.22–28. *LW* 11:17. For Luther's use of medieval Old Testament exegesis, leading to his discovery of the "faithful synagogue," see Preus, *From Shadow to Promise*, chap. 14.

12. "First Lectures on the Psalms," 1513–15. *WA* 3:68.4–7. *LW* 10:77. For more evidence on Luther's early attitude toward the Jews and how it affected his writings, see Maurer, "Die Zeit der Reformation."

13. "Lectures on Romans," 1515–16. *WA* 56:199.10–13. *LW* 25:182.

14. *WA* 56:199.28–30. *LW* 25:183.

15. "The Magnificat," 1521. *WA* 7:600.33–601.2. *LW* 21:354–55. On Luther's view of the Old Testament patriarchs as the "spiritual Israel," see ibid., *WA* 7:597.1–18. *LW* 21:351.

16. Letter written in February 1514 to George Spalatin. *WA.BR* 1:23.2–19. *SJ* 1:28–29. The Reuchlin controversy began in 1509, when the emperor decreed the confiscation of Jewish books, and ended in the 1520s with the condemnation of Reuchlin's writings by the pope. The satirical "Letters of Obscure Men," issued by the humanist Ulrich von Hutten, fueled the controversy after 1515 and made it look ridiculous. See the collection of letters in Hutten, *On the Eve of the Reformation*, especially the introduction by Holborn; and Spitz, *Renaissance and Reformation Movements*, 280–81.

17. "First Lectures on the Psalms," 1513–15. *WA* 3:203.27–29. *LW* 10:173.

18. "That Jesus Christ Was Born a Jew," 1523. *WA* 11:315.3–9. *LW* 45:200.

19. *WA* 11:325.25–331.22. *LW* 45:213–21.

20. *WA* 11:331.23–336.5. *LW* 45:221–28.

21. *WA* 11:336.6–36. *LW* 45:228–29.

22. *WA* 11:336.16–19. *LW* 45:229.

23. *WA* 11:336.30–34. *LW* 45:229.

24. "Sermon on Jer. 23:5–9," 25 November 1526. *WA* 20:569.36–37. "Table Talk," 21 May–11 June 1540, no. 5026. *WA.TR* 4:620.5–8.

25. In a letter to Nicholas von Amsdorf, dated 23 January 1535, Luther reported that a Polish Jewish physician had been sent to Wittenberg to poison him but had been arrested before he could carry out his plan. *WA.BR* 3:428.14–17.

26. "Lectures on Genesis," 1535–36. *WA* 42:520.22–35. *LW* 2:361–62.

27. *WA.BR* 8:89.9–90.13.

28. "Table Talk," 27 May–18 June 1537, no. 3597. *WA.TR* 3:442.4–5, 12. *LW* 54:239.

29. "Against the Sabbatarians: Letter to a Good Friend," 1538. *WA* 50:322.31–34. *LW* 47:78.

30. *WA* 50:323.30–324.10. *LW* 47:79–80.

31. *WA* 50:330.35–37. *LW* 47:89. On "natural law," Luther shared the basic view of Aquinas. See McNeill, "Natural Law," 220–21.

32. *WA* 50:336.2–6. *LW* 47:96.

33. *WA* 53:412–552. *LW* 47:123–306. The kind of pamphlet Luther received and read is not known.

34. *WA* 53:418.30–32. *LW* 47:139.

35. *WA* 53:419.10–11. *LW* 47:139.

36. *WA* 53:420.13–16. *LW* 47:141.

37. *WA* 53:431.32–432.6. *LW* 47:154–55.

38. *WA* 53:433.19–21. *LW* 47:157.

39. *WA* 53:441.7–12. *LW* 47:166.

40. *WA* 53:443.14–22. *LW* 47:169. On usury, see Exod. 22:25 and Deut. 23:19–20, which allow Jews to take interest from Gentiles, but not from fellow Jews.

41. *WA* 53:448.20–22. *LW* 47:175.

42. *WA* 53:462.3. *LW* 47:192.

43. *WA* 53:482.8–14. *LW* 47:217.

44. *WA* 53:511.19–24. *LW* 47:254.

45. *WA* 53:514.18–19. *LW* 47:257.

46. *WA* 53:514.1–8. *LW* 47:257.

47. See, for example, "Table Talk" during the winter of 1542/43, no. 5504. *WA.TR* 5:198.18–19. *LW* 54:436.

48. *WA* 53:522.8.10–17. *LW* 47:267.

49. *WA* 53:522.30–37. *LW* 47:268.

50. *WA* 53:526.14–16. *LW* 47:272.

51. *WA* 53:528.33–34. *LW* 47:275.

52. *WA* 53:529.28–31. *LW* 47:276.

53. *WA* 53:536.23–537.17. *LW* 47:286.

54. *WA* 53:539.31–540.4. *LW* 47:289–90.

55. Quoted in *LW* 47:135, no. 30 from Josel's petition to the magistrates of Strassburg requesting the prohibition of the circulation of Luther's treatise.

56. Lewin, *Luthers Stellung zu den Juden*, 97ff.

57. *Vom Schem Hamphoras und vom Geschlecht Christi*, 1543. *WA* 53:573–648. *Von den letzten Worten Davids*, 1543. *WA* 54:16–100.

58. *WA* 53:581.7–586.18.

59. *WA* 53:596.8–598.27. The scheme is based on 216 Hebrew letters, divided by three in order to arrive at the number 72. Luther was aware of the tetragram for "God," YHWH.

60. "Wo hat er's gelesen? Der Sau im Hintern." *WA* 53:601.4–5. See the description and a photograph of the relief in *WA* 53:600.26–601.5.

61. Ibid, 609.14–17.

62. Ibid., 613.16–32

63. See Luther's chart, ibid., 629.

64. Ibid., 634.19–644.19.

65. Ibid., 644.20–33.

66. Ibid., 646.19–31.

67. Ibid., 648.11–15.

68. *WA* 54:67.39–68.20.

69. Ibid., 70.9–39.

70. Ibid., 100.21–27. See also ibid., 30.27–31.2.

71. Quoted in *WA* 53:574. On the Bucer-Bullinger correspondence, see *WA* 54:20–21.

72. "A Warning to the Jews" (*Eine Vermahnung an die Juden*), 1546. *WA* 51:196.14–17.

73. For an overview of the scholarly debate, see the extensive treatment by Brosseder, *Luthers Stellung zu den Juden;* also, Sucher, *Luthers Stellung zu den Juden,* pt. 3; and Meier, "Zur Interpretation von Luthers Judenschriften." See also the critical assessment of the "old" anti-Semitic Luther by Oberman, *Wurzeln des Antisemitismus,* chap. 16. One unsuccessful attempt has been made to view Luther's treatises against the Jews as "missionary" enterprises. See Holmio, *Lutheran Reformation and the Jews.* But Holmio's thesis was based on an error of translation;

he translated "Sendebrief" as "mission epistle" (ibid., 131). "Sendungsbrief" is "mission letter," but "Sendebrief" is a "circulatory, or open letter." For a detailed critique of Holmio's thesis, see Brosseder, *Luthers Stellung zu den Juden*, 264–66.

74. Oberman, *Wurzeln des Antisemitismus*, 155–56; and Gerhard Müller, "Antisemitismus," 146–49.

75. The typical racist ideology, expressed in the Aryan/Semite dichotomy, can be traced to the French philosopher A. de Gobineau, who used the dichotomy in his work "An Essay on the Inequality of the Human Races" (*Essai sur l'inégalité des races humaines*), 1853–55. His tendency to view "Aryan" as synonymous with "German" provided the foundation for political German anti-Semitism; its first ideological proponent was Wilhelm Marr (1818–1904), founder of the first League of Anti-Semites (*Antisemitenliga*) in 1879. For a brief illustrated history of anti-Semitism, see Schwarz and Ahimeir, "Antisemitism"; and Mosse, *Toward the Final Solution*, esp. chap. 1.

76. See Oberman, *Wurzeln des Antisemitismus*, epilogue on "the stony road to co-existence," 185–92; also Siirala, "Luther and the Jews."

CHAPTER 8

1. "Commentaries on the Activities and Writings of Martin Luther" (*Commentaria de actis et scriptis M. Lutheri*), 1549. Denifle, *Luther und Luthertum*. Grisar, *Luther*. How Cochlaeus influenced Catholic Luther biographers, who in turn influenced others, has been shown by Herte, *Das katholische Lutherbild*.

2. Lortz, *Reformation in Germany*, 1:458.

3. "Table Talk," date unknown, no. 6024. *WA.TR* 5:445.8–11.

4. This is the conclusion of Ebstein, *Dr. Martin Luthers Krankheiten*. Ebstein investigated the relation of physical illness to depression. See also Halder, *Das Harnsteinleiden Martin Luthers* on kidney stones.

5. Their findings are summarized by Spitz, "Psychohistory and History," 63–64 n. 19.

6. Preserved Smith, "Luther's Early Development," 362.

7. Reiter, *Martin Luther*. This work was heavily influenced by the polemics of Denifle and Grisar.

8. Ibid., 2:121.

9. Grisar, *Luther* (German ed.) 3:598.

10. Huizinga, *Waning of the Middle Ages*, 138, 150.

11. Erikson, *Young Man Luther*. See the discussion of this work in Johnson, *Psychohistory and Religion*.

12. Erikson, *Young Man Luther*, 14.

13. Ibid., 22.

14. "Table Talk," May 1532, no. 1159. *WA.TR* 2:134.5–7. Translated by Bainton. The translation of the saying has been a matter of debate. See Bainton, "Psychiatry and History," 35; and Spitz, "Psychohistory and History," 71.

15. "Table Talk," 28 March–27 May 1537, no. 3566A. *WA.TR* 3:415.29–416.2. *LW* 54:235. Erikson, *Young Man Luther*, 67–73.

16. "Table Talk," 28 March–27 May 1537, no. 3566B. *WA.TR* 3:417.2–3. Erikson, *Young Man Luther*, 79.

17. Ibid., 57–97, especially 97.
18. "Table Talk," 20 May 1532, no. 1558. *WA.TR* 2:133.38–134.2. *LW* 54:157. There are variants. The fullest account in *SD*, nos. 420, 450, quoted and translated by Bainton, "Psychiatry and History," 41.
19. Erikson, *Young Man Luther*, 140.
20. *SD* no. 533, critically analyzed by Bainton, "Psychiatry and History," 42.
21. Erikson, *Young Man Luther*, 38.
22. Ibid., 94
23. Ibid., 213.
24. Ibid., 201–14.
25. Ibid., 221–22.
26. Ibid., 257.
27. Ibid., 255–61, esp. 261.
28. In addition to the critique of Bainton and Spitz, see Bornkamm, "Luther und sein Vater"; Lindbeck, "Erikson's *Young Man Luther*." Few historians have reviewed Erikson's book. See Spitz, "Psychohistory and History," 69 n. 31.
29. "Table Talk," 21–28 March 1537, no. 3556A. *WA.TR* 3:410.39–40.
30. 5 June 1530. *WA.BR* 5:351.22–24. *LW* 49:319.
31. Letter of 20 May 1531. *WA.BR* 6:103–6. *LW* 50:17–21.
32. "Table Talk," 28 March–27 May 1537, no. 3566B. *WA.TR* 3:416.13–14.
33. Erikson, *Young Man Luther*, 66.
34. Bornkamm, "Luther und sein Vater," 21.
35. Erikson, *Young Man Luther*, 148.
36. "The Misuse of the Mass," 1521. *WA* 8:483.2–3. *LW* 36:134.
37. Holl, "Luther on Luther," 19.
38. Bainton, "Psychiatry and History," 52–54.
39. Oberman, "Wir sein Pettler," 237–38.
40. Bainton, "Psychiatry and History," 20.
41. *WA.BR* 2:333.34–37. *LW* 48:217.
42. *WA.BR* 8:51.1–15. *LW* 50:167.
43. "Table Talk" in February 1537, no. 3543A. *WA.TR* 3:390.7. *LW* 54:227.
44. Mühlhaupt, "Luthers Kampf mit der Krankheit," 115.
45. Letter to Elector John Frederick, 28 March 1532. *WA.BR* 6:277.19–20. Letter to Caspar Cruciger, 1 May 1541. *WA.BR* 9:390.24–25. Cruciger had been pastor at the Castle Church in Wittenberg and professor at the University since 1528.
46. The bubonic plague, known as "black death," killed one fourth of the population in Europe when it came from China or India via Russia in 1347–50. Rats and fleas were principal carriers. Without any known cure, the plague killed humans within days, through fever and boils infiltrating into the lymph glands. Wittenberg was struck on 2 August 1527; the epidemic lasted several weeks. See *LW* 43:115–16.
47. "Table Talk," no. 157. *WA.TR* 1:75.8–11. *LW* 54:23.
48. "Whether One May Flee From a Deadly Plague" (*Ob man vor dem Sterben fliehen möge*), 1527. *WA* 23:370.10–375.10. *LW* 43:134–36.
49. "Eight Sermons at Wittenberg," 1522. *WA* 10/3:62.1–2. *LW* 51:98. Luther loved to tell how "Pomeranus" (John Bugenhagen's home territory was Pomerania) consoled him when, as father confessor, he reminded him of the power of God's grace.

Pomeranus was "like a voice from heaven." "Table Talk," 30 November 1531, no. 122. *WA.TR* 1:47.25–29. *LW* 54:15–16.

50. This is the convincing conclusion of Hans-Martin Barth, *Der Teufel und Jesus Christus*, 208–10. See also Obendiek, *Der Teufel bei Martin Luther*, 235–54. Luther's whole life has been portrayed as that of "a man between God and the devil." See the subtitle of Oberman, *Luther*.

51. "Table Talk" from the 1530s, no. 4784. *WA.TR* 4:501.21.

52. "Whether One May Flee From a Deadly Plague," 1527. *WA* 23:357.27–32. *LW* 43:128.

53. Mühlhaupt, "Luthers Kampf mit der Krankheit," 121.

54. The statistics have been assembled by Dieck, "Luthers Schaffenskraft," 36–39, based on the chronology in Buchwald and Kawerau, *Luther-Kalendarium*, 17–159.

55. "Fourteen Consolations For Those Who Labor and Are Heavy-laden" (*Tessaradecas consolatoria pro laborantibus et oneratis*), 1520 (reprinted 1530). *WA* 6:105.14–19. *LW* 42:122.

56. "Table Talk," 6 August 1538, no. 3945. *WA.TR* 4:26.9–13.

57. *WA.BR* 3:394.22–26. *LW* 49:93.

58. See the account of Luther's marriage in Bainton, *Here I Stand*, 287–93; by the same author, "Katharine von Bora." Schwiebert, *Luther and His Times*, 583–93. Lazareth, *Luther on the Christian Home*, 11–33. Most details in Boehmer, "Luthers Ehe." Sources in Knolle, "Luthers Heirat."

59. *WA.BR* 3:541.2–8. *LW* 49:117.

60. A remark heard by Luther's friend Nicholas Amsdorf. See Boehmer, "Luthers Ehe," 65.

61. "The War of Whoring Monks" (*Monachopornomachia*). Lemnius was in Wittenberg after 1538. He had fled the city after Luther had had him put under house arrest. See Luther's "Declaration Against Simon Lemnius" (*Erklärung gegen Simon Lemnius*), 1538. *WA* 50:350–51.

62. The letters were dated 10 August 1528 and were delivered by special messenger. *WA.BR* 4:517.25; 526–36. *SJ* 2:451–53. Luther answered with a "New Fable of Aesop, Recently Translated Into German, About the Lion and the Ass" (*Eine neue Fabel Aesops, neulich deutsch gefunden: Vom Löwen und Esel*), 1528. *WA* 26:534–54. Reference to "toilet paper," 540.13–18.

63. "Table Talk," no. 49. *WA.TR* 1:17.10–15. *LW* 54:7–8.

64. "Table Talk," 30 November 1531, no. 121. *WA.TR* 1:47.15–18. *LW* 54:15.

65. "Table Talk," 24 February 1538, no. 3777. *WA.TR* 3:607.16–17. *LW* 54:271.

66. "Judgment of Martin Luther on Monastic Vows," 1521. *WA* 8:585. 24–27. *LW* 44:264.

67. "Commentary on 1 Cor. 7" (*Das siebente Kapitel S. Pauli zu den Korinthern ausgelegt*), 1523. *WA* 12:109.8–9. *LW* 28:21.

68. "Lectures on Genesis," 1543. *WA* 43:315.30–32. *LW* 4:251.

69. "The Babylonian Captivity," 1520. *WA* 6:558.31. *LW* 36:104. Luther made detailed pronouncements about sexual behavior. See Boehmer, *Luthers Ehebuch*; Seeberg, "Luthers Anschauung von dem Geschlechtsleben und der Ehe"; and Lähteenmäki, *Sexus und Ehe bei Luther*.

70. German "Answer to King Henry's Book" (*Antwort auf König Heinrichs Buch*),

1522. *WA* 10/2:238.13–23. Henry VIII had written "A Defense of Seven Sacraments Against Martin Luther" (*Assertio septem sacramentorum adversus Martinum Lutherum*), 1521. "Lectures on Genesis" (2:22), 1542. *WA* 42:99.23–36. *LW* 1:133.

71. "Table Talk," 15 or 16 July 1539, no. 4709. *WA.TR* 4:441.14–16.

CHAPTER 9

1. Luther does theology in historical contexts. On the risks of systematizing his theology, see Pesch, *Hinführung zu Luther,* 316–22.

2. "Table Talk," 14 December 1531–22 January 1532, no. 153. *WA.TR* 1:72.16–19. *LW* 54:22.

3. "Lectures on Galatians," 1535. *WA* 40/1:77.11–20. *LW* 26:28–29.

4. "Lectures on Romans," 1515–16. *WA* 56:371.27. *LW* 25:361.

5. "Sermon on Baptism," 1534. *WA* 37:661.20–26.

6. Luther opposed the distortions of late medieval sacramentology with the Augustinian notion that one must first receive the grace of Christ in the sacrament before one can follow him in a moral life. He therefore opted for a particular position in the Roman Catholic tradition. See Iserloh, "Luthers Stellung in der Theologischen Tradition," 46.

7. "Table Talk," 11–19 June 1540, no. 5070. *WA.TR* 4:641.14–18, 20–642.2. *LW* 54:385.

8. See Gerrish, *Grace and Reason,* 169.

9. That is why Luther's theology has been called "dialectical": he thinks in "twos." Loeschen, *Wrestling With Luther,* 16–17.

10. "Lectures on Romans," 1515–16. *WA* 56:274.11–18. *LW* 25:261–62.

11. Text in Brandi, *Der Augsburger Religionsfriede.* Partial English translation in Kidd, *Documents Illustrative of the Continental Reformation,* no. 149, 363–64. See also Pfeiffer, "Augsburger Religionsfriede 1555."

12. "Sermons on the Gospel of St. John" (3:14), 1539. *WA* 47:66.21–24. *LW* 22:339.

13. "Lectures on Psalms" (Ps. 130:1), 1532–33. *WA* 40/3:337.11.

14. "Lectures on Galatians," 1535. *WA* 40/1:181.11–13, 19–21. *LW* 26:99.

15. Ibid., *WA* 40/1:589.25–28. *LW* 26:387.

16. Smalcald Articles, 1537, pt. 2, I.1–5. *BS* 415. *BC* 292.

17. Small Catechism, 1529, pt. 2.4 (Second Article of the Creed). *BS* 511. *BC* 345.

18. "Preface to the Doctoral Disputation of Palladius and Tilemann," 1537. *WA* 39/1:205.2–5.

19. "... *quia isto articulo stante stat Ecclesia, ruente ruit Ecclesia.*" "Commentary on Psalm 130" (:4), 1533. *WA* 40/3:352.3.

20. See chap. 4, n. 29. For a summary of Luther texts and their interpretation, see Pesch, *Die Theologie der Rechtfertigung,* 152–59. On the impact of the Epistle to the Romans on Luther, see Holl, "Die Rechtfertigungslehre."

21. By Heinrich Boehmer and Anders Nygren. See Watson, *Let God Be God,* 33–34. How important Luther's study of Paul was has been shown by Grane, *Modus Loquendi Theologicus,* chaps. 2–3, esp. 199.

22. This question was debated at the 1963 Assembly of the Lutheran World

Federation in Helsinki. See *Justification Today*. For an assessment of the discussion, see Peters, "Zu einer Neuinterpretation der reformatorischen Rechtfertigungslehre."

23. See the history of the doctrine in Müller, *Die Rechtfertigungslehre*, esp. 113–16.

24. The theological assumption that God's grace moves even free will has been called an "anti-Pelagian codicil." See Gritsch and Jenson, *Lutheranism*, 39–40, 46–47. Pelagius (ca. A.D. 410) stressed human response over against Augustine's insistence on absolute divine initiative in the relationship between sin and grace. Pelagianism became a heresy in the Middle Ages even though historical-critical study discloses that Pelagius did not teach "free will" to sin or not to sin. See Robert F. Evans, *Pelagius*, 120–21.

25. "Forensic" (from the Latin *forum*, the marketplace where citizens met to transact legal and other business) means pronouncing the verdict that a sinner is righteous on account of Christ rather than on account of merit acquired through good works. Luther echoed Paul (Rom. 3:21–28) and old German practices. See Elert, "Deutschrechtliche Züge in Luthers Rechtfertigungslehre."

26. "A Treatise on the New Testament, That Is, the Holy Mass," 1520. *WA* 6:357.14–15. *LW* 35:84.

27. Letter to John Spenlein, a fellow friar, dated 8 April 1516. *WA.BR* 1:35.24–32. *LW* 48:12–13.

28. See Brecht, "Der rechtfertigende Glaube"; Wolf, "Die Rechtfertigungslehre," 215; Pesch, *Hinführung zu Luther*, 265–67. For ecumenical implications, see Kantzenbach, "Christusgemeinschaft und Rechtfertigung." See also Forde, "The Exodus from Virtue to Grace" and *Justification*. On the implications for anthropology, see Joest, *Ontologie der Person*, esp. 351–53 on the relation to eschatology. See also the constructive Roman Catholic approach in Bogdahn, *Die Rechtfertigungslehre Luthers*, especially on "solus Christus," 250–60.

29. "Lectures on Galatians," 1535. *WA* 40/1:209.16–23. *LW* 26:117.

30. "Die höchste Kunst in der Christenheit," sermon on Gal. 3:23–29, January 1531. *WA* 36:9.28–29.

31. *WA* 40/1:509.17–20, 27–28. *LW* 26:329.

32. See Althaus, *Theology of Martin Luther*, 227–33.

33. "Third Disputation Against the Antinomians," 1538. *WA* 39/1:521.5–522.3. Quoted and translated in Ebeling, *Luther*, 163–64.

34. "Disputation on Matt. 22:1–14," 1537. *WA* 39/1:283.18–19.

35. "The Freedom of the Christian," 1520. *WA* 7:25.34. *LW* 31:351.

36. Luther stressed the soteriological aspects of the dogma of the Trinity (what God did in Christ for salvation). See Maurer, "Die Einheit der Theologie Luthers," 17–19, and "Luthers Theologie," 25–26.

37. Smalcald Articles, 1537, pt. 2.II.15 (The Mass). *BS* 421. *BC* 295. Italics mine.

38. There seems to be consensus on this view. See, for example, Pesch, *Hinführung zu Luther*, 269.

39. What follows is a summary of Müller, *Die Rechtfertigungslehre*, 54–63.

40. "Confession Concerning Christ's Supper," 1528. *WA* 26:340.1–2. *LW* 37:228.

41. "Lectures on Romans" (4:7), 1515–16. *WA* 56:272.17–18. *LW* 25:260.

42. Müller, *Die Rechtfertigungslehre*, 56.

43. Large Catechism, 1529, pt. 2.65 (Third Article of the Creed). *BS* 660. *BC* 419.

44. Apology of the Augsburg Confession, 1530, IV.1–2 (Justification). *BS* 158–59. *BC* 107.

45. Confutation (*Confutatio*), 1530, 6:3. Text in Immenkötter, *Die Confutatio der Confessio Augustana*, 90:18–21. English by Reu, *Augsburg Confession*, 352.

46. See Gritsch and Jenson, *Lutheranism*, 42–43.

47. Ibid., 44.

48. Augsburg Confession, 1530, VII.2 (The Church). *BS* 61. *BC* 32.

49. See the detailed evaluation of Catholic reactions in Bogdahn, *Die Rechtfertigungslehre Luthers,* esp. 273; Pesch, *Hinführung zu Luther,* 270–71. An official theological commission of the Federated Lutheran Churches of Germany offered a reinterpretation of the doctrine of justification in 1972, using a terminology which differs from sixteenth-century language, and focuses on "unconditional acceptance" (*vorbehaltloses Angenommenwerden*). See Lohff and Walther, *Rechtfertigung im neuzeitlichen Zusammenhang.* Summary by G. Müller, "Rechtfertigungslehre heute."

50. Willebrands, "Gesandt in die Welt," 459. Speech at the Assembly of the Lutheran World Federation in Geneva, 1970. Translation mine.

CHAPTER 10

1. "Concerning the Order of Public Worship," 1523. *WA* 12:35–37. *LW* 53:11–14. On Luther's "principles of worship," see Vajta, *Luther on Worship*, chaps. 1–2.

2. "Concerning Rebaptism," 1528. *WA* 26:147.15–16. *LW* 40:231.

3. Preface to the "Ordinance of a Common Chest," 1523. *WA* 12:15.26–31. *LW* 45:176. See also Grimm, "Organization of Poor Relief."

4. See pts. 4, 6 in the Small Catechism, and pts. 4, 5 in the Large Catechism of 1529. *BS* 515–17, 519–21. *BC* 348–49, 351–53. See also Gritsch, "Luther's Catechisms of 1529."

5. Preface to the Large Catechism, 1529. *BS* 553.19. *BC* 361.19.

6. "Address to the German Nobility," 1520. *WA* 6:408.27–28. *LW* 44:129. For a brief summary of the difference, see my introduction to Haendler, *Luther on Ministerial Office,* 11–12.

7. For a summary of the literature and an analysis, see Gritsch, "The Ministry in Luther's Theological Perspective"; also Pesch, *Hinführung zu Luther,* 212–17.

8. Exorcism was the first act in Luther's order of baptism. "The Order of Baptism, Newly Revised," 1526. *WA* 19:539.4. *LW* 53:107.

9. Small Catechism, 1529, pt. 4.84–86 (Baptism). *BS* 707. *BC* 446.

10. See Grane, "Luther, Baptism, and Christian Formation," 196.

11. Large Catechism, 1529, pt. 5.15, 18 (Confession). *BS* 729–30. *BC* 458–59.

12. Smalcald Articles, 1537, pt. 3, IV (The Gospel). *BS* 449. *BC* 310.

13. "Commentary on Psalm 2" (:11), 1532. *WA* 40/2:285.15–20. *LW* 12:72.

14. Large Catechism, 1529, pt. 2.1–2 (Creed); pt. 3.1 (Lord's Prayer). *BS* 647, 662. *BC* 411, 420.

15. Ibid., pt. 4.1. *BS* 691. *BC* 436.

16. Ibid., pt. 5.24 (Lord's Supper). *BS* 712. *BC* 449.

17. Ibid., pt. 5.79. *BS* 723. *BC* 455.

18. "A Sermon on Preparing to Die," 1529. *WA* 2:688.35–37. *LW* 42:103.

19. For a review of this issue in the context of the question of infant communion, see Gritsch, "Infant Communion."

20. Large Catechism, 1529, pt. 5.87 (Lord's Supper). *BS* 725. *BC* 456–57.

21. Term used by Jenson, "The Return to Baptism," 223.

22. Large Catechism, 1529, pt. 3.65 (Lord's Prayer). *BS* 677. *BC* 429.

23. "Lectures on Isaiah," 1529. *WA* 31/2:448.9–10. *LW* 17:241.

24. Ibid., *WA* 31/2:448.20. *LW* 17:242.

25. "Confession Concerning Christ's Supper," 1528. *WA* 26:504.30–31. *LW* 37:364.

26. "A Sermon on Keeping Children in School," 1530. *WA* 30/2:526.34–527.13. *LW* 46:219–20.

27. "On the Councils and the Church," 1539. *WA* 50:632.35–633.11. *LW* 41:154.

28. Wilhelm Löhe and John Höffding were engaged in an intensive debate over the question of whether the office of the ministry is divinely instituted or derives from the power of the local congregation. This nineteenth-century debate has been described by Fagerberg, *Bekenntnis, Kirche und Amt*.

29. "Concerning the Ministry," 1523. *WA* 12:189.21–27. *LW* 40:34. Luther stressed the "common" ministry in his critique of the Catholic priesthood, and he emphasized the "special" ministry in his critique of the *Schwärmer*. Some Luther scholars hold that Luther refused to grant the right to celebrate the Eucharist to the unordained. See Pesch, *Hinführung zu Luther*, 213. Other Luther scholars maintain that Luther did grant this right to the laity. See Fagerberg, "Amt," *TRE* 2:554–55. There are many Luther texts which limit the right to the ordained. See Manns, "Amt und Eucharistie."

30. Large Catechism, 1529, pt. 3.56 (Creed). *BS* 658. *BC* 418. For a definition of "ministry *of* the gospel," derived from Luther, see Gritsch and Jenson, *Lutheranism*, 117–23.

31. "On the Councils and the Church," 1539. *WA* 50:642.27–32. *LW* 41:165.

32. Large Catechism, 1529, pt. 1.22 (First Commandment). *BS* 564. *BC* 367.

33. Smalcald Articles, 1537, pt. 3, XII (The Church). *BS* 459–60. *BC* 315.

34. A slogan coined by William of Durant in the fifteenth century. See Spitz, *Renaissance and Reformation Movements* 2:313.

35. "Dedicatory Letter, Explanations of the Ninety-five Theses," 1518. *WA* 1:529.22–26.

36. Cited in Lohse, "Die Einheit der Kirche," 15.

37. "Against the Execrable Bull of the Antichrist," 1520. *WA* 6:604.22–23.

38. Preface to the Latin Edition of Luther's Writings, 1545. *WA* 54:184.34–185.5. *LW* 34:335–36. On Luther's intercession for Tetzel, see "Against Goat Emser" (*Ad aegocerstem Emserianum*), 1519. *WA* 2:667.16.

39. For a study of Luther's dialectic between the visible and the invisible church, see Kattenbusch, *Die Doppelschichtigkeit*. On the relationship between church and church law, see G. Müller, "Ekklesiologie und Kirchenrecht."

40. Smalcald Articles, 1537, pt. 2, IV.9, 14. *BS* 430, 431. *BC* 300, 301.

41. This was the stipulation which Philip Melanchthon appended to the Smalcald Articles of 1537. See *BS* 463–64. *BC* 316–17.

42. Lohse, "Office of Leadership," 52–53.

43. Bornkamm, "What is the Church?," 151.

44. Large Catechism, 1529, pt. 2.48 (Creed). *BS* 656. *BC* 416. It has been noted that Luther leaned towards a "congregationalist" and "preconstantinian" view of the church because of the emphasis on the local congregation. See Grane, "Luther und Luthertum," thesis 8, 42.

45. Large Catechism, 1529, pt. 2.58 (Creed). *BS* 659. *BC* 418.

46. "Commentary on Psalm 45" (:10), 1532. *WA* 40/2:560.10. *LW* 12:263.

47. "Commentary on Psalm 110," 1518. *WA* 1:697.1–14. See also Althaus, *Theology of Martin Luther,* 312–13.

48. That Luther was committed to "catholicity" has been argued by Brandenburg, *Die Zukunft Martin Luthers,* 60.

49. "The Three Symbols or Creeds of the Church," 1538. *WA* 50:270.17–22. *LW* 34:212. Italics mine.

50. "On the Councils and the Church," 1539. *WA* 50:642.1–7. *LW* 41:164–65.

51. "Sermon on the Third Sunday After Trinity 1 Peter 5:5–11," 1539. *WA* 22:32.1–12, 19–21.

CHAPTER 11

1. Luther used the phrase to describe the anthropological implications of the doctrine of justification. Passages and interpretations in Althaus, *Theology of Martin Luther,* 242–45; and in Pesch, *Hinführung zu Luther,* chap. 11.

2. "Preface to the Epistle of St. Paul to the Romans," 1546 (1522). *WA.DB* 7:11.16–19. *LW* 35:370–71.

3. "Against the Heavenly Prophets in the Matter of Images and Sacraments," 1525. *WA* 18:136.9–18, 24–25. *LW* 40:146.

4. See Olsson, *Schöpfung, Vernunft und Gesetz,* 17.

5. "Treatise on Good Works," 1520. *WA* 6:207.3–5. *LW* 44:27.

6. "Lectures on Galatians," 1535. *WA* 40/1:174.13–14. *LW* 26:95. Luther spoke of "masquerade" (*Mummenschantz*) and a "face mask" (*larva*).

7. The title of an essay on Luther's "Table Talks" by Bainton, "Luther on Birds, Babies and Dogs."

8. "Table Talk," 18 May 1532, no. 274. *WA.TR* 1:115.31. *LW* 54:38.

9. "Table Talk," 11 December 1532–2 January 1533, no. 2849b. *WA.TR* 3:27.1–6. *LW* 54:175.

10. "Table Talk," 2–17 September 1540, no. 5227. *WA.TR* 5:17.20–23. *LW* 54:400.

11. "Table Talk," fall 1533, no. 3390b. *WA.TR* 3:301.3–8. *LW* 54:199–200.

12. "Table Talk," 28 December 1531–1 January 1532, no. 2342a. *WA.TR* 2:425.1–2.

13. "Martin Luther to the Devotees of Music" (*Martinus Luther Musicae Studiosis*). Preface to Georg Rhau's Delightful Symphonies (*symphoniae iucundae*), 1538. *WA* 50:371.1–13. *LW* 53:323.

14. Ibid., *WA* 50:370.2–4. *LW* 53:322.

15. See Blankenburg, "Luther und die Musik," 17.

16. Walter, *In Praise of the Art of Music (Lob und Preis der löblichen Kunst Musica),* 1538? Quoted in Gurlitt, "Johannes Walter," 93.

17. "A Preface for All Good Hymnals," 1538. WA 35:483.29–30. LW 53:320.

18. "First Lectures on Psalms," 1513–15. WA 4:140.31–34. LW 11:294.

19. "To the Councilmen of All Cities in Germany That They May Establish and Maintain Christian Schools," 1524. WA 15:46.13–18. LW 45:369–70.

20. Well documented by Nettl, *Luther and Music*, chap. 6.

21. This is the judgment of Buszin, "Luther on Music," 97.

22. "Table Talk," 1530–35, no. 1160. WA.TR 1:573.31–33; 574.1–4.

23. How the wholistic view is linked to eschatology, in contrast to Greco-Roman and Enlightenment anthropologies, has been shown by Spitz, "Views of Modern Man," esp. 33, 40.

24. See, for example, Lienhardt, "Luther und die Menschenrechte."

25. For a useful sketch of the "orders," see Althaus, *The Ethics of Martin Luther*, chap. 3. The relation of the orders to the endtime has been convincingly argued by Wingren, *Luther on Vocation*, 164–69.

26. "A Sermon on Keeping Children in School," 1530. WA 30/2:569.10–12. LW 46:246.

27. "Martin Luther's Judgment on Monastic Vows," 1521. WA 8:585.24–27. LW 44:264.

28. "Confession Concerning Christ's Supper," 1528. WA 26:505.18–23. LW 37:365.

29. "Commentary on Psalm 111" (:3), 1530. WA 31/1:399.34–400.3. LW 13:358.

30. "Sermons on the Sermon on the Mount" (Matt. 5–7), 1530. WA 32:495.29–496.2. LW 21:237.

31. Luther began to understand all vocations as "divine callings" after 1522 when he rejected monasticism as a special vocation. Mystics like John Tauler influenced this understanding of vocation. See Althaus, *Ethics of Martin Luther*, 39.

32. Small Catechism, 1529. 9:1–15. BS 522–27. BC 354–56.

33. "Wedding Sermon on Hebr. 13:4," 8 (?) January 1531. WA 34/1:71.29–31.

34. This is the critique of Thielicke, *Theological Ethics* 1:378–79. That Luther did not encourage a stance of uncritical obedience to existing orders has been argued by Holl, "Reconstruction of Morality," esp. 113–21. On the difficulties of relating Luther's views to the modern world, see Wingren, "Beruf," *TRE* 5:663–66.

35. Thesis 29 of "Theses Concerning Faith and Law," 1535. WA 39/1:46.18–19. LW 34:111. Cited as the motto of Luther's ethical stance by Althaus, *Ethics of Martin Luther*, v. That the article of justification normed Luther's ethics has been shown by Thielicke, *Theological Ethics* 1:10–12.

36. "Exposition of Psalm 127, for the Christians at Riga in Livonia" (*Der hundertsiebenundzwanzigste Psalm ausgelegt an die Christen zu Rigen im Livland*), 1524. WA 15:367.15–19. LW 45:326.

37. "Commentary on Psalm 147," 1532. WA 31/1:436.7–11, 13–19. LW 14, 114–15.

38. Large Catechism, 1529, pt. 1.117 (Fourth Commandment). BS 590. BC 381.

39. "Table Talk," 16 June–14 August 1531, no. 2029. WA.TR 2:299.4–7.

40. Large Catechism, 1529, pt. 1.147 (Fourth Commandment). BS 598. BC 385.

41. "New Newspaper from the Rhine" (*Neue Zeitung vom Rhein*), 1542. WA 53:404–5. See also Hendrix, "Martin Luther und Albrecht von Mainz," 112–13. A *Quentlein* is a small fraction of something; *Lot* is about 10 grams.

42. For a comprehensive study of Luther's sense of humor as a counterbalance to melancholy, see Söderblom, *Humor och melanckoli och andra Lutherstudier,* chaps. 1–3.

43. "Meditation at Table" on Christmas Day, 1538, no. 4201. *WA.TR* 4:197.18–25. *LW* 54:326–27.

44. See Blanke, *Luthers Humor,* 43–44.

45. Letter to George Spalatin, 24 April 1530. *WA.BR* 5:290.5–291.1. *LW* 49:293.

46. Ibid., *WA.BR* 5:291:39–41. *LW* 49:294–95.

47. Ibid., *WA.BR* 5:291.46–47. *LW* 49:295.

48. *Klageschrift der Vögel gegen Wolfgang Sieberger,* 1534? WA 38:292–93.

49. Ibid., WA 38:293.19–23.

50. Dated 9 July 1535. *WA.BR* 7:207.11–14.

51. "Eight Sermons at Wittenberg," 1522. WA 10/3:18.15–19.7. *LW* 51:77.

52. Ibid., WA 10/3:47.9–16. *LW* 51:91.

53. Letter of 4 December 1539. *WA.BR* 8:625.20–25, 26–626.36.

54. Letter of 10 February 1546. *WA.BR* 11:291.1–3. *LW* 50:305.

55. Ibid., *WA.BR* 11:291.12–16. *LW* 50:306.

56. Letter to Philip Melanchthon, 1 August 1521. *WA.BR* 2:372.82–85. *LW* 48:281–82.

CHAPTER 12

1. Address to students on 19 February 1546. *CR* 6:59.

2. Matthesius, *D. Martin Luthers Leben,* v–vi.

3. Ibid., 362.

4. Cochlaeus, *Activities and Works of Martin Luther,* 317.

5. The history of Cochlaeus's influence has been described by Herte, *Das katholische Lutherbild.*

6. See Jedin, "Wandlungen des Lutherbildes," 83.

7. This view originated in nineteenth-century France. See Herte, *Das katholische Lutherbild* 3:23.

8. Döllinger, *Die Reformation* 3:176.

9. Some of these historians were influenced by Enlightenment philosophy. See Jedin, "Wandlungen des Lutherbildes," 86.

10. This is the judgment of Hasler, *Luther in der katholischen Dogmatik,* 105.

11. Grisar, *Luther* (German ed.) 3:650.

12. Lortz, "Luther's Intellectual Style," 7.

13. Lortz, *Reformation in Germany* 1:200.

14. Lortz, "Basic Elements of Luther's Intellectual Style," 33.

15. The transition from a "destructive critique" to "interest and respect" in Germany, France, and the English-speaking countries has been sketched by Stauffer, *Luther As Seen By Catholics.*

16. Memorial coin in 1617, commemorating the one hundredth anniversary of the "Ninety-five Theses." See Zeeden, *Legacy of Luther,* 37.

17. Ibid., 47–48.

18. Spener, *Pia Desideria,* 51–52.

19. See Zeeden, *Legacy of Luther*, 132–35.

20. Walch published a Luther biography in 1751. See Zeeden, *Legacy of Luther*, chap. 3, esp. 113.

21. *Letters for the Improvement of Humanity (Briefe zur Beförderung der Humanität)*, 1792. Quoted in and translated from Bornkamm, *Luther im Spiegel der deutschen Geistesgeschichte*, 211.

22. See Williams, "Joseph Priestley and Luther," 147.

23. Bornkamm, *Luther im Spiegel der deutschen Geistesgeschichte*, 34.

24. Hegel, *Lectures on the History of Philosophy (Vorlesungen über die Geschichte der Philosophie)*, 20, 50.

25. Ranke emphasized Luther's political influence, which was greatest on Elector Frederick. See *History of the Reformation in Germany*, 613. See also Bornkamm, *Luther im Spiegel der deutschen Geistesgeschichte*, 41–48.

26. See Bornkamm, *Luther im Spiegel der deutschen Geistesgeschichte*, 88–90.

27. Troeltsch, *Social Teaching of the Christian Churches* 2:552.

28. See the detailed analysis of Engels and his disciples by Friesen, *Reformation and Utopia*, chaps. 7–9.

29. *Theses Concerning Martin Luther*, 17.

30. See the description of this change in Bornkamm, *Luther im Spiegel der deutschen Geistesgeschichte*, chaps. 9–11.

31. This is the judgment of Pelikan, "Adolf von Harnack and Luther," 253.

32. See Gritsch, "Luther und die Schwärmer," 105–6. For a detailed study of Holl's theology and philosophy of history, see Bodenstein, *Die Theologie Karl Holls*, esp. pt. 2.

33. Barth, "Lutherfeier 1933," 12.

34. See, for example, Deutelmoser, *Luther: Staat und Glaube*.

35. See Carlson, *Reinterpretation of Luther*, 58–59. Chaps. 3–4 describe the impact of "motif research" on Luther studies.

36. Scheel collected and edited all available evidence until 1512. See *SD* and *SML*. Boehmer told the life of Luther until 1521. See *Martin Luther*.

37. See Bornkamm, *Luther im Spiegel der deutschen Geistesgeschichte*, 133.

38. Ritter, "Luther und der deutsche Geist."

39. See Thiel, *Luther*.

40. The interesting German history of this *Lutherania* has been told by Bornkamm, *Luther im Spiegel der deutschen Geistesgeschichte*, chaps. 16–18.

41. See Vajta, *Lutherforschung heute*, 10.

42. Ibid., 126.

43. Named after Peter Waldes, a French merchant who founded a Bible-oriented reform movement which took the vow of poverty and stressed community life. The Waldensians were excommunicated by Pope Lucius III in 1184.

44. Vajta, *Lutherforschung heute*, 135.

45. Ibid., 141.

46. Ibid., 149.

47. Ibid., 151.

48. Ibid., 172–82.

49. The second congress was held in Münster, Westphalia, in 1960. See Vajta, *Luther und Melanchthon*.

50. These were the themes for a third congress in Järvenpää, Finland, in 1966. See Asheim, *The Church, Mysticism, Sanctification and the Natural*.

51. This was the topic of the fourth congress, which was held in St. Louis in 1971. See Oberman, *Dawn of the Modern Era*.

52. The fifth congress took place in Lund, Sweden, in 1977. See Grane and Lohse, *Luther und die Theologie der Gegenwart*. The sixth congress will take place in Erfurt, German Democratic Republic, on the theme "Luther—Impact and Work" (*Werk und Wirkung*), in commemoration of Luther's five hundredth birthday.

53. Three international journals help to keep Luther scholars in touch with each other: *Archiv für Reformationsgeschichte* (with annual "Literature Reviews" which include a section on Luther); the *Lutherjahrbuch;* and *Luther*, the *Zeitschrift* of the *Luthergesellschaft*. See, for example, the reports on international Luther research, including reports from the Netherlands, Spain, and Japan, in the 1977 *Lutherjahrbuch*.

54. The somewhat complex series of events has been summarized and analyzed by Iserloh, "Aufhebung des Lutherbannes?" 69–72.

55. Ibid., 78.

56. For the plurality of points of view on the Catholic side, see Manns, *Lutherforschung heute*.

57. This is the judgment of Pesch, *Ketzerfürst und Kirchenvater*, 42–43.

58. This was the observation of Brunner, "Die Reformation Luthers," 82.

59. Pesch, *Hinführung zu Luther*, 273.

60. This is acknowledged on the Catholic side. See Fries, "Das Grundanliegen der Theologie Luthers," 166–67.

61. Brandenburg, *Die Zukunft Martin Luthers*, 83.

62. Speech of Cardinal Willebrands at the Fifth Assembly of the Lutheran World Federation in 1970 in Evian. See Willebrands, "Gesandt in die Welt," 458.

63. "To the Christian Nobility of the German Nation," 1520. WA 6:404.24–25. LW 44:123.

64. Sermon on the Third Sunday After Trinity on 1 Peter 5:5–11. "Cruciger's Summer Postil" (*Crucigers Sommerpostille*), 1544. WA 22:33.23–27.

BIBLIOGRAPHY

(See also sources listed under "Abbreviations" at the beginning of the book.)

Aland, Kurt. *Martin Luther's 95 Theses: With the Pertinent Documents from the History of the Reformation*. Translated by P. J. Schroeder. St. Louis and London: Concordia Pub. House, 1967.

———. "Der deutsche Luther." *Luther* 51 (1980):115–29.

Althaus, Paul. *The Theology of Martin Luther*. Translated by Robert C. Schultz. Philadelphia: Fortress Press, 1966.

———. *The Ethics of Martin Luther*. Translated by Robert C. Schultz. Philadelphia: Fortress Press, 1972.

Asendorf, Ulrich. *Eschatologie bei Luther*. Göttingen: Vandenhoeck & Ruprecht, 1967.

Asheim, Ivar, ed. *The Church, Mysticism, Sanctification and the Natural in Luther's Thought: Lectures Presented to the Third International Congress on Luther Research, Järvenpää, Finland, August 11–16, 1966*. Philadelphia: Fortress Press, 1967.

Atkinson, James. *The Trial of Luther*. New York: Stein & Day, 1971.

Bainton, Roland H. "The Left Wing of the Reformation." *Journal of Religion* 21(1941):124–34.

———. *Here I Stand: A Life of Martin Luther*. New York: Abingdon & Cokesbury, 1950.

———. *The Travail of Religious Liberty*. Philadelphia: Westminster Press, 1951.

———. "Luther on Birds, Dogs and Babies." In *Martin Luther Lectures*, edited by Roland H. Bainton et al., vol. 1, *Luther Today*, 3–12. Decorah, Ia: Luther College Press, 1957.

———. "Luther's Attitudes on Religious Liberty." In *Collected Papers in Church History*, vol. 2, *Studies on the Reformation*, 20–45. Boston: Beacon Press, 1963.

———. "Katherine von Bora." In *Women of the Reformation in Germany and Italy*, 23–43. Minneapolis: Augsburg Pub. House, 1971.

———. "Psychiatry and History: An Examination of Erikson's *Young Man Luther*." In *Psychohistory and Religion: The Case of Young Man Luther*, edited by Roger A. Johnson, 19–56. Philadelphia: Fortress Press, 1977.

———. "Luther, Begin and the Jews." *Christianity and Crisis* 41, no. 10 (5 October 1981):258, 270–71.

Baron, Salo W. *A Social and Religious History of the Jews*. vol. 13, *Inquisition, Renaissance, and Reformation*. New York: Columbia Univ. Press, 1969.

Barth, Hans-Martin. *Der Teufel und Jesus Christus in der Theologie Martin Luthers*. Göttingen: Vandenhoeck & Ruprecht, 1967.

Barth, Karl. "Lutherfeier 1933." *Theologische Existenz heute* 4 (1933). Munich: Chr. Kaiser.

———. *Eine Schweizer Stimme, 1938–1945*. Zollikon-Zürich: Evangelischer Verlag, 1948.

Bauer, Karl. *Die Wittenberger Universitätstheologie und die Anfänge der deutschen Reformation*. Tübingen: Mohr, 1928.

Baumer, Remigius, ed. *Lutherprozess und Lutherbann: Vorgeschichte, Ergebnis, Nachwirkung*. Münster: Aschendorff, 1972.

Baylor, Michael G. *Action and Person: Conscience in Late Scholasticism and the Young Luther*. Leiden: Brill, 1977.

Beer, Theobald. *Der fröhliche Wechsel und Streit. Grundzüge der Theologie Luthers*. 2 vols. Leipzig: St. Benno Verlag, 1974.

Beintker, Horst. *Die Überwindung der Anfechtung bei Luther*. Berlin: Evangelische Verlagsanstalt, 1954.

———. "Anfechtung III: Reformation und Neuzeit." In *TRE* 2, 695–708.

Benrath, Gustav A. "Ablass." In *TRE* 1, 347–64.

Bergrav, Eivind. *Man and State*. Translated by George Aus. Philadelphia: Muhlenberg Press, 1951.

Bizer, Ernst. *Studien zur Geschichte des Abendmahlsstreits im 16. Jahrhundert*. Gütersloh, 1940. Reprint, Darmstadt: Wissenschaftliche Buchgesellschaft, 1962.

Blanke, Fritz. *Luthers Humor: Scherz und Schalk in Luthers Seelsorge*. Hamburg: Furche Verlag, 1957.

Blankenburg, Walter. "Luther und die Musik." *Luther* 28 (1957):14–27.

Bluhm, Heinz. *Martin Luther: Creative Translator*. St. Louis: Concordia, 1965.

Bodenstein, Walter. *Die Theologie Karl Holls im Spiegel des antiken und reformatorischen Christentums*. Berlin, W. de Gruyter, 1968.

Boehmer, Heinrich. "Luthers Ehe." *Lutherjahrbuch* 7 (1925):40–76.

———. *Luther and the Reformation in the Light of Modern Research*. Translated by E. S. G. Potter. London: G. Bell and Sons, 1930.

———. *Der junge Luther*. 3d ed., rev. by Heinrich Bornkamm. Leipzig: Koehler & Amelang, 1939.

———. *Martin Luther: Road to Reformation*. Translated by John W. Doberstein and Theodore G. Tappert. Philadelphia: Muhlenberg Press, 1957.

Boehmer, Julius, ed. *Luthers Ehebuch. Was Martin Luther Ehelosen, Eheleuten und Eltern zu sagen hat. Ein Buch zur Geschlechts-und Geschlechterfrage*. Zwickau: Johann Hermann, 1935.

Bogdahn, Martin. *Die Rechtsfertigungslehre Luthers im Urteil der neueren katholischen Theologie: Möglichkeiten und Tendenzen der katholischen Lutherdeutung in evangelischer Sicht*. Göttingen: Vandenhoeck & Ruprecht, 1971.

Bonhoeffer, Dietrich. *No Rusty Swords: Letters, Lectures and Notes, 1928–1936*. Translated by Edwin H. Robertson and John Bowden. New York: Harper & Row, 1965.

Bornkamm, Heinrich. "Luther und sein Vater: Bemerkungen zu Erik H. Erikson, *Young Man Luther: A Study in Psychoanalysis and History.*" In *Luther: Gestalt und Wirkungen. Gesammelte Aufsätze,* 11-32. Gütersloh: Gerd Mohn, 1975.

—————. "Luther und sein Landesherr Kurfürst Friedrich der Weise." *Gesammelte Aufsätze,* 33–38.

—————. "Luther als Schriftsteller." *Gesammelte Aufsätze,* 39–64.

—————. "Das Wort Gottes bei Luther." *Gesammelte Aufsätze,* 147–86.

—————. "What is the Church?" In *Luther's World of Thought,* translated by Martin H. Bertram, 134–55. Philadelphia: Fortress Press, 1958.

—————. "The Nation." In *Luther's World of Thought,* 218–36.

—————. "The State." In *Luther's World of Thought,* 237–57.

—————. *Luther's Doctrine of the Two Kingdoms.* Translated by Karl H. Hertz. Philadelphia: Fortress Press, 1966.

—————. *Thesen und Thesenanschlag Luthers.* Berlin: A Töppelmann, 1967.

—————. *Luther and the Old Testament.* Translated by Eric W. and Ruth C. Gritsch, and edited by Victor I. Gruhn. Philadelphia: Fortress Press, 1969.

—————. *Luther im Spiegel der deutschen Geistesgeschichte: Mit ausgewählten Texten von Lessing bis zur Gegenwart.* 2d ed., rev. Göttingen: Vandenhoeck & Ruprecht, 1970.

—————. *Luther in der Mitte seines Lebens: Das Jahrzent zwischen dem Wormser und dem Augsburger Reichstag.* Göttingen: Vandenhoeck & Ruprecht, 1979. (English edition forthcoming. Philadelphia: Fortress Press, 1983.)

Borth, Wilhelm. *Die Luthersache, 1517–24: Die Anfänge der Reformation als Frage von Politik und Recht.* Lübeck: Matthiessen Verlag, 1970.

Brandenburg, Albert. *Die Zukunft des Martin Luthers: Luther, Evangelium und die Katholizität.* Kassel: J. Stande; Münster: Aschendorff, 1977.

—————, and Gritsch, Eric W. "Luther's Success and Failure as a Reformer of the Church: Disputation." In *Luther und die Theologie der Gegenwart: Referate und Berichte des Fünften Internationalen Kongresses für Lutherforschung, Lund, Schweden, 14.–20. August, 1977,* edited by Leif Grane and Bernhard Lohse, 97–111. Göttingen: Vandenhoeck & Ruprecht, 1980.

Brandi, Karl, ed. *Der Augsburger Religionsfriede vom 25. September 1555.* 2d ed. Munich: G. Himmer, 1927.

—————. *The Emperor Charles V: The Growth and Destiny of a Man and of a World Empire.* Translated by C. V. Wedgewood. New York: Jonathan Cape, 1965; London, 1939.

Brecht, Martin. "Der rechtfertigende Glaube an das Evangelium von Jesus Christus als Mitte von Luthers Theologie." *Zeitschrift für Kirchengeschichte* 89 (1978):45–77.

—————. *Martin Luther: Sein Weg zur Reformation, 1483–1521.* Stuttgart: Calwer Verlag, 1981.

—————. "Der Schimpfer Luther." *Luther* 52(1981):97–113.

Bring, Ragnar. "Der paulinische Hintergrund der lutherischen Lehre von den zwei Reichen." *Studia Theologica* 27(1973):107–26.

Brosseder, Johannes. *Luthers Stellung zu den Juden im Spiegel seiner Interpretation.* Munich: M. Hueber, 1972.

Brunner, Peter. *Nicholaus von Amsdorf als Bischof von Naumburg: Eine Unter-suchung zur Gestalt des evangelischen Bischofsamtes*. Gütersloh: Gerd Mohn, 1961.

———. "Die Reformation Martin Luthers als kritische Frage an die Zukunft." *Fuldaer Hefte* 18(1968):60–83.

Buchwald, Georg and Gustav Kawerau, eds. *Luther Kalendarium: Verzeichnis von Luthers Schriften*. 2d ed., rev. Leipzig: M. Heinsius Nachfolger Eher & Sievers, 1929.

Buszin, W. E. "Luther on Music." *Musical Quarterly* 32(1946):80–97.

Carlson, Edgar M. *The Reinterpretation of Luther*. Philadelphia: Muhlenberg Press, 1948.

Clasen, Martin, ed. *Luther-Nachkommenbuch, 1525–1960*. Limburg: A. Starke, 1960.

Cochlaeus, Johannes. *Commentaria de actis et scripturis Martini Lutheri*. Mainz, 1549. Copy at Gettysburg Library.

Cranz, Ferdinand E. *An Essay on the Development of Luther's Thought on Justice, Law and Society*. Cambridge, Mass.: Harvard Univ. Press, 1959.

Davies, Rupert E. *The Problem of Authority in the Continental Reformers. Luther, Zwingli and Calvin*. London: Epworth Press, 1946.

Delius, Hans-Ulrich. "Zu Luthers historischen Quellen." *Lutherjahrbuch* 42(1975):71–125.

Denifle, Heinrich. *Luther und Luthertum in der ersten Entwicklung, quellenmässig dargestellt*. Mainz: F. Kirchheim, 1904.

Deutelmoser, Arnold. *Luther: Staat und Glaube*. Jena: Diederichs, 1937.

Dickens, A. G. *The German Nation and Martin Luther*. New York: Harper & Row, 1974.

Dieck, Alfred. "Luthers Schaffenskraft." *Luther* 27(1956):35–39.

Döllinger, Ignaz. *Die Reformation, ihre innere Entwicklung und ihre Wirkungen im Umfang des Lutherischen Bekenntnisses*. 3 vols. Frankfurt am Main: Minerva, 1962. Reprint of 1846–48 ed.

Dörries, Hermann. "Luther und das Widerstandsrecht." In *Wort und Stunde*, vol. 3, *Beiträge zum Verständnis Luthers*, 195–270. Göttingen: Vandenhoeck & Ruprecht, 1970.

Drews, Paul. *Die Disputationen Dr. Martin Luthers*. Göttingen: Vandenhoeck & Ruprecht, 1895.

Duchrow, Ulrich, and Heiner Hoffmann, eds. *Die Vorstellung von zwei Reichen und Regimenten bis Luther*. Gütersloh: Gerd Mohn, 1972.

———. *Two Kingdoms: The Use and Misuse of a Lutheran Theological Concept*. Geneva: Lutheran World Federation, 1977.

Ebeling, Gerhard. "Sola Scriptura and Tradition." In *The Word of God and Tradition*, translated by S. H. Hooke, 102–47. Philadelphia: Fortress Press, 1964.

———. "Das Problem des Natürlichen bei Luther." In *The Church, Mysticism, Sanctification and the Natural in Luther's Thought*, edited by Ivar Asheim, 169–79. Philadelphia: Fortress Press, 1967.

———. *Evangelische Evangelienauslegung: Eine Untersuchung zu Luthers Her-meneutik*. 1942. Reprint. Darmstadt: Wissenschaftliche Buchgesellschaft, 1969.

————. *Luther, An Introduction to His Thought*. Translated by R. A. Wilson. Philadelphia: Fortress Press, 1970.

————. "Die Anfänge von Luthers Hermeneutik." In *Lutherstudien*, vol. 1, 1–68. Tübingen: Mohr, 1971.

————. "Luthers Psalterdruck vom Jahre 1513." In *Lutherstudien*, vol. 1, 69–131.

————. "Luther und die Bibel." In *Lutherstudien*, vol. 1, 286–301.

————. "Luther und der Anbruch der Neuzeit." In *Wort und Glaube: Gesammelte Aufsätze,* vol. 3, 29–59. Tübingen: Mohr, 1975.

————. *Lutherstudien.* vol. 2, *Disputatio de homine.* Tübingen: Mohr, 1977.

Ebon, Martin, trans. *The Last Days of Luther by Justus Jonas, Michael Coelius, and Others*. Garden City, New York: Doubleday & Co., 1970.

Ebstein, Wilhelm. *Dr. Martin Luthers Krankheiten und deren Einfluss auf seinen körperlichen Zustand*. Stuttgart: Enke, 1908.

Edwards, Mark U. *Luther and the False Brethren*. Stanford, Calif.: Stanford Univ. Press, 1975.

Elert, Werner. "Deutschrechtliche Züge in Luthers Rechtfertigungslehre." *Zeitschrift für systematische Theologie* 12(1935):22–35.

Elliger, Walter. *Thomas Müntzer: Leben und Werk*. Göttingen: Vandenhoeck & Ruprecht, 1975.

Elton, G.R. *Reformation Europe 1517–1559*. New York: Harper & Row, 1966.

Erikson, Erik H. *Young Man Luther: A Study in Psychoanalysis and History*. New York: Norton, 1958.

Eschenhagen, Edith. "Beiträge zur Sozial- und Wirtschaftsgeschichte der Stadt Wittenberg in der Reformationszeit." *Lutherjahrbuch* 9(1927):9–118.

Evans, Robert F. *Pelagius. Inquiries and Reappraisals*. (New York: Seabury Press, 1968).

Fabian, Ekkehard. *Die Entstehung des schmalkaldischen Bundes und seiner Verfassung 1524/29–1531/35*. Tübingen: Selbstverlag, 1962.

Fagerberg, Holsten. "Amt IV: Reformationszeit." *TRE* 2:552–74.

————. *Bekenntnis, Kirche und Amt in der deutschen konfessionellen Theologie des 19. Jahrhunderts*. Uppsala: Lundequistka Bokhandeln, 1952.

Faulkner, John A. "Luther and the Bigamous Marriage of Philip of Hesse." *American Journal of Theology* 17(1913):206–31.

Fischer-Galati, Stephen. "Ottoman Imperialism and the Religious Peace of Nürnberg." *ARG* 47(1956):160–79.

Forde, Gerhard O. "The Exodus From Virtue to Grace: Justification By Faith Today." *Interpretation* 34(1980):32–44.

————. *Justification By Faith—a Matter of Death and Life*. Philadelphia: Fortress Press, 1982.

Forell, George W. "Luther and the War Against the Turks." *Church History* 14(1945):256–71.

————. "Luther and Conscience." In *Encounters With Luther*, edited by Eric W. Gritsch, vol. 1, *Lectures, Discussions and Sermons at the Martin Luther Colloquia 1970–1974*, 218–35. Gettysburg: Institute for Luther Studies, 1980.

Franz, Günther. *Der deutsche Bauernkrieg*. 6th ed. Darmstadt: Wissenschaftliche Buchfesellsch, 1962.

————, ed. *Quellen zur Geschichte des Bauernkrieges*. Munich: R. Oldenburg, 1963.

————. *Thomas Müntzer: Schriften und Briefe. Kritische Gesamtausgabe*. Gütersloh: Gerd Mohn, 1968.

Freund, Michael. "Zur Geschichte der Lutherrose." *Luther* 42(1972):37–39.

Friedensburg, Walter. "Die Reformation und der Reichstag zu Speyer 1526." *Lutherjahrbuch* 8(1926):120–95.

Fries, Heinrich. "Das Grundanliegen der Theologie Luthers in der Sicht der katholischen Theologie der Gegenwart." In *Wandlungen des Lutherbildes*, edited by Karl Forster, 157–91. Würzburg: Echter Verlag, 1966.

Friesen, Abraham. *Reformation and Utopia: The Marxist Interpretation of the Reformation and Its Antecedents*. Wiesbaden: Franz Steiner, 1974.

Gebhardt, Bruno. *Die Gravamina der deutschen Nation gegen den römischen Hof*. Breslau, 1884.

Gerrish, Brian A. *Grace and Reason: A Study in Luther's Theology*. Oxford: At the Clarendon Press, 1962.

Gloege, Gerhard. "Die Grundfrage der Reformation Heute." *Kerygma und Dogma* 12(1966):1–13.

Grane, Leif. *Modus Loquendi Theologicus; Luthers Kampf um die Erneuerung der Theologie (1515–1518)*. Leiden: Brill, 1975.

————. "Lutherforschung und Geistesgeschichte, Auseinandersetzung mit Heiko A. Oberman." *ARG* 68(1977):302–15.

————. "Luther und das Luthertum." *Zeitschrift für Kirchengeschichte* 89(1978):36–44.

————. "Luther und Latomus." In *Luther und die Theologie der Gegenwart*, edited by Grane and Lohse, 170–77.

————. "Luther, Baptism and Christian Formation." In *Encounters with Luther*, edited by Eric W. Gritsch, vol. 2, *Lectures, Discussions and Sermons at the Martin Luther Colloquia 1975–1979*, 189–98. Gettysburg: Institute for Luther Studies, 1982.

Grane, Leif, and Bernhard Lohse, eds. *Luther und die Theologie der Gegenwart: Referate und Berichte des Fünften Internationalen Kongresses für Luther-forschung, Lund, Schweden, 14.–20. August, 1977*. Göttingen: Vandenhoeck & Ruprecht, 1980.

Grimm, Harold J. "Luther's Contribution to Sixteenth Century Organization of Poor Relief." *ARG* 61(1971):222–33.

Grisar, Hartmann. *Luther*. 3 vols. Frieburg i.Br.: Herdersche Buchhandlung, 1911–12.

————. *Luther: His Life and Work*. 3 vols. in 1. Translated by E. M. Lammond, and edited by Luigi Cappadelta. St. Louis: Herder, 1930.

Gritsch, Eric W. *Reformer Without a Church: The Life and Thought of Thomas Müntzer (1488?–1525)*. Philadelphia: Fortress Press, 1967.

————. "Luther and Violence: A Reappraisal of a Neuralgic Theme." *The Sixteenth Century Journal* 3(1972):37–55.

————. "Luther und die Schwärmer: Verworfene Anfechtung? Zum 50. Todesjahr Karl Holls." *Luther* 3(1976):105–21.

————. "Infant Communion: What Shape Tradition?" *Academy* (The Lutheran Academy of Scholarship) 36(1979):85–108.

————. "The Ministry in Luther's Theological Perspective." In *Encounters With Luther*, edited by Eric W. Gritsch, 1:180–94. Gettysburg: Institute for Luther Studies, 1982.

————. "Luther's Catechisms of 1529: Whetstones of the Church." In *Encounters With Luther* 2: 237–48.

Gritsch, Eric W., and Robert W. Jenson. *Lutheranism: The Theological Movement and Its Confessional Writings*. Philadelphia: Fortress Press, 1976.

Günter, Wolfgang. *Martin Luthers Vorstellung von der Reichsverfassung*. Münster: Aschendorff, 1976.

Gurlitt, Willibald. "Johannes Walter und die Musik der Reformationszeit." *Lutherjahrbuch* 15(1933):1–101.

Haendler, Gert. *Luther on Ministerial Office and Congregational Function*. Translated by Ruth C. L. Gritsch, and edited by Eric W. Gritsch. Philadelphia: Fortress Press, 1981.

Haikola, Lauri. "Luther und das Naturrecht." In *Vierhundertfünfzig Jahre lutherische Reformation, 1517–1967: Festschrift für Franz Lau zum 60. Geburtstag*, edited by Helmar Junghans et al., 126–34. Göttingen: Vandenhoeck & Ruprecht, 1967.

Haile, Harry G. "The Great Martin Luther Spoof, or, Philosophical Limits to Knowledge." *Yale Review* 67(1978):236–46.

————. *Luther: An Experiment in Biography*. New York: Doubleday & Co., 1980.

Halder, Annemarie. *Das Harnsteinleiden Martin Luthers*. Munich: Dissertation, Urologische Klinik, 1969.

Hall, S. "The Common Chest Concept: Luther's Contribution to 16th Century Poor Relief." *Social Thought* 5(1979):43–53.

Harley, W. N. *Little Journeys With Martin Luther*. Columbus, Oh.: Hans Lufft, 1916.

Hasler, August. *Luther in der katholischen Dogmatik*. Munich: Hueber Verlag, 1968.

Hauffen, Adolf. "Husz eine Gans—Luther ein Schwan." *Prager deutsche Studien* 9(1908):1–28.

Headley, John M. *Luther's View of Church History*. New Haven, Conn., and London: Yale Univ. Press, 1963.

Hegel, George F. W. *Werke*. Vol. 20, *Vorlesungen über die Geschichte der Philosophie*. Frankfurt am Main: Surkamp, 1971.

Heick, Otto W. "The Just Shall Live By Faith." *Concordia Theological Monthly* 43(1972):579–90.

Hendrix, Scott H. *Luther and the Papacy: Stages in a Reformation Conflict*. Philadelphia: Fortress Press, 1981.

————. "Martin Luther and Albrecht von Mainz." *Lutherjahrbuch* 49(1982):96–114.

Henning, Gerhard. *Cajetan und Luther: ein historischer Beitrag zur Begegnung von Thomismus und Reformation*. Stuttgart: Calwer Verlag, 1966.

Herte, Adolf. *Das katholische Lutherbild im Bann der Lutherkommentare des Cochlaeus*. 3 vols. Münster: Aschendorff, 1943.

Hertz, Karl H., ed. *Two Kingdoms and One World. A Sourcebook in Christian Social Ethics*. Minneapolis: Augsburg Pub. House, 1976.

Hillerbrand, Hans J. "Thomas Müntzer's Last Tract Against Luther." *The Mennonite Quarterly Review* 38(1964):20–36.

––––––. "The Spread of the Protestant Reformation of the Sixteenth Century: A Historical Case Study in the Transfer of Ideas." *The South Atlantic Quarterly* 67(1968):265–86.

Hillerdal, Gunnar. "Römer 13 und Luthers Lehre von den zwei Reichen." *Lutherische Rundschau* 13(1963):17–34.

Hoffman, Bengt. *The Theologia Germanica of Martin Luther: Translation, Introduction and Commentary*. New York/Ramsey/Toronto: Paulist Press, 1980.

Holborn, Louise W. "Printing and the Growth of a Protestant Movement in Germany From 1517 to 1524." *Church History* 11(1942):123–37.

Holl, Karl. "Die Rechtfertigungslehre in Luthers Vorlesung über den Römerbrief mit besonderer Rücksicht auf die Frage der Heilsgewissheit." In *Gesammelte Aufsätze zur Kirchengeschichte*, vol. 1, *Luther*, 4th and 5th eds., 111–54. Tübingen: Mohr, 1927.

––––––. "Luthers Bedeutung für den Fortschrift der Auslegungskunst." In *Gesammelte Aufsätze*, 1:154–82.

––––––. *The Cultural Significance of the Reformation*. Translated by Karl and Barbara Hertz and John H. Lichtblau. New York: Meridian, 1959.

––––––. "Luther on Luther." Translated by H. C. Erik Middlefort. In *Interpreters of Luther: Essays in Honor of Wilhelm Pauck*, 9–34. Philadelphia: Fortress Press, 1968.

––––––. *What Did Luther Understand by Religion?* Edited by James L. Adams and Walter F. Bense, and translated by Fred W. Meuser and Walter R. Wietzke. Philadelphia: Fortress Press, 1977.

––––––. *The Reconstruction of Morality*. Edited by James L. Adams and Walter F. Bense, and translated by Fred W. Meuser and Walter R. Wietzke. Minneapolis: Augsburg Pub. House, 1979.

Holmio, Armas, K. E. *The Lutheran Reformation and the Jews: The Birth of the Protestant Jewish Mission*. Hancock, Mich.: Finnish Lutheran Book Concern, 1949.

Höss, Irmgard. "Georg Spalatins Verhältnis zu Luther und zur Reformation." *Luther* 31(1960):67–80.

Huizinga, Johan. *The Waning of the Middle Ages*. New York: Doubleday & Co., 1956.

Hutten, Ulrich von, ed. *On the Eve of the Reformation: "Letters of Obscure Men."* Translated by Francis G. Stokes. New York: Harper & Row, 1964.

Hyma, Albert. *The Brethren of the Common Life*. Grand Rapids: Wm. B. Eerdmans, 1950.

Ihlenfeld, Kurt. "Martin Luther und Lucas Cranach." *Luther* 44 (1973):42–44.

Immenkötter, Herbert. *Die Confutatio der Confessio Augustana vom 3. August, 1530*. Münster: Aschendorff, 1979.

Iserloh, Erwin. "Luthers Stellung in der theologischen Tradition." In *Wandlungen des Lutherbildes*, edited by Karl Forster, 15–37. Würzburg: Echter Verlag, 1966.

––––––. *The Theses Were Not Posted: Luther Between Reform and Reformation*. Translated by Jared Wicks. Boston: Beacon Press, 1968.

––––––. "Aufhebung des Lutherbannes? Kirchengeschichtliche Überlegungen zu einer aktuellen Frage." In *Lutherprozess und Lutherbann*, edited by Remigius Bäumer, 69–80. Münster: Aschendorff, 1972.

———. *Luther und die Reformation: Beiträge zu einem ökumenischen Lutherverständnis*. Aschaffenburg: Pattloch, 1974.

Jansen, Reiner. *Studien zu Luthers Trinitätslehre*. Frankfurt am Main: Lang, 1976.

Jedin, Hubert. "Wandlungen des Lutherbildes in der katholischen Geschichtsschreibung." In *Wandlungen des Lutherbildes*, edited by Karl Forster, 77–101. Würzburg: Echter Verlag, 1966.

Jensen, De Lamar, ed. *Confrontation at Worms: Martin Luther and the Diet of Worms*. Provo, Utah: Brigham Young University Press, 1973.

Jenson, Robert W. *The Triune Identity: The God of the Gospel*. Philadelphia: Fortress Press, 1982.

———. "The Return to Baptism." In *Encounters With Luther*, edited by Eric W. Gritsch, vol. 2, *Lectures, Discussions and Sermons at the Luther Colloquia 1975–1979*, 217–25. Gettysburg: Institute for Luther Studies, 1982.

———. "Of Another Spirit." The Martin Luther Colloquium 1981. Institute for Luther Studies. Lutheran Theological Seminary at Gettysburg. *Bulletin* 62(Winter 1982):3–13.

Joest, Wilfried. *Ontologie der Person bei Luther*. Göttingen: Vandenhoeck & Ruprecht, 1967.

Johns, Christa T. *Luthers Konzilsidee in ihrer historischen Bedingtheit und ihrem reformatorischen Neuansatz*. Berlin: Töpelmann, 1966.

Johnson, Roger A., ed. *Psychohistory and Religion: The Case of Young Martin Luther*. Philadelphia: Fortress Press, 1977.

Junghans, Helmar. "Das mittelalterliche Vorbild für Luthers Lehre von den zwei Reichen." In *Vierhundertfünfzig Jahre Reformation, 1517–1967: Festschrift für Franz Lau zum 60. Geburtstag*, edited by Helmar Junghans et al, 135–53. Göttingen: Vandenhoeck & Ruprecht, 1967.

———. *Wittenberg als Lutherstadt*. Göttingen: Vandenhoeck & Ruprecht, 1979.

———. "Luther als Bibelhumanist." *Luther* 53(1982):1–9.

Justification Today. Studies and Reports. Lutheran World. Supplement No. 1. Geneva: Lutheran World Federation, 1965.

Kalkoff, Paul, ed. *Die Depeschen des Nuntius Aleander vom Wormser Reichstage 1521*. Halle: Niemeyer, 1886.

Kantzenbach, Friedrich W. "Christusgemeinschaft und Rechtfertigung: Luthers Gedanke vom fröhlichen Wechsel als Frage an unsere Rechtfertigungsbotschaft." *Luther* 35(1964):34–45.

———. *Martin Luther. Der bürgerliche Reformator*. Göttingen: Musterschmidt, 1972.

———. "Jesus Christus Haupt der Kirche: Erwägungen zu Ansatz und Einheit der Kirchen." *Lutherjahrbuch* 41(1974):7–44.

Kattenbusch, Ferdinand. *Die Doppelschichtigkeit in Luthers Kirchenbegriff*. Gotha: Leopold Klotz, 1928.

Kidd, B. J., ed. *Documents Illustrative of the Continental Reformation*. Oxford: At the Clarendon Press, 1911.

Kirchner, Hubert. *Luther and the Peasants' War*. Translated by Darrell Jodock. Philadelphia: Fortress Press, 1972.

Kirn, Paul. *Friedrich der Weise und die Kirche*. Leipzig: G. Teubner, 1926.

Knolle, Theodor. "Luthers Heirat nach seinen und seiner Zeitgenossen Aussagen." *Luther* 7 (1925):21–47.

Köhler, Walter, ed. *Dokumente zum Ablasstreit von 1517*. 2d ed. Tübingen: Mohr, 1934.

Kohls, Ernst-Wilhelm. "Die Deutungen des Verhaltens Luthers in Worms innerhalb der neueren Historiographie." *ARG* 63(1972):43–71.

————. *Luther oder Erasmus: Luthers theologische Auseinandersetzung mit Erasmus*. 2 vols. Basel Reinhardt, 1972–78.

Kolde, Theodor. "Luther und sein Ordensgeneral in Rom in den Jahren 1518 und 1520." *Zeitschrift für Kirchengeschichte* 2(1878):472–80.

Kooiman, Willem J. "Luther At Home." In *The Martin Luther Lectures*, edited by Roland H. Bainton et al., vol. 3, *The Mature Luther*, 59–75. Decorah, Ia.: Luther College Press, 1959.

————. *Luther and the Bible*. Translated by John Schmidt. Philadelphia: Muhlenberg Press, 1961.

Kunst, Hermann. *Evangelischer Glaube und politische Verantwortung. Martin Luther als politischer Berater*. Stuttgart: Evangelisches Verlagswerk, 1977.

Lähteenmäki, Olavi. *Sexus und Ehe bei Luther*. Translated by Martha Römer. Turku: Agricola Gesellschaft, 1955.

Lazareth, William H. *Luther on the Christian Home: An Application of the Social Ethics of the Reformation*. Philadelphia: Muhlenberg Press, 1960.

————. "Luther on Civil Righteousness and Natural Law." In *The Church, Mysticism, Sanctification and the Natural in Luther's Thought*, edited by Ivar Asheim, 180–88. Philadelphia: Fortress Press, 1967.

Leder, Hans-Günther. *Ausgleich mit dem Papst? Luthers Haltung in den Verhandlungen mit Miltitz 1520*. Stuttgart: Calwer Verlag, 1969.

Lewin, Reinhold. *Luthers Stellung zu den Juden: Ein Beitrag zur Geschichte der Juden in Deutschland während des Reformationszeitalters*. Berlin: Trowitsch & Son, 1911.

Lienhard, Marc. *Luther's Witness to Jesus Christ*. Translated by Edwin H. Robertson. Minneapolis: Augsburg Pub. House, 1982.

————. "Luther und die Menschenrechte." *Luther* 48(1977):12–28.

Liermann, Hans. "Luther ordnet seine Kirche." *Lutherjahrbuch* 31(1964):29–46.

Lietzmann, Hans, ed. *Die Wittenberger und Leisniger Kastenordnung*. Berlin: Marcus & Weber, 1935.

Lindbeck, George A. "Erikson's *Young Man Luther*: A Historical and Theological Reappraisal." *Soundings* (Summer 1973):210–27.

Loeschen, John R. *Wrestling With Luther: An Introduction to the Study of His Thought*. St. Louis: Concordia Pub. House, 1976.

Loewenich, Walter von. *Duplex Iustitia: Luthers Stellung zu einer Unionsformel des 16. Jahrhunderts*. Wiesbaden: Franz Steiner, 1972.

————. "Luthers Heirat: Geschehnis und Geschichte." *Luther* 47(1976):47–60.

————. *Luther's Theology of the Cross*. Translated by Herbert J. Bouman. Minneapolis: Augsburg Pub. House, 1976.

Lohff, Wenzel, and Christian Walther, eds. *Rechtfertigung im neuzeitlichen*

Zusammenhang: Studien zur Interpretation der Rechtfertigungslehre im Auftrag des theologischen Ausschuss der Vereinigten Evang.-Lutherischen Kirchen Deutschlands. Gütersloh: Gerd Mohn, 1974.

Lohse, Bernhard. "The Development of the Offices of Leadership in the German Lutheran Churches: 1517–1918." In *Episcopacy in the Lutheran Church? Studies in the Development and Definition of the Office of Leadership,* edited by Ivar Asheim and Victor R. Gold, 51–71. Philadelphia: Fortress Press, 1970.

————. "Conscience and Authority in Luther." In *Luther and the Dawn of the Modern Era,* edited by Heiko A. Obermann, 158–83. Leiden: Brill, 1974.

————. "Die Einheit der Kirche bei Luther." *Luther* 50 (1979):10–24.

————. *Martin Luther: Eine Einführung in sein Leben und Werk.* Munich: C. H. Beck, 1981.

Lönning, Inge. *"Kanon im Kanon": Zum dogmatischen Grundproblem des neutestamentlichen Kanons.* Munich: Kaiser Verlag, 1971.

Loofs, Friedrich. "Der Articulus stantis et cadentis ecclesiae." *Theologische Studien und Kritiken* 90(1917):323–420.

Lortz, Joseph. *The Reformation in Germany.* 2 vols. Translated by Ronald Walls. New York and London: Herder & Herder, 1968.

————. "The Basic Elements of Luther's Intellectual Style." In *Catholic Scholars Dialogue with Luther,* edited by Jared Wicks, 3–33. Chicago: Loyola Univ. Press, 1970.

Lotz, David W. "Sola Scriptura: Luther on Biblical Authority." *Interpretation* 35(1981):458–73.

Luther, Johannes. "Die Nachkommenschaft Martin Luthers des Reformators." *Lutherjahrbuch* 7(1925):123–28.

Mackinnon, James. *Luther and the Reformation.* 4 vols. New York and London: Longmans, Green & Co., 1928–30.

Maier, Paul C., ed. *Caspar Schwenckfeld: On the Person and Work of Christ.* Assen: Royal Van Gorcum, 1959.

Manns, Peter. *Lutherforschung Heute: Krise und Aufbruch.* Wiesbaden: Steiner Verlag, 1967.

————. "Amt und Eucharistie in der Theologie Luthers." In *Amt und Eucharistie,* edited by Peter Bläser et al., 68–173. Paderborn: Bonifacius, 1973.

————. *Martin Luther—An Illustrated Biography.* Translated by Michael Shaw. New York: Crossroad, 1982.

Manschreck, Clyde C. *Melanchthon: The Quiet Reformer.* Nashville and New York: Abingdon Press, 1958.

Maron, Gottfried. "Bauernkrieg." *TRE* 5:319–38.

Matheson, Peter C. "Luther and Hitler: A Controversy Reviewed." *Journal of Ecumenical Studies* 17(1980):445–53.

Matthesius, Johann M. *D. Martin Luthers Leben: In siebzehn Predigten dargestellt.* Berlin: Evangelischer Buchverlag, 1885.

Mau, Rudolf. "Autorität II: Reformationszeit." *TRE* 5:32–36.

Maurer, Wilhem. *Der junge Melanchthon zwischen Humanismus und Reformation.* 2 vols. Göttingen: Vandenhoeck & Ruprecht, 1967–69.

————. "Die Einheit der Theologie Luthers." In *Kirche und Geschichte:*

Gesammelte Aufsätze, edited by Ernst-Wilhelm Kohls and Gerhard Müller, vol. 1, *Luther und das evangelische Bekenntnis,* 11–21. Göttingen: Vandenhoeck & Ruprecht, 1970.

———. "Die Anfänge von Luthers Theologie." In *Kirche und Geschichte,* vol. 1, 22–37.

———. "Die Zeit der Reformation." In *Kirche und Synagoge: Handbuch zur Geschichte von Christen und Juden,* edited by Karl H. Rengstorf and Siegfried von Kortzfleisch, vol. 1, *Darstellung mit Quellen,* 363–78. Stuttgart: Kohlhammer, 1968.

May, Gerhard, ed. *Das Marburger Religionsgespräch 1529.* Gütersloh: Gerd Mohn, 1969.

McCracken, George E., ed. *Early Medieval Theology: The Library of Christian Classics.* Vol. 9. Philadelphia: Westminster Press, 1953.

McNeill, John T. "Natural Law in the Thought of Luther." *Church History* 10(1941):211–22.

Meier, Kurt. "Zur Interpretation von Luthers Judenschriften." In *Vierhundertfünfzig Jahre lutherische Reformation 1517–1967,* edited by Helmar Junghans et al., 233–50. Göttingen: Vandenhoeck & Ruprecht, 1967.

Meinhold, Peter. *Die Genesisvorlesung Luthers und ihre Herausgeber.* Stuttgart: Kohlhammer, 1936.

———. *Luthers Sprachphilosophie.* Berlin: Lutherisches Verlagshaus, 1958.

———. *Luther Heute: Wirken und Theologie Martin Luthers, des Reformators der Kirche, in ihrer Bedeutung für die Gegenwart.* Berlin and Hamburg: Lutherisches Verlagshaus, 1967.

Meissinger, Karl A. *Luthers Exegese in der Frühzeit.* Leipzig: M. Heinsius, 1910.

Migne, J. P. *Patrologia.* Series *Latina.* 221 vols. in 222. Paris, 1844-1904.

Moeller, Bernd. *Imperial Cities and the Reformation.* Edited and translated by Erik Middlefort and Mark U. Edwards. Philadelphia: Fortress Press, 1972.

Moellering, Ralph. "Luther's Attitude Toward the Jews." *Concordia Theological Monthly* 19(1948):920–34. 20(1949):45–59; 194–215; 579.

Montgomery, John W. *In Defense of Martin Luther: Essays.* Milwaukee: Northwestern Pub. Co., 1970.

Mostert, Walter. "Scriptura sacra sui ipsius interpres: Bemerkungen zum Verständnis der Heiligen Schrift durch Luther." *Lutherjahrbuch* 46(1979):60–96.

Mosse, George L. *Toward the Final Solution. A History of European Racism.* New York: Fertig, 1978.

Mühlhaupt, Erwin. "Luthers Kampf mit der Krankheit." *Luther* 29(1958):115–23.

———. *Luther über Müntzer, erläutert und an Thomas Müntzers Schrifttum nachgeprüft.* Witten: Luther Verlag, 1973.

Müller, Gerhard. "Ekklesiologie und Kirchenrecht beim jungen Luther." *Zeitschrift für systematische Theologie* 7(1968):100–128.

———. "Rechtfertigungslehre heute: Eine moderne Interpretation." *Luther* 46(1975):1–4.

———. *Die Rechtfertigungslehre: Geschichte und Probleme.* Gütersloh: Gerd Mohn, 1977.

———. "Antisemitismus VI: 16. und 17. Jahrhundert." *TRE* 3:143–55.

Müller, Nikolaus. *Die Wittenberger Bewegung, 1521–1522: Die Vorgänge in und um Wittenberg während Luthers Wartburg Aufenthaltes*. Leipzig: M. Heinsius, 1911.

Nembach, Ulrich. *Predigt des Evangeliums: Luther als Prediger, Pädagoge und Rhetor*. Neukirchen: Neukirchener Verlag, 1972.

Nettl, Paul. *Luther and Music*. Translated by Frida Best and Ralph Wood. Philadelphia: Muhlenberg Press, 1948.

Niebuhr, Reinhold. *The Nature and Destiny of Man*. 2 vols. New York: Charles Scribner's Sons, 1953.

Nilsson, Kjell O. *Simul: Das Miteinanderwirken von Göttlichem und Menschlichem in Luthers Theologie*. Göttingen: Vandenhoeck & Ruprecht, 1966.

Obendiek, Harmannus. *Der Teufel bei Luther*. Berlin: Furche Verlag, 1931.

Oberman, Heiko A. "'Wir sein Pettler. Hoc est verum.' Bund und Gnade in der Theologie des Mittelalters und der Reformation." *Zeitschrift für Kirchengeschichte* 78(1967):232–52.

———. "Reformation: Epoche oder Episode." *ARG* 68(1977):50–109.

———. *Masters of the Reformation: The Emergence of a New Intellectual Climate in Europe*. Translated by Dennis Martin. New York: Cambridge Univ. Press, 1981.

———. *Wurzeln des Antisemitismus: Christenangst und Judenplage im Zeitalter von Humanismus und Reformation*. Berlin: Severin & Siedler, 1981.

———. *Luther: Mensch zwischen Gott und Teufel*. Berlin: Severin & Siedler, 1982.

———, ed. *Luther and the Dawn of the Modern Era: Papers for the Fourth International Congress for Luther Research* [in St. Louis, Missouri, 22–27 August 1971]. Leiden: Brill, 1974.

———, ed. *Deutscher Bauernkrieg 1525. Zeitschrift für Kirchengeschichte* 85(1975).

Ohlig, Rudolf. *Die zwei-Reiche Lehre Luthers in der Auslegung der deutschen lutherischen Theologie der Gegenwart seit 1945*. Bern and Frankfurt am Main: Lang, 1974.

Olivier, Daniel. *The Trial of Luther*. Translated by John Tonkin. St. Louis: Concordia Pub. House, 1978.

Olsson, Herbert. *Schöpfung, Vernunft und Gesetz in Luthers Theologie*. Uppsala: Appelbergs Boktryckeri, 1971.

Østergaard-Nielson, H. *Scriptura sacra et viva vox: Eine Lutherstudie*. Munich: Chr. Kaiser, 1957.

Oyer, John S. *Lutheran Reformers Against Anabaptists: Luther, Melanchthon and Menius and the Anabaptists of Central Germany*. The Hague: Nijhoff, 1964.

Pelikan, Jaroslav. *Obedient Rebels: Catholic Substance and Protestant Principle in Luther's Reformation*. New York: Harper & Row, 1964.

———. "Adolf von Harnack on Luther." In *Interpreters of Luther: Essays in Honor of Wilhelm Pauck*, edited by Jaroslav Pelikan, 253–74. Philadelphia: Fortress Press, 1968.

———. "Luther Comes to the New World." In *Luther and the Dawn of the Modern Era*, edited by Heiko A. Oberman, 1–10. Leiden: Brill, 1974.

Penzel, Klaus. "Ernst Troeltlsch on Luther." In *Interpreters of Luther: Essays in Honor of Wilhelm Pauck*, edited by Jaroslav Pelikan, 275–303. Philadelphia: Fortress Press, 1968.

Pesch, Otto H. *Die Theologie der Rechtfertigung bei Martin Luther und Thomas von*

Aquin: Versuch eines systematisch-theologischen Dialogs. Mainz: Matthias-Grünewald Verlag, 1967.

————. *Ketzerfürst und Kirchenlehrer: Wege katholischer Begegnung mit Luther.* Stuttgart: Calwer Verlag, 1971.

————. *The God Question in Thomas Aquinas and Martin Luther.* Translated by Gottfried G. Krodel. Philadelphia: Fortress Press, 1972.

————. *Hinführung zu Luther.* Mainz: Matthias-Grünewald Verlag, 1982.

Peters, Albrecht. "Systematische Besinnung zu einer Neuinterpretation der reformatorischen Rechtfertigungslehre im neuzeitlichen Lebenszusammenhang." In *Studien zur Neuinterpretation der Rechtfertigungslehre,* edited by W. Lohff and C. Walther, 107–25. Gütersloh: Gerd Mohn, 1974.

Pfeiffer, Gerhard. "Augsburger Religionsfriede 1555." *TRE* 4:639–45.

Pfnür, Vinzenz. *Die Einigung bei den Religionsgesprächen von Worms und Regensburg 1540/41: Eine Täuschung?* Gütersloh: Gerd Mohn, 1980.

Pinomaa, Lennart. *Der existentielle Charakter der Theologie Luthers: Das Hervorbrechen der Theologie der Anfechtung und ihre Bedeutung für das Lutherverständnis.* Helsinki: Finnische Akademie der Wissenschaften, 1940.

Preus, James H. *From Shadow to Promise: Old Testament Interpretation from Augustine to Luther.* Cambridge, Mass.: Harvard Univ. Press, 1969.

————. *Carlstadt's Ordinances and Luther's Liberty: A Study of the Wittenberg Movement, 1521–1522.* Cambridge, Mass.: Harvard Univ. Press, 1974.

Preuss, Hans. *Martin Luther: Der Künstler. Der Prophet. Der Deutsche.* 3 vols. Gütersloh: Bertelsmann, 1931–34.

Ranke, Leopold von. *History of the Reformation in Germany.* Translated by Sarah Austin. London: Longman, Brown, Green, 1905.

Reiter, Paul J. *Martin Luther: Umwelt, Charakter und Psychose.* 2 vols. Copenhagen: Leren & Munksgaard, 1937–41.

Reu, Michael J. *Luther's German Bible: An Historical Presentation Together With a Collection of Sources.* Columbus, Oh.: Lutheran Book Concern, 1934.

————. *Luther and the Scriptures.* Columbus, Oh.: Wartburg Press, 1944.

————. *The Augsburg Confession: A Collection of Sources.* St. Louis: Concordia Pub. House, 1960.

Reuter, Fritz, ed. *Der Reichstag zu Worms 1521: Reichspolsitik und Luthersache. Im Auftrag der Stadt Worms zum 450. Jahrgedenken.* Worms: Stadtarchiv, 1971.

Ritter, Gerhard. "Luther und der deutsche Geist." In *Die Weltwirkung der Reformation,* 2d ed., rev., 66–80. Darmstadt, 1959.

Rogge, Joachim, ed. *1521-1971: Luther in Worms.* Berlin: W. de Gruyter, 1971.

Rohr, John von. "The Sources of Luther's Self: Depression in the Monastery." *Journal of Bible and Religion* 19(1951):6–11.

Roth, Cecil. "The Jews in the Middle Ages." In *The Cambridge Medieval History,* edited by I. Burn and John Bagnell, vol. 7, *Decline of the Middle Ages,* 632–63. New York: Macmillan Co., 1861–1927.

Rupp, Gordon E. "Luther: The Contemporary Image." In *The Church, Mysticism, Sanctification and the Natural,* edited by Ivar Asheim, 9–19. Philadelphia: Fortress Press, 1967.

————. *The Righteousness of God: Luther Studies.* 3d ed. London: Hodder & Stoughton, 1968.

————. *Patterns of Reformation*. Philadelphia: Fortress Press, 1969.

————. "Luther at the Castle Coburg, 1530." *Bulletin of the John Rylands University Library* 61(1979):182–205.

————. "Martin Luther and the Jews." *Nederlands Theologisch Tijdschrift* 31(1977):121–35.

Rupp, Gordon E., and Philip S. Watson, eds. *Luther and Erasmus: Free Will and Salvation*. Library of Christian Classics. Vol. 17. Philadelphia: Westminster Press, 1969.

Saarnivaara, Uuras. *Luther Discovers the Gospel: New Light on Luther's Way From Medieval Catholicism to Evangelical Faith*. St. Louis: Concordia Pub. House, 1951.

Sauter, Gerhard. *Zur zwei-Reiche-Lehre Luthers*. Munich: Chr. Kaiser, 1973.

Scheible, Heinz, ed. *Das Widerstandsrecht als Problem der deutschen Protestanten 1523–46*. Gütersloh: Gerd Mohn, 1969.

Scheurl, Siegfried, Freiherr von. "Martin Luthers Doktoreid." *Zeitschrift für bayrische Kirchengeschichte* 32(1963):46–52.

Schubert, Hans von, and Karl Meissinger. *Zu Luthers Vorlesungstätigkeit*. Heidelberg: Carl Winters Universitätsbuchhandlung, 1920.

Schulze, Wilhelm A. "Luther und der Zins." *Luther* 42(1971):139–46.

Schwarz, Karl, and Abba Ahimeir, "Antisemitism." In *Encyclopedia Judaica*, 3:87–160. New York: Macmillan Co., 1971–72.

Schwarz, Reinhard. *Vorgeschichte der reformatorischen Busstheologie*. Berlin: W. de Gruyter, 1968.

Schwiebert, Ernest G. *Luther and His Times*. St. Louis: Concordia, 1950.

Scribner, Bob, and Gerhard Benecke, eds. *The German Peasant War of 1525: New Viewpoints*. London: George Allen & Unwin, 1979.

Seeberg, Reinhold. "Luthers Anschauung von dem Geschlechtsleben und der Ehe und ihre geschichtliche Stellung." *Lutherjahrbuch* 7(1925):77–122.

Seitz, Otto, ed. *Der authentische Text der Leipziger Disputation 1519*. Berlin: Schwetschke & Sohn, 1903.

Selge, Kurt-Victor. "Capta conscientia in verbo Dei: Luthers Widerrufsverweigerung in Worms." In *Der Reichstag zu Worms 1521: Reichspolitik und Luthersache*, edited by Fritz Reuter. Worms: Stadtarchiv, 1971.

————. "Die Leipziger Disputation zwischen Luther und Eck." *Zeitschrift für Kirchengeschichte* 86(1975):26–40.

Shirer, William L. *The Rise and Fall of the Third Reich*. New York: Charles Scribner's Sons, 1959, 1960.

Shoenberger, Cynthia G. "Luther and the Justifiability of Resistance to Legitimate Authority." *Journal of the History of Ideas* 40(1979):3–20.

Sider, Ronald. *Andreas Bodenstein von Karlstadt: The Development of His Thought, 1517–1525*. Leiden: Brill, 1974.

————. *Karlstadt's Battle With Luther: Documents in a Liberal-Radical Debate*. Philadelphia: Fortress Press, 1978.

Siggins, Ian D. *Martin Luther's Doctrine of Christ*. New Haven, Conn., and London: Yale Univ. Press, 1970.

————. *Luther and His Mother*. Philadelphia: Fortress Press, 1981.

Siirala, Aarne. "Luther and the Jews." *Lutheran World* 11(1964): 337–58.

Smith, Preserved. "Luther's Early Development in the Light of Psychoanalysis." *American Journal of Psychology* 24(1913):360–77.

Söderblom, Nathan. *Humor och Melankoli och andra Lutherstudier.* Uppsala: Sveriges kristliga Studentrörelses Skriftserie, 1919.

Spener, Philip J. *Pia Desideria.* Edited and translated by Theodore G. Tappert. Philadelphia: Fortress Press, 1964.

Spitz, Lewis W. *The Renaissance and Reformation Movements.* 2 vols. Chicago: Rand McNally Co., 1971.

———. "Psychohistory and History: The Case of *Young Man Luther.*" In *Psychohistory and Religion,* edited by Roger A. Johnson, 57–87. Philadelphia: Fortress Press, 1977.

———. "Luther's Impact on Modern Man." *Concordia Theological Monthly* 41(1977)1:26-43.

Stauffer, Richard. *Luther As Seen By Catholics.* Richmond: John Knox Press, 1967.

Stein, Wolfgang. *Das kirchliche Amt bei Luther.* Wiesbaden: Franz Steiner, 1974.

Steinmetz, David M. *Misericordia Dei: The Theology of Johannes von Staupitz in Its Late Medieval Setting.* Leiden: Brill, 1968.

———. *Luther and Staupitz: An Essay in the Intellectual Origins of the Reformation.* Durham, N.C.: Duke Univ. Press, 1980.

Stephan, Horst. *Luther in den Wandlungen seiner Kirche.* 2d ed., rev. Berlin: Töpelmann, 1952.

Stern, Selma. *Josel of Rosheim: Commander of Jewry in the Holy Roman Empire of the German Nation.* Translated by Gertrud Hirschler. Philadelphia: Jewish Publication Society, 1965.

Strauss, Gerhard, ed. *Manifestations of Discontent in Germany on the Eve of the Reformation.* Bloomington: Indiana Univ. Press, 1972.

Strohl, Henri. *L'Évolution Religieuse de Luther jusqu'en 1515.* Strasbourg: Librairie Istra, 1922.

Sucher, Bernd C. *Luthers Stellung zu den Juden: Eine Interpretation aus germanistischer Sicht.* Niewkoop: de Graaf, 1977.

Tappert, Theodore G. "The Professor and His Students." In *Martin Luther Lectures,* edited by Roland H. Bainton et al., vol 3, *The Mature Luther,* 3–20. Decorah, Ia.: Luther College Press, 1959.

Tavard, George H. *Holy Writ and Holy Church: The Crisis of the Protestant Reformation.* New York: Harper & Row, 1959.

Tentler, Thomas N. *Sin and Confession on the Eve of the Reformation.* Princeton: Princeton Univ. Press, 1977.

Theses Concerning Martin Luther 1483–1983. The Luther Quincentenary in the German Democratic Republic. Berlin and Dresden: Verlag Zeit im Bild, 1983.

Thiel, Rudolf. *Luther.* 2 vols. Berlin: Neff, 1941.

Thielicke, Helmut. *Theological Ethics.* 3 vols. Edited and translated by William H. Lazareth. Philadelphia: Fortress Press, 1979.

Tillich, Paul. *The Protestant Era.* Chicago: University of Chicago Press, 1948.

Tillmanns, Walter C. *The World and Men Around Luther.* Minneapolis: Augsburg Pub. House, 1959.

Todd, John M. *Martin Luther: A Biographical Study*. London: Burns & Oates, 1964.

———. *Luther: A Life*. New York: Crossroad, 1982.

Trachtenberg, Joshua. *The Devil and the Jews: The Medieval Conception of the Jew and Its Relation to Modern Antisemitism*. New Haven, Conn.: Yale University Press, 1943.

Troeltsch, Ernst. *The Social Teaching of the Christian Churches*. 2 vols. Translated by Oliver Wyon. New York: Macmillan Co., 1931.

Vajta, Vilmos. *Luther on Worship: An Interpretation*. Philadelphia: Muhlenberg Press, 1954.

———, ed. *Lutherforschung heute: Referate und Berichte des 1. Internationalen Lutherforschungskongresses, Aarhus, 18.–23. August, 1956*. Berlin: Lutherisches Verlagshaus, 1958.

———, ed. *Luther and Melanchthon in the History and Theology of the Reformation*. [Second International Congress for Luther Research, Münster, 8–13 August 1960.] Philadelphia: Muhlenberg Press, 1961.

Volz, Hans. *Luthers deutsche Bibel: Entstehung und Geschichte der deutschen Lutherbibel*. Edited by Henning Wendland. Hamburg: Wittig, 1978.

Walch, Johann G. *D. Martin Luthers sämtliche Schriften*. 23 vols. in 25. 2d ed. St. Louis: J. J. Gebauer, 1880–1919.

Watson, Philip J. *Let God Be God: An Interpretation of the Theology of Martin Luther*. 1947. Reprint. Philadelphia: Fortress Press, 1966.

Wenger, John C. "The Schleitheim Confession of Faith." *The Mennonite Quarterly Review* 19(1945):243–53.

Wicks, Jared, ed. and trans. *Cajetan Responds: A Reader in Reformation Controversy*. Washington: Catholic Univ. of America Press, 1978.

Willebrands, Cardinal Jan. "Gesandt in die Welt." *Lutherische Rundschau* 20(1970):447–60.

Williams, George H. *The Radical Reformation*. Philadelphia: Westminster Press, 1962.

———. "Joseph Priestley on Luther." In *Interpreters of Luther,* edited by Jaroslav Pelikan, 121–58. Philadelphia: Fortress Press, 1968.

Wingren, Gustav. *Luther on Vocation*. Translated by Carl Rasmussen. Philadelphia: Muhlenberg Press, 1959.

———. "Das Problem des Natürlichen bei Luther." In *The Church, Mysticism, Sanctification and the Natural in Luther's Thought,* edited by Ivar Asheim, 156–79. Philadelphia: Fortress Press, 1967.

———. "Beruf II: Historische und ethische Aspekte." *TRE* 5:657–71.

Woerner, Bernhard, and Rudolf Poser. *Wegweiser in Buchwalds Lutherkalendarium: Synoptisches Inhaltsverzeichnis der gebräuchlichsten Lutherausgaben*. Leipzig: M. Heinsius Nachfolger, 1935.

Wolf, Ernst. "Die Rechtfertigungslehre als Mitte und Grenze reformatorischer Theologie." In *Peregrinatio: Studien zur reformatorischen Theologie und zum Kirchenproblem*. 2d ed. Munich: Chr. Kaiser, 1962.

Wolf, Günther, ed. *Luther und die Obrigkeit*. Darmstadt: Wissenschaftliche Buchgesellschaft, 1972.

Wolgast, Eike. *Die Wittenberger Theologie und die Politik der evangelischen Stände:*

Studien zu Luthers Gutachten in politischen Fragen. Gütersloh: Gerd Mohn, 1977.

————. *Die Religionsfrage als Problem des Widerstandsrechts im 16. Jahrhundert.* Heidelberg: Carl Winters Universitätsbuchhandlung, 1980.

Wood, Skevington A. *Captive to the Word: Martin Luther, Doctor of Sacred Scripture.* Grand Rapids: Wm. B. Eerdmans, 1969.

Zeeden, Ernst W. *The Legacy of Luther: Martin Luther and the Reformation in the Estimation of the German Lutherans From Luther's Death to the Beginning of the Age of Goethe.* Translated by Ruth M. Bethell. London: Hollis & Carter, 1954.

Zumkeller, Adolar. "Martin Luther und sein Orden." *Analecta Augustiniana* 25(1962): 254–90.

————. "Erbsünde, Gnade und Rechtfertigung im Verständnis der Erfurter Augustinertheologen des Spätmittelalters." *Zeitschrift für Kirchengeschichte* 92(1981):39–59.

INDEXES

INDEX OF NAMES

INDEX OF SUBJECTS